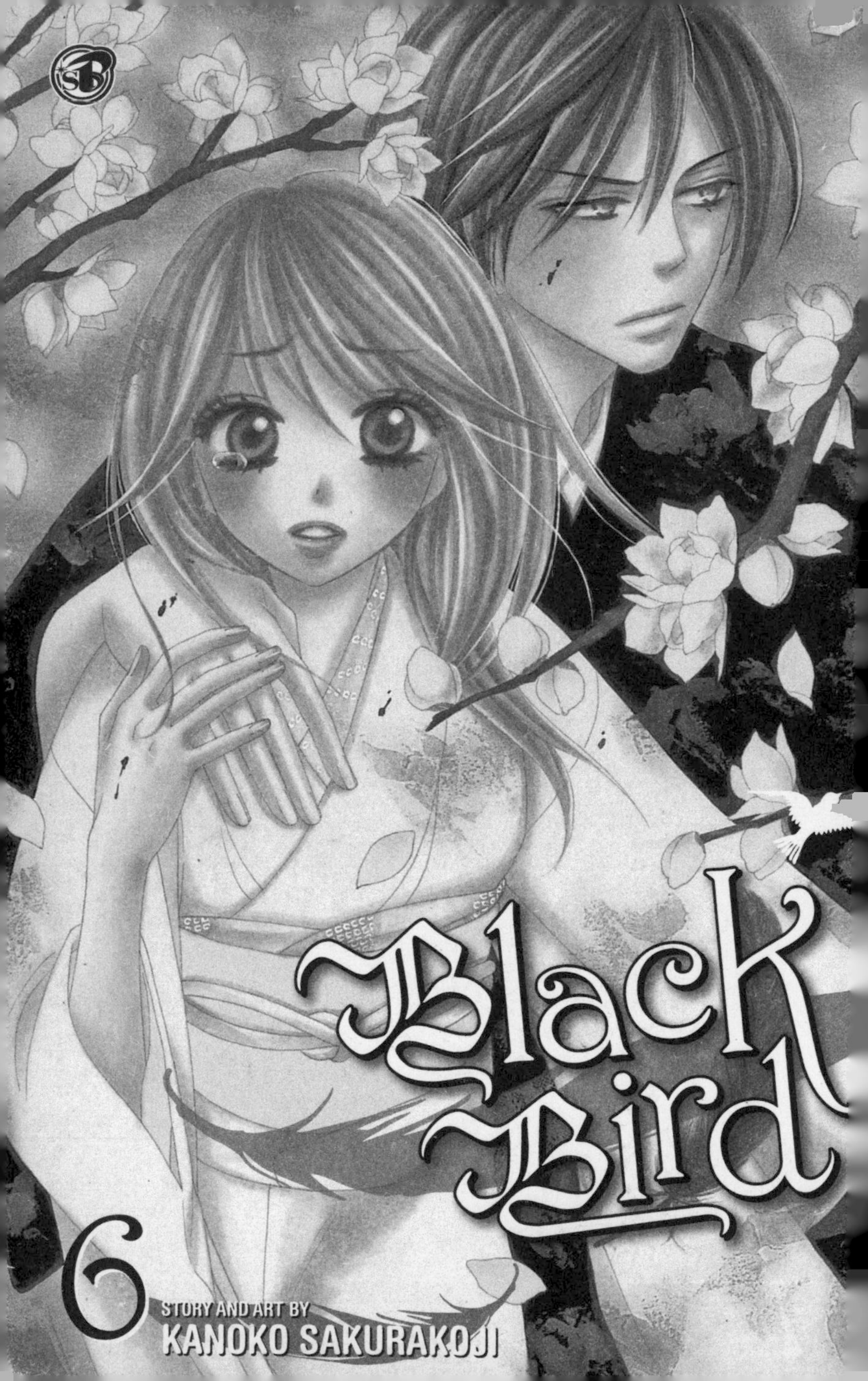
Black Bird
6
STORY AND ART BY
KANOKO SAKURAKOJI

Black Bird

CONTENTS

CHARACTERS

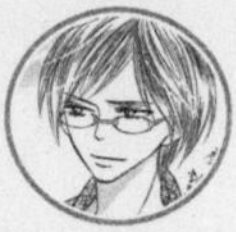

TADANOBU KUZUNOHA
Kyo's close friend since childhood. Current leader of the Kitsune clan.

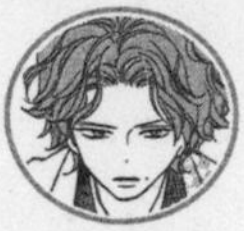

KOH
Sho's lieutenant. Is he siding with Kyo for political gain?

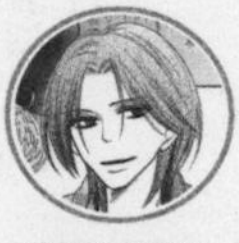

SHO USUI
Kyo's older brother and a member of the Eight Daitengu. He is also known as Sojo. He is currently incarcerated after injuring Misao in an attempt to gain leadership of the clan.

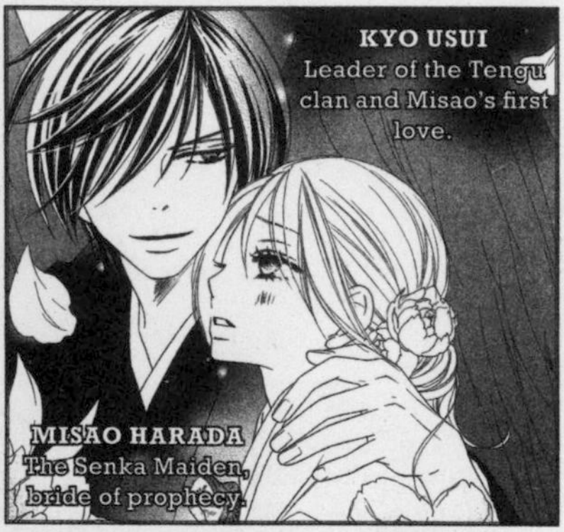
KYO USUI
Leader of the Tengu clan and Misao's first love.
MISAO HARADA
The Senka Maiden, bride of prophecy.

THE EIGHT DAITENGU
Kyo's bodyguards. Their names designate their official posts.

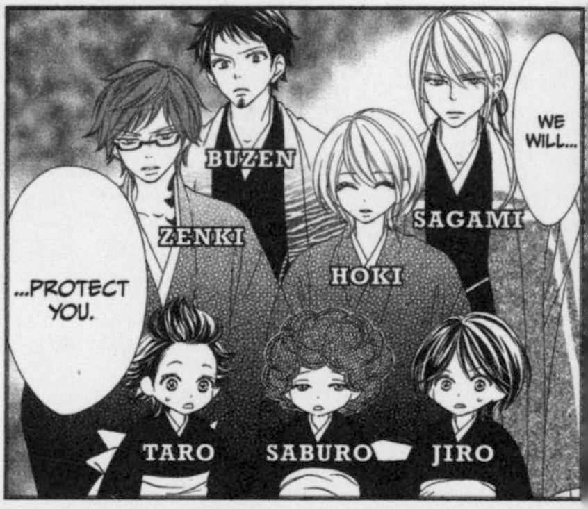
WE WILL...
...PROTECT YOU.
SAGAMI
BUZEN
ZENKI
HOKI
JIRO
SABURO
TARO

STORY THUS FAR
Misao can see spirits and demons, and her childhood sweetheart Kyo has been protecting her since she was little.

"Someday, I'll come for you, I promise." Kyo reappears the day before Misao's 16th birthday to tell her, "Your 16th birthday marks 'open season' on you." She is the Senka Maiden, and if a demon drinks her blood, he is granted a long life. If he eats her flesh, he gains eternal youth. And if he makes her his bride, his clan will prosper...

Misao discovers that Kyo is a *tengu*, a crow demon, with his sights firmly set on her. But no one knows if Misao, a human, will survive being bedded by a demon. The answer can only be found in the *Senka Roku*, the record of the previous Senka Maiden kept by the Kuzunoha clan. During a battle between Kyo and Tadanobu, the head of the Kuzunoha clan, the *Senka Roku* is stolen by unidentified demons!

Kyo is under a lot of pressure to bed Misao and solidify his position as leader of the Usui clan. But Kyo decides he will destroy his brother Sho instead. With no rival to his claim, it won't matter if he doesn't sleep with Misao.

Kyo returns to his home village, Tengu no Sato, with Misao. Sho, who has been imprisoned there, already has a plan in motion to steal the leadership from Kyo. When Misao learns of it, she uses herself as bait in order to approach Sho, but...?!

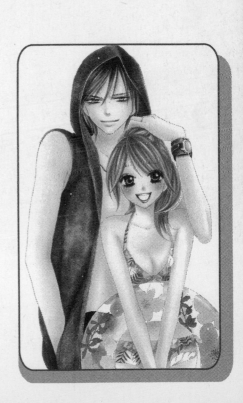

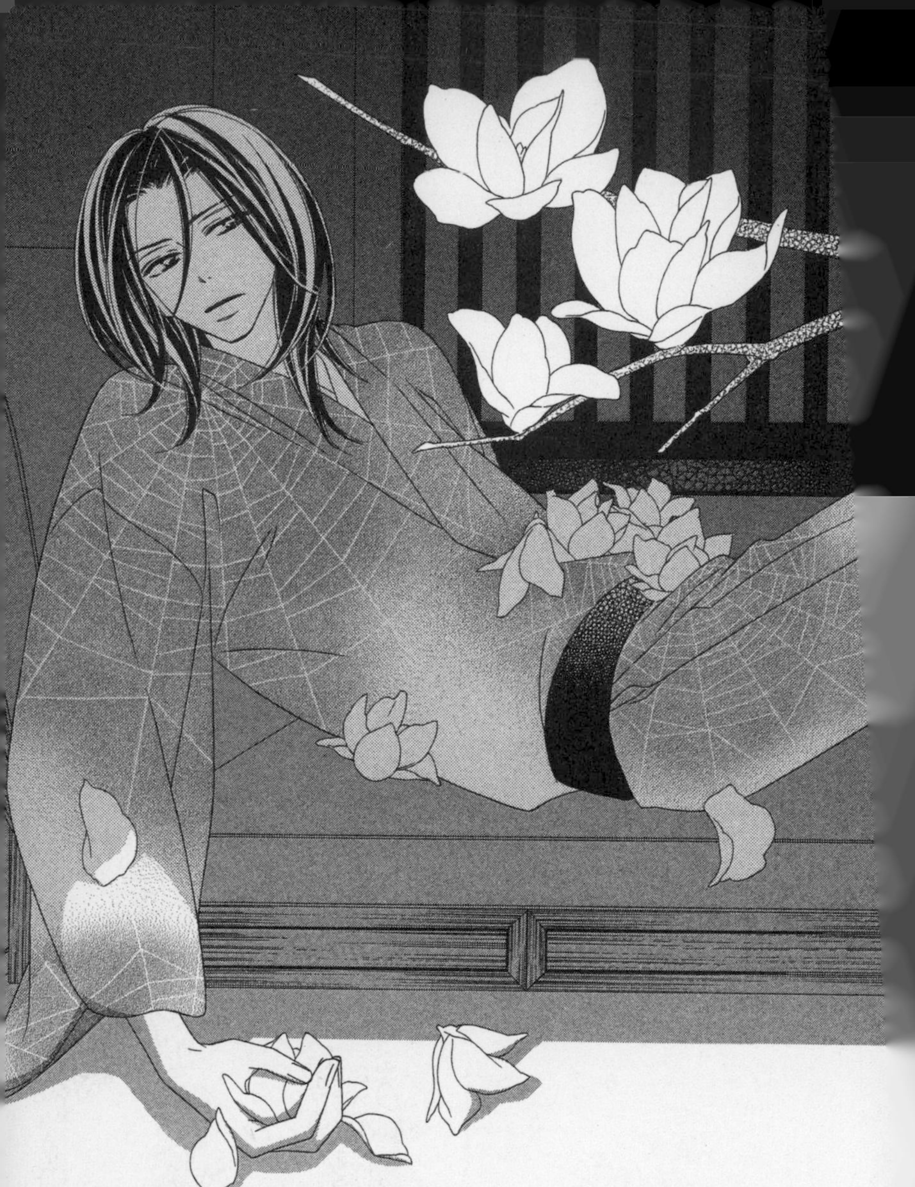

Black Bird

Chapter 22

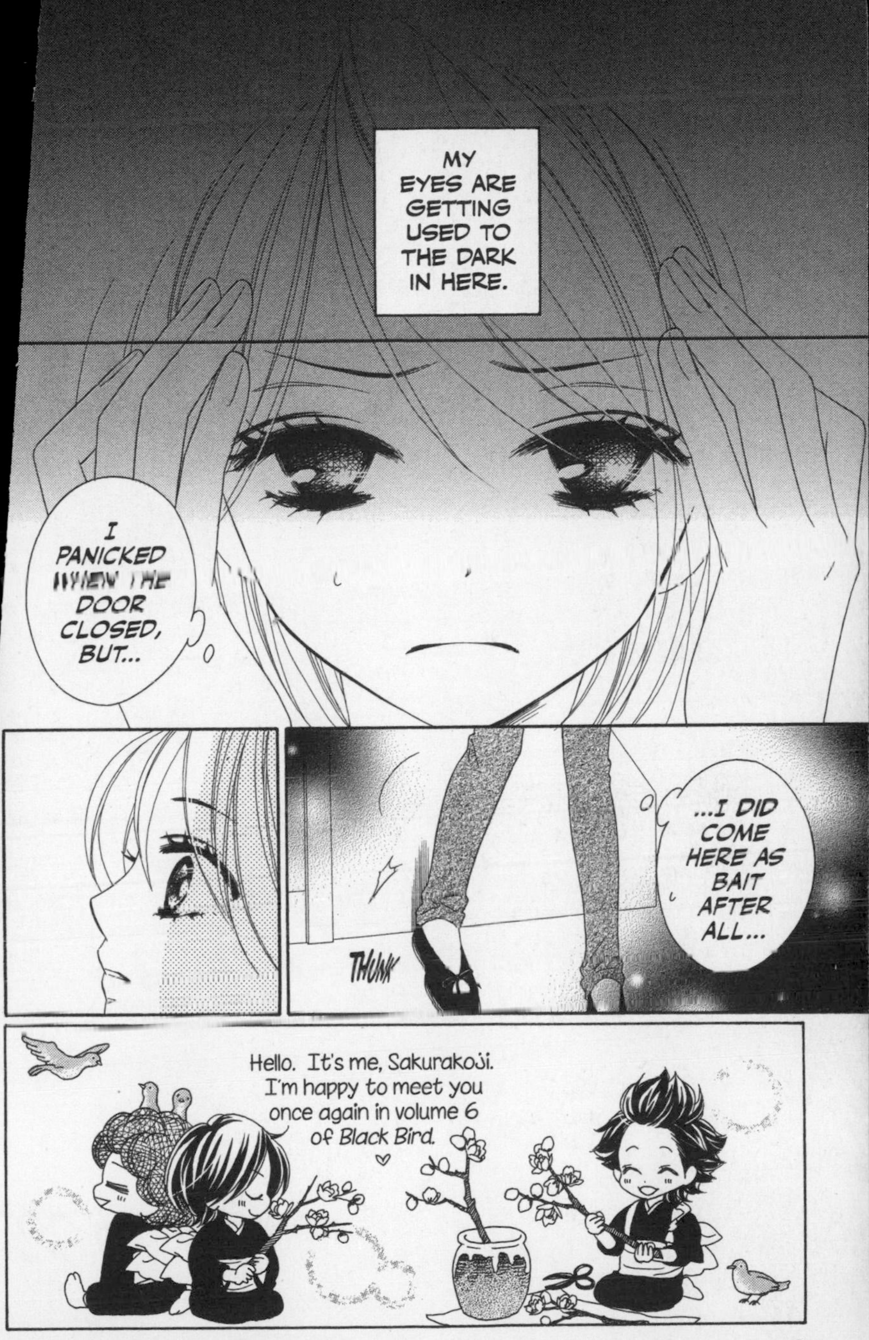
MY EYES ARE GETTING USED TO THE DARK IN HERE.
I PANICKED WHEN THE DOOR CLOSED, BUT...
...I DID COME HERE AS BAIT AFTER ALL...
THUNK
Hello. It's me, Sakurakoji. I'm happy to meet you once again in volume 6 of *Black Bird*.

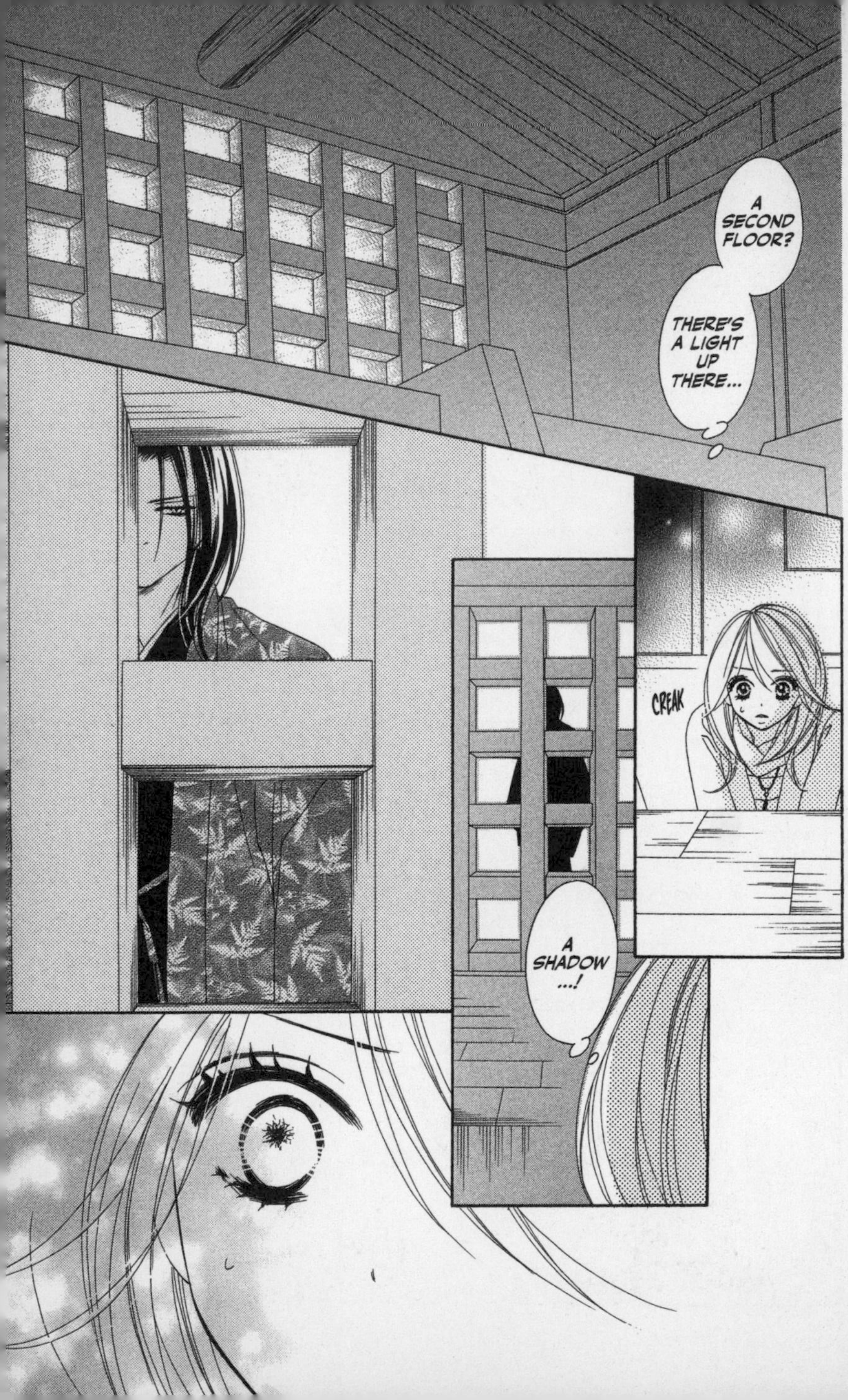
A SECOND FLOOR?
THERE'S A LIGHT UP THERE...
CREAK
A SHADOW ...!

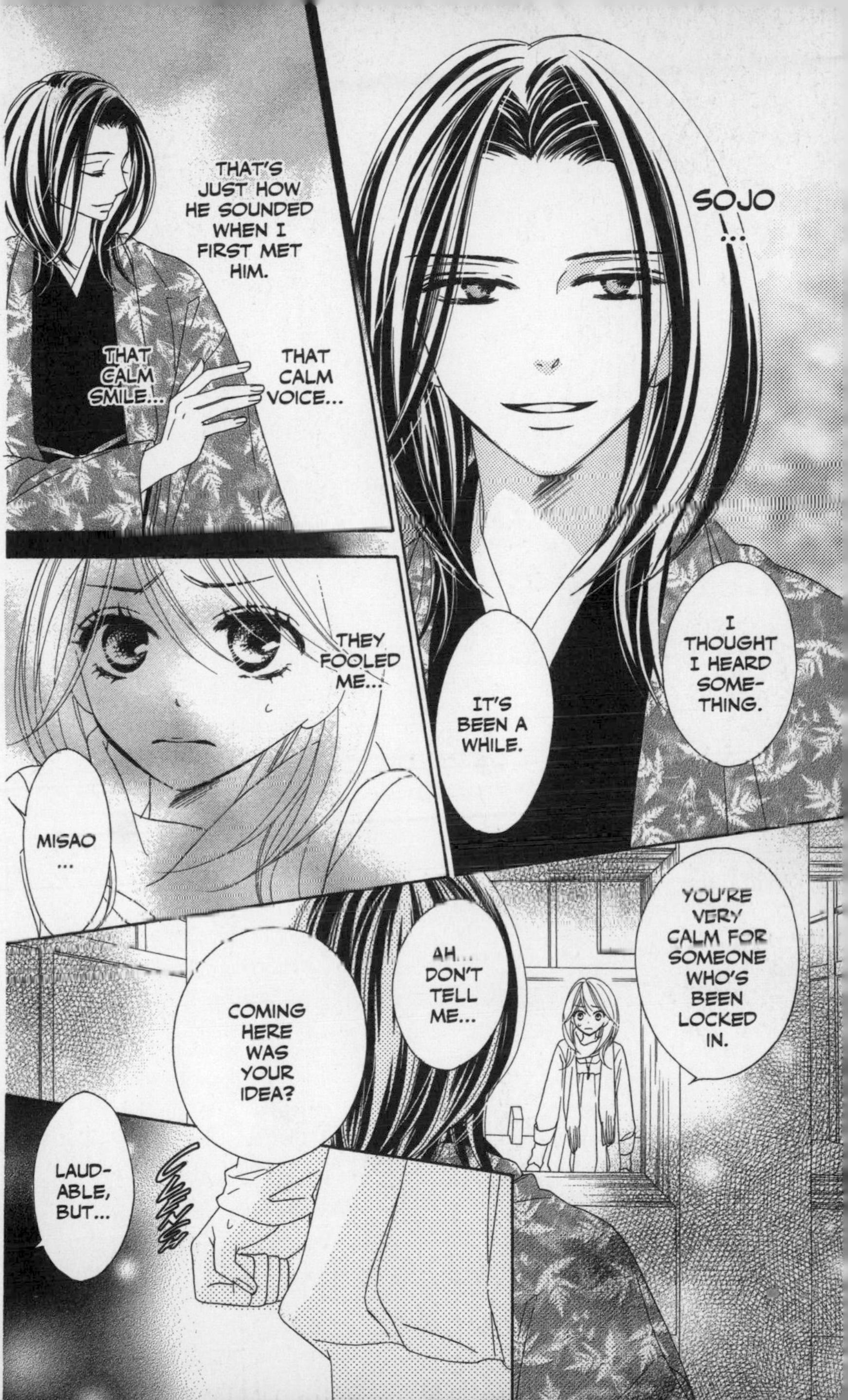
SOJO...
I THOUGHT I HEARD SOME-THING.
IT'S BEEN A WHILE.
THAT'S JUST HOW HE SOUNDED WHEN I FIRST MET HIM.
THAT CALM VOICE...
THAT CALM SMILE...
THEY FOOLED ME...
MISAO...
YOU'RE VERY CALM FOR SOMEONE WHO'S BEEN LOCKED IN.
AH... DON'T TELL ME...
COMING HERE WAS YOUR IDEA?
LAUD-ABLE, BUT...

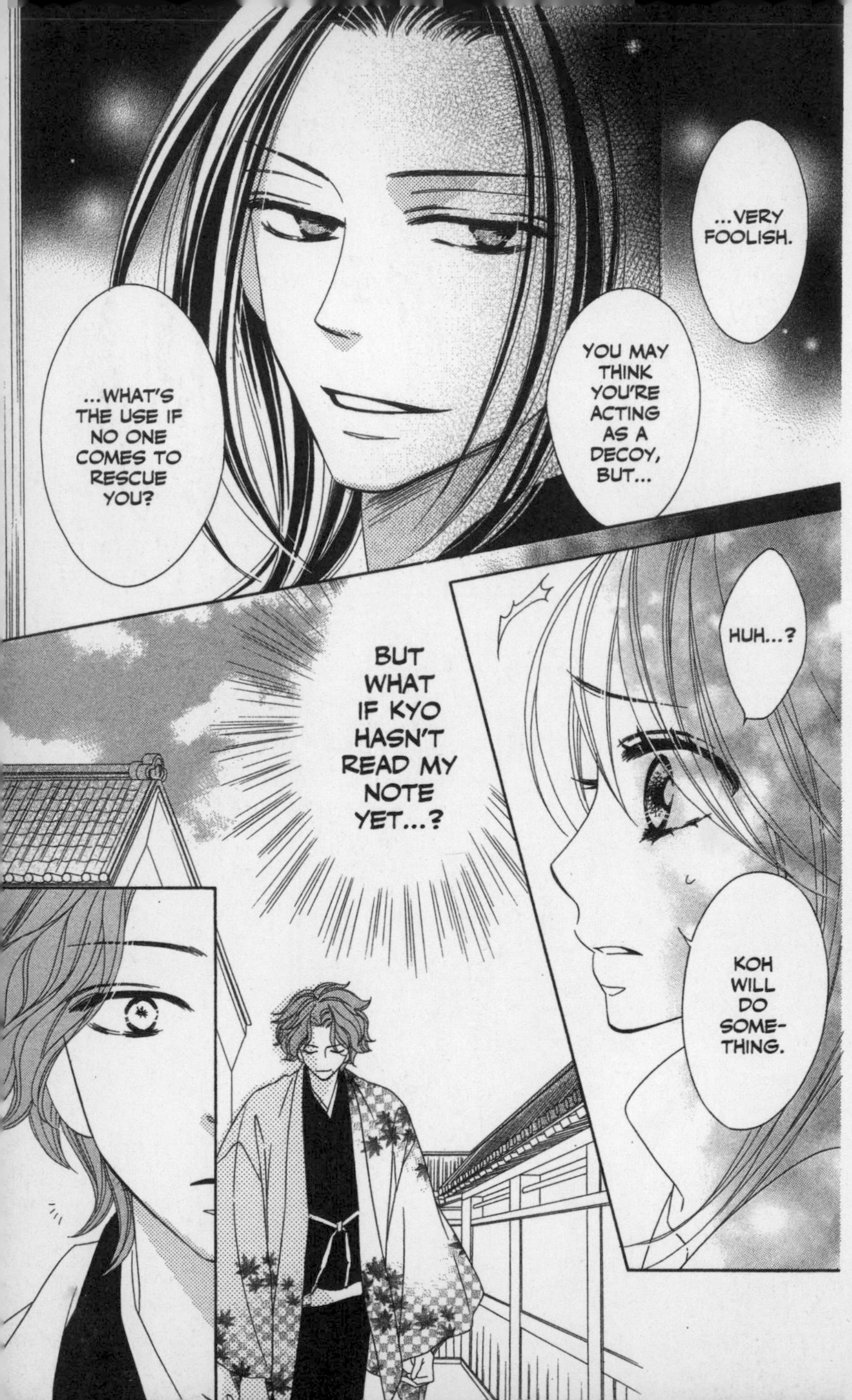
...VERY FOOLISH.
YOU MAY THINK YOU'RE ACTING AS A DECOY, BUT...
...WHAT'S THE USE IF NO ONE COMES TO RESCUE YOU?
HUH...?
KOH WILL DO SOME-THING.
BUT WHAT IF KYO HASN'T READ MY NOTE YET...?

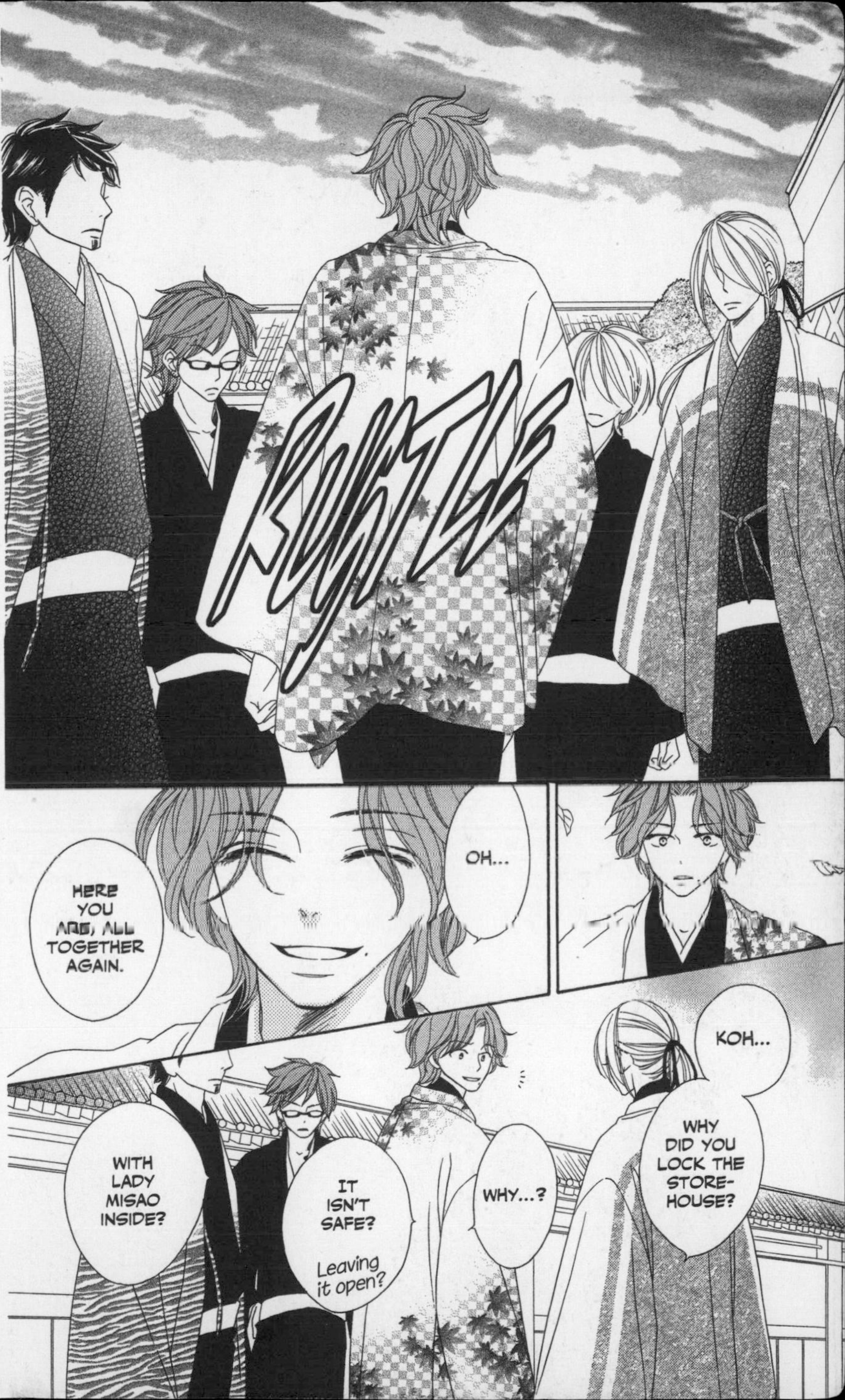
RUSTLE
OH...
HERE YOU ARE, ALL TOGETHER AGAIN.
KOH...
WHY DID YOU LOCK THE STORE-HOUSE?
WHY...?
IT ISN'T SAFE?
Leaving it open?
WITH LADY MISAO INSIDE?

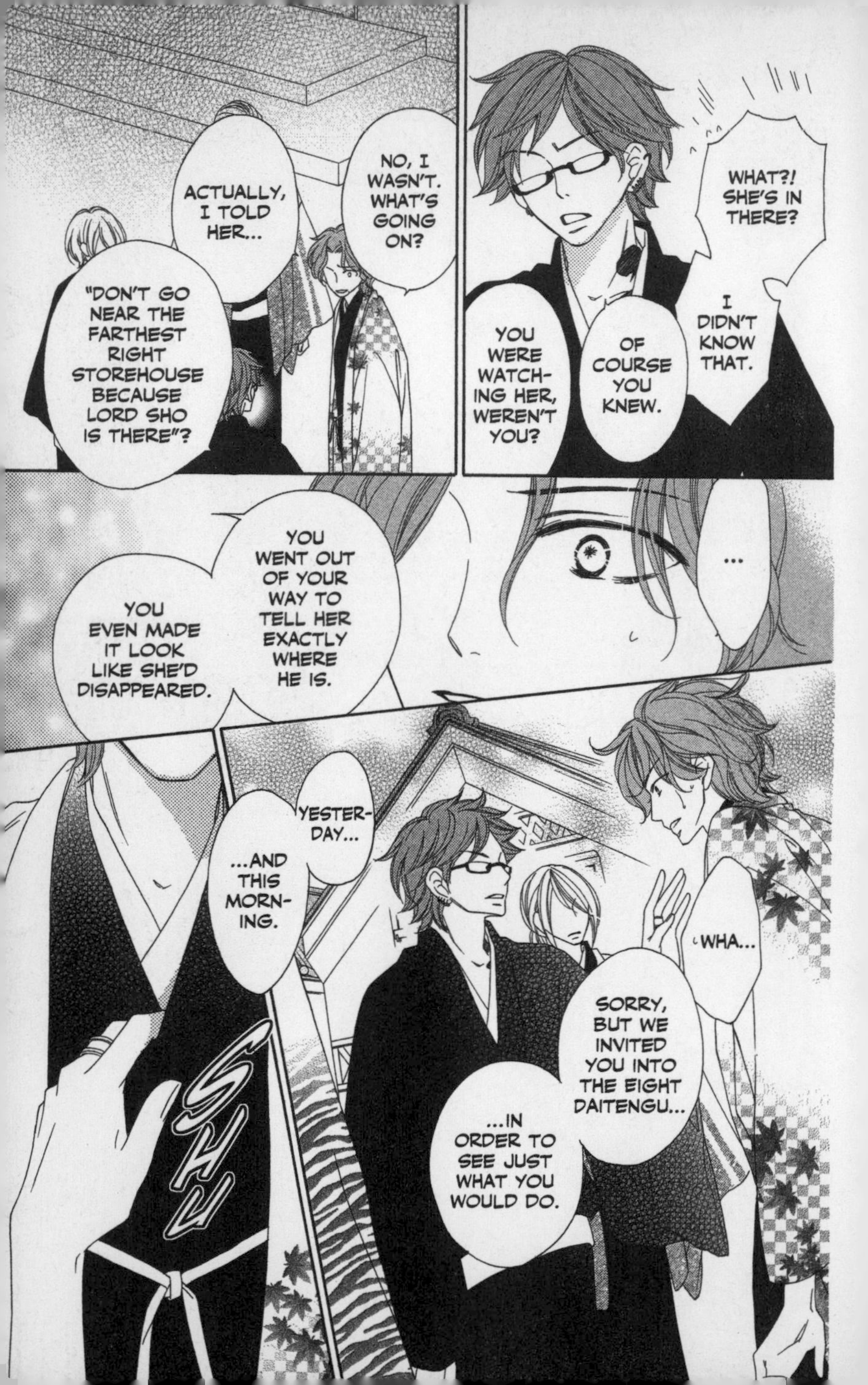
WHAT?! SHE'S IN THERE?
I DIDN'T KNOW THAT.
OF COURSE YOU KNEW.
YOU WERE WATCHING HER, WEREN'T YOU?
NO, I WASN'T. WHAT'S GOING ON?
ACTUALLY, I TOLD HER...
"DON'T GO NEAR THE FARTHEST RIGHT STOREHOUSE BECAUSE LORD SHO IS THERE"?
...
YOU WENT OUT OF YOUR WAY TO TELL HER EXACTLY WHERE HE IS.
YOU EVEN MADE IT LOOK LIKE SHE'D DISAPPEARED.
YESTER-DAY...
...AND THIS MORN-ING.
WHA...
SORRY, BUT WE INVITED YOU INTO THE EIGHT DAITENGU...
...IN ORDER TO SEE JUST WHAT YOU WOULD DO.
SHU

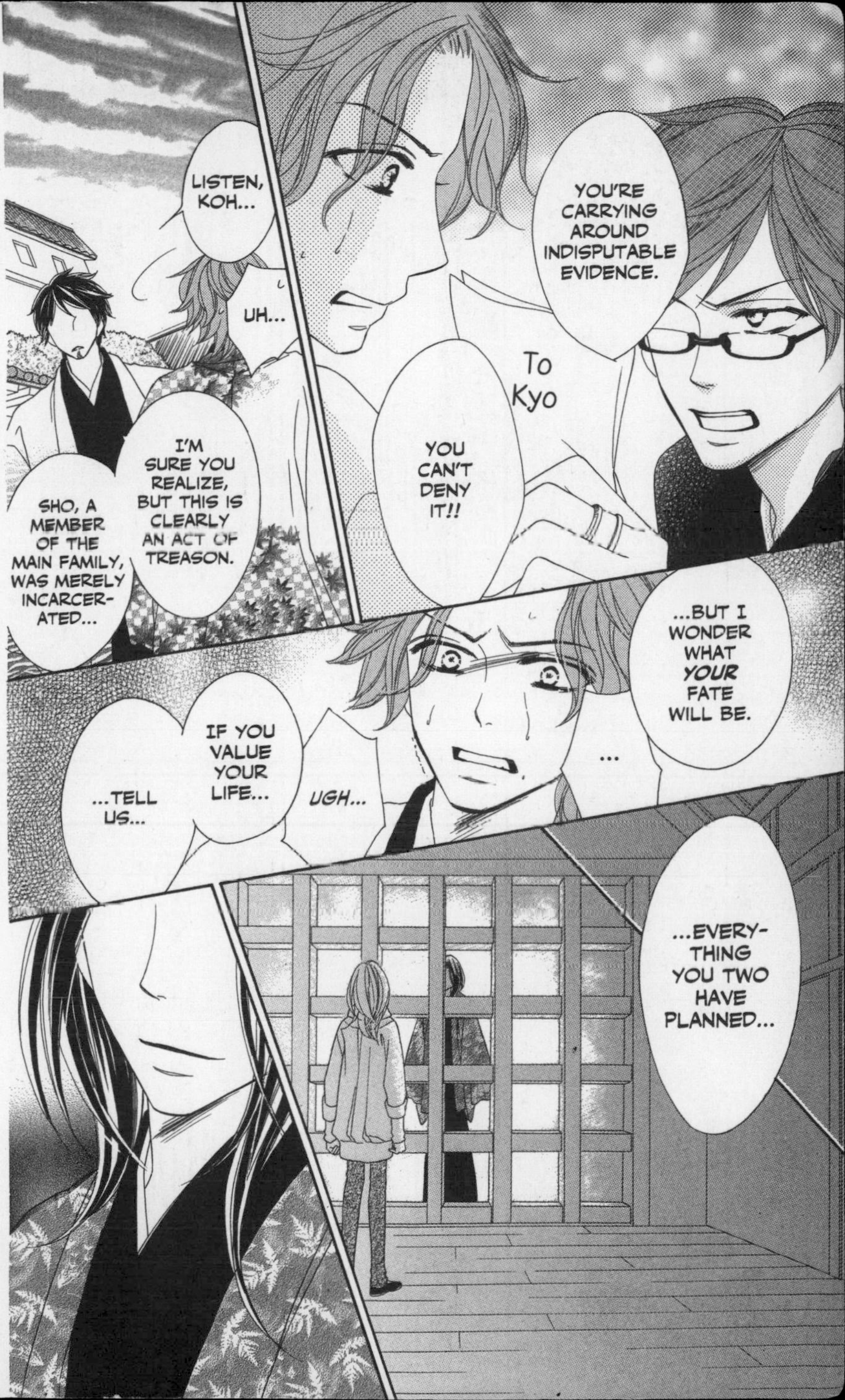
YOU'RE CARRYING AROUND INDISPUTABLE EVIDENCE.
To Kyo
YOU CAN'T DENY IT!!
LISTEN, KOH...
UH...
I'M SURE YOU REALIZE, BUT THIS IS CLEARLY AN ACT OF TREASON.
SHO, A MEMBER OF THE MAIN FAMILY, WAS MERELY INCARCERATED...
...BUT I WONDER WHAT *YOUR* FATE WILL BE.
...
UGH...
IF YOU VALUE YOUR LIFE...
...TELL US...
...EVERYTHING YOU TWO HAVE PLANNED...

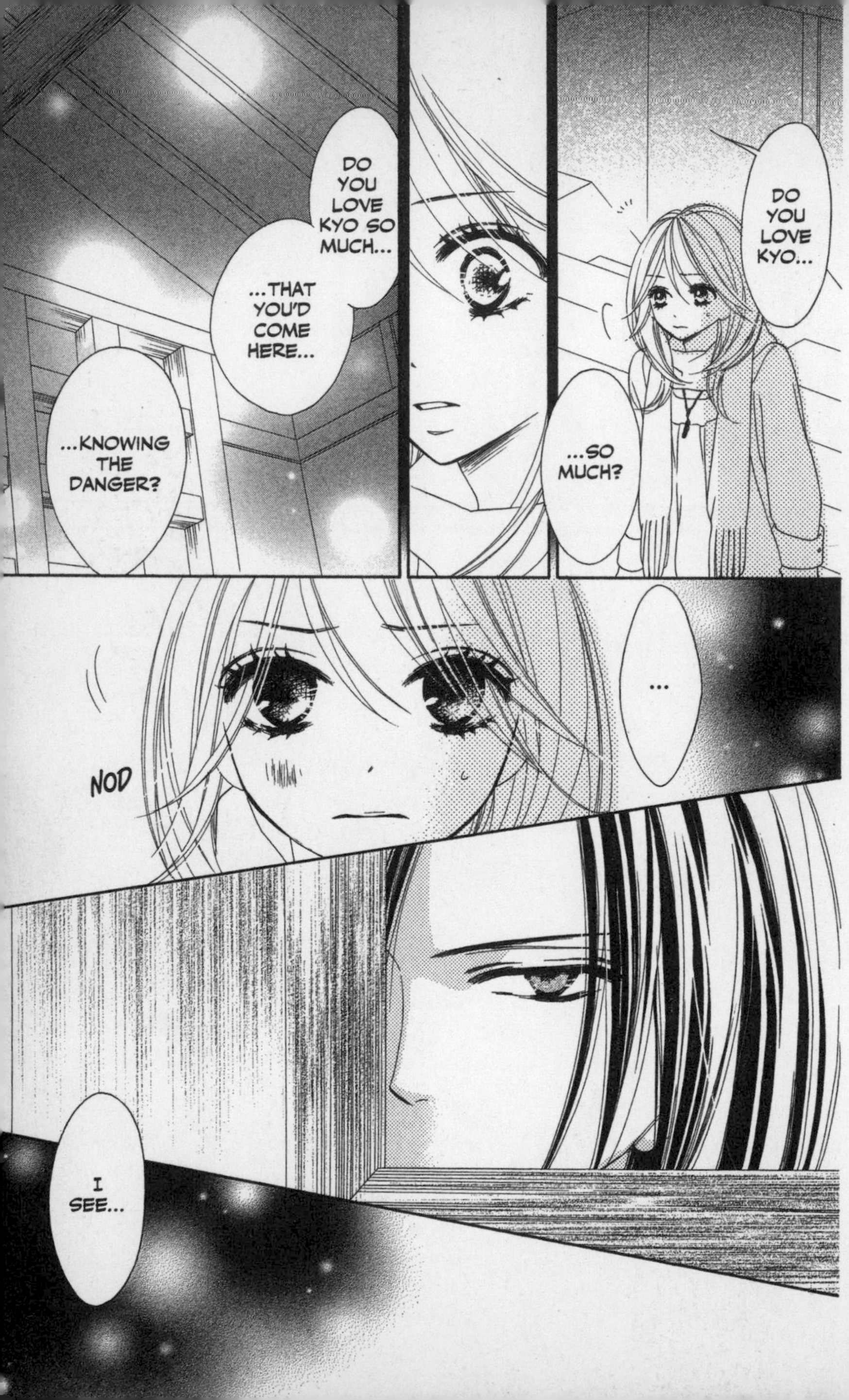
DO YOU LOVE KYO...
...SO MUCH?
DO YOU LOVE KYO SO MUCH...
...THAT YOU'D COME HERE...
...KNOWING THE DANGER?
...
NOD
I SEE...

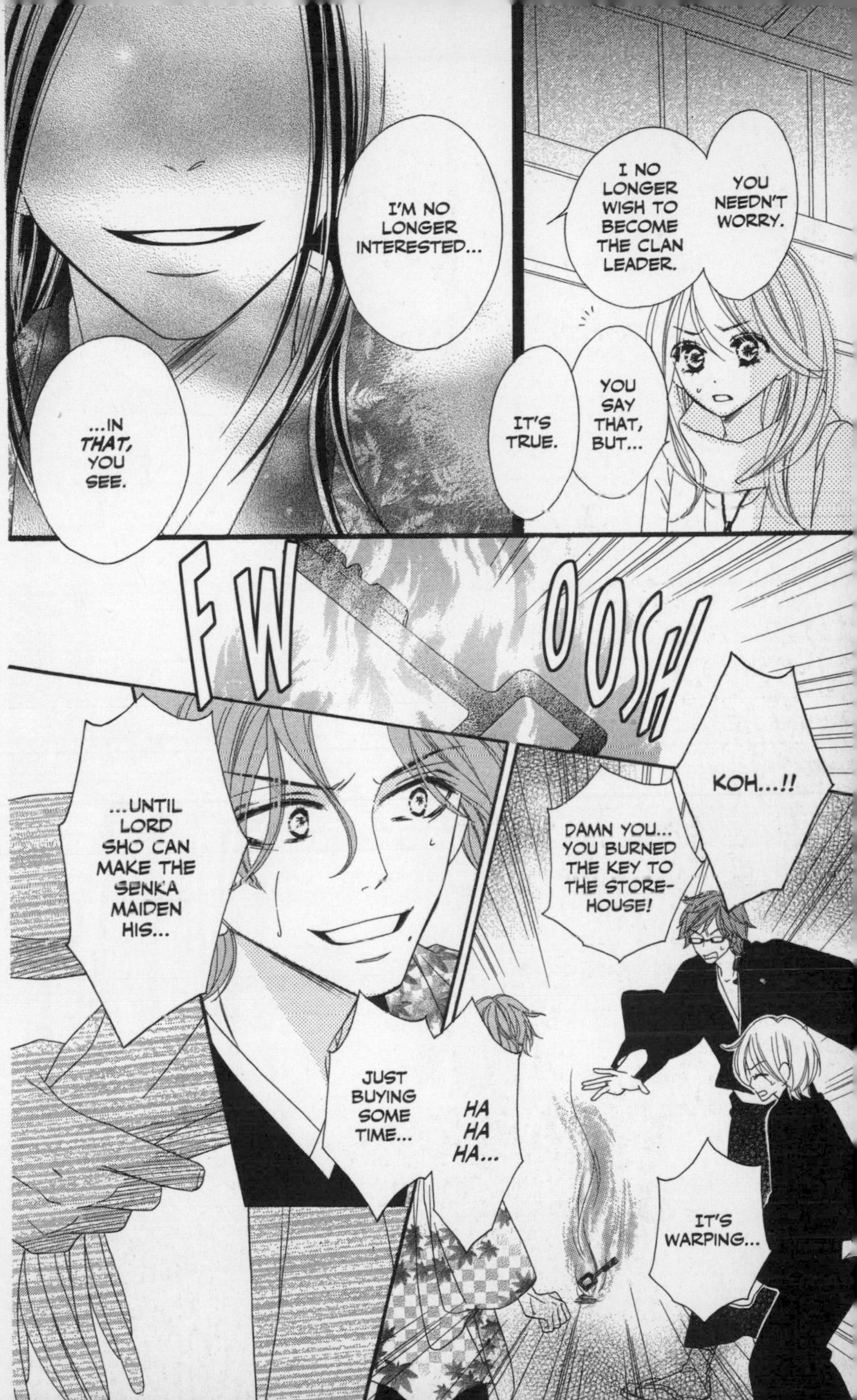
YOU NEEDN'T WORRY.
I NO LONGER WISH TO BECOME THE CLAN LEADER.
YOU SAY THAT, BUT...
IT'S TRUE.
I'M NO LONGER INTERESTED...
...IN *THAT*, YOU SEE.
FWOOSH
KOH...!!
DAMN YOU... YOU BURNED THE KEY TO THE STORE-HOUSE!
IT'S WARPING...
JUST BUYING SOME TIME...
HA HA HA...
...UNTIL LORD SHO CAN MAKE THE SENKA MAIDEN HIS...

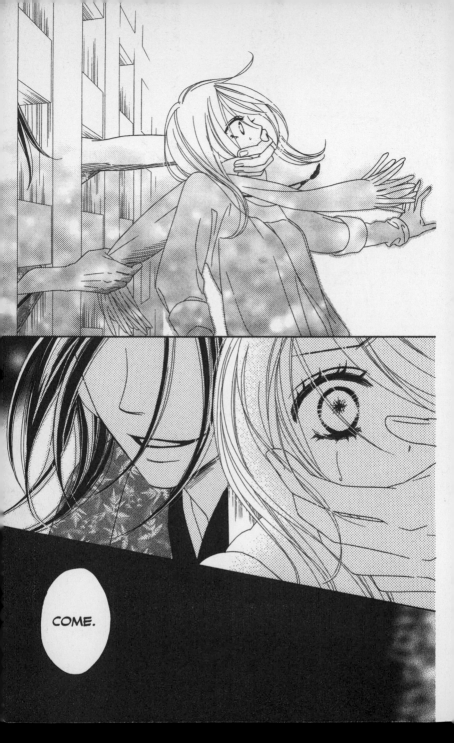

COME.

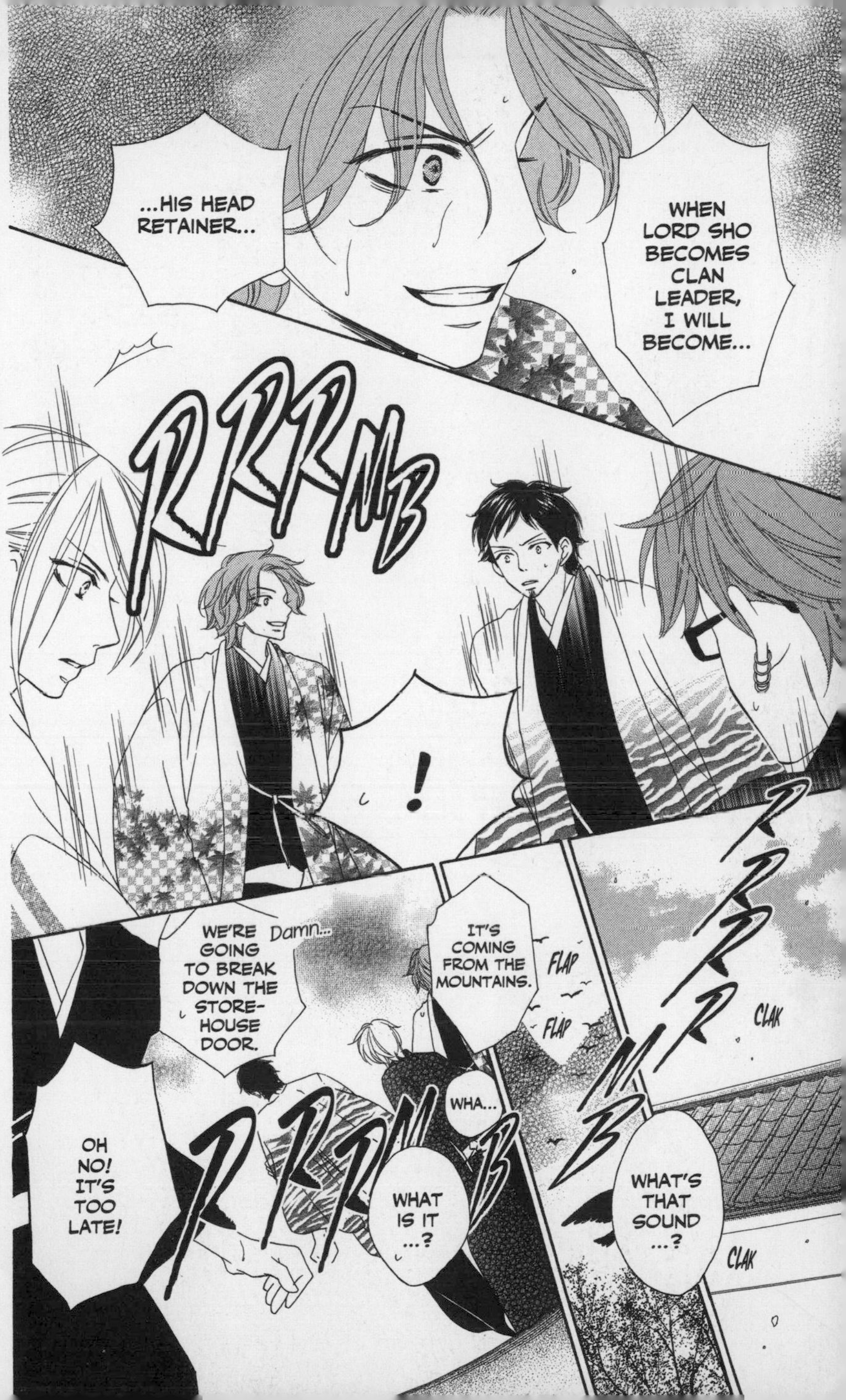
WHEN LORD SHO BECOMES CLAN LEADER, I WILL BECOME...
...HIS HEAD RETAINER...
RRRMB
!
RRRRRMB
CLAK
WHAT'S THAT SOUND ...?
CLAK
IT'S COMING FROM THE MOUNTAINS.
FLAP
FLAP
WE'RE GOING TO BREAK DOWN THE STORE-HOUSE DOOR.
Damn...
WHA...
WHAT IS IT ...?
RRRMB
OH NO! IT'S TOO LATE!

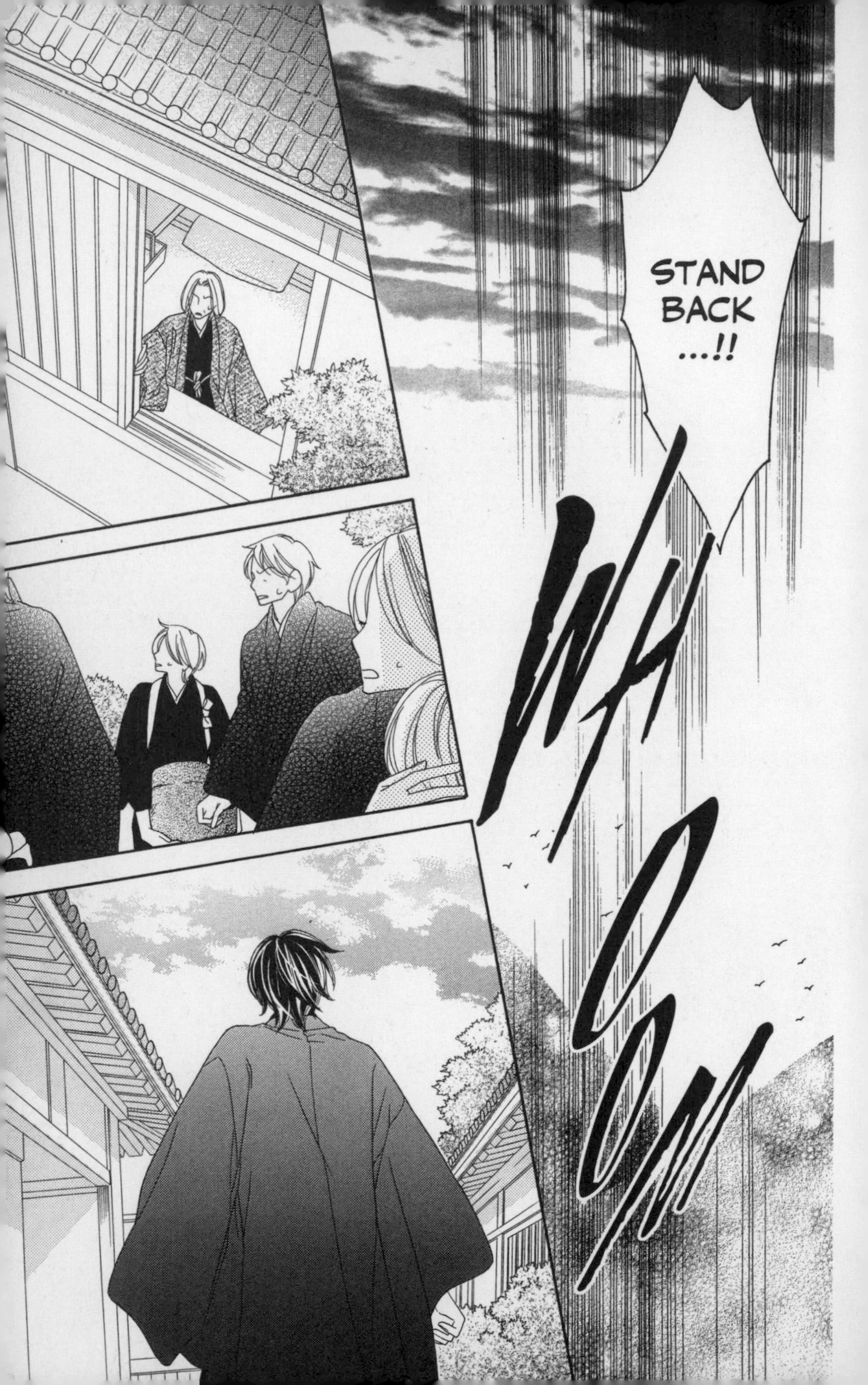
STAND BACK ...!!
WHOOSH

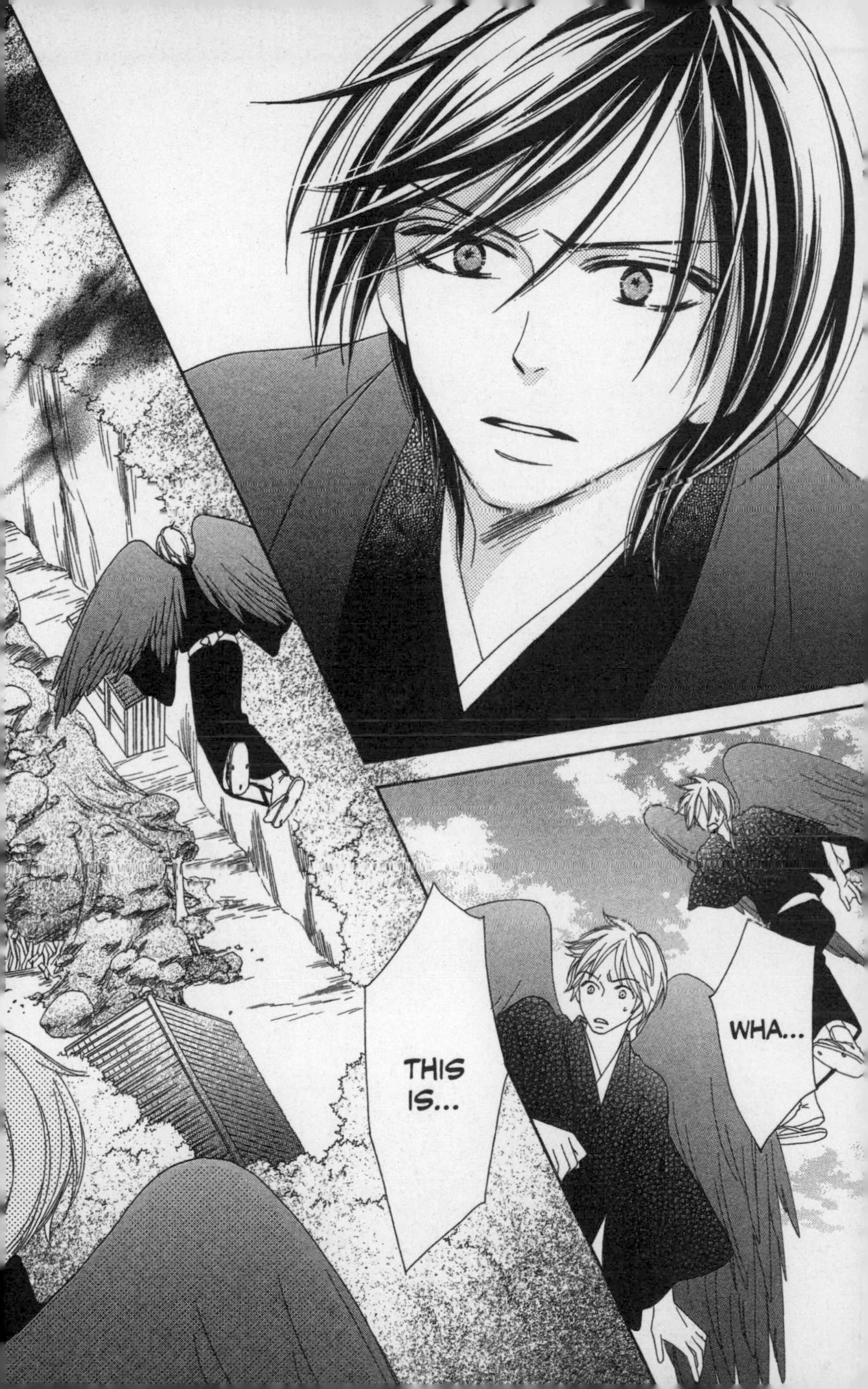
WHA...
THIS IS...

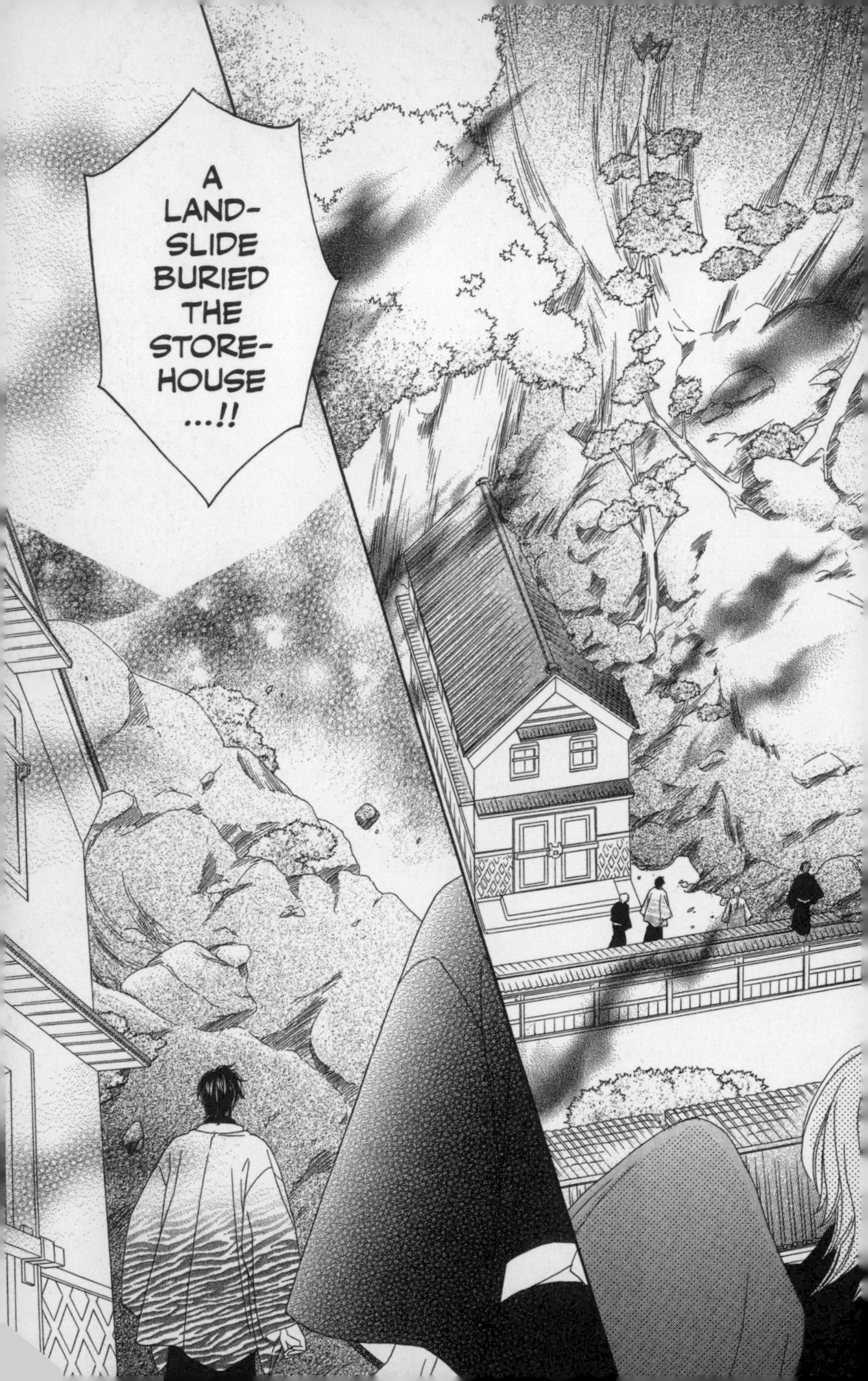
A LAND-SLIDE BURIED THE STORE-HOUSE ...!!

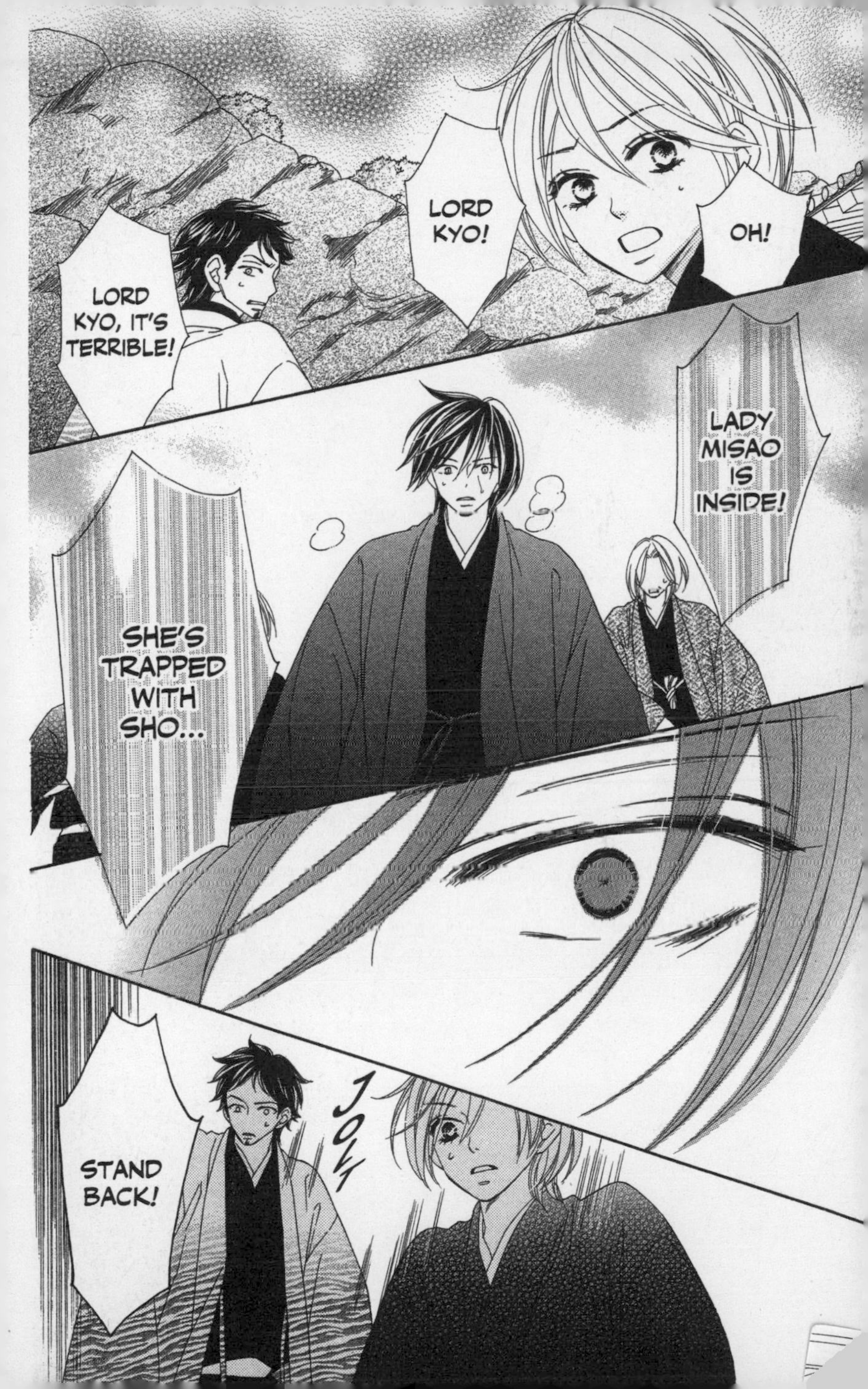
OH!
LORD KYO!
LORD KYO, IT'S TERRIBLE!
LADY MISAO IS INSIDE!
SHE'S TRAPPED WITH SHO...
JOLT
STAND BACK!

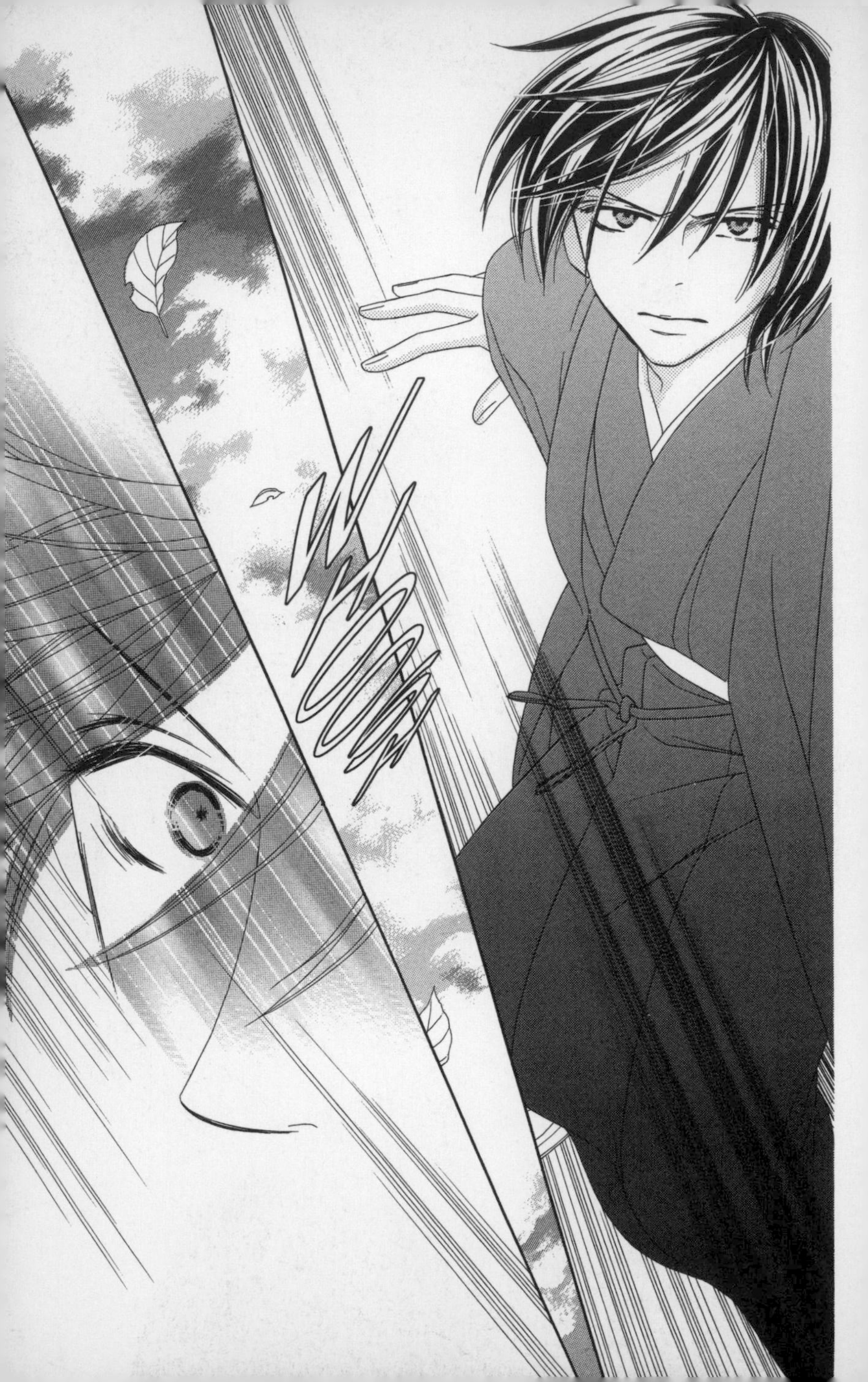

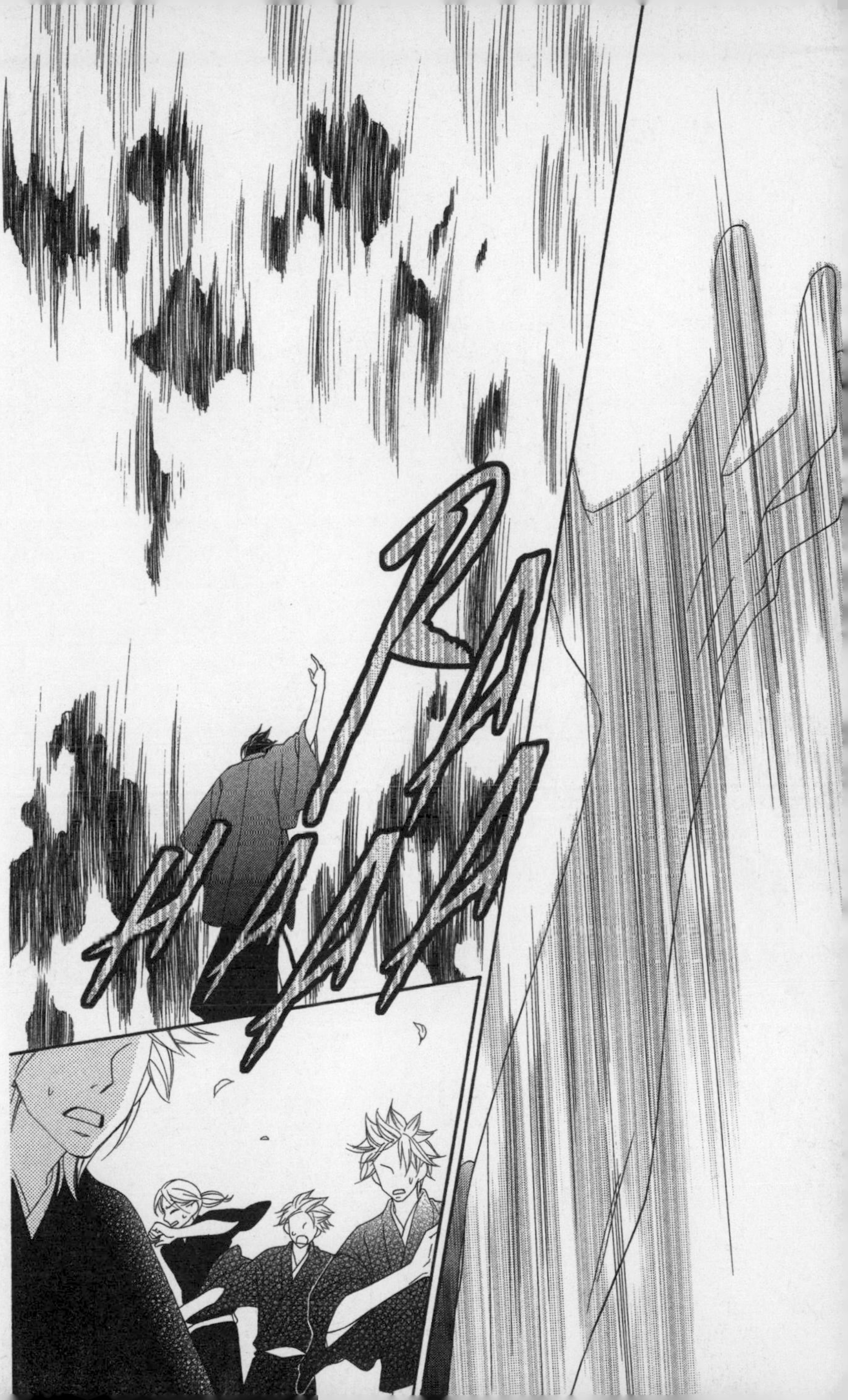
BAHAAA

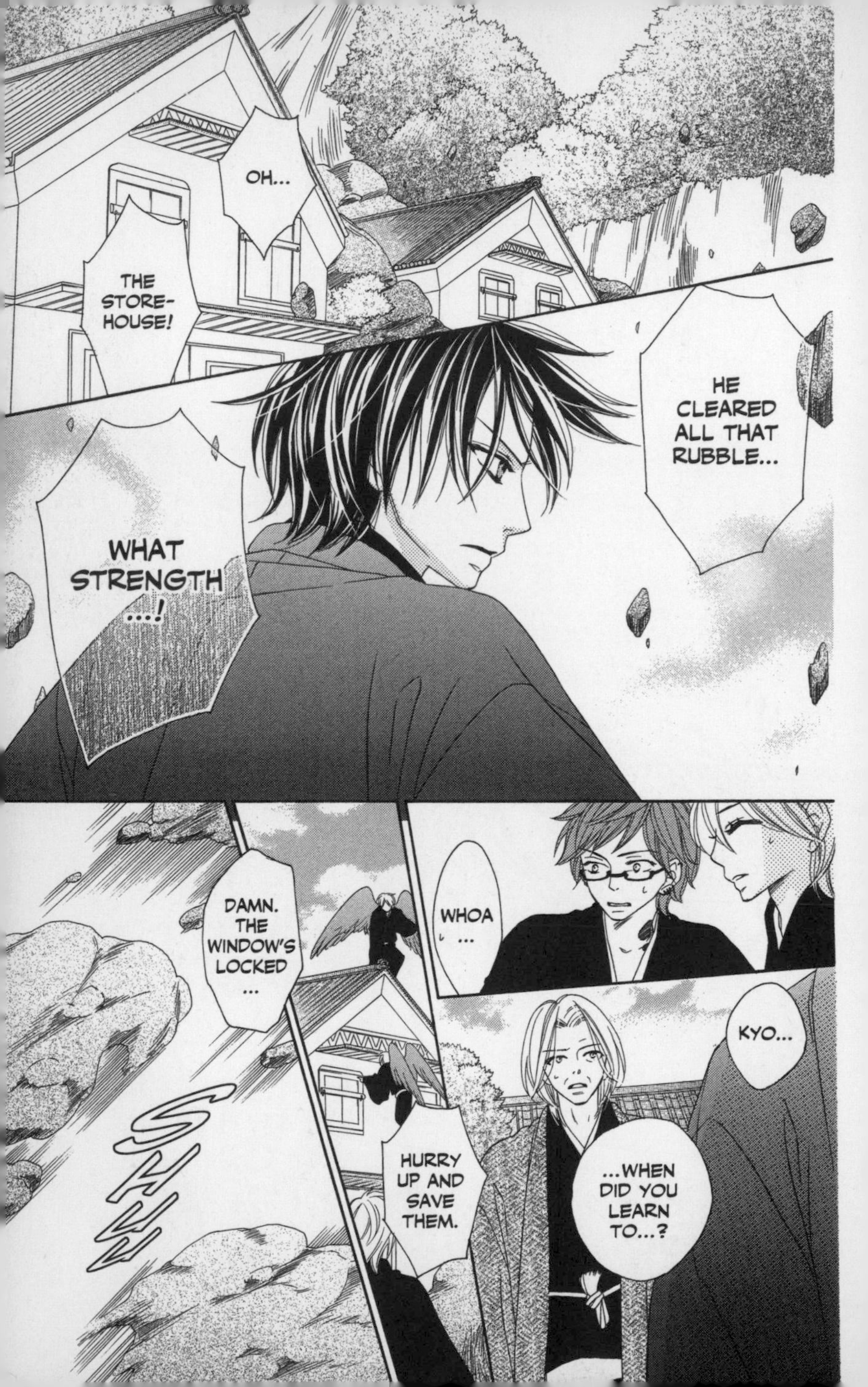
OH...
THE STORE-HOUSE!
HE CLEARED ALL THAT RUBBLE...
WHAT STRENGTH ...!
WHOA ...
KYO...
...WHEN DID YOU LEARN TO...?
DAMN. THE WINDOW'S LOCKED ...
HURRY UP AND SAVE THEM.
SHUU

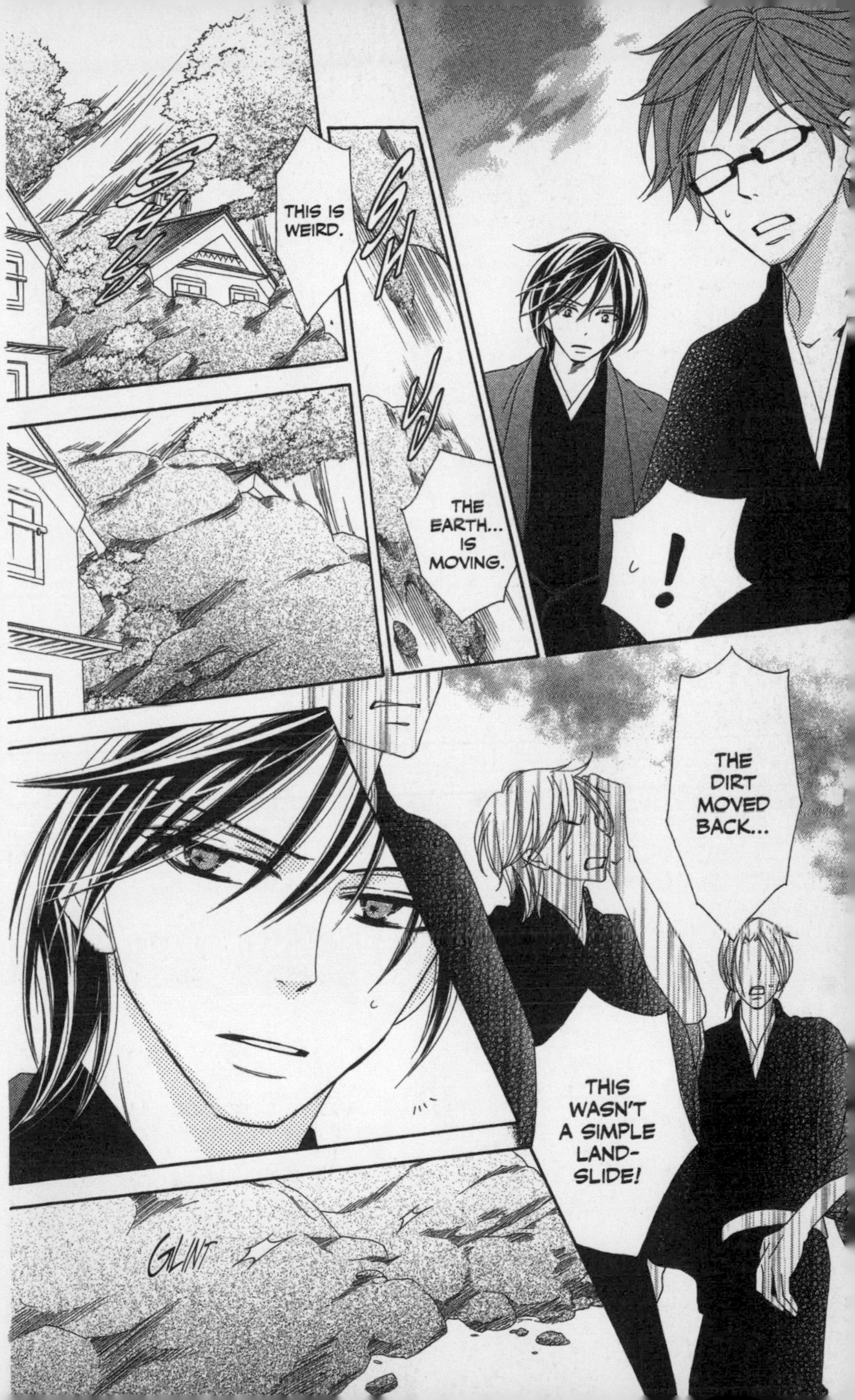
!
THIS IS WEIRD.
THE EARTH... IS MOVING.
THE DIRT MOVED BACK...
THIS WASN'T A SIMPLE LAND-SLIDE!
GLINT

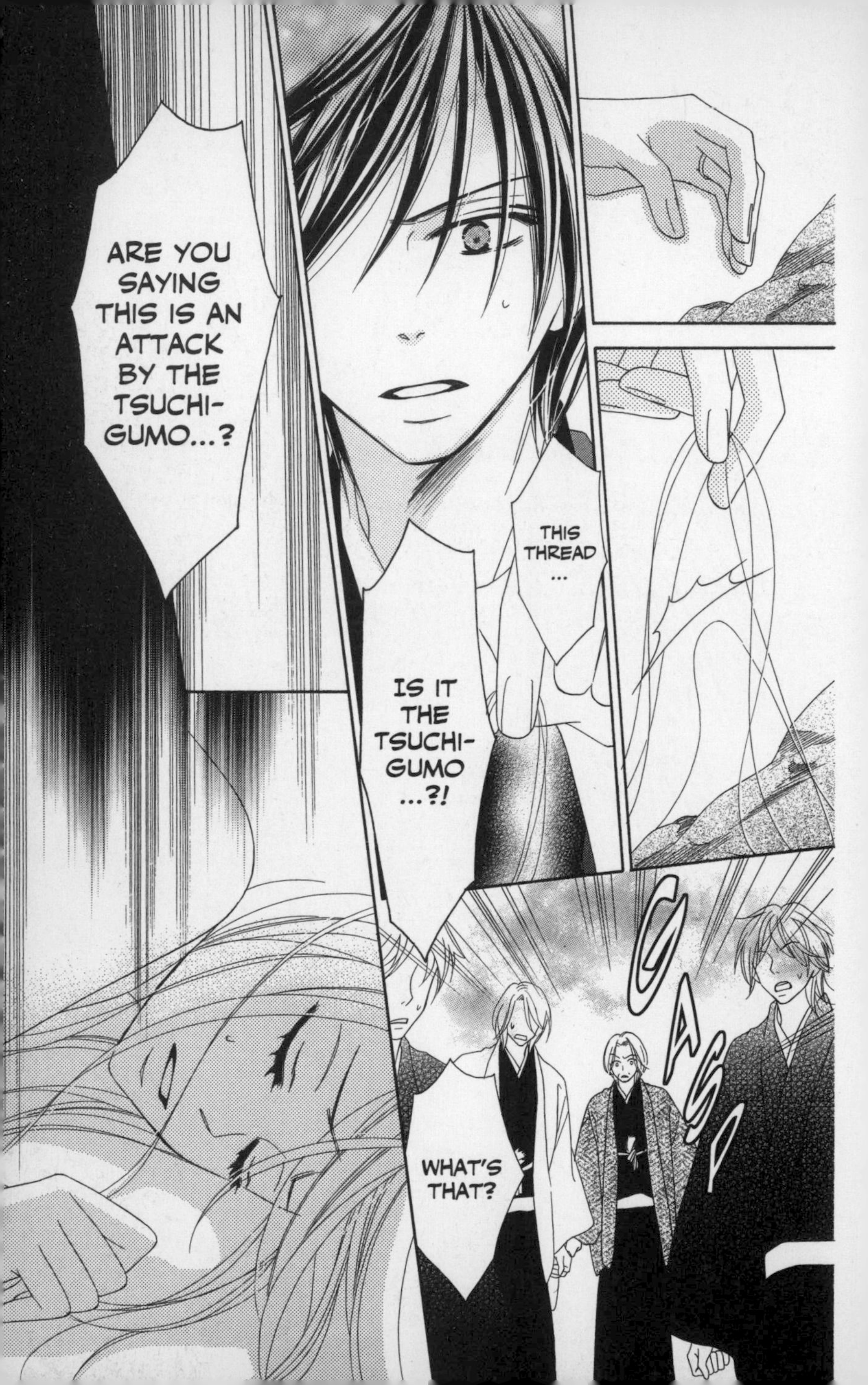
THIS THREAD ...
IS IT THE TSUCHI-GUMO ...?!
GASA
WHAT'S THAT?
ARE YOU SAYING THIS IS AN ATTACK BY THE TSUCHI-GUMO...?

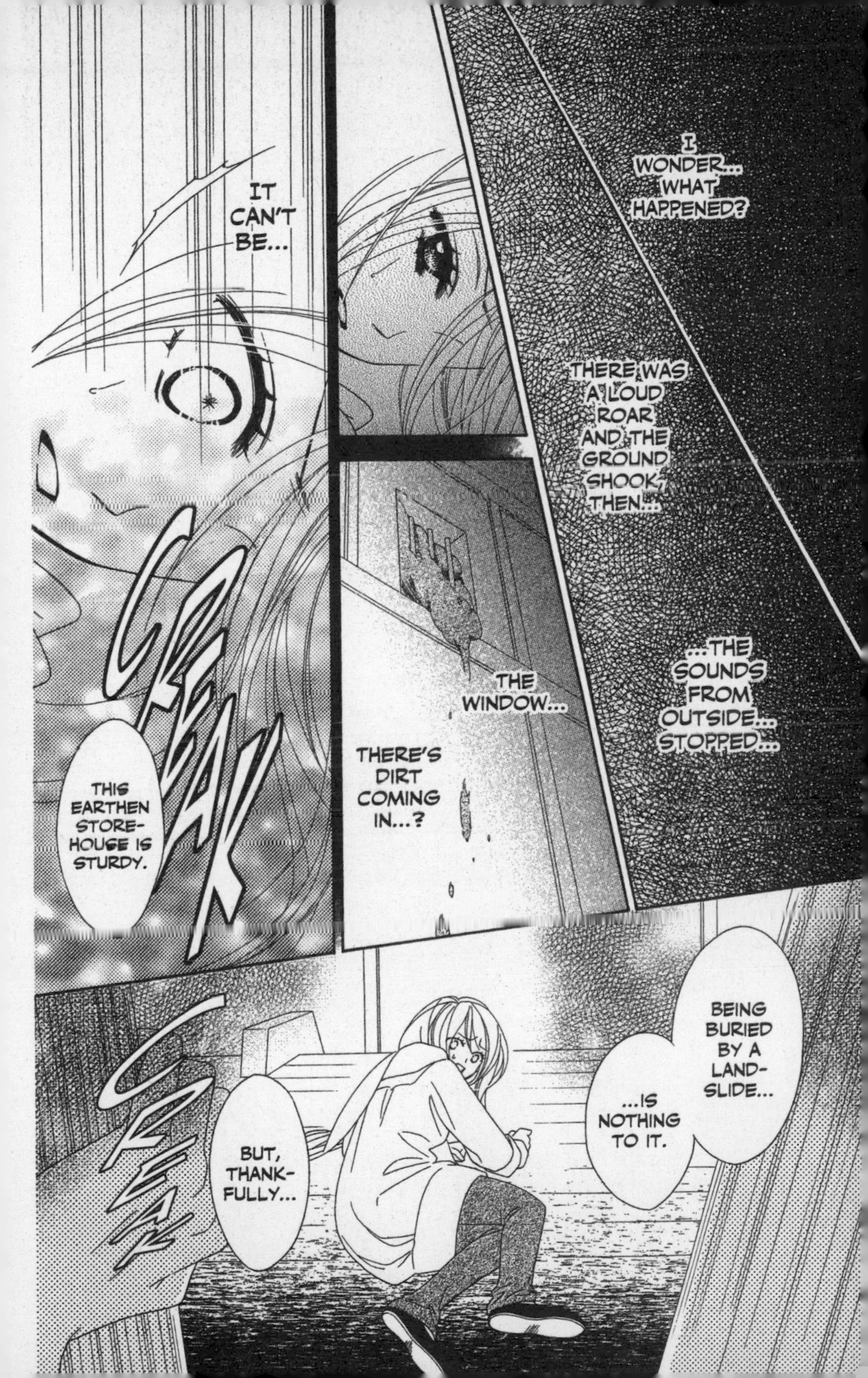
I WONDER... WHAT HAPPENED?
THERE WAS A LOUD ROAR AND THE GROUND SHOOK, THEN...
...THE SOUNDS FROM OUTSIDE... STOPPED...
THE WINDOW...
THERE'S DIRT COMING IN...?
IT CAN'T BE...
CREAK
THIS EARTHEN STOREHOUSE IS STURDY.
BEING BURIED BY A LANDSLIDE...
...IS NOTHING TO IT.
BUT, THANKFULLY...

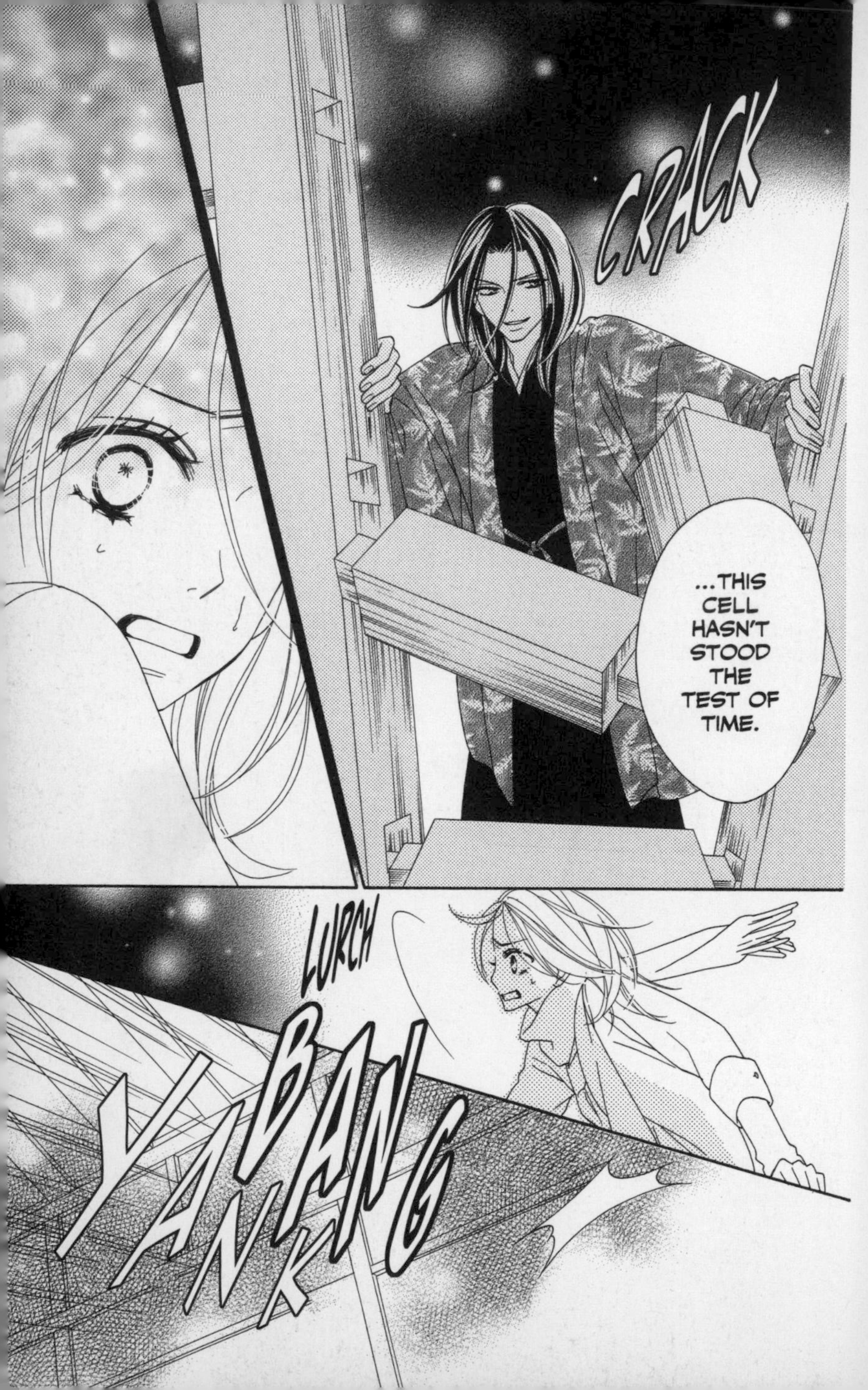
CRACK
...THIS CELL HASN'T STOOD THE TEST OF TIME.
LURCH
BANG
YANK

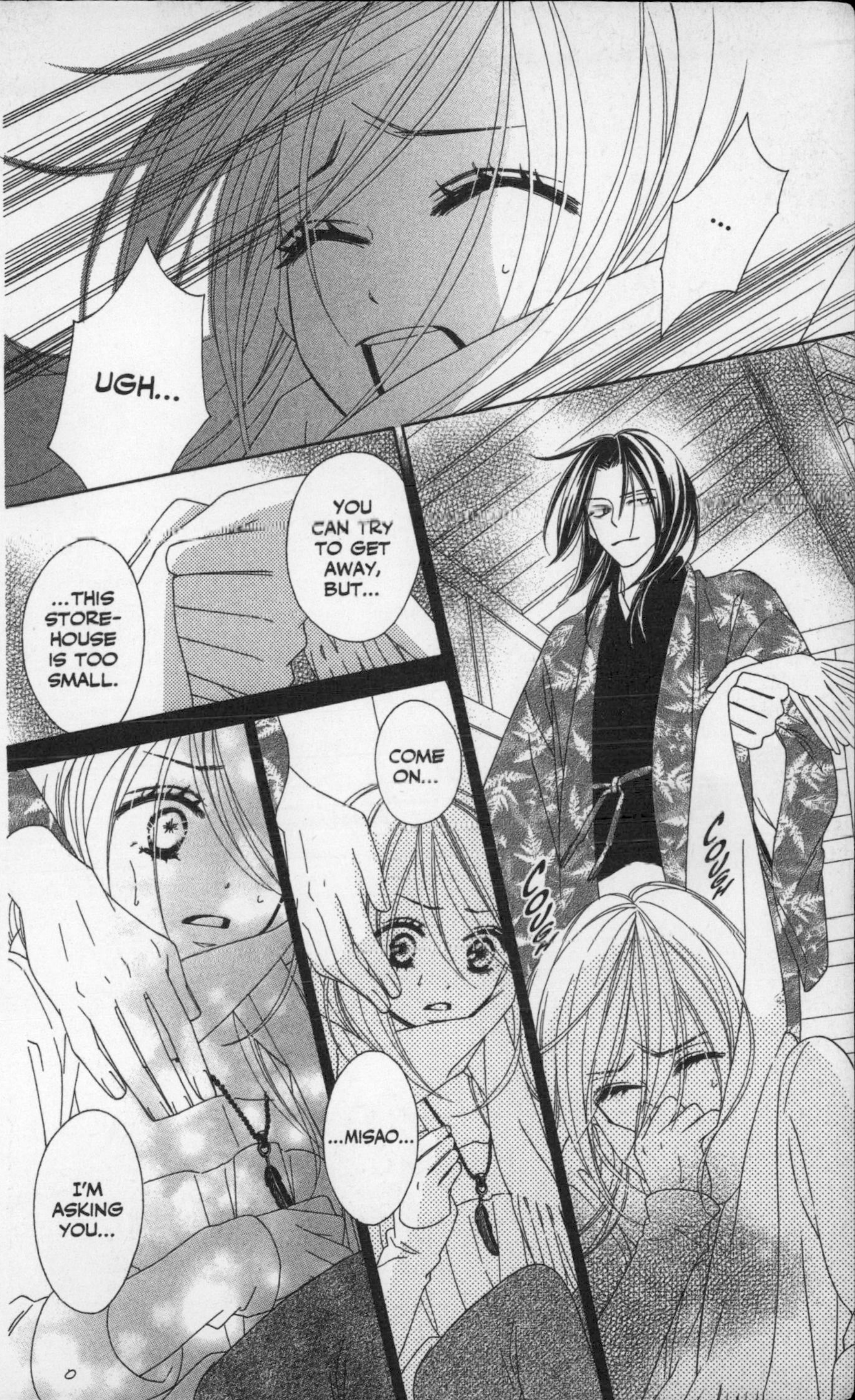
...
UGH...
COUGH
COUGH
YOU CAN TRY TO GET AWAY, BUT...
...THIS STORE-HOUSE IS TOO SMALL.
COME ON...
...MISAO...
I'M ASKING YOU...

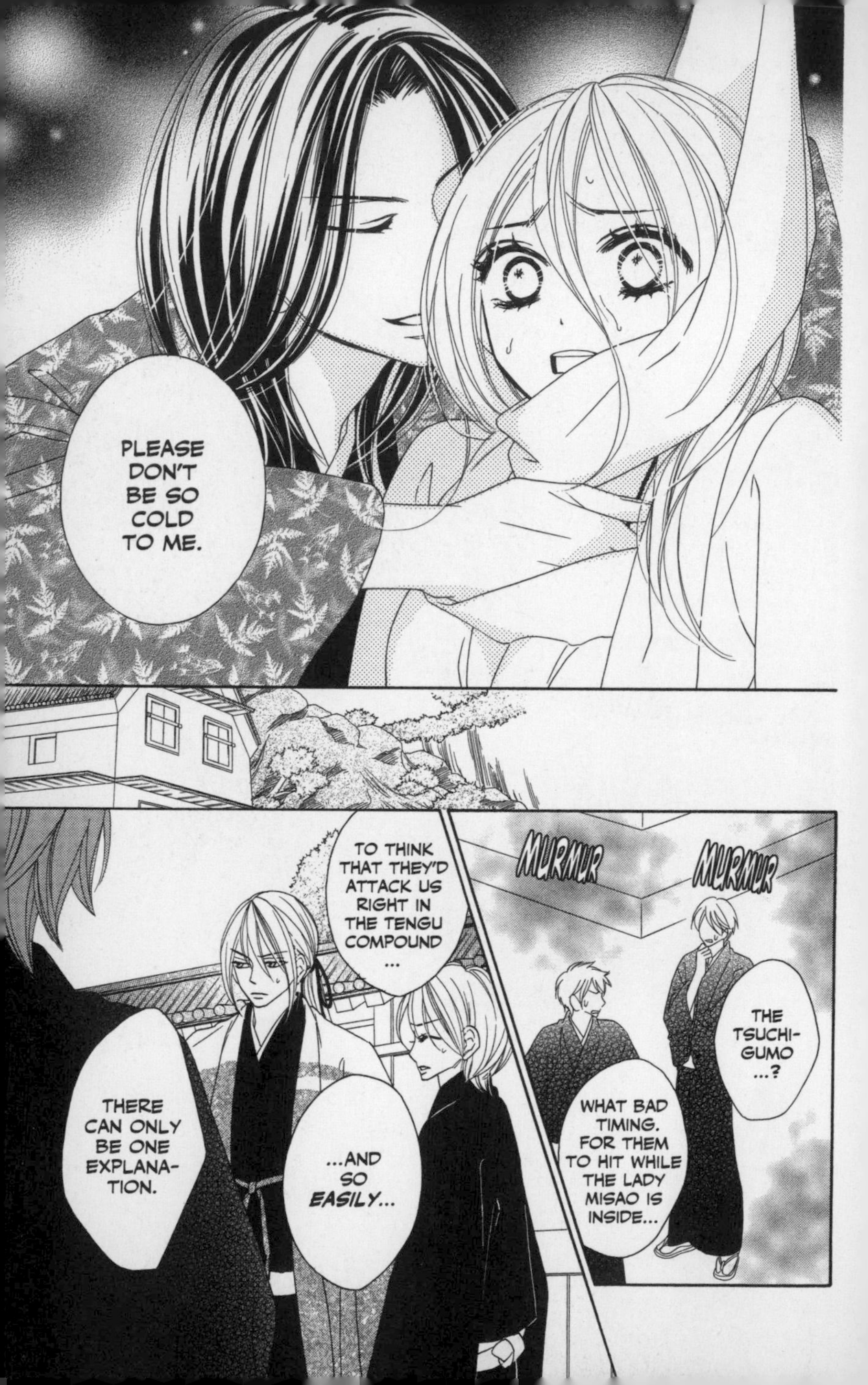
PLEASE DON'T BE SO COLD TO ME.
MURMUR
MURMUR
THE TSUCHI-GUMO ...?
WHAT BAD TIMING. FOR THEM TO HIT WHILE THE LADY MISAO IS INSIDE...
TO THINK THAT THEY'D ATTACK US RIGHT IN THE TENGU COMPOUND ...
...AND SO *EASILY*...
THERE CAN ONLY BE ONE EXPLANA-TION.

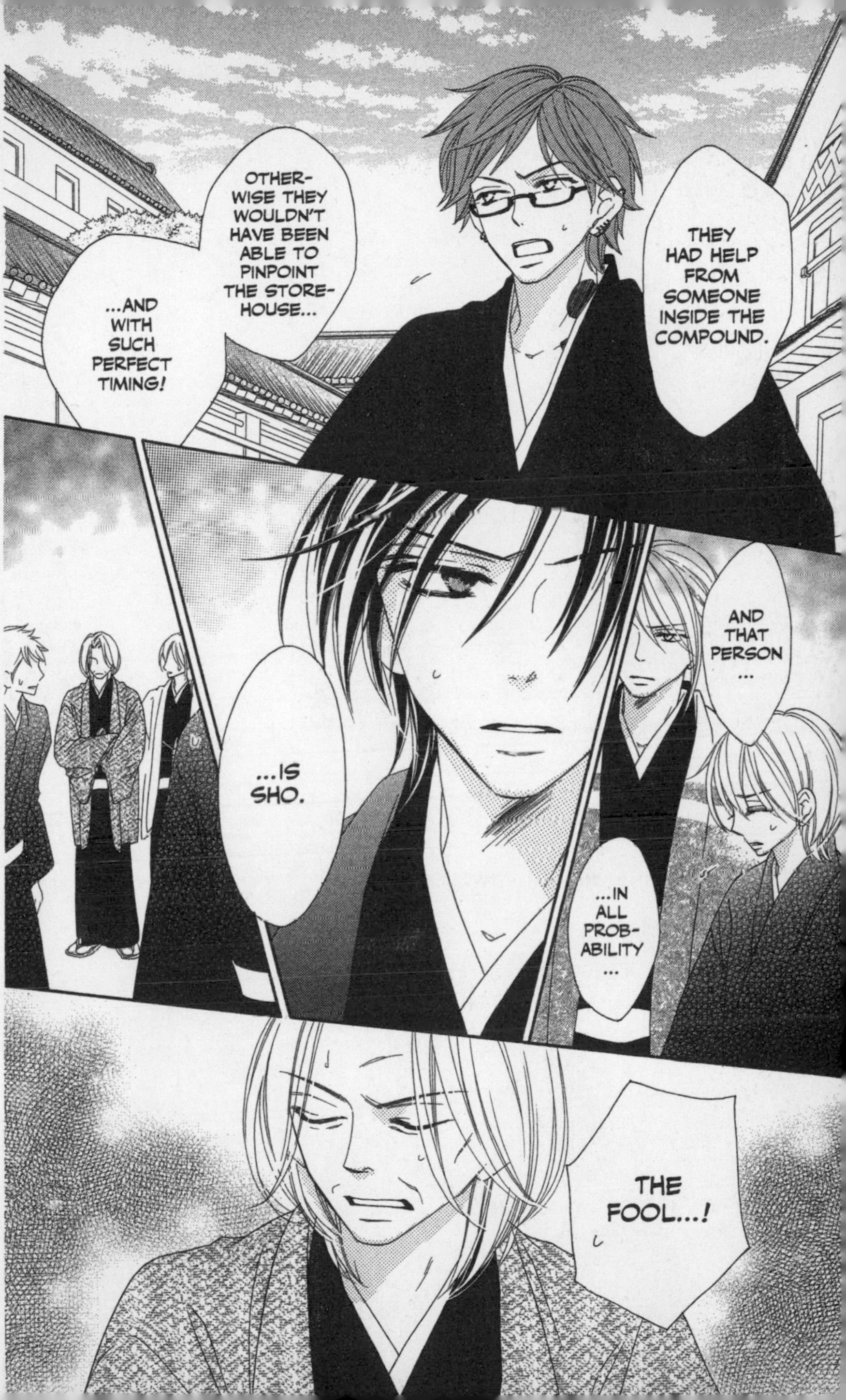
THEY HAD HELP FROM SOMEONE INSIDE THE COMPOUND.
OTHER-WISE THEY WOULDN'T HAVE BEEN ABLE TO PINPOINT THE STORE-HOUSE...
...AND WITH SUCH PERFECT TIMING!
AND THAT PERSON ...
...IN ALL PROB-ABILITY ...
...IS SHO.
THE FOOL...!

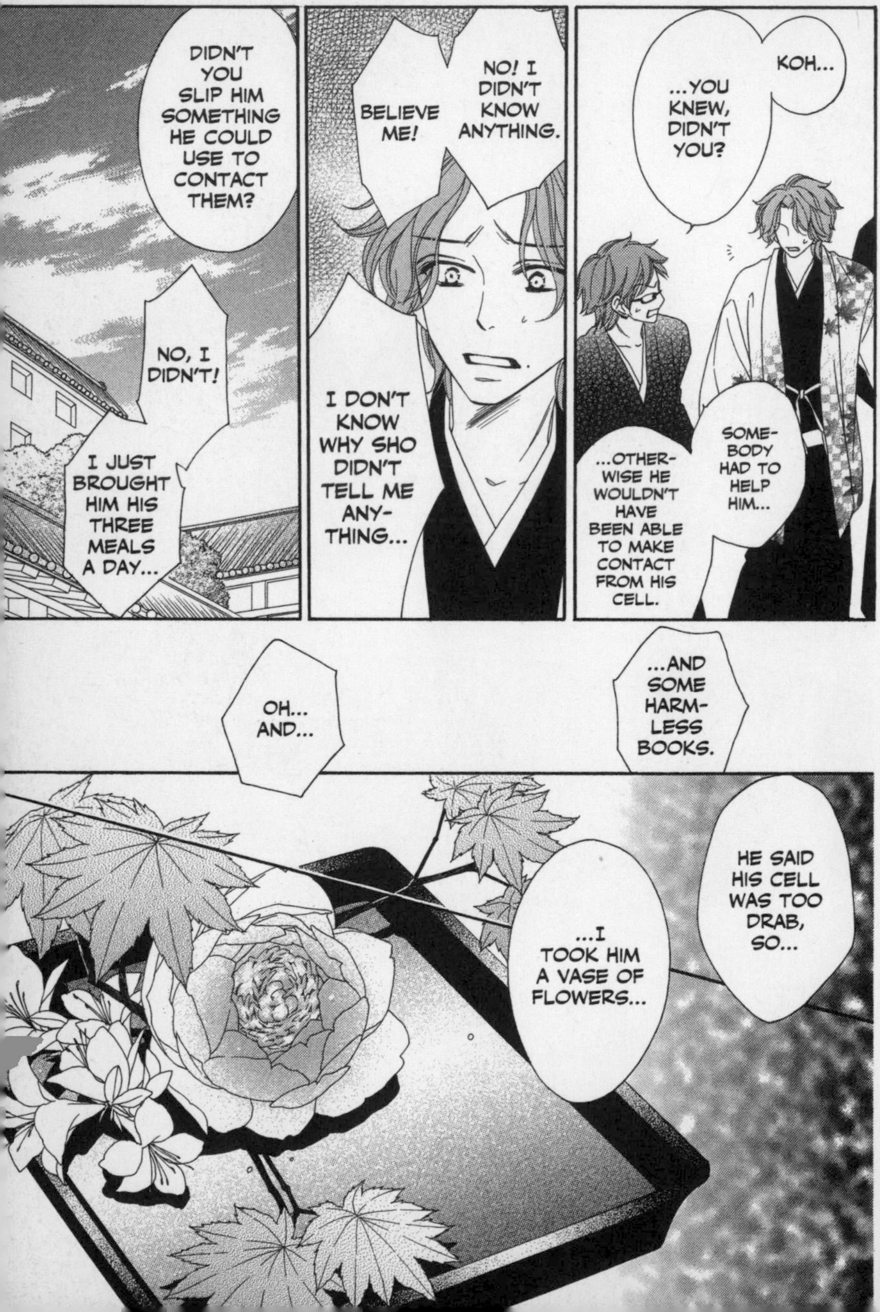
KOH...
...YOU KNEW, DIDN'T YOU?
SOMEBODY HAD TO HELP HIM...
...OTHERWISE HE WOULDN'T HAVE BEEN ABLE TO MAKE CONTACT FROM HIS CELL.
NO! I DIDN'T KNOW ANYTHING.
BELIEVE ME!
I DON'T KNOW WHY SHO DIDN'T TELL ME ANYTHING...
DIDN'T YOU SLIP HIM SOMETHING HE COULD USE TO CONTACT THEM?
NO, I DIDN'T!
I JUST BROUGHT HIM HIS THREE MEALS A DAY...
...AND SOME HARMLESS BOOKS.
OH... AND...
HE SAID HIS CELL WAS TOO DRAB, SO...
...I TOOK HIM A VASE OF FLOWERS...

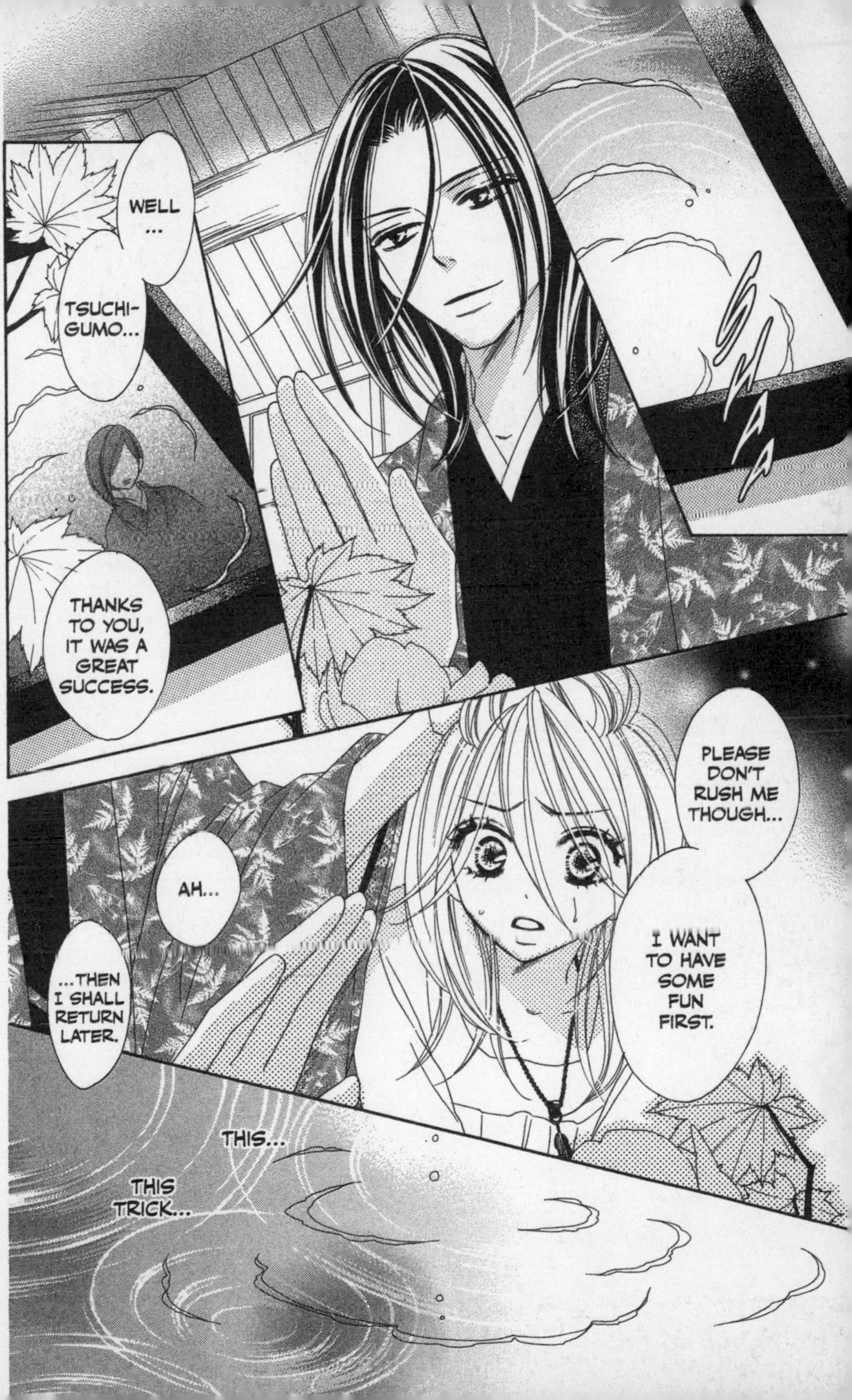
WELL ...
TSUCHI-GUMO...
THANKS TO YOU, IT WAS A GREAT SUCCESS.
PLEASE DON'T RUSH ME THOUGH...
I WANT TO HAVE SOME FUN FIRST.
AH...
...THEN I SHALL RETURN LATER.
THIS...
THIS TRICK...

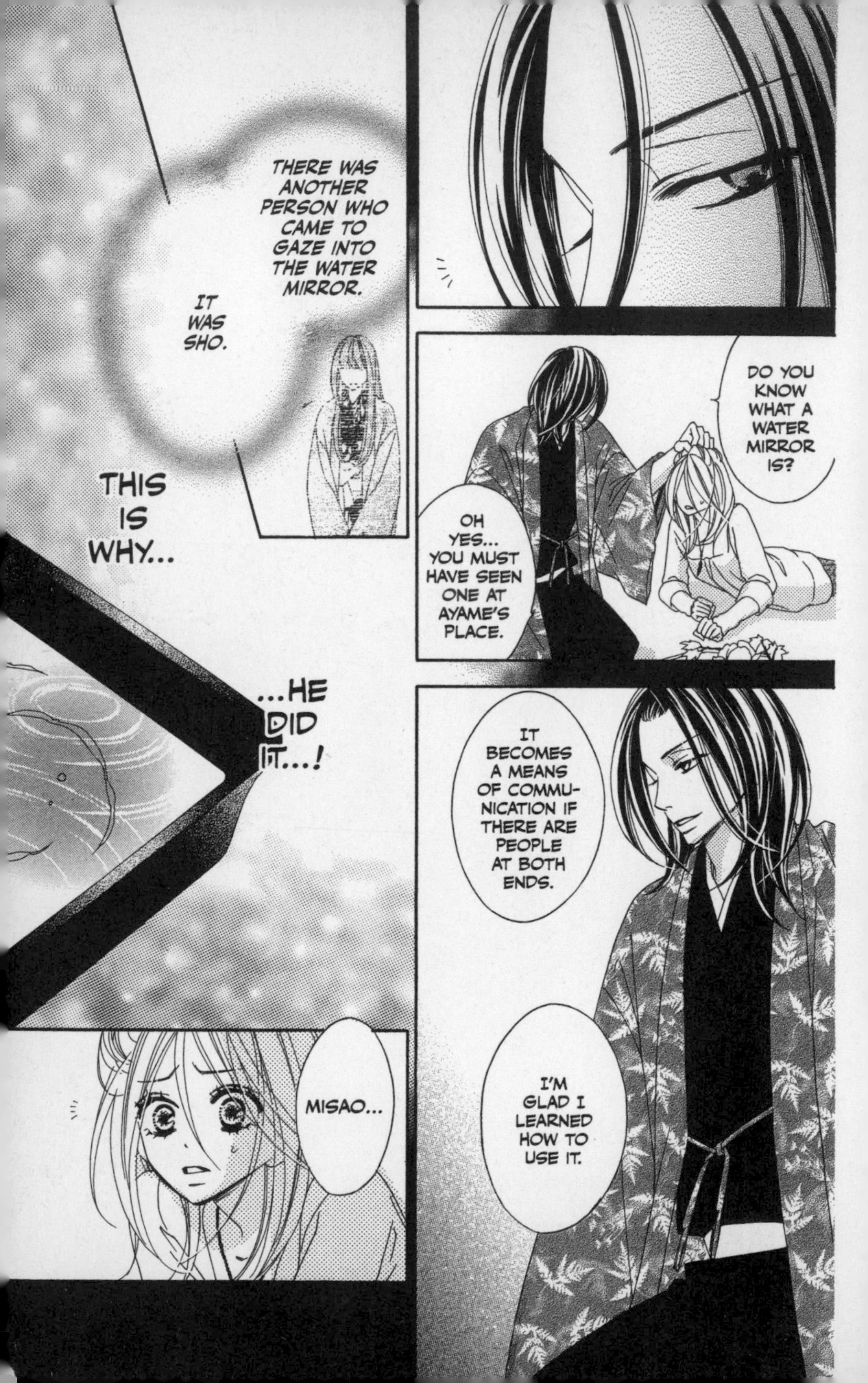
DO YOU KNOW WHAT A WATER MIRROR IS?
OH YES... YOU MUST HAVE SEEN ONE AT AYAME'S PLACE.
IT BECOMES A MEANS OF COMMU-NICATION IF THERE ARE PEOPLE AT BOTH ENDS.
I'M GLAD I LEARNED HOW TO USE IT.
THERE WAS ANOTHER PERSON WHO CAME TO GAZE INTO THE WATER MIRROR.
IT WAS SHO.
THIS IS WHY...
...HE DID IT...!
MISAO...

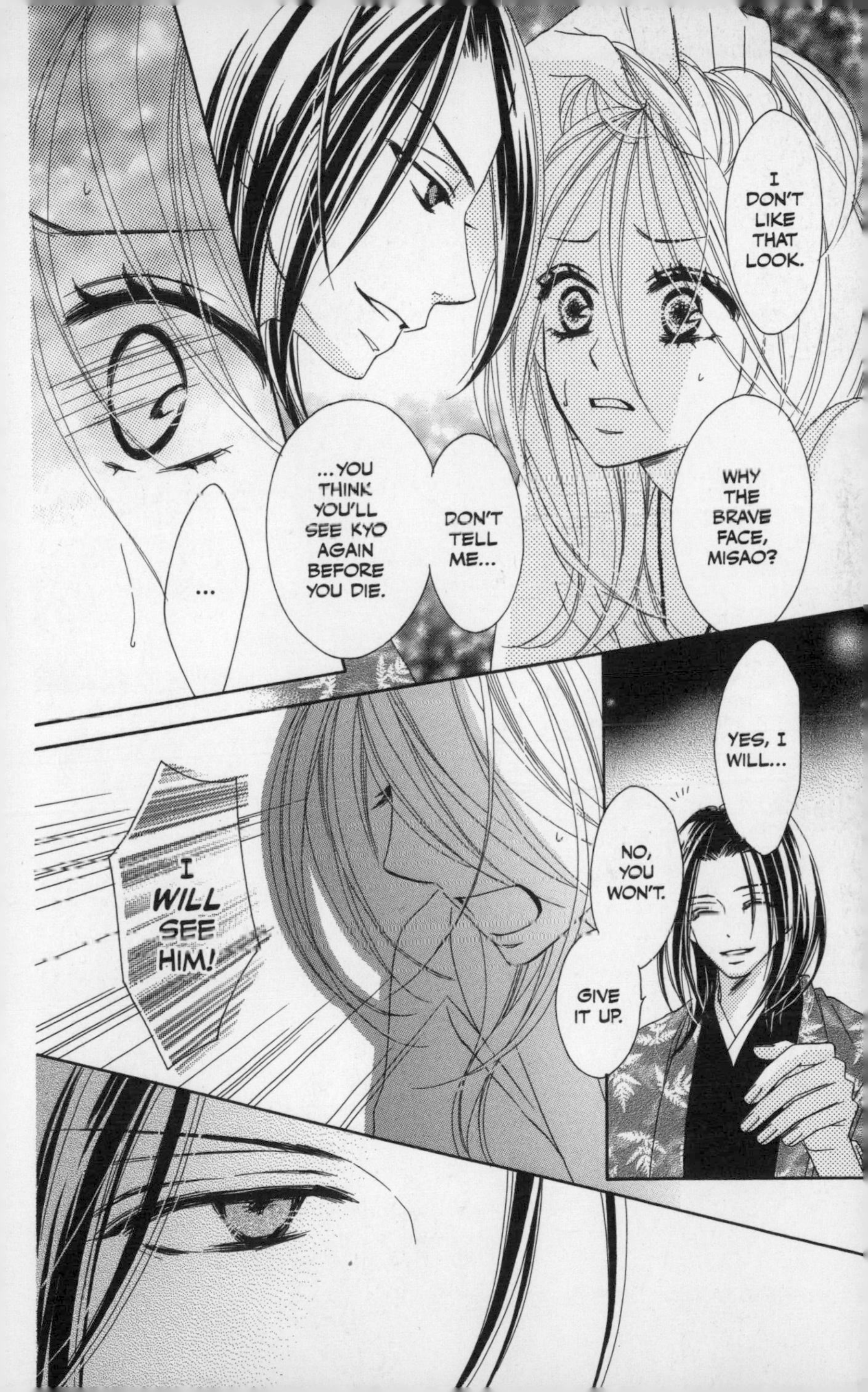
I DON'T LIKE THAT LOOK.
WHY THE BRAVE FACE, MISAO?
DON'T TELL ME...
...YOU THINK YOU'LL SEE KYO AGAIN BEFORE YOU DIE.
...
YES, I WILL...
NO, YOU WON'T.
GIVE IT UP.
I WILL SEE HIM!

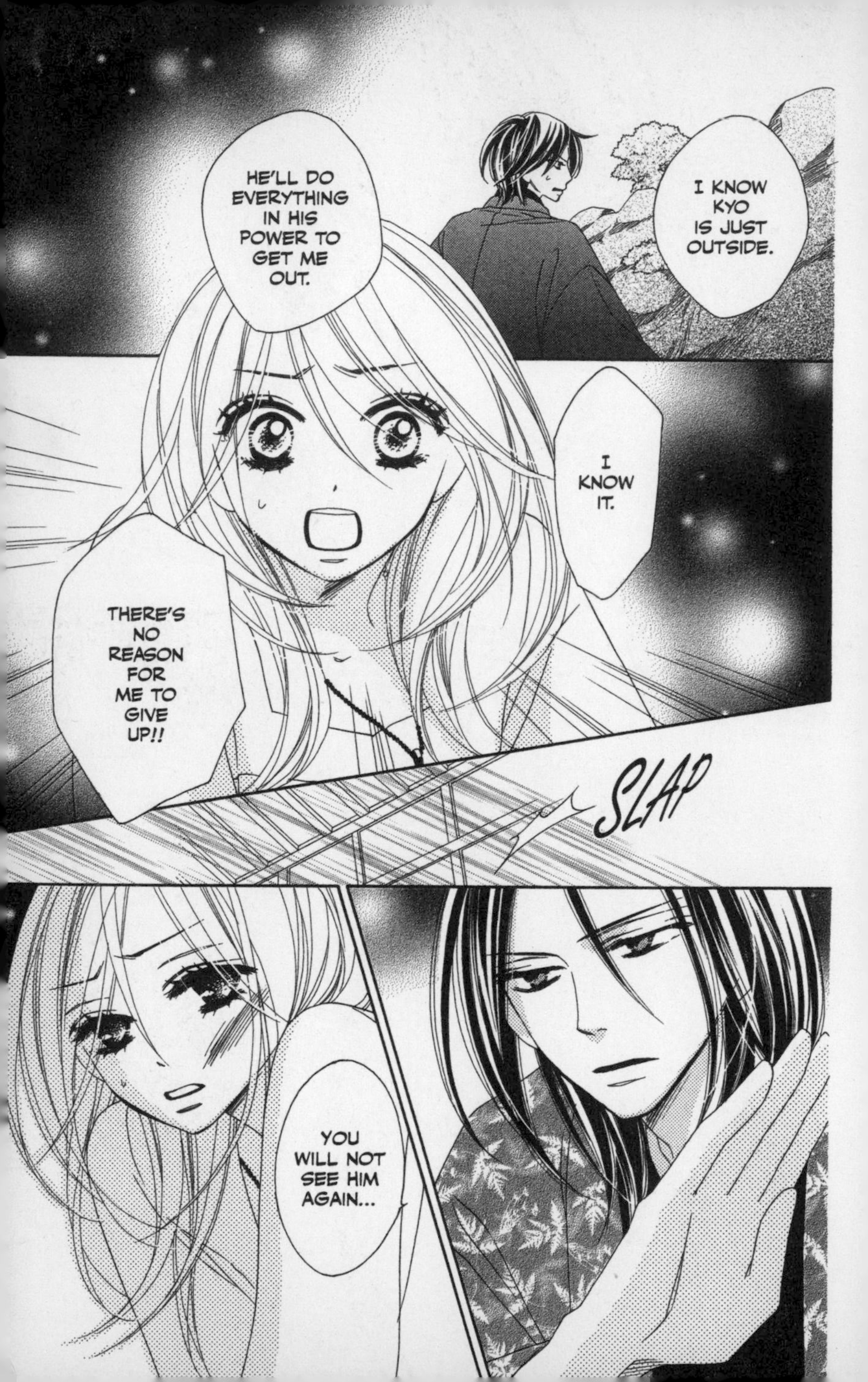
I KNOW KYO IS JUST OUTSIDE.
HE'LL DO EVERYTHING IN HIS POWER TO GET ME OUT.
I KNOW IT.
THERE'S NO REASON FOR ME TO GIVE UP!!
SLAP
YOU WILL NOT SEE HIM AGAIN...

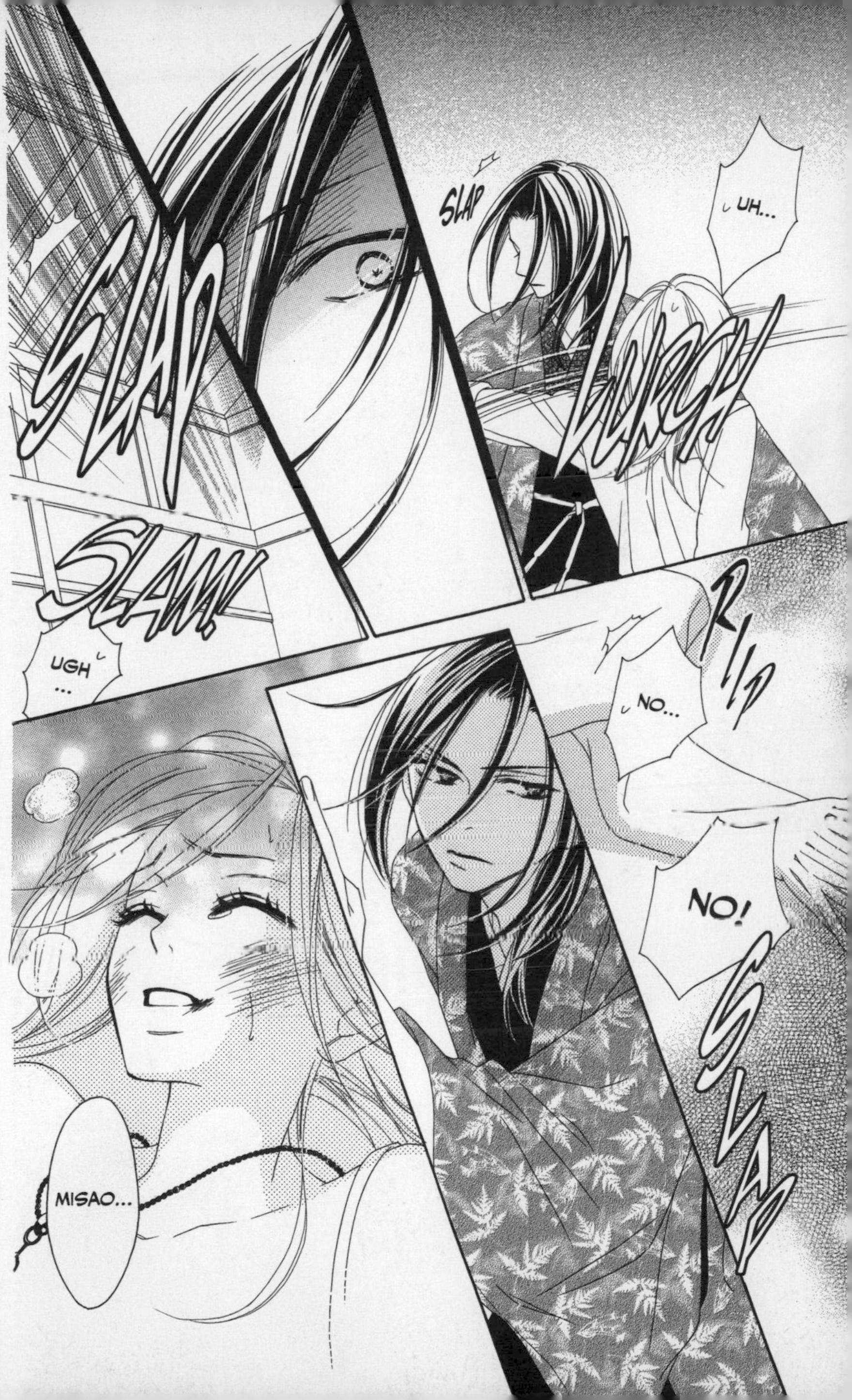
SLAP
UH...
LURCH
SLAP
SLAM!
UGH...
RIP
NO...
NO!
MISAO...

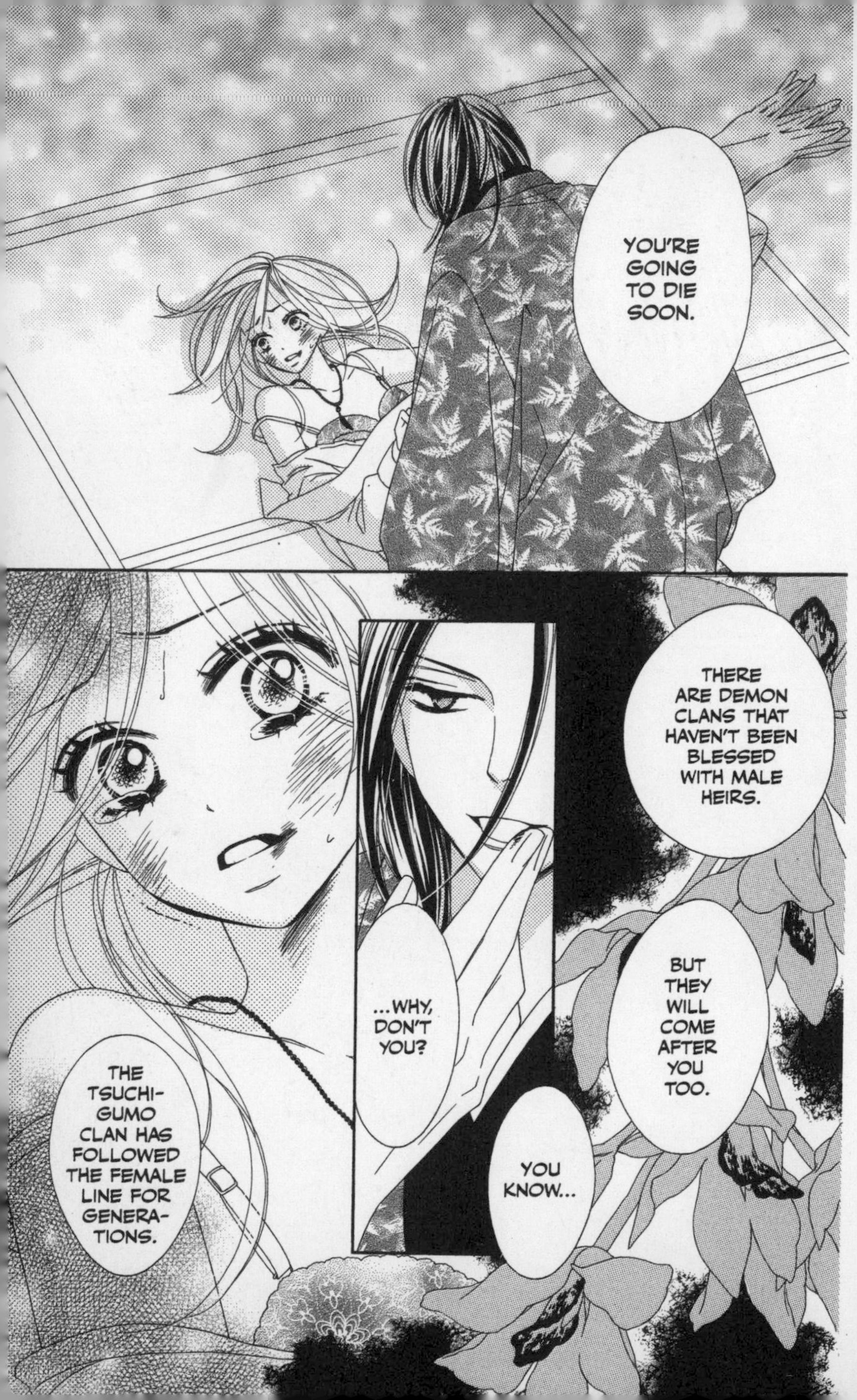
YOU'RE GOING TO DIE SOON.
THERE ARE DEMON CLANS THAT HAVEN'T BEEN BLESSED WITH MALE HEIRS.
BUT THEY WILL COME AFTER YOU TOO.
YOU KNOW...
...WHY, DON'T YOU?
THE TSUCHI-GUMO CLAN HAS FOLLOWED THE FEMALE LINE FOR GENERA-TIONS.

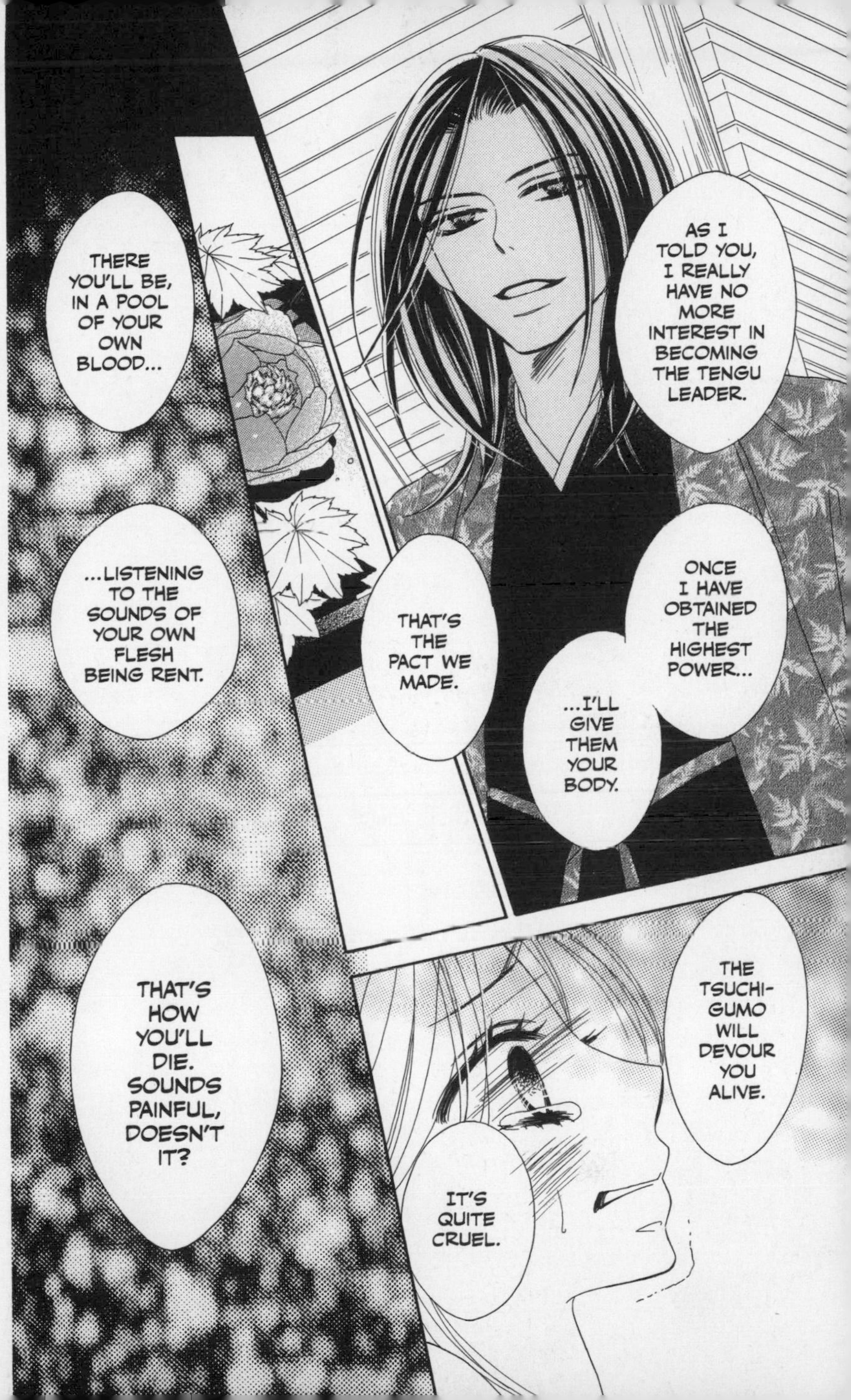
AS I TOLD YOU, I REALLY HAVE NO MORE INTEREST IN BECOMING THE TENGU LEADER.
ONCE I HAVE OBTAINED THE HIGHEST POWER...
...I'LL GIVE THEM YOUR BODY.
THAT'S THE PACT WE MADE.
THE TSUCHI-GUMO WILL DEVOUR YOU ALIVE.
IT'S QUITE CRUEL.
THERE YOU'LL BE, IN A POOL OF YOUR OWN BLOOD...
...LISTENING TO THE SOUNDS OF YOUR OWN FLESH BEING RENT.
THAT'S HOW YOU'LL DIE. SOUNDS PAINFUL, DOESN'T IT?

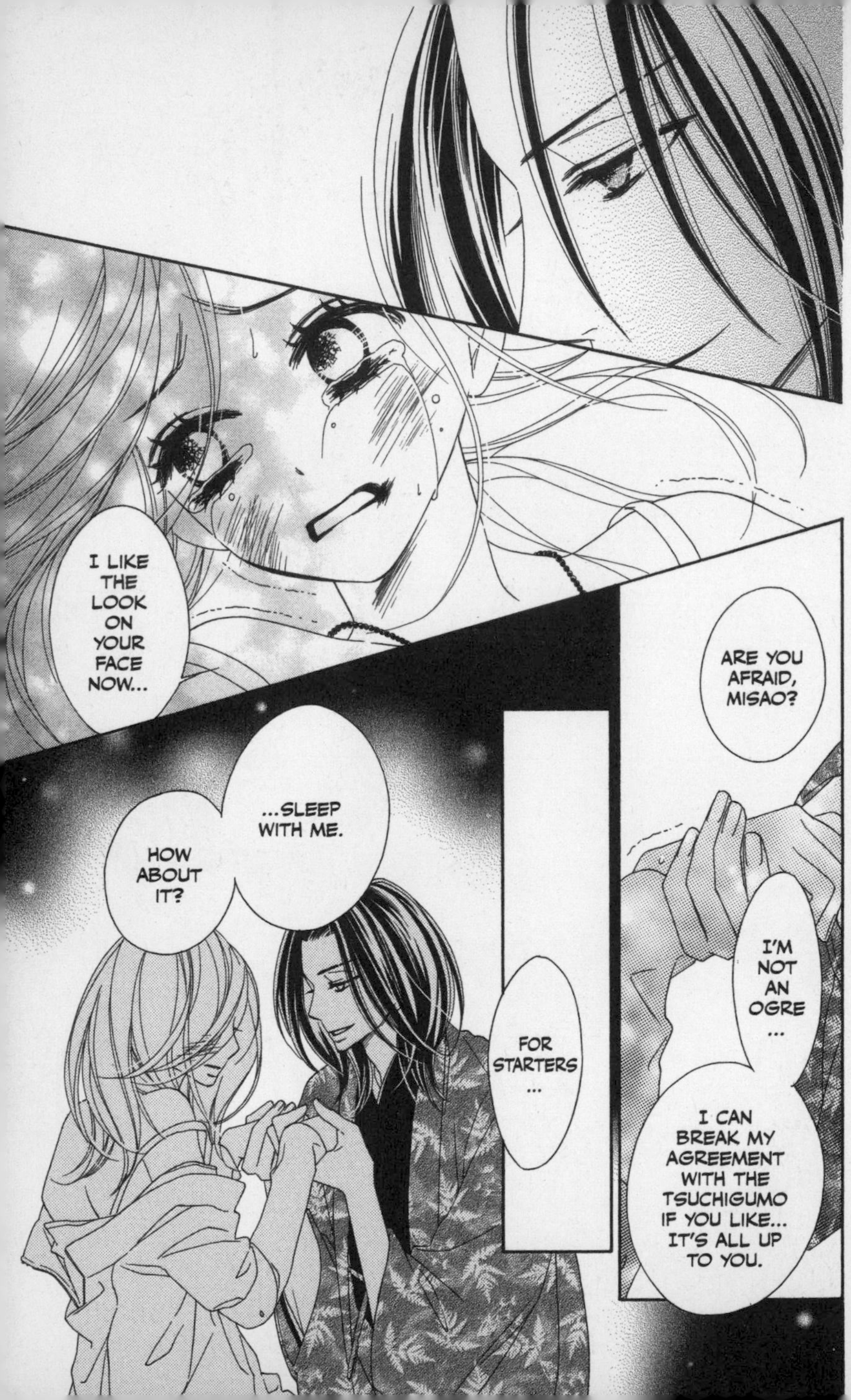
I LIKE THE LOOK ON YOUR FACE NOW...
ARE YOU AFRAID, MISAO?
I'M NOT AN OGRE...
I CAN BREAK MY AGREEMENT WITH THE TSUCHIGUMO IF YOU LIKE... IT'S ALL UP TO YOU.
FOR STARTERS...
...SLEEP WITH ME.
HOW ABOUT IT?

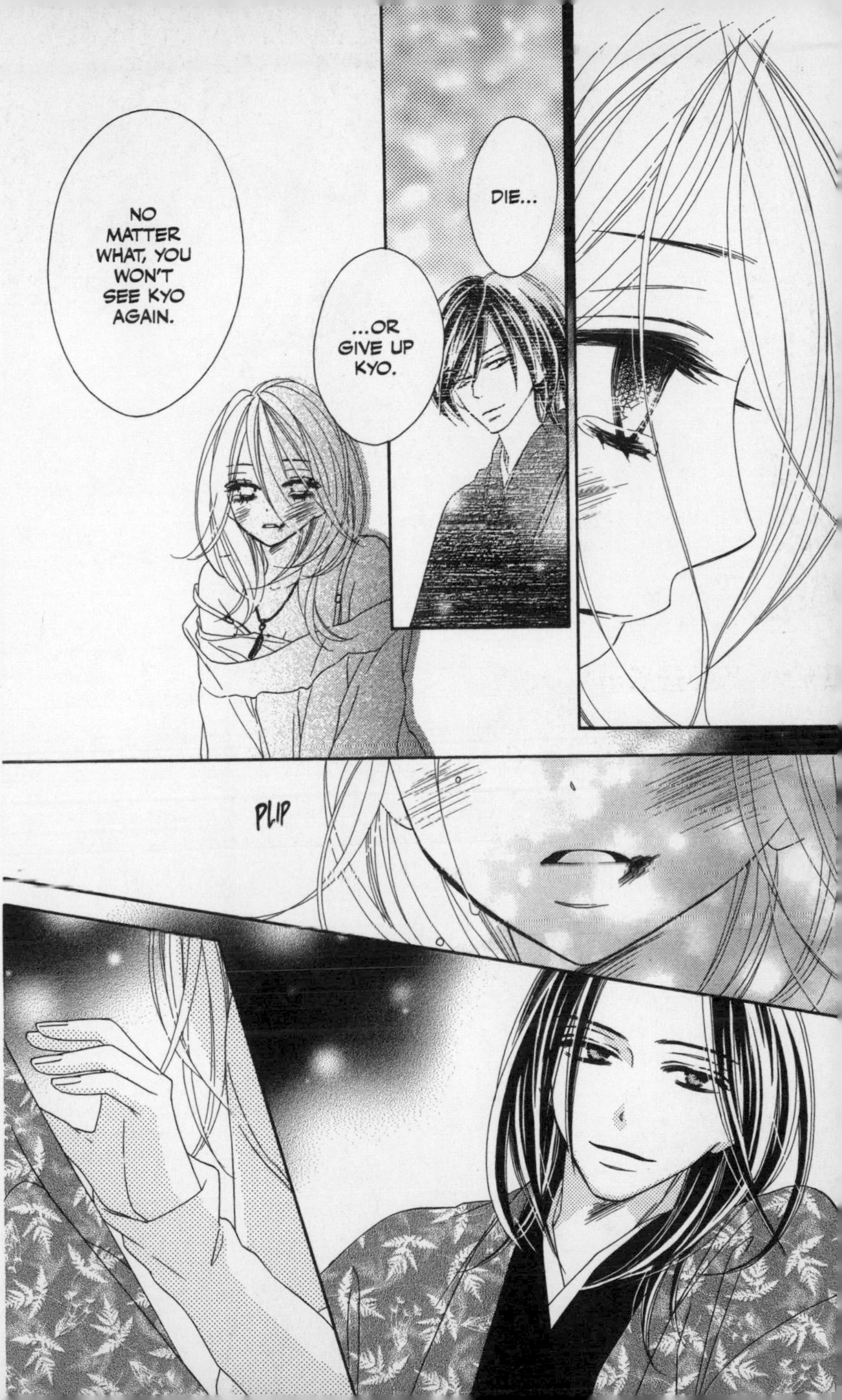
DIE...
...OR GIVE UP KYO.
NO MATTER WHAT, YOU WON'T SEE KYO AGAIN.
PLIP

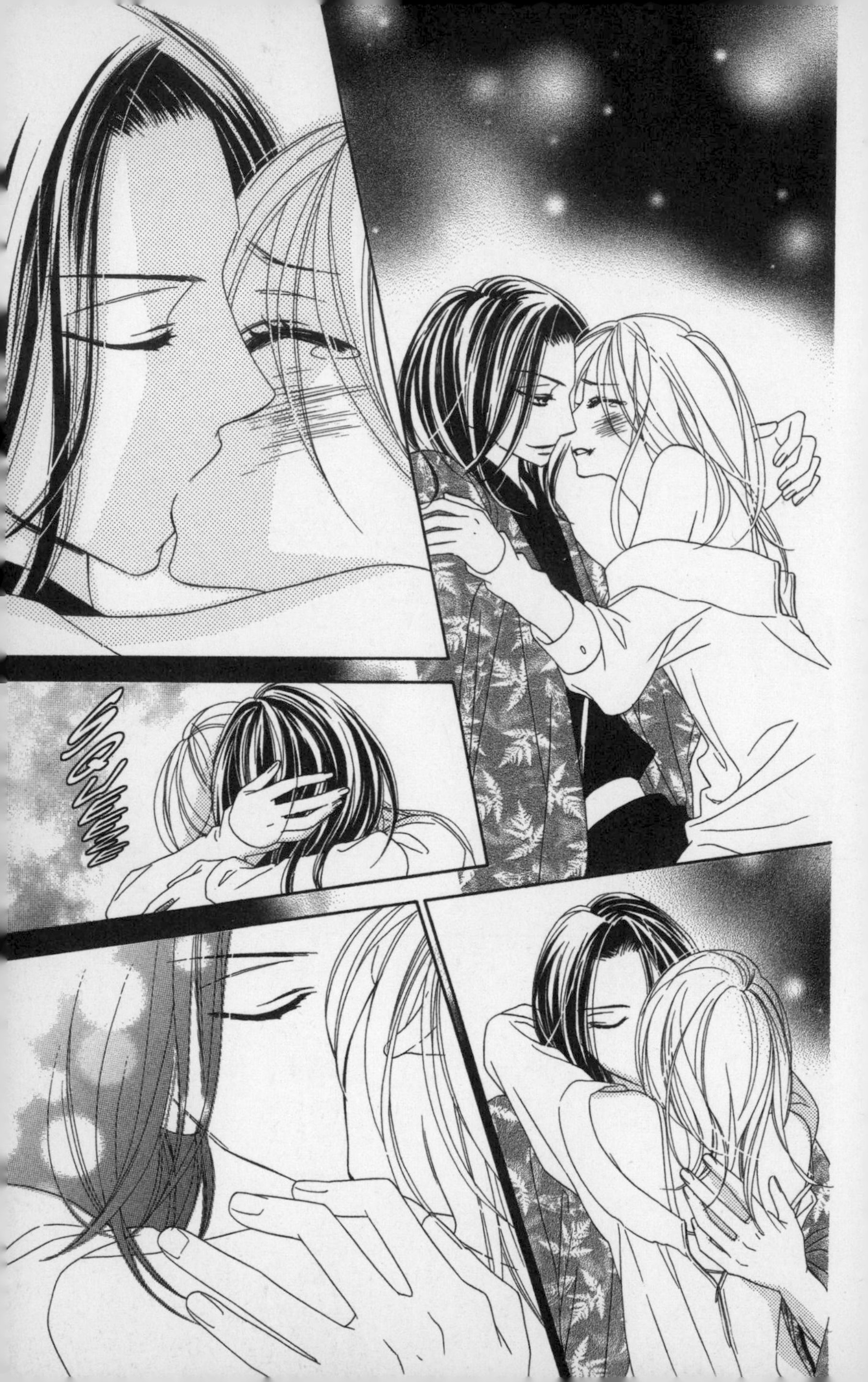

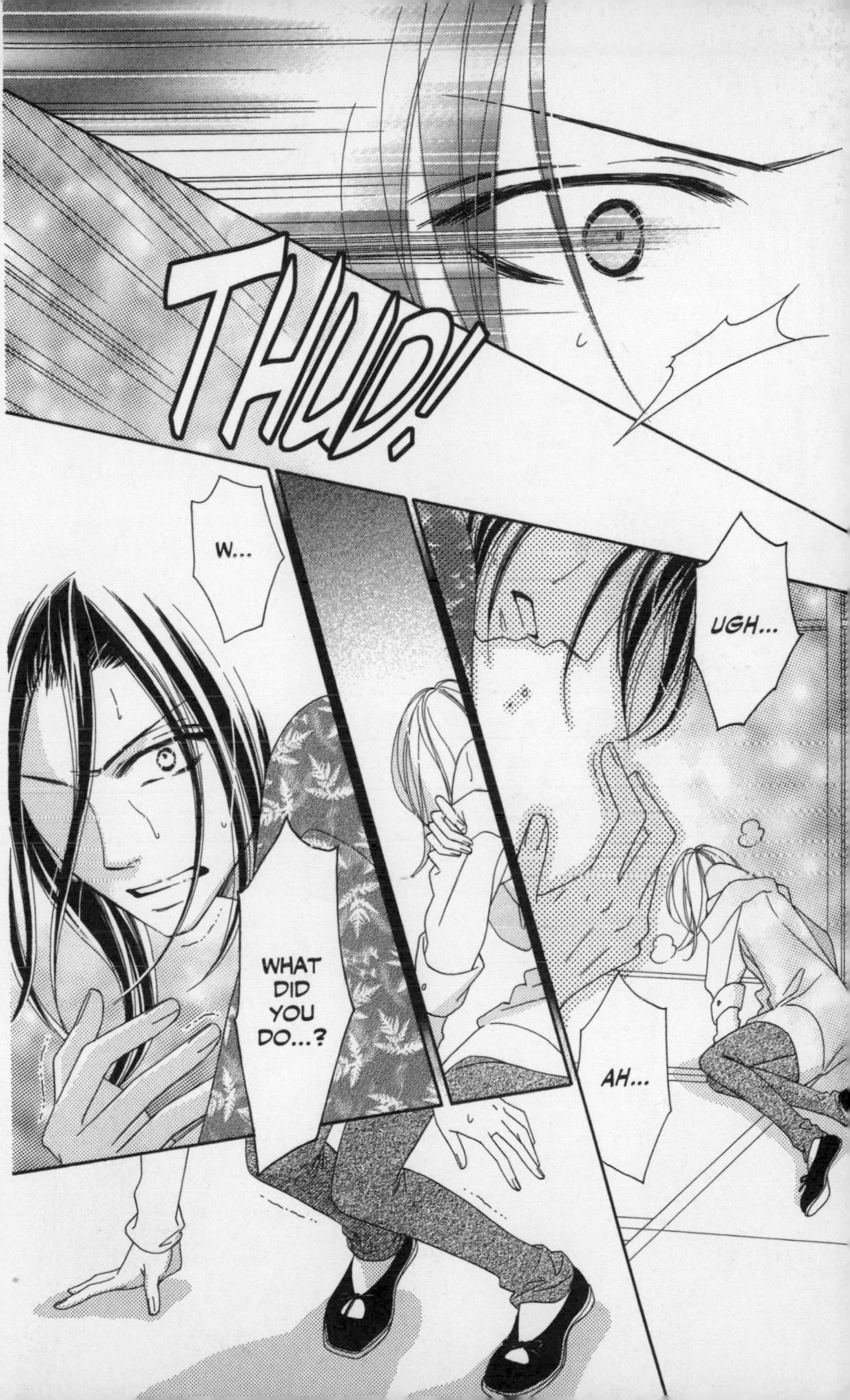
THUD!
UGH...
AH...
W...
WHAT DID YOU DO...?

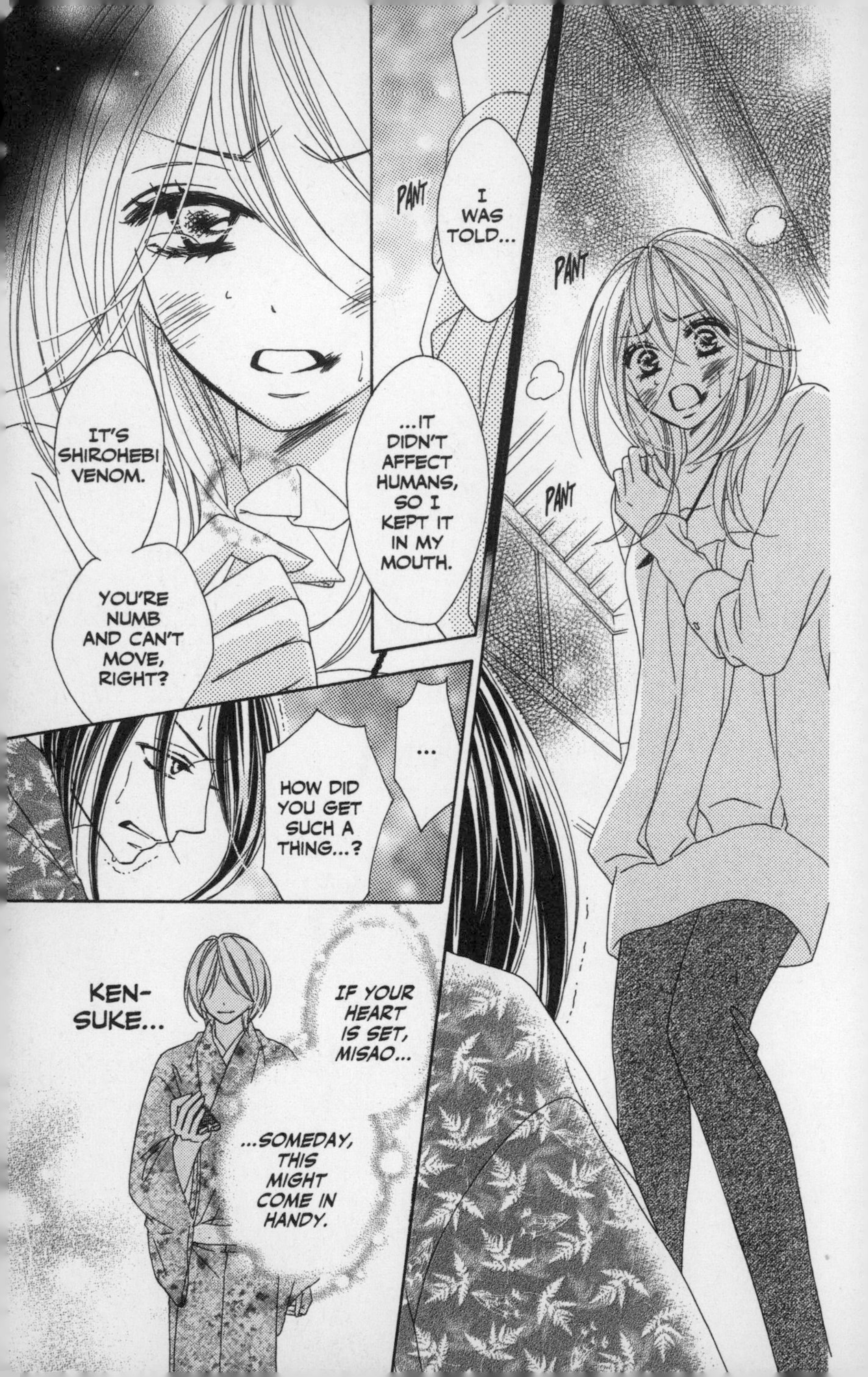
PANT
PANT
PANT
I WAS TOLD...
...IT DIDN'T AFFECT HUMANS, SO I KEPT IT IN MY MOUTH.
IT'S SHIROHEBI VENOM.
YOU'RE NUMB AND CAN'T MOVE, RIGHT?
...
HOW DID YOU GET SUCH A THING...?
IF YOUR HEART IS SET, MISAO...
KEN-SUKE...
...SOMEDAY, THIS MIGHT COME IN HANDY.

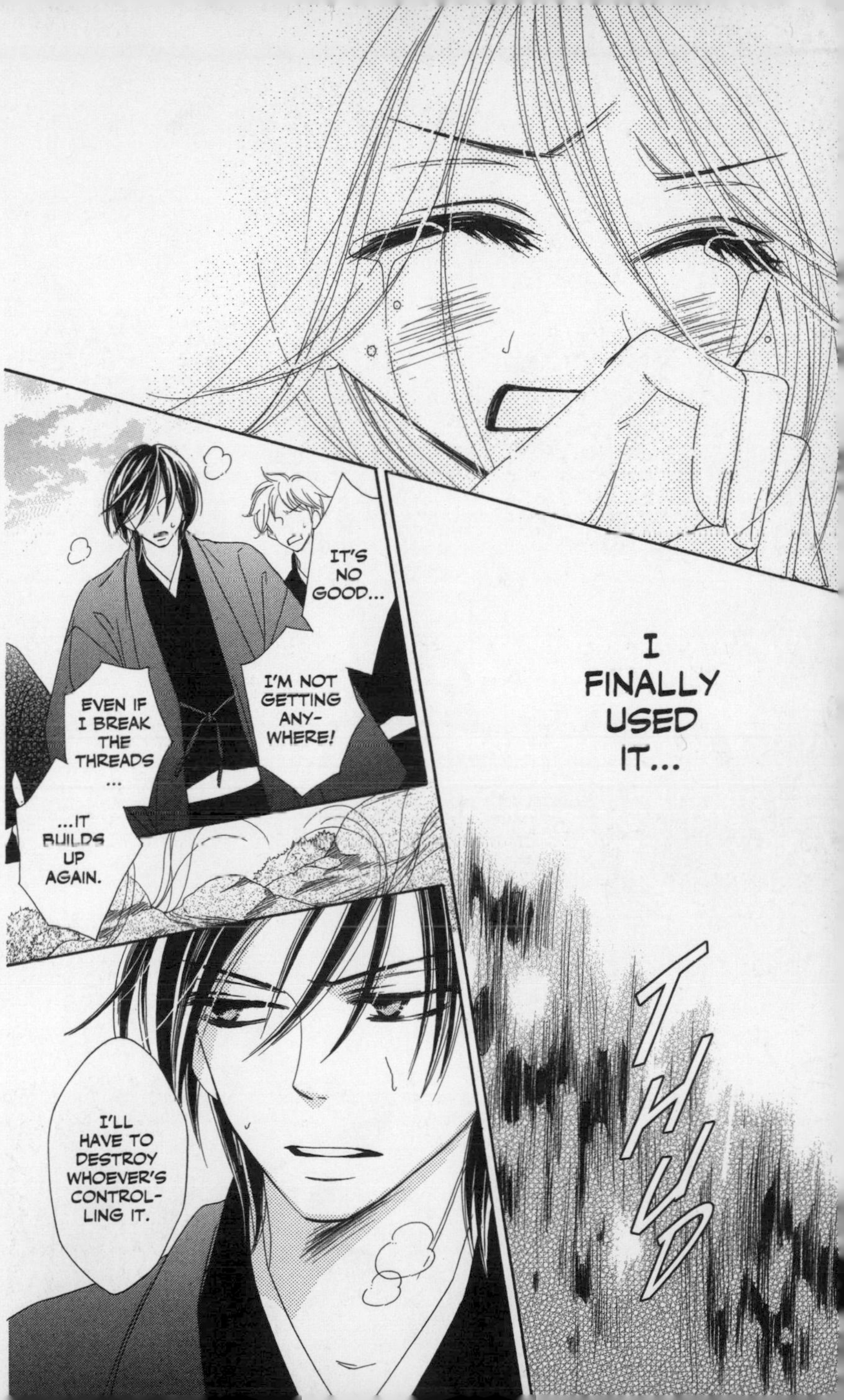
I FINALLY USED IT...
THUD
IT'S NO GOOD...
I'M NOT GETTING ANY-WHERE!
EVEN IF I BREAK THE THREADS...
...IT BUILDS UP AGAIN.
I'LL HAVE TO DESTROY WHOEVER'S CONTROL-LING IT.

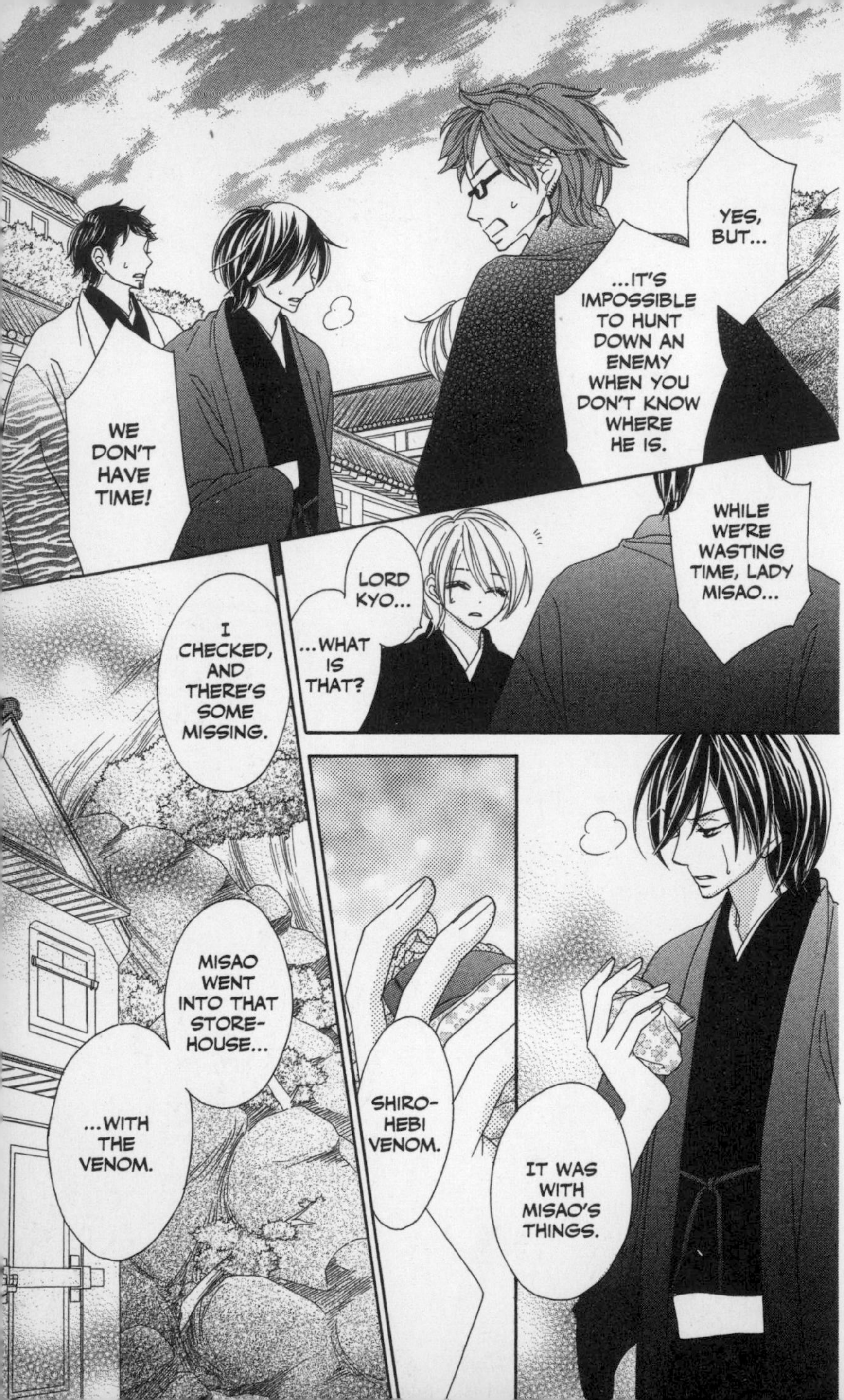
YES, BUT...
...IT'S IMPOSSIBLE TO HUNT DOWN AN ENEMY WHEN YOU DON'T KNOW WHERE HE IS.
WE DON'T HAVE TIME!
WHILE WE'RE WASTING TIME, LADY MISAO...
LORD KYO...
...WHAT IS THAT?
IT WAS WITH MISAO'S THINGS.
SHIRO-HEBI VENOM.
I CHECKED, AND THERE'S SOME MISSING.
MISAO WENT INTO THAT STORE-HOUSE...
...WITH THE VENOM.

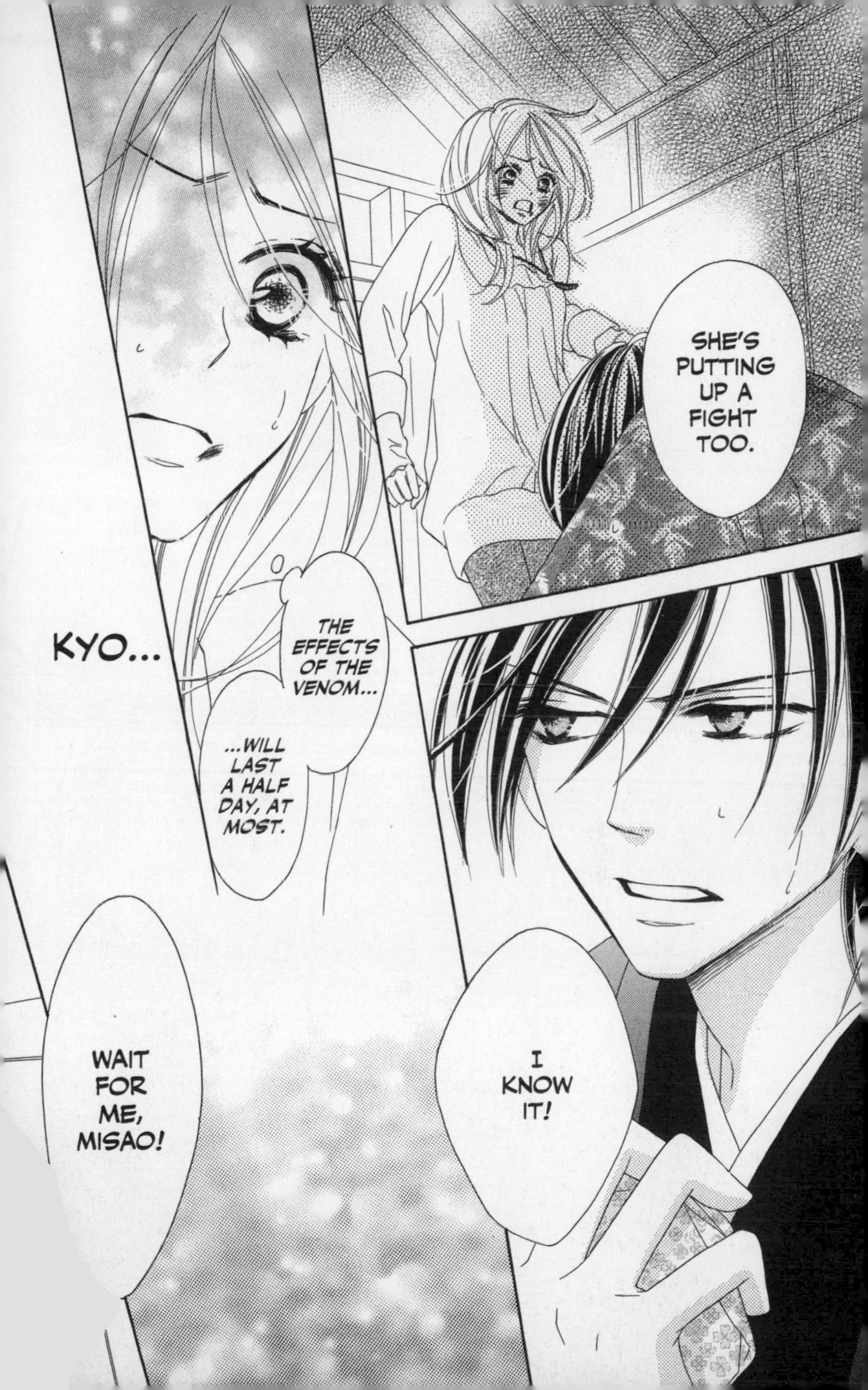
SHE'S PUTTING UP A FIGHT TOO.
THE EFFECTS OF THE VENOM...
...WILL LAST A HALF DAY, AT MOST.
KYO...
I KNOW IT!
WAIT FOR ME, MISAO!

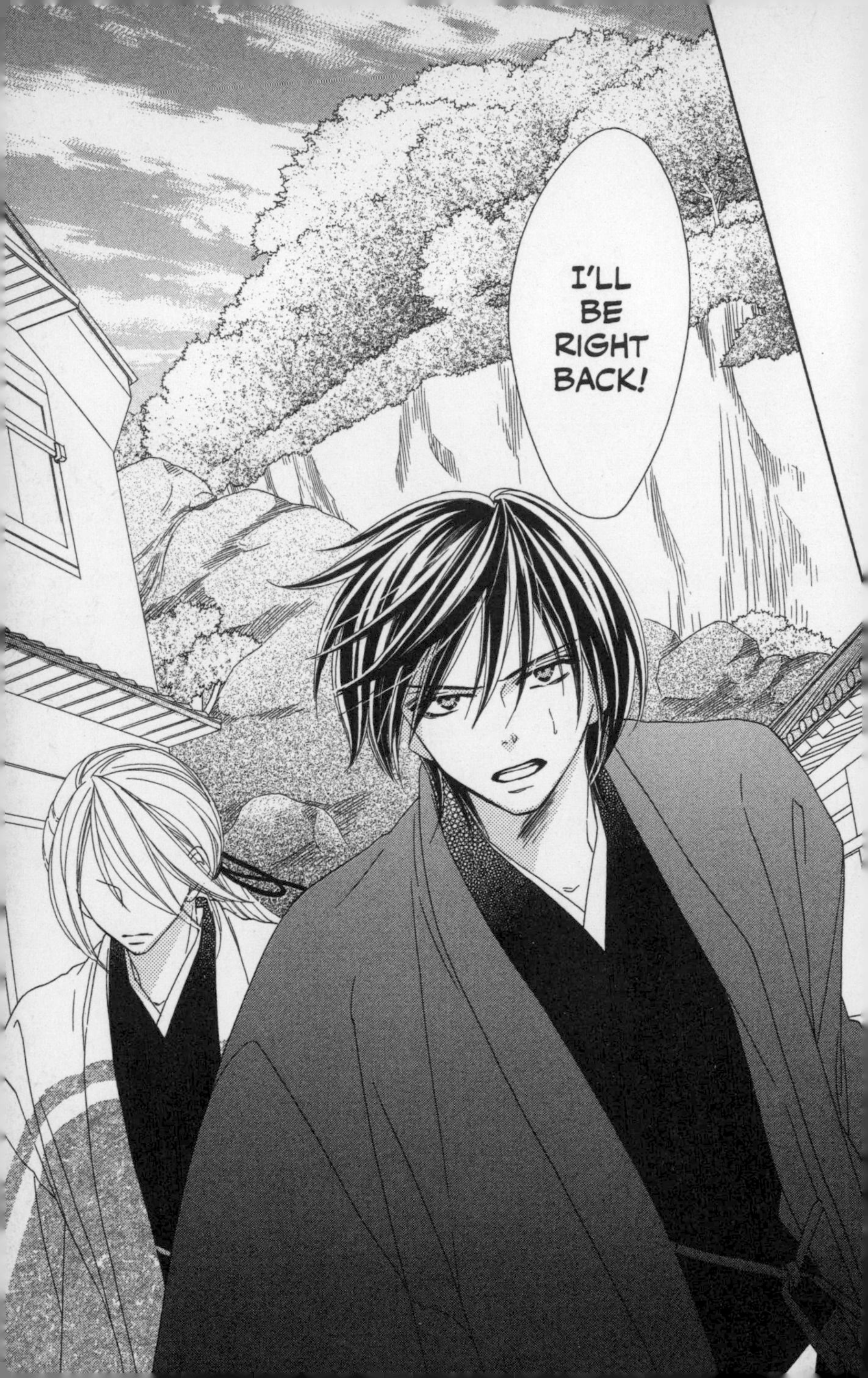
I'LL BE RIGHT BACK!

Illustration Request Number Eight

"Kensuke Now"

He's sniffing Misao's hanky in a small, dark place...

I was finally able to use the venom in the seal case in the story!

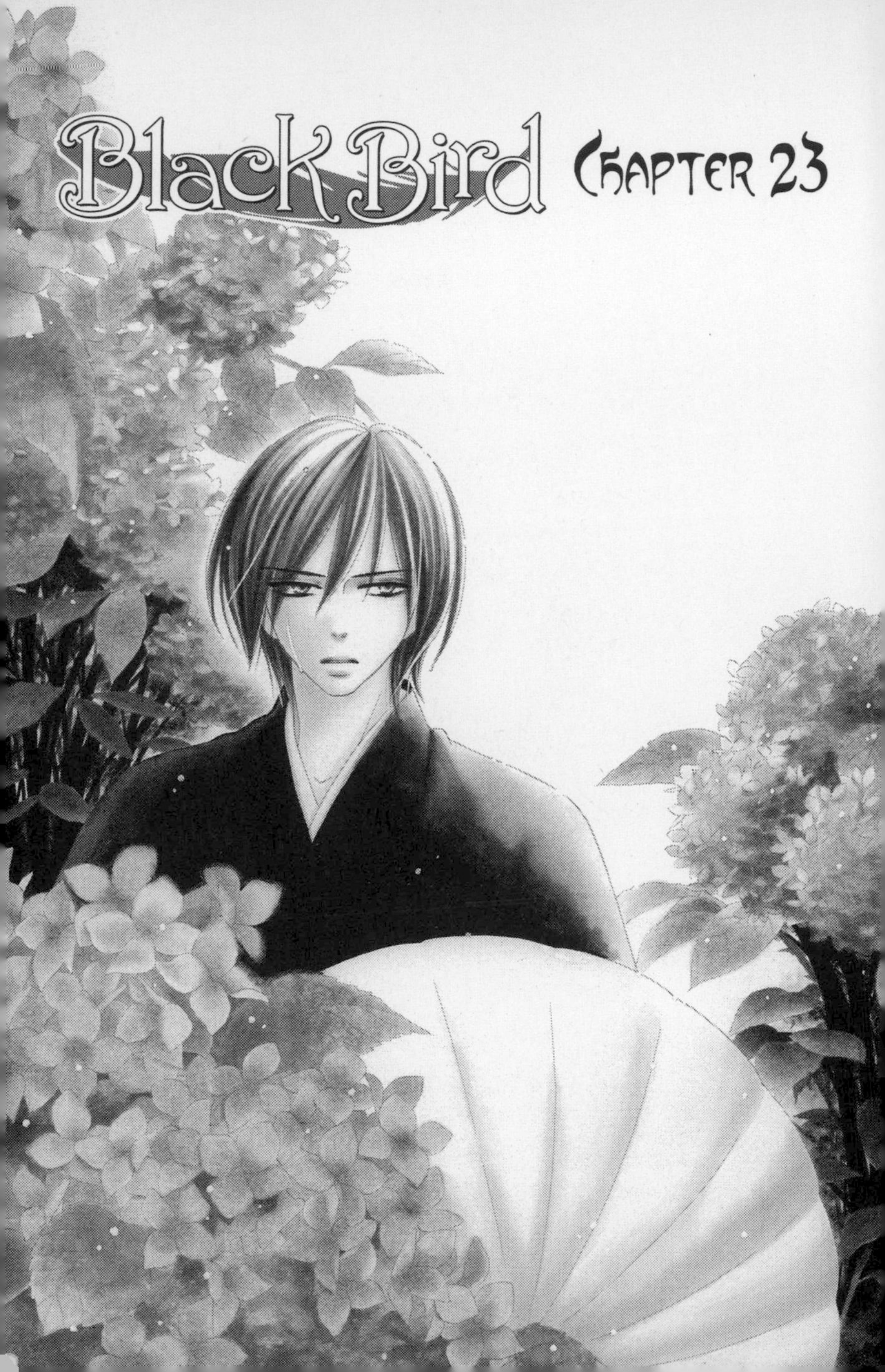
Black Bird
Chapter 23

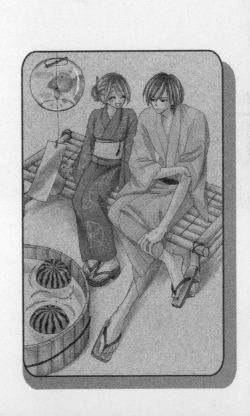

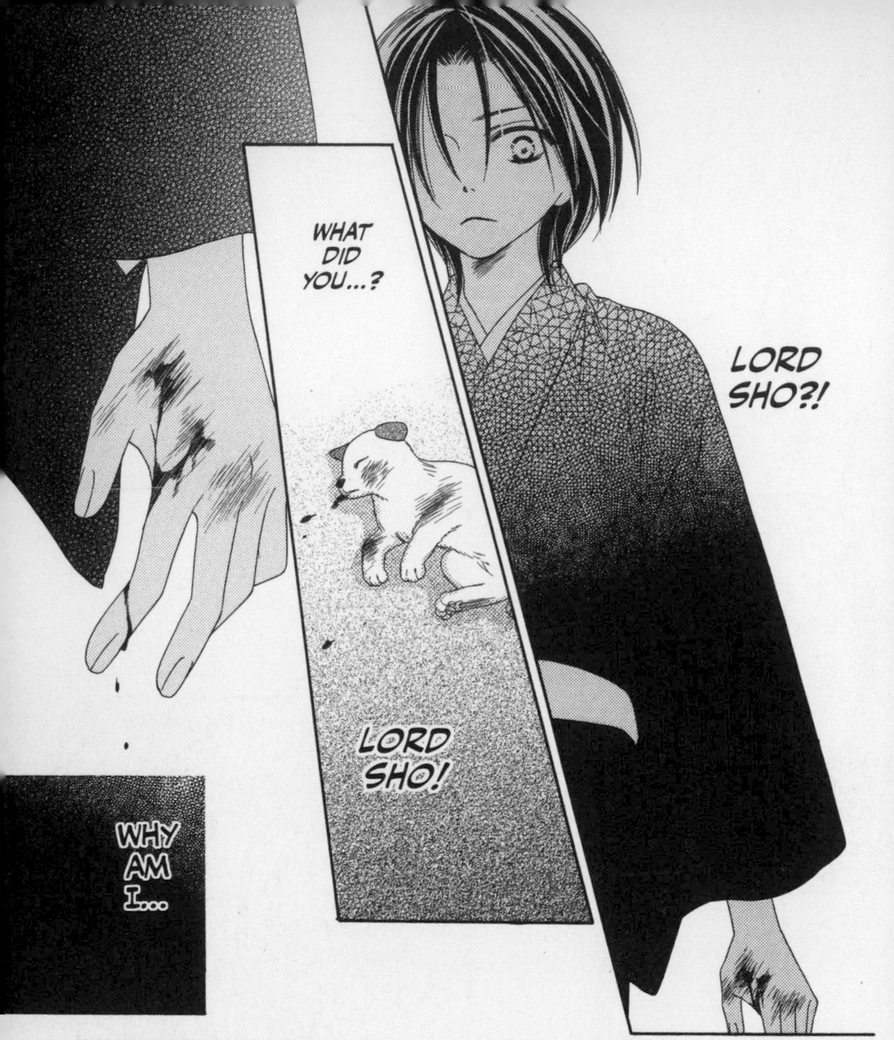
LORD SHO?!
WHAT DID YOU...?
LORD SHO!
WHY AM I...

The characters and composition in the cover illustrations are always the same... I've been trying to think of a way out of this rut.
How is it that I seem to put more effort into the cover, I wonder...?

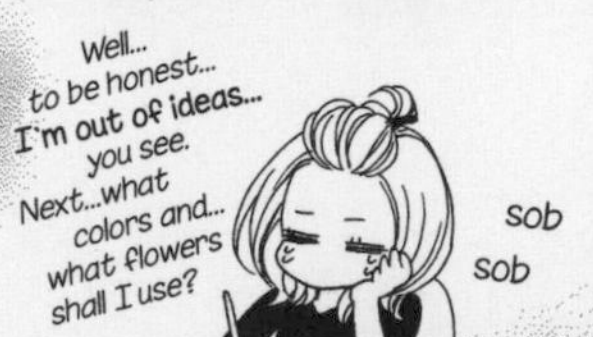
Well... to be honest... I'm out of ideas... you see. Next...what colors and... what flowers shall I use?
sob
sob

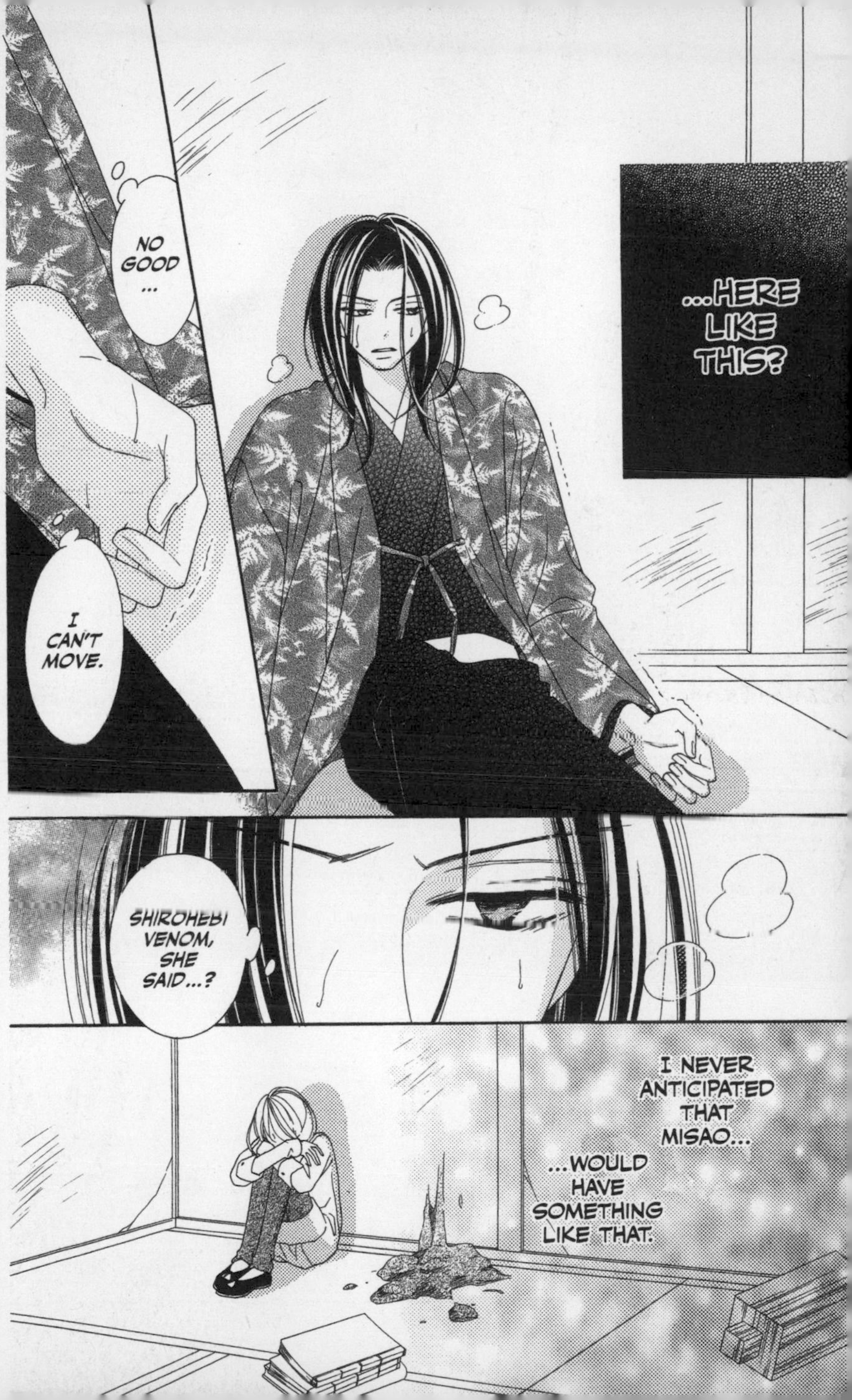
...HERE LIKE THIS?
NO GOOD ...
I CAN'T MOVE.
SHIROHEBI VENOM, SHE SAID...?
I NEVER ANTICIPATED THAT MISAO...
...WOULD HAVE SOMETHING LIKE THAT.

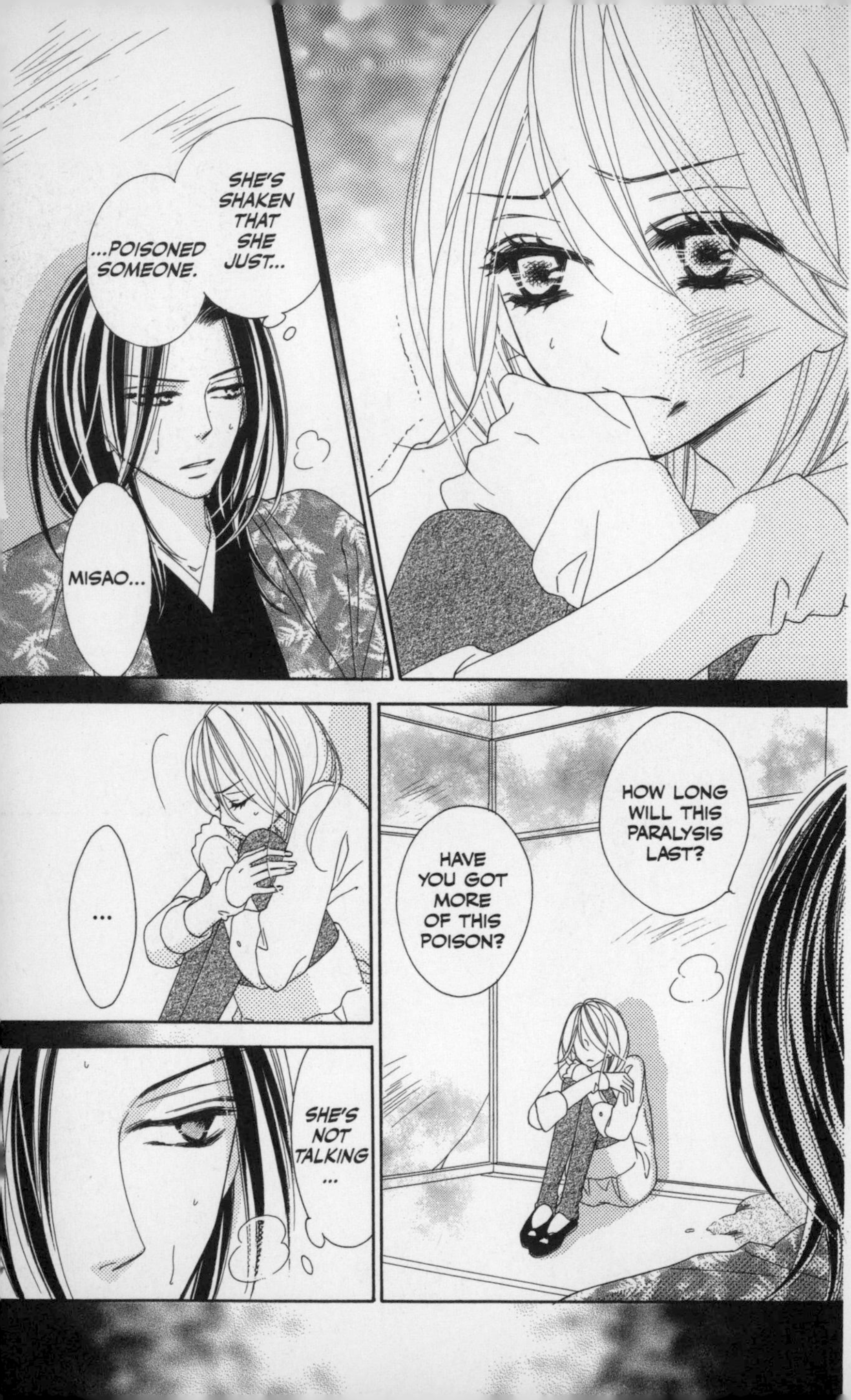
SHE'S SHAKEN THAT SHE JUST...
...POISONED SOMEONE.
MISAO...
HOW LONG WILL THIS PARALYSIS LAST?
HAVE YOU GOT MORE OF THIS POISON?
...
SHE'S NOT TALKING ...

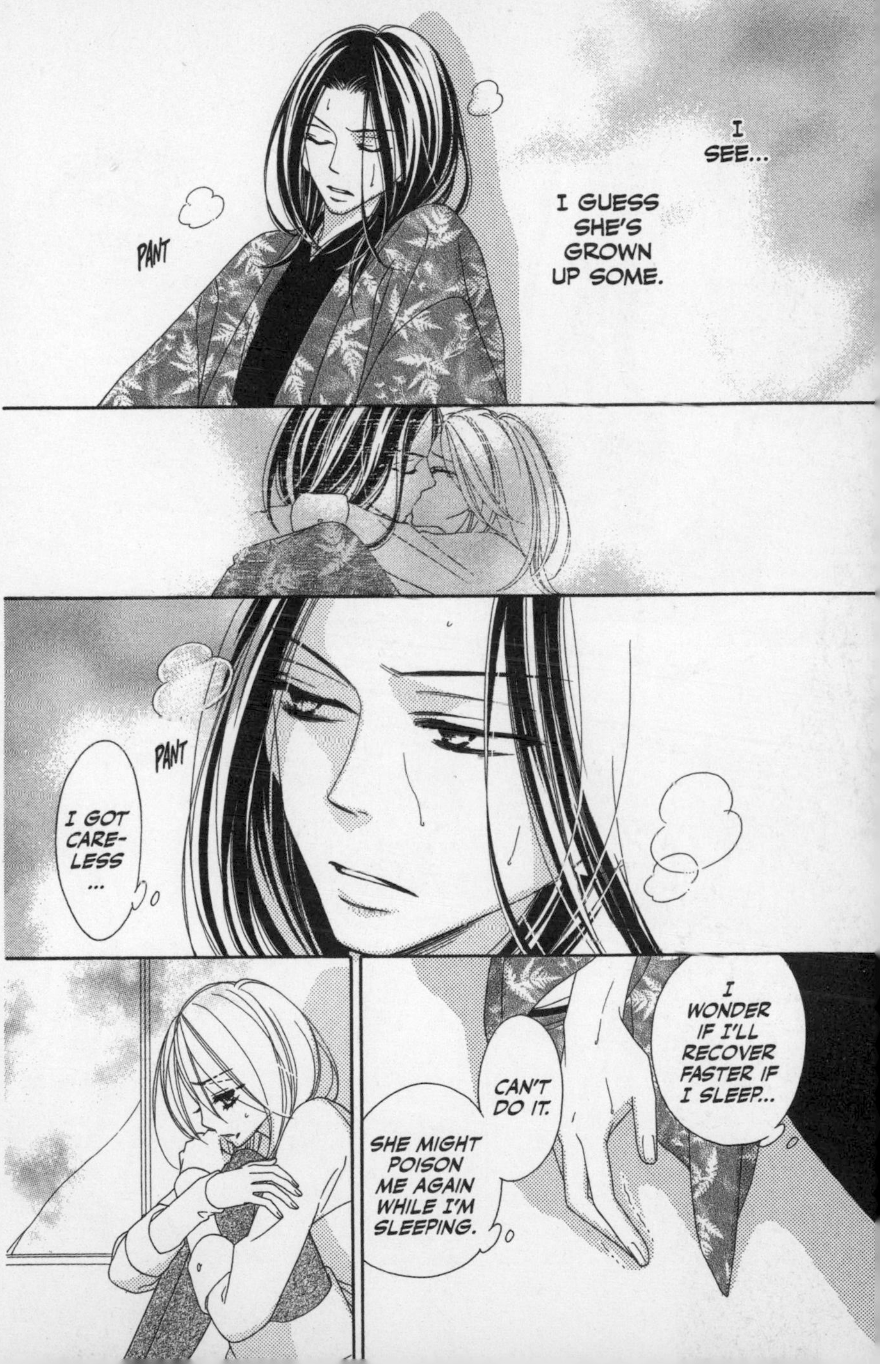
I SEE...
I GUESS SHE'S GROWN UP SOME.
PANT
PANT
I GOT CARE-LESS ...
I WONDER IF I'LL RECOVER FASTER IF I SLEEP...
CAN'T DO IT.
SHE MIGHT POISON ME AGAIN WHILE I'M SLEEPING.

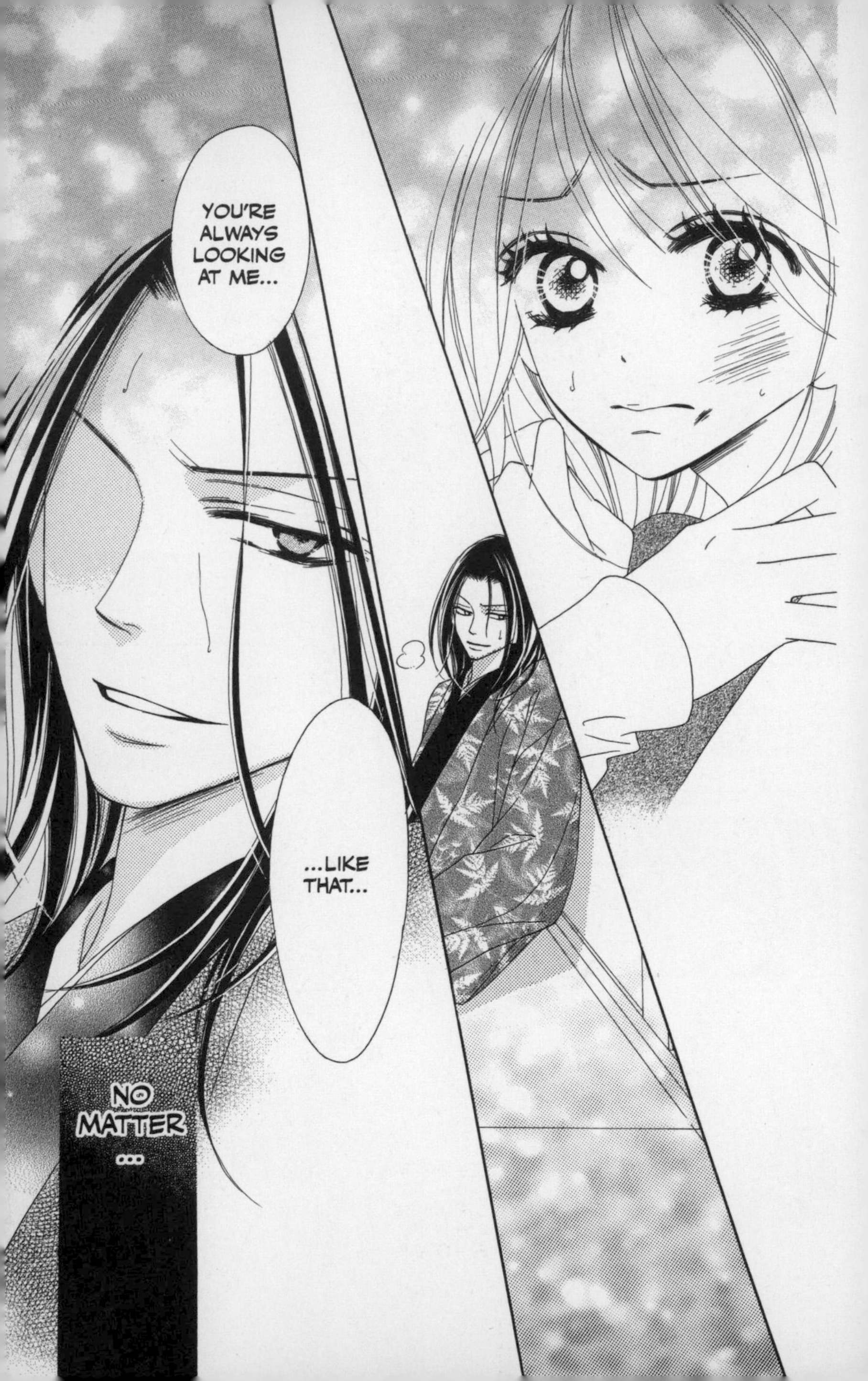
YOU'RE ALWAYS LOOKING AT ME...
...LIKE THAT...
NO MATTER ...

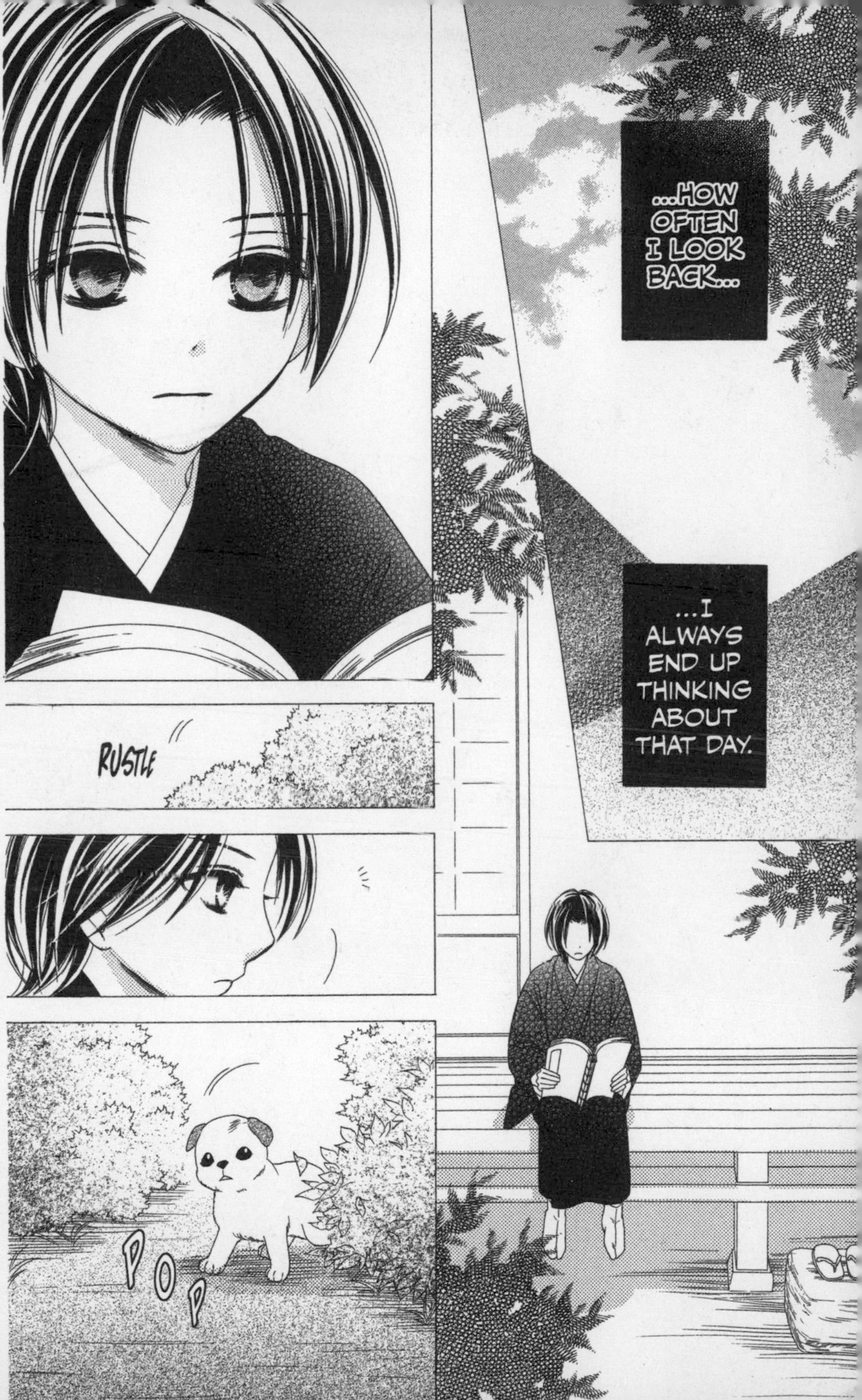
...HOW OFTEN I LOOK BACK...
...I ALWAYS END UP THINKING ABOUT THAT DAY.
RUSTLE
POP

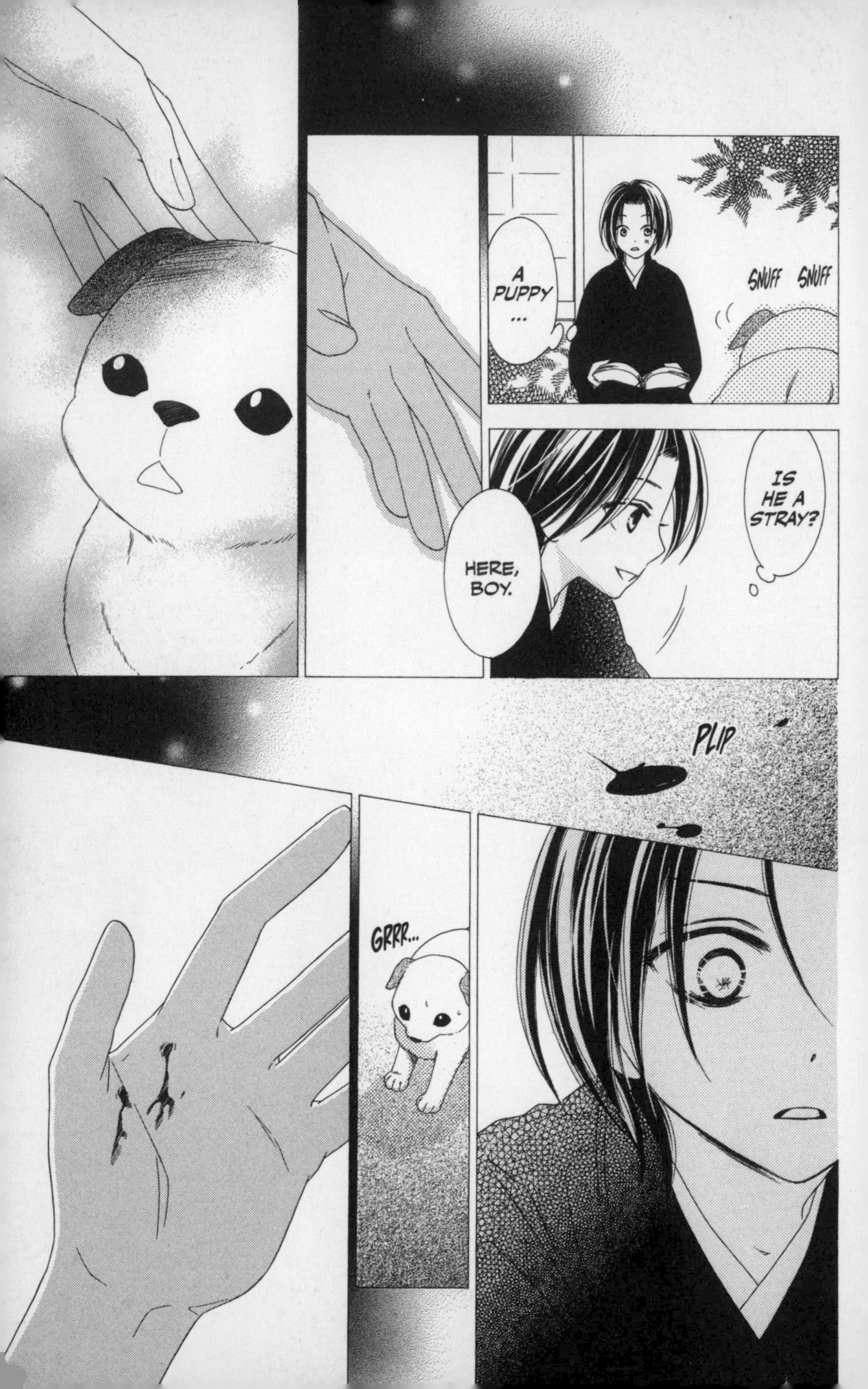

SNUFF SNUFF
A PUPPY ...
IS HE A STRAY?
HERE, BOY.
PLIP
GRRR...

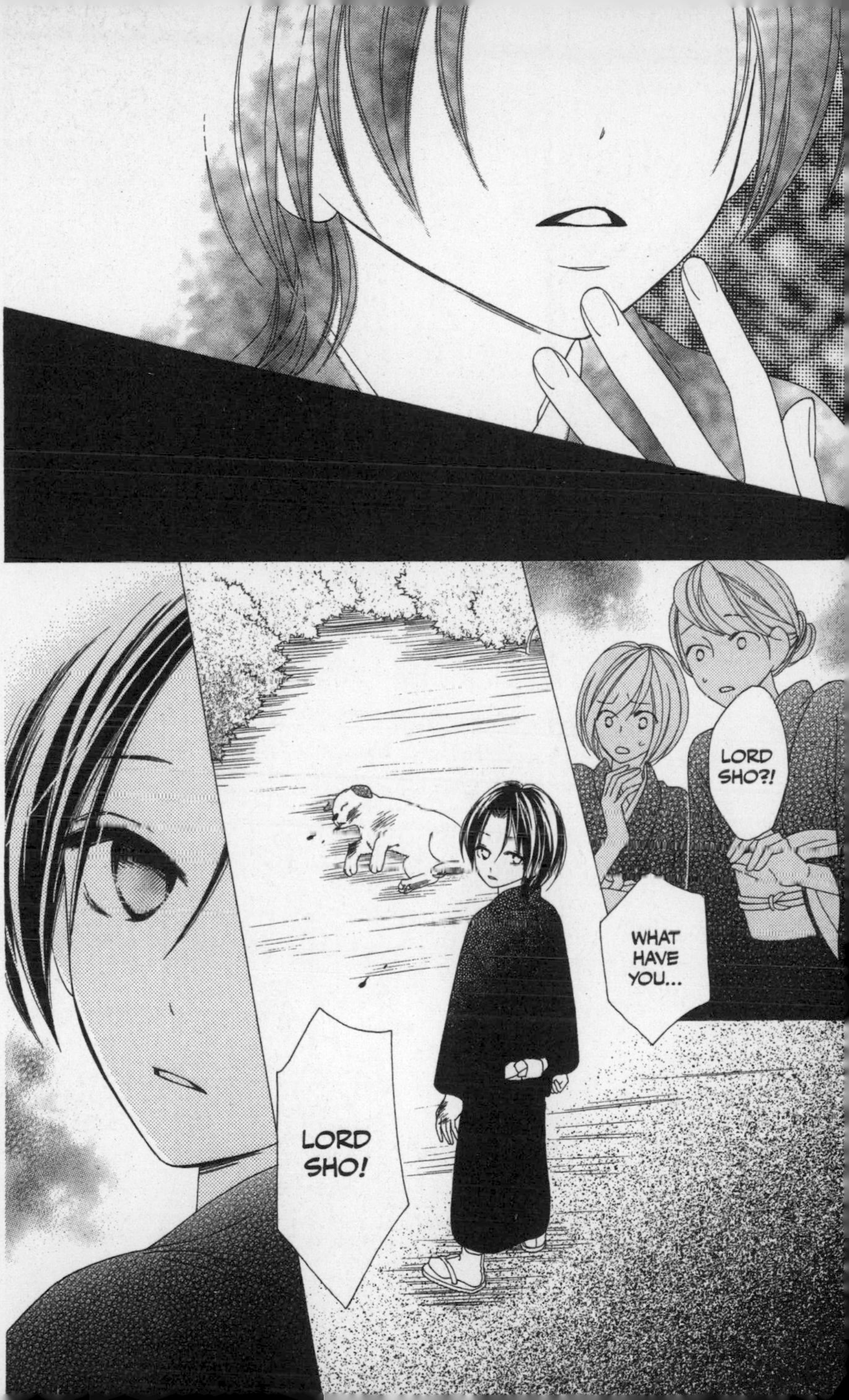
LORD SHO?!
WHAT HAVE YOU...
LORD SHO!

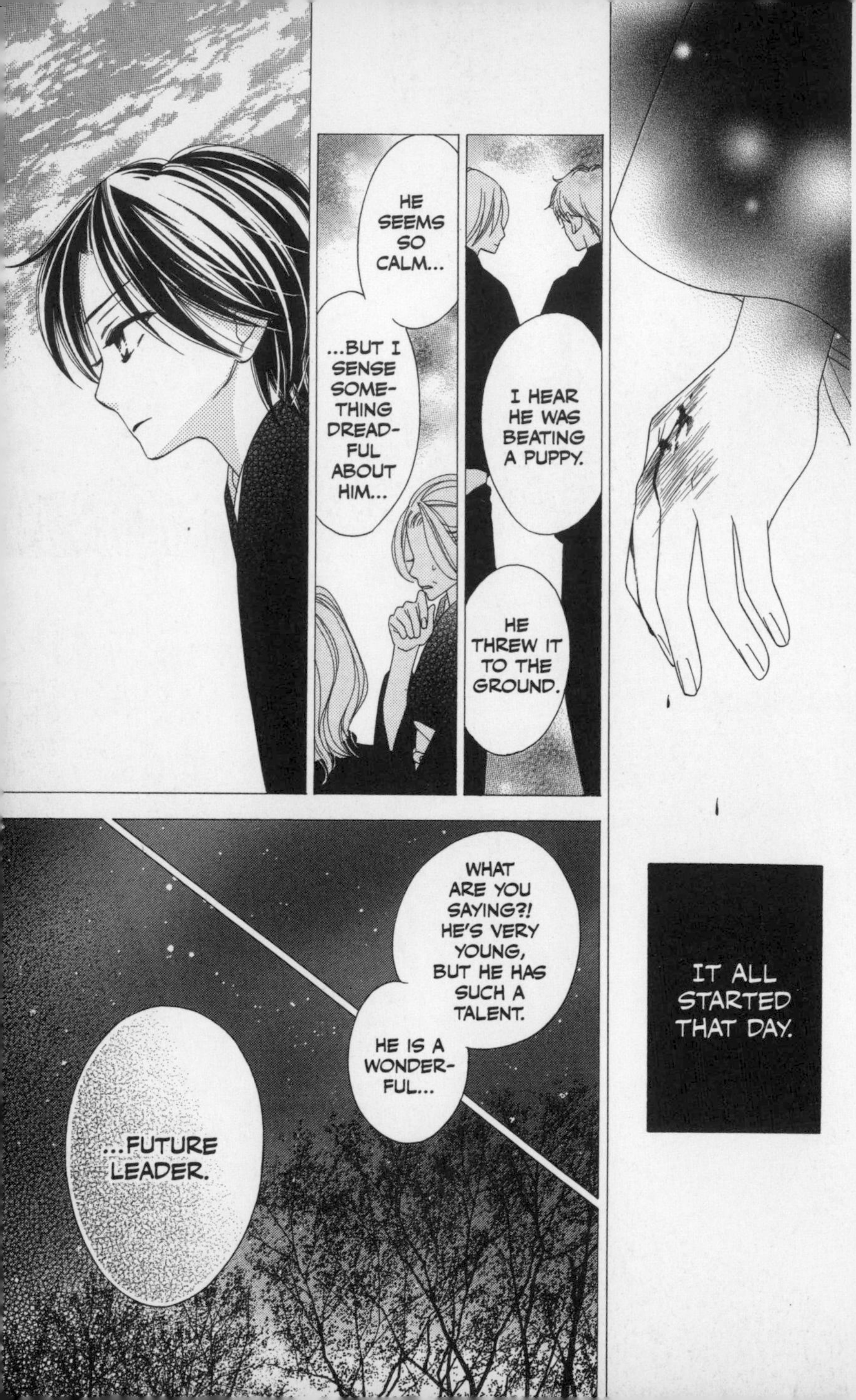
IT ALL STARTED THAT DAY.
I HEAR HE WAS BEATING A PUPPY.
HE THREW IT TO THE GROUND.
HE SEEMS SO CALM...
...BUT I SENSE SOMETHING-THING DREADFUL ABOUT HIM...
WHAT ARE YOU SAYING?! HE'S VERY YOUNG, BUT HE HAS SUCH A TALENT.
HE IS A WONDERFUL...
...FUTURE LEADER.

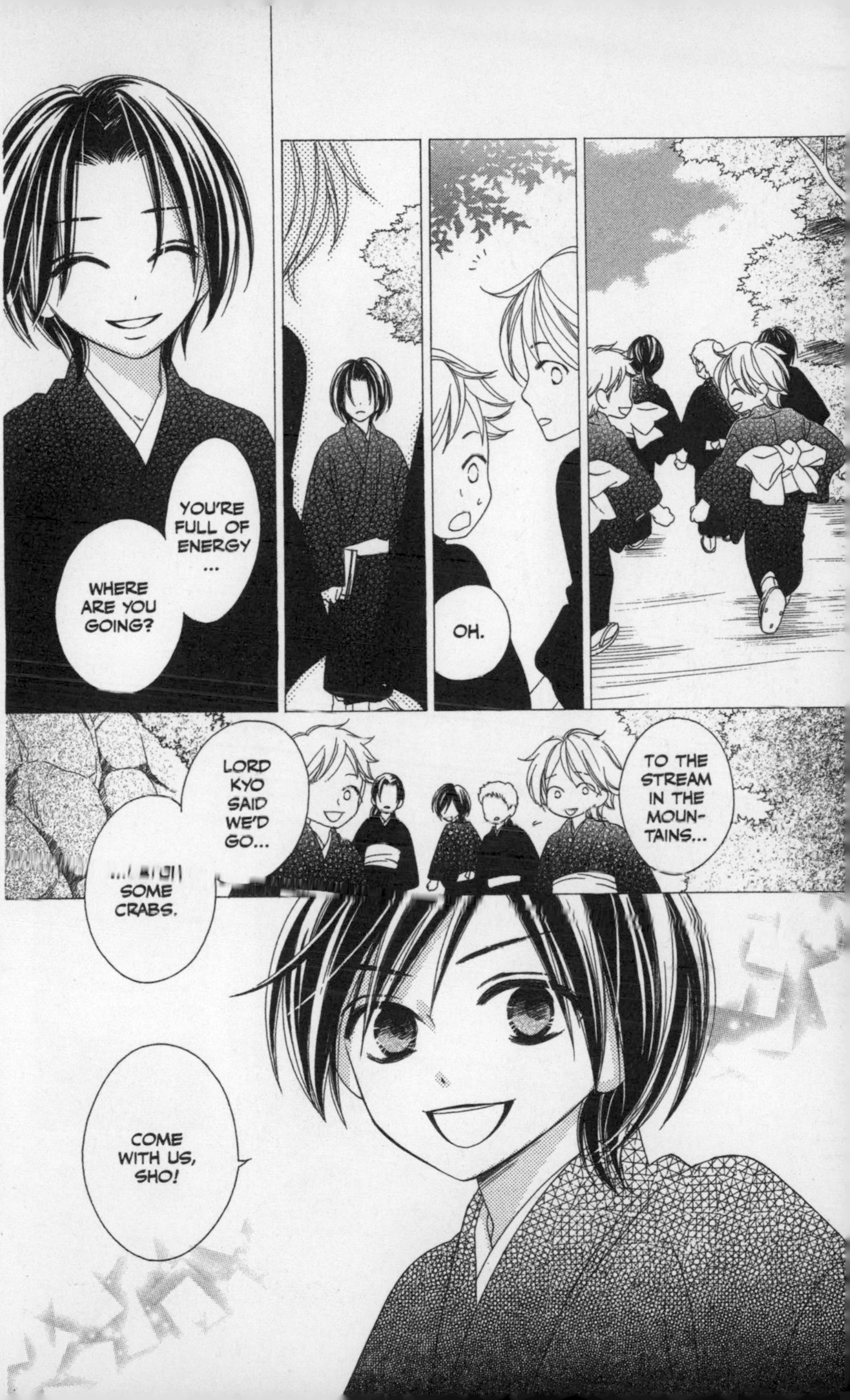
OH.
YOU'RE FULL OF ENERGY ...
WHERE ARE YOU GOING?
TO THE STREAM IN THE MOUNTAINS...
LORD KYO SAID WE'D GO...
SOME CRABS.
COME WITH US, SHO!

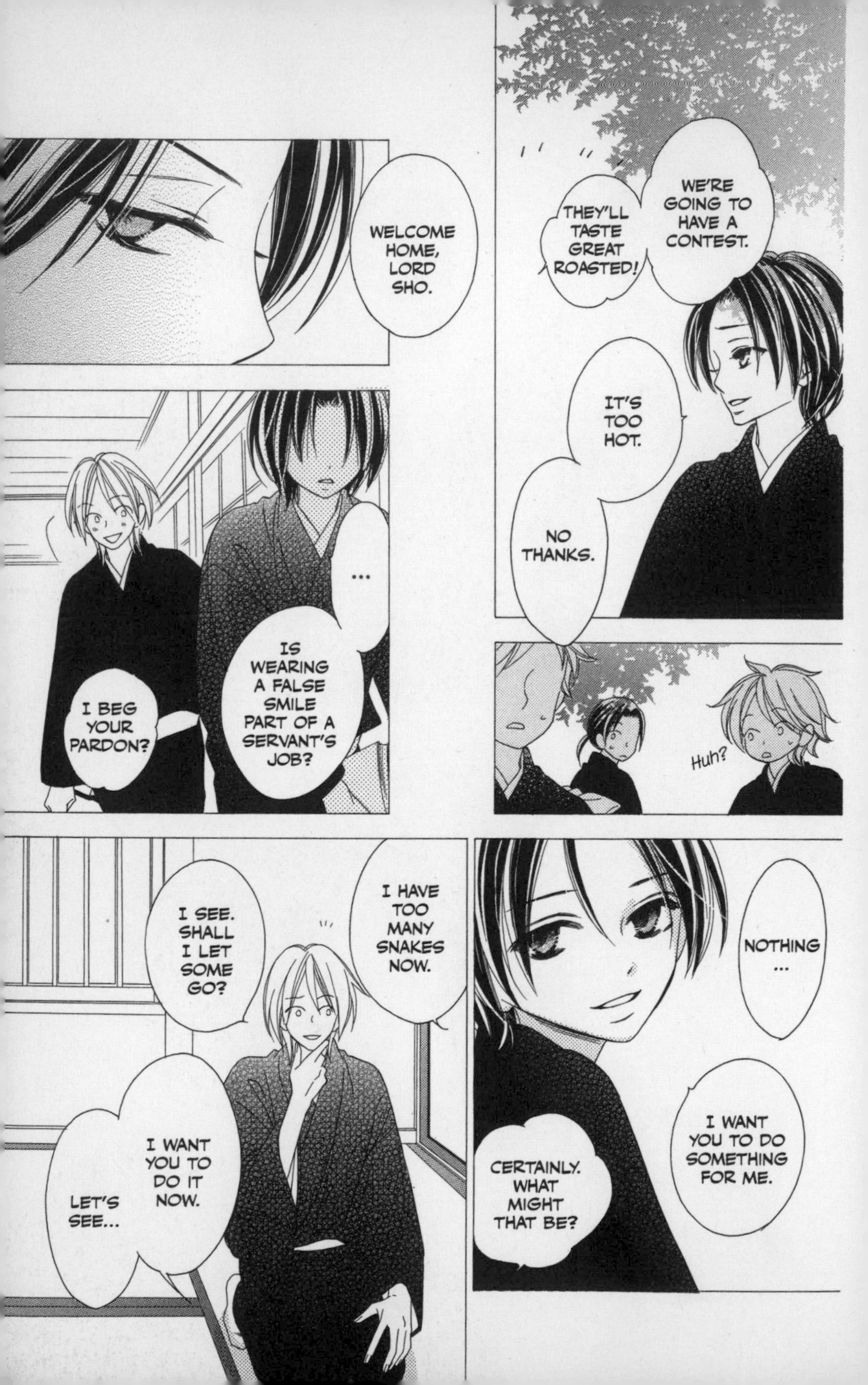
WE'RE GOING TO HAVE A CONTEST.
THEY'LL TASTE GREAT ROASTED!
IT'S TOO HOT.
NO THANKS.
Huh?
WELCOME HOME, LORD SHO.
...
IS WEARING A FALSE SMILE PART OF A SERVANT'S JOB?
I BEG YOUR PARDON?
NOTHING...
I WANT YOU TO DO SOMETHING FOR ME.
CERTAINLY. WHAT MIGHT THAT BE?
I HAVE TOO MANY SNAKES NOW.
I SEE. SHALL I LET SOME GO?
I WANT YOU TO DO IT NOW.
LET'S SEE...

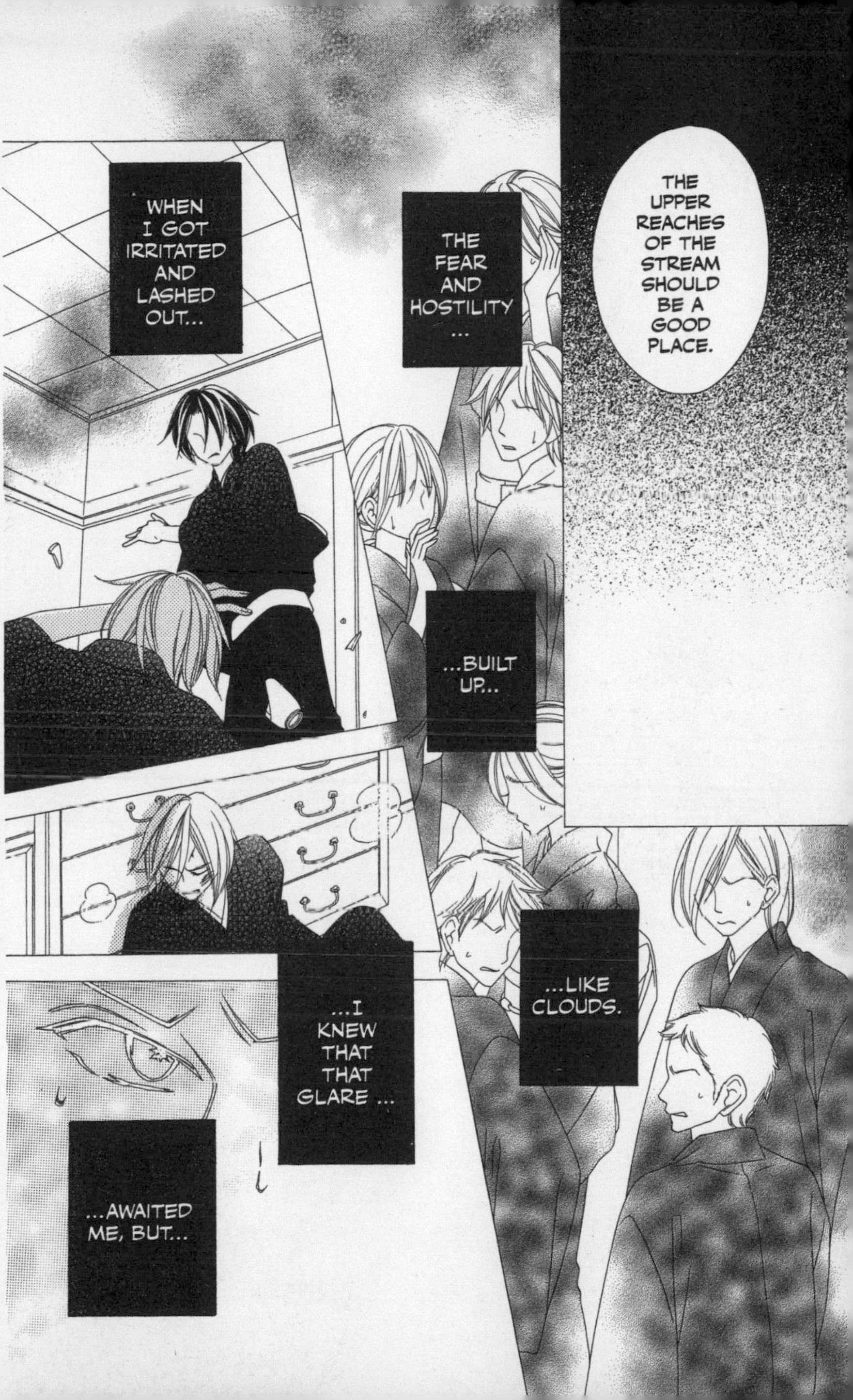
THE UPPER REACHES OF THE STREAM SHOULD BE A GOOD PLACE.
WHEN I GOT IRRITATED AND LASHED OUT...
THE FEAR AND HOSTILITY ...
...BUILT UP...
...LIKE CLOUDS.
...I KNEW THAT THAT GLARE ...
...AWAITED ME, BUT...

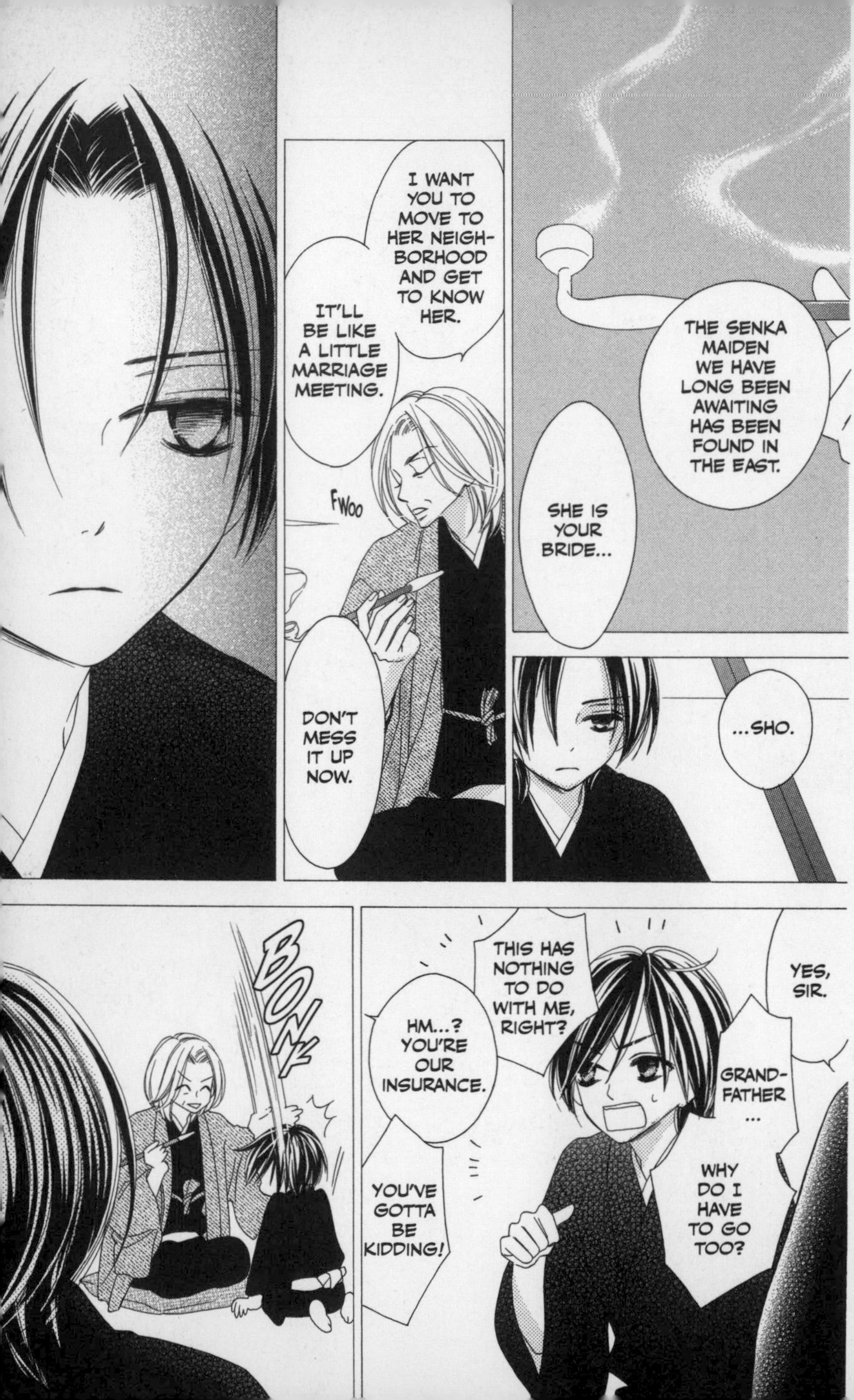
THE SENKA MAIDEN WE HAVE LONG BEEN AWAITING HAS BEEN FOUND IN THE EAST.
SHE IS YOUR BRIDE...
...SHO.
I WANT YOU TO MOVE TO HER NEIGH-BORHOOD AND GET TO KNOW HER.
IT'LL BE LIKE A LITTLE MARRIAGE MEETING.
FWOO
DON'T MESS IT UP NOW.
YES, SIR.
GRAND-FATHER ...
WHY DO I HAVE TO GO TOO?
THIS HAS NOTHING TO DO WITH ME, RIGHT?
HM...? YOU'RE OUR INSURANCE.
YOU'VE GOTTA BE KIDDING!
BONK

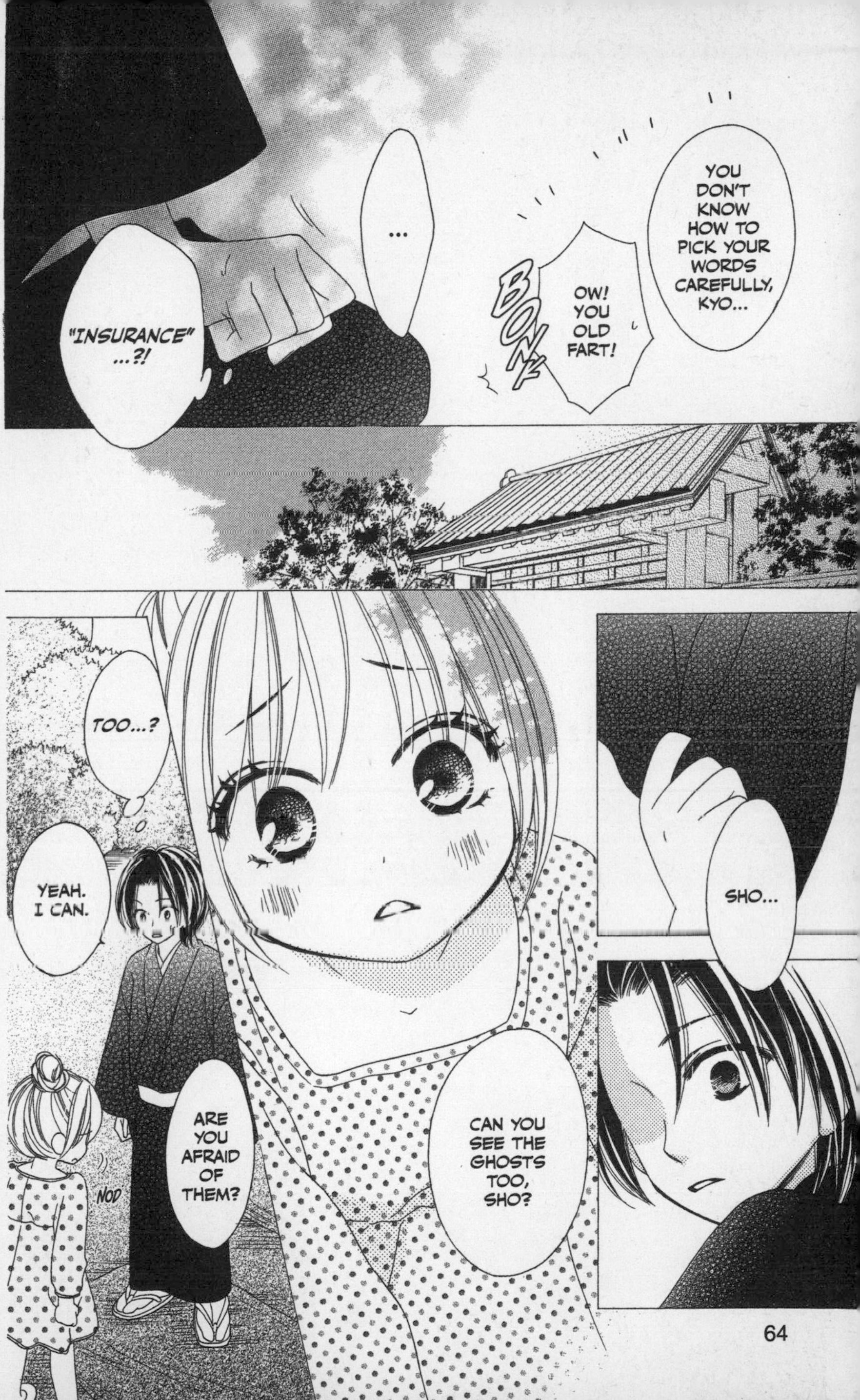
YOU DON'T KNOW HOW TO PICK YOUR WORDS CAREFULLY, KYO...
OW! YOU OLD FART!
BONK
...
"INSURANCE" ...?!
SHO...
CAN YOU SEE THE GHOSTS TOO, SHO?
TOO...?
YEAH. I CAN.
ARE YOU AFRAID OF THEM?
NOD

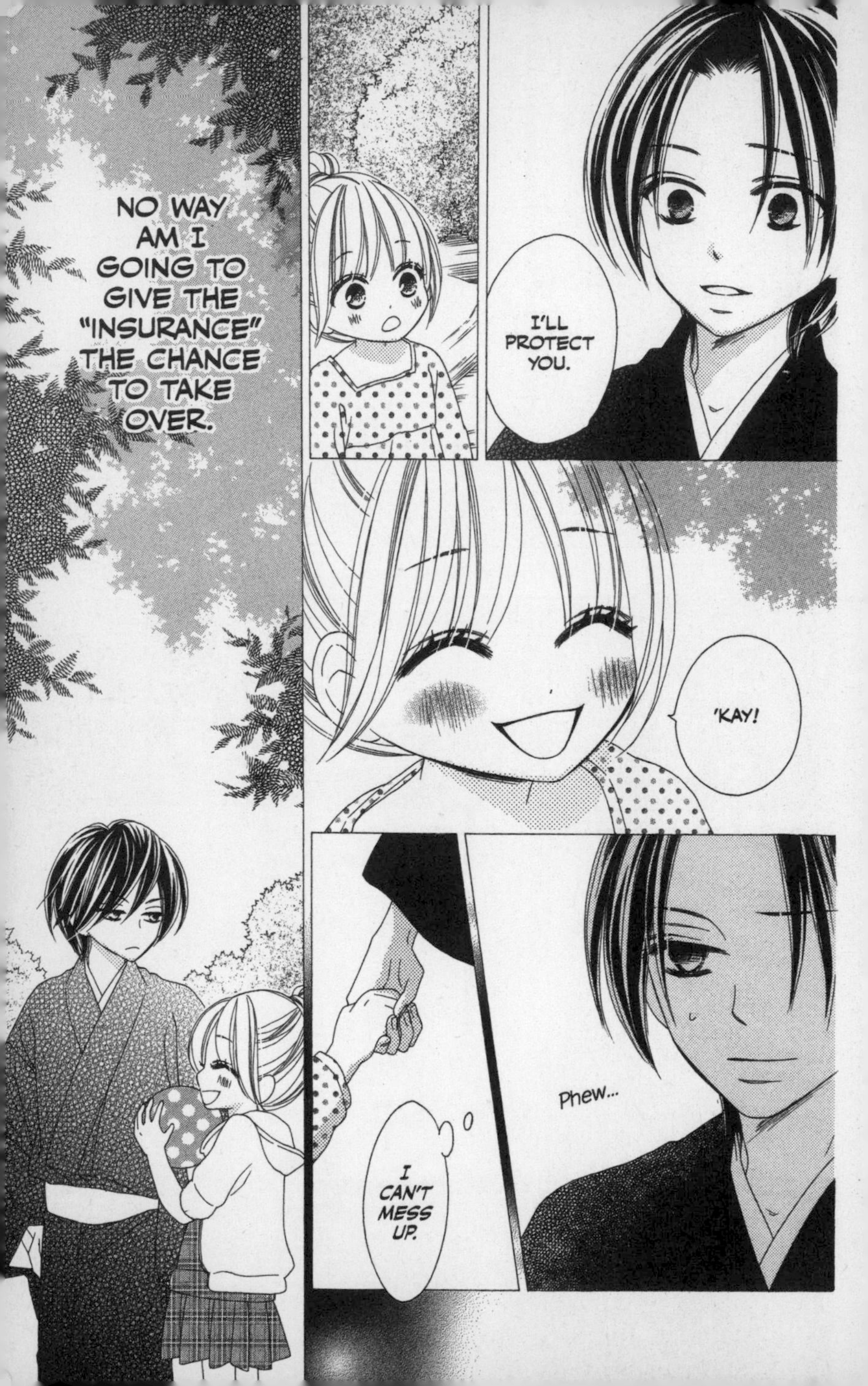
I'LL PROTECT YOU.
'KAY!
Phew...
I CAN'T MESS UP.
NO WAY AM I GOING TO GIVE THE "INSURANCE" THE CHANCE TO TAKE OVER.

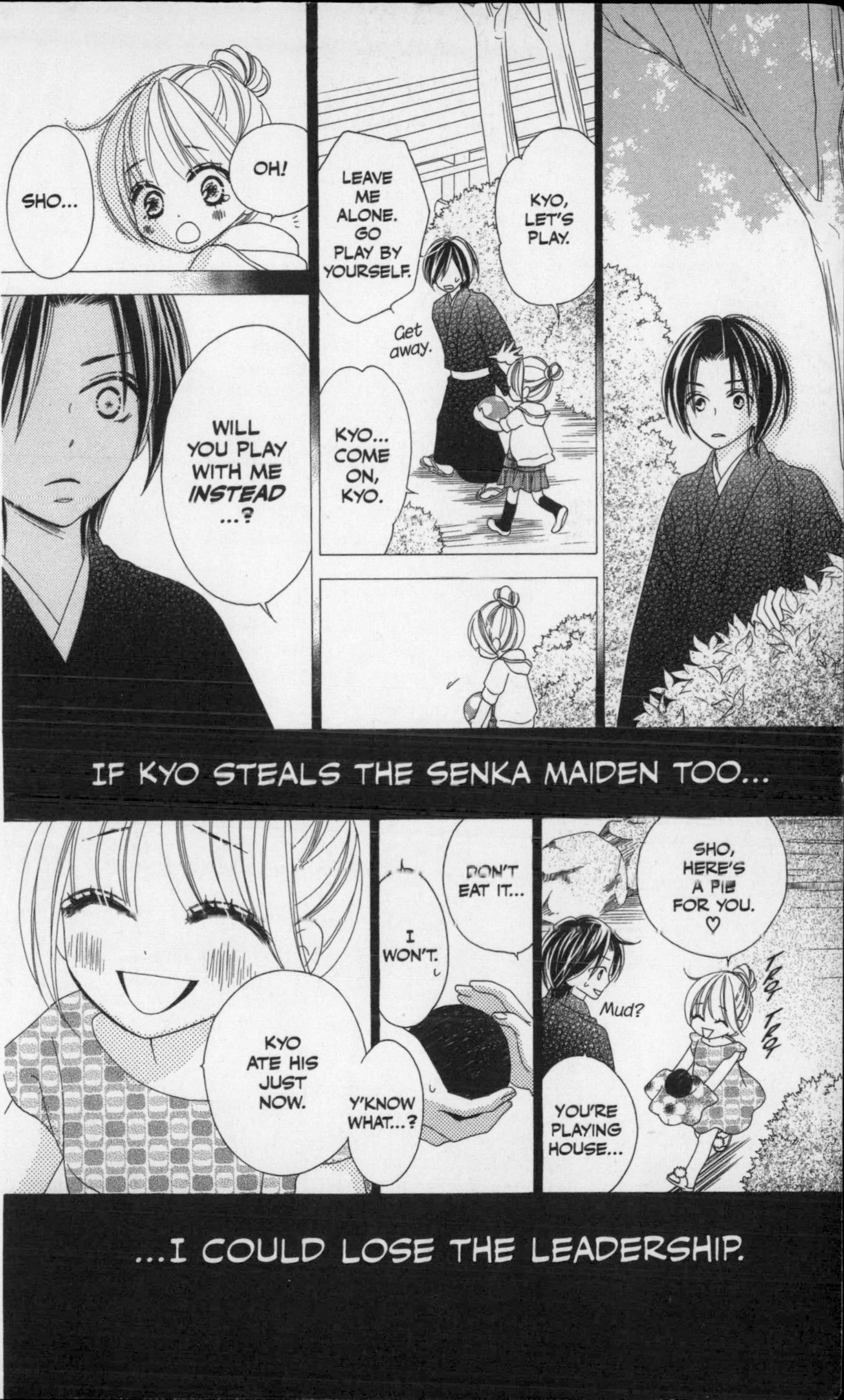
KYO, LET'S PLAY.
LEAVE ME ALONE. GO PLAY BY YOURSELF.
Get away.
KYO... COME ON, KYO.
OH!
SHO...
WILL YOU PLAY WITH ME INSTEAD ...?
IF KYO STEALS THE SENKA MAIDEN TOO...
SHO, HERE'S A PIE FOR YOU. ♡
TROT TROT
Mud?
YOU'RE PLAYING HOUSE...
DON'T EAT IT...
I WON'T.
Y'KNOW WHAT...?
KYO ATE HIS JUST NOW.
...I COULD LOSE THE LEADERSHIP.

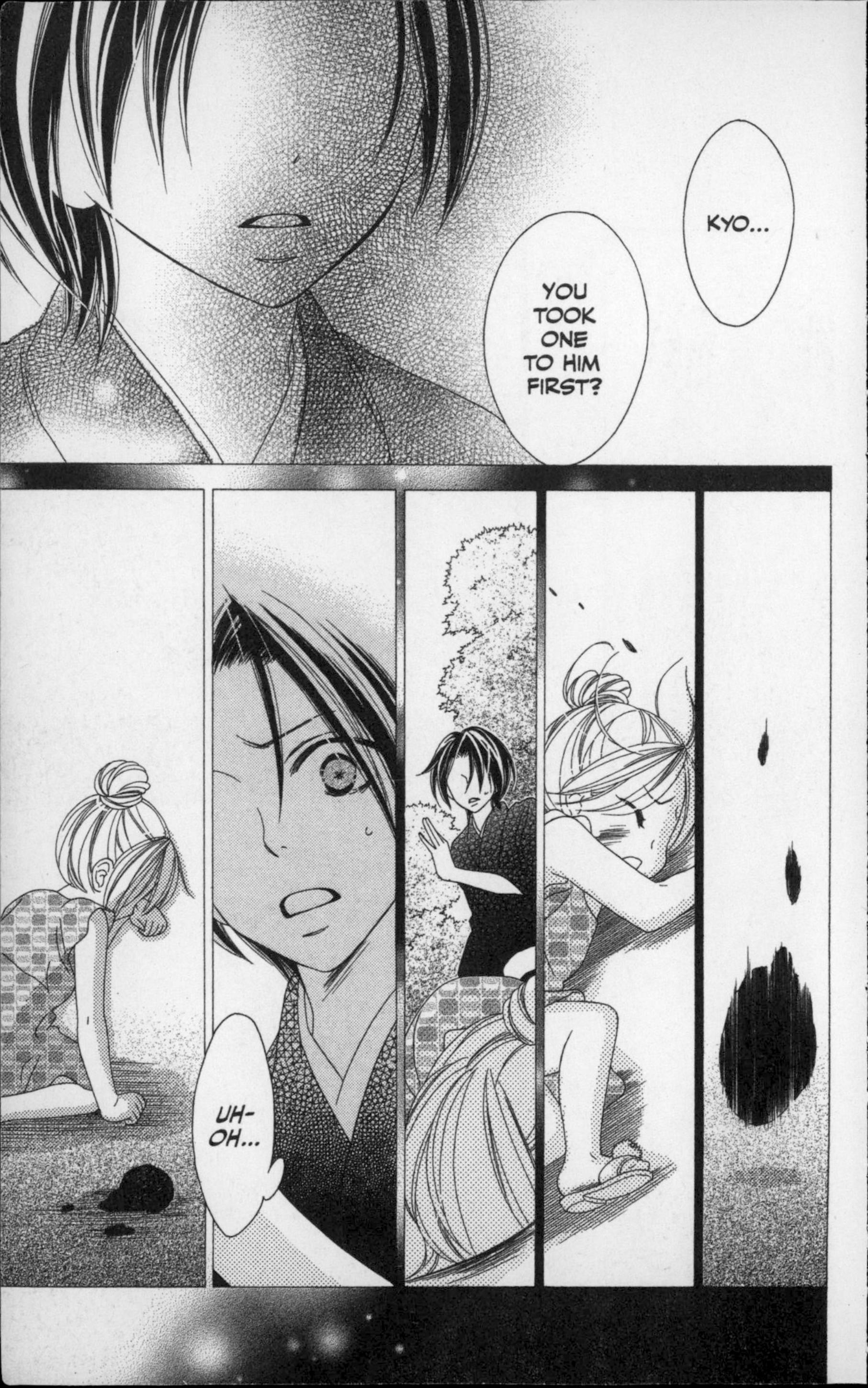
KYO...
YOU TOOK ONE TO HIM FIRST?
UH-OH...

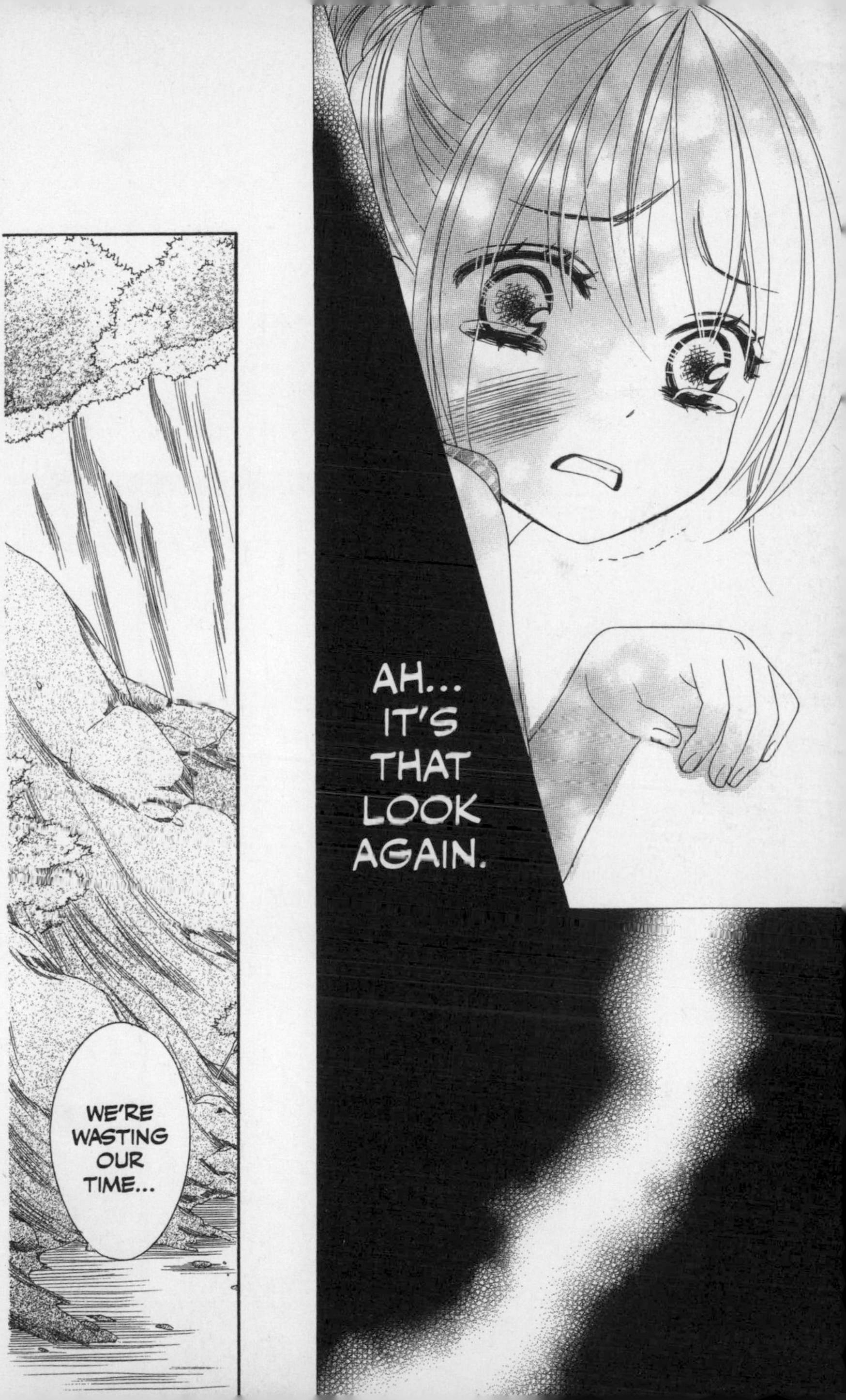
AH... IT'S THAT LOOK AGAIN.
WE'RE WASTING OUR TIME...

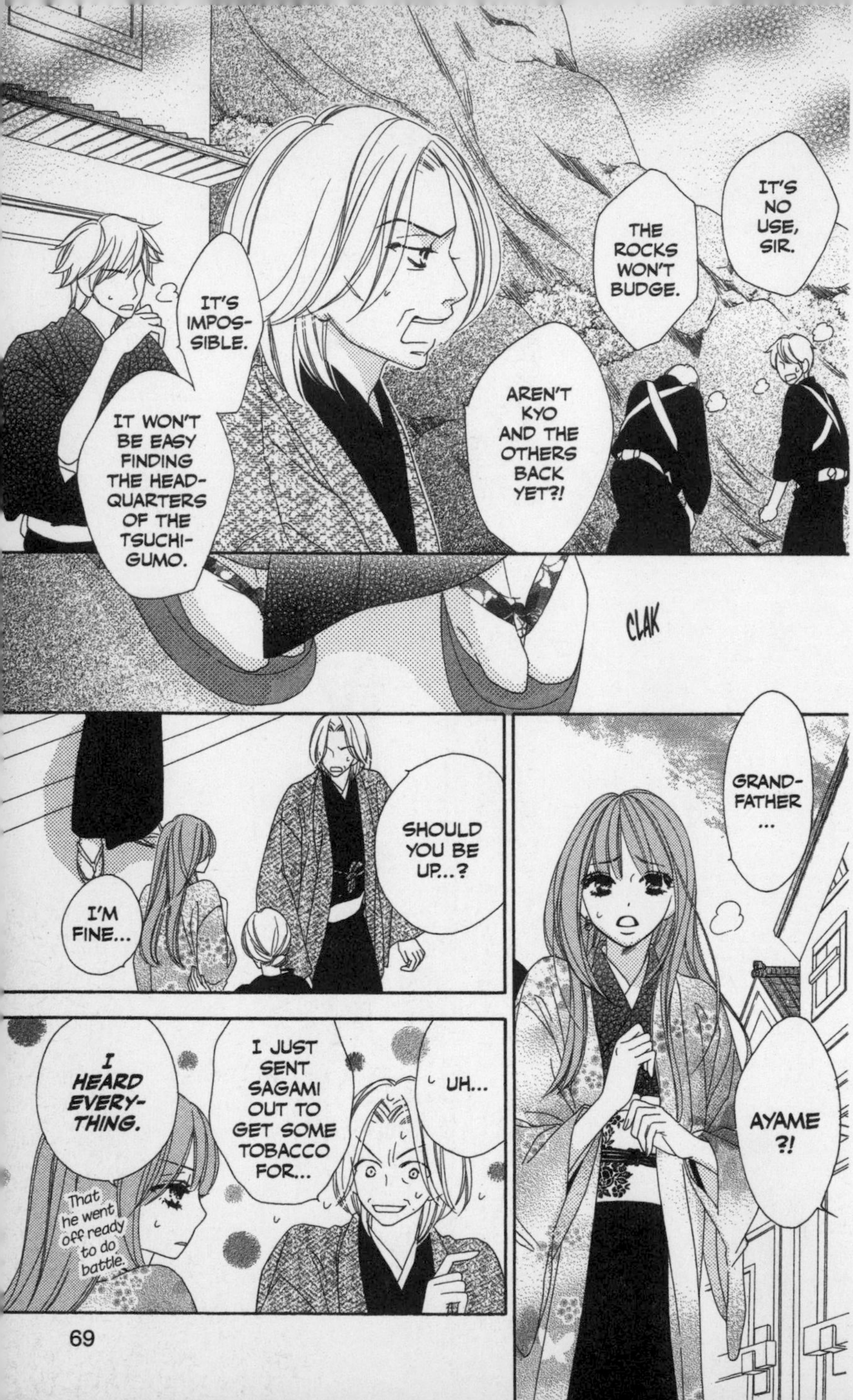
IT'S NO USE, SIR.
THE ROCKS WON'T BUDGE.
AREN'T KYO AND THE OTHERS BACK YET?!
IT'S IMPOSSIBLE.
IT WON'T BE EASY FINDING THE HEADQUARTERS OF THE TSUCHIGUMO.
CLAK
GRANDFATHER...
AYAME?!
SHOULD YOU BE UP...?
I'M FINE...
UH...
I JUST SENT SAGAMI OUT TO GET SOME TOBACCO FOR...
I HEARD EVERYTHING.
That he went off ready to do battle.

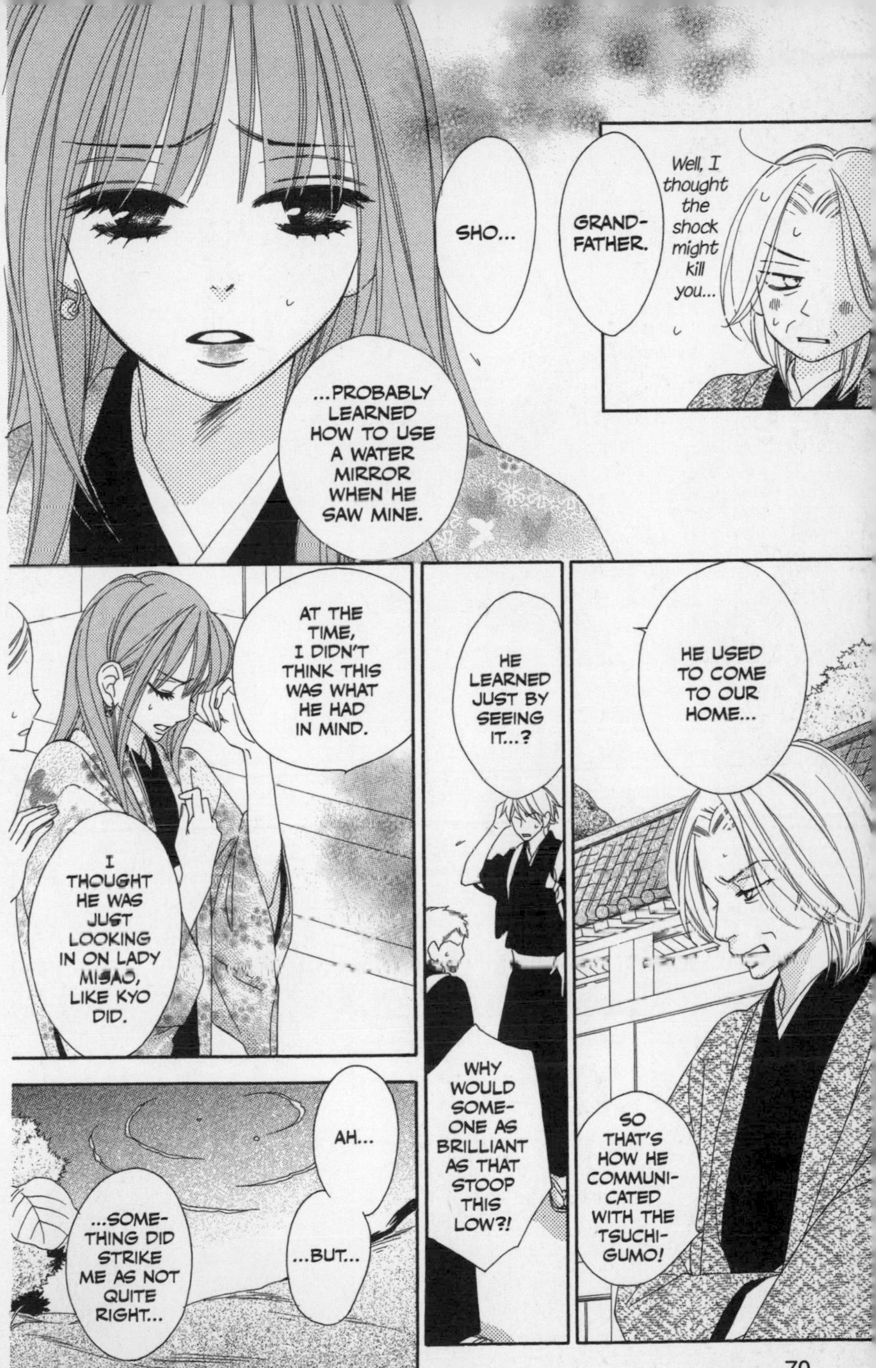
Well, I thought the shock might kill you...
GRAND-FATHER.
SHO...
...PROBABLY LEARNED HOW TO USE A WATER MIRROR WHEN HE SAW MINE.
HE USED TO COME TO OUR HOME...
SO THAT'S HOW HE COMMUNICATED WITH THE TSUCHIGUMO!
HE LEARNED JUST BY SEEING IT...?
WHY WOULD SOMEONE AS BRILLIANT AS THAT STOOP THIS LOW?!
AT THE TIME, I DIDN'T THINK THIS WAS WHAT HE HAD IN MIND.
I THOUGHT HE WAS JUST LOOKING IN ON LADY MISAO, LIKE KYO DID.
AH...
...BUT...
...SOMETHING DID STRIKE ME AS NOT QUITE RIGHT...

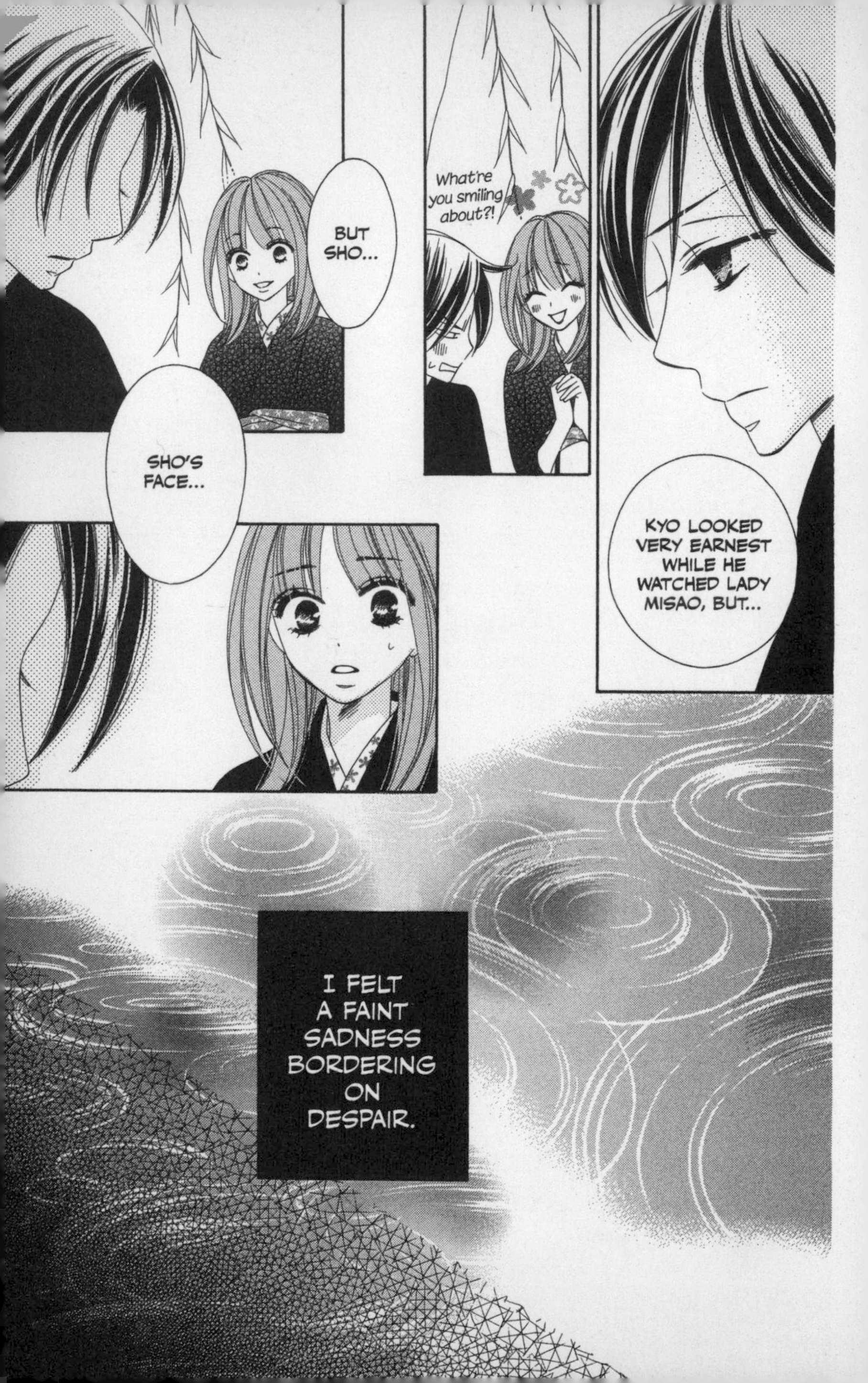
KYO LOOKED VERY EARNEST WHILE HE WATCHED LADY MISAO, BUT...
What're you smiling about?!
BUT SHO...
SHO'S FACE...
I FELT A FAINT SADNESS BORDERING ON DESPAIR.

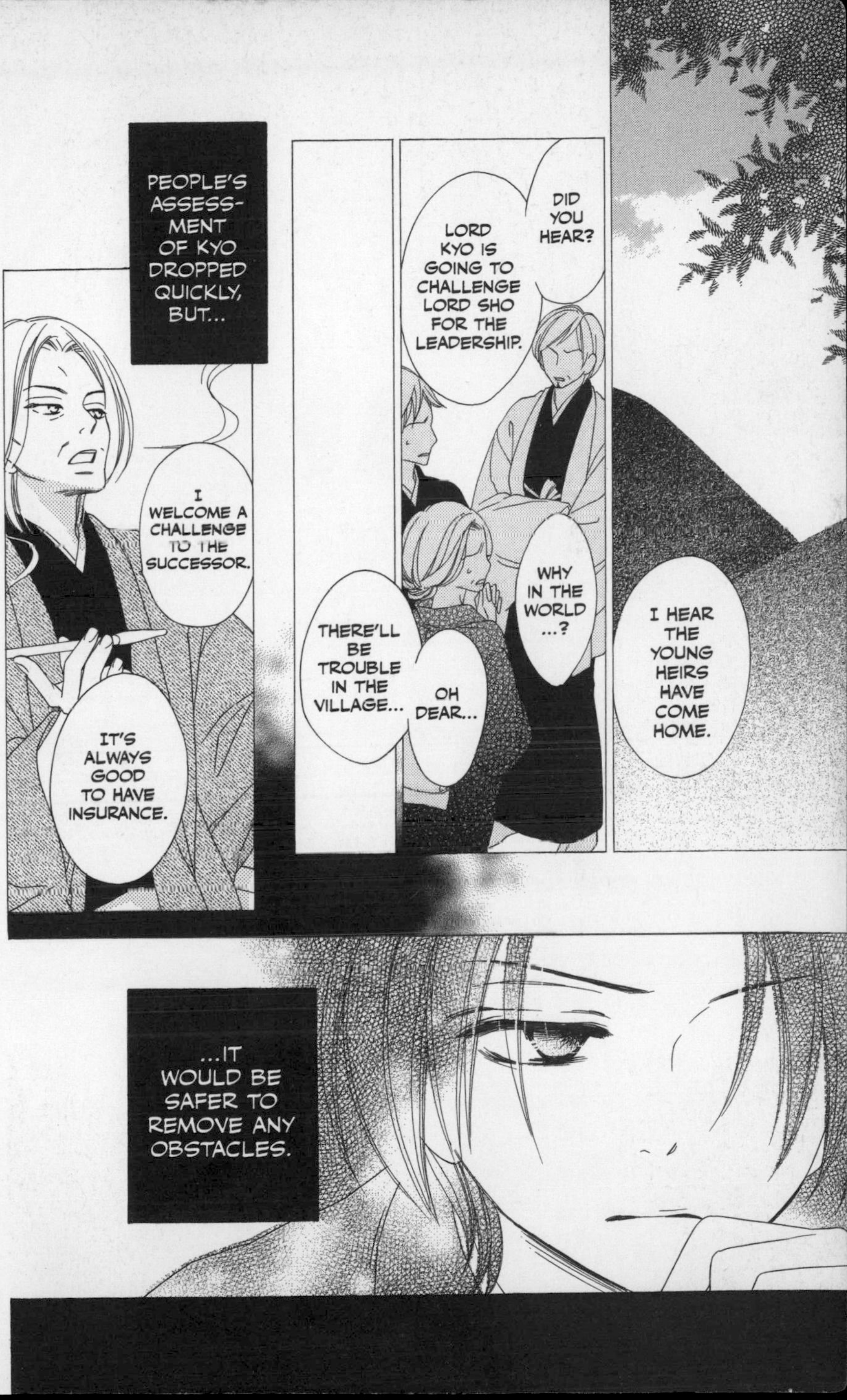
I HEAR THE YOUNG HEIRS HAVE COME HOME.
DID YOU HEAR?
LORD KYO IS GOING TO CHALLENGE LORD SHO FOR THE LEADERSHIP.
WHY IN THE WORLD ...?
OH DEAR...
THERE'LL BE TROUBLE IN THE VILLAGE...
PEOPLE'S ASSESS-MENT OF KYO DROPPED QUICKLY, BUT...
I WELCOME A CHALLENGE TO THE SUCCESSOR.
IT'S ALWAYS GOOD TO HAVE INSURANCE.
...IT WOULD BE SAFER TO REMOVE ANY OBSTACLES.

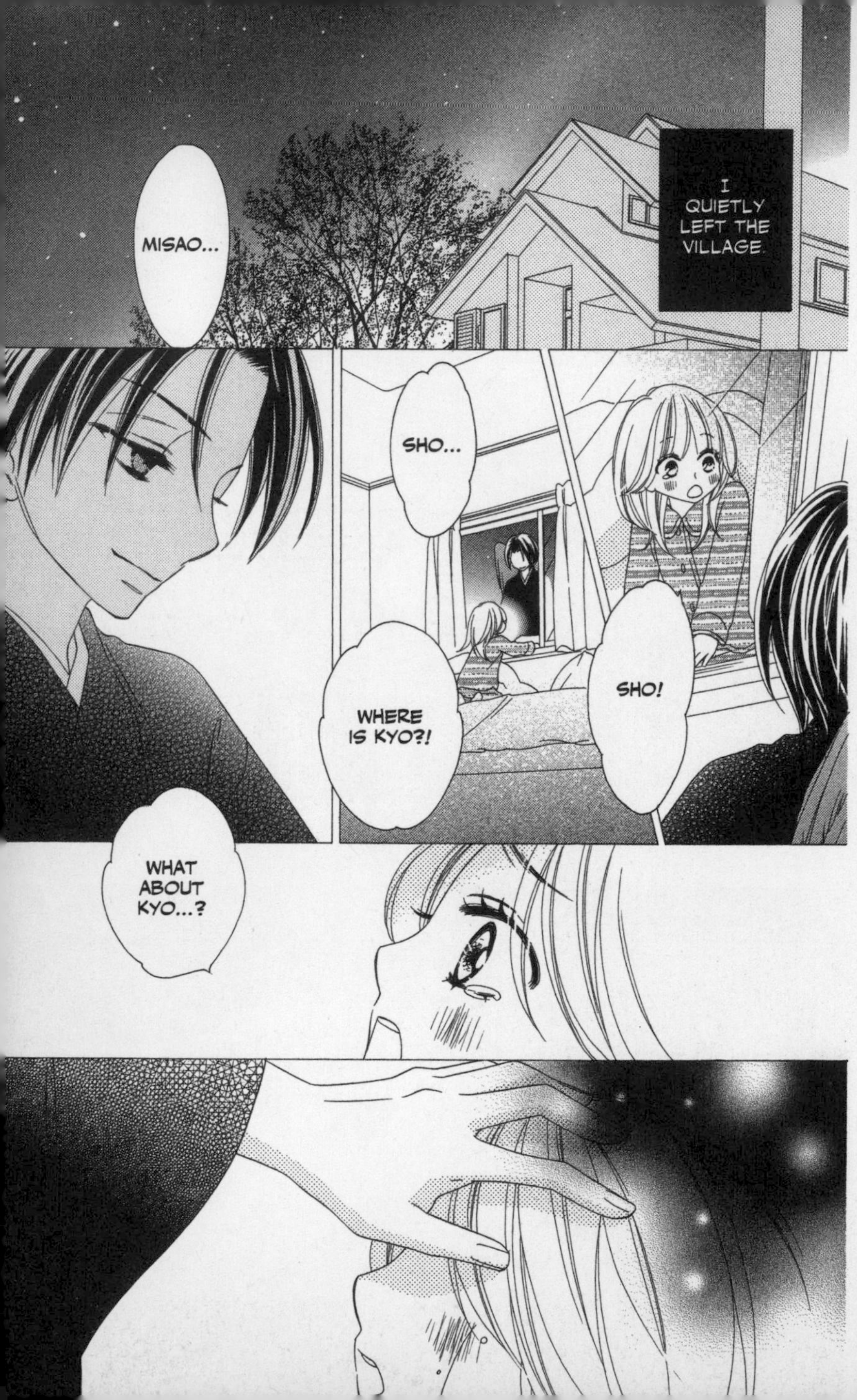
I QUIETLY LEFT THE VILLAGE.
MISAO...
SHO!
SHO...
WHERE IS KYO?!
WHAT ABOUT KYO...?

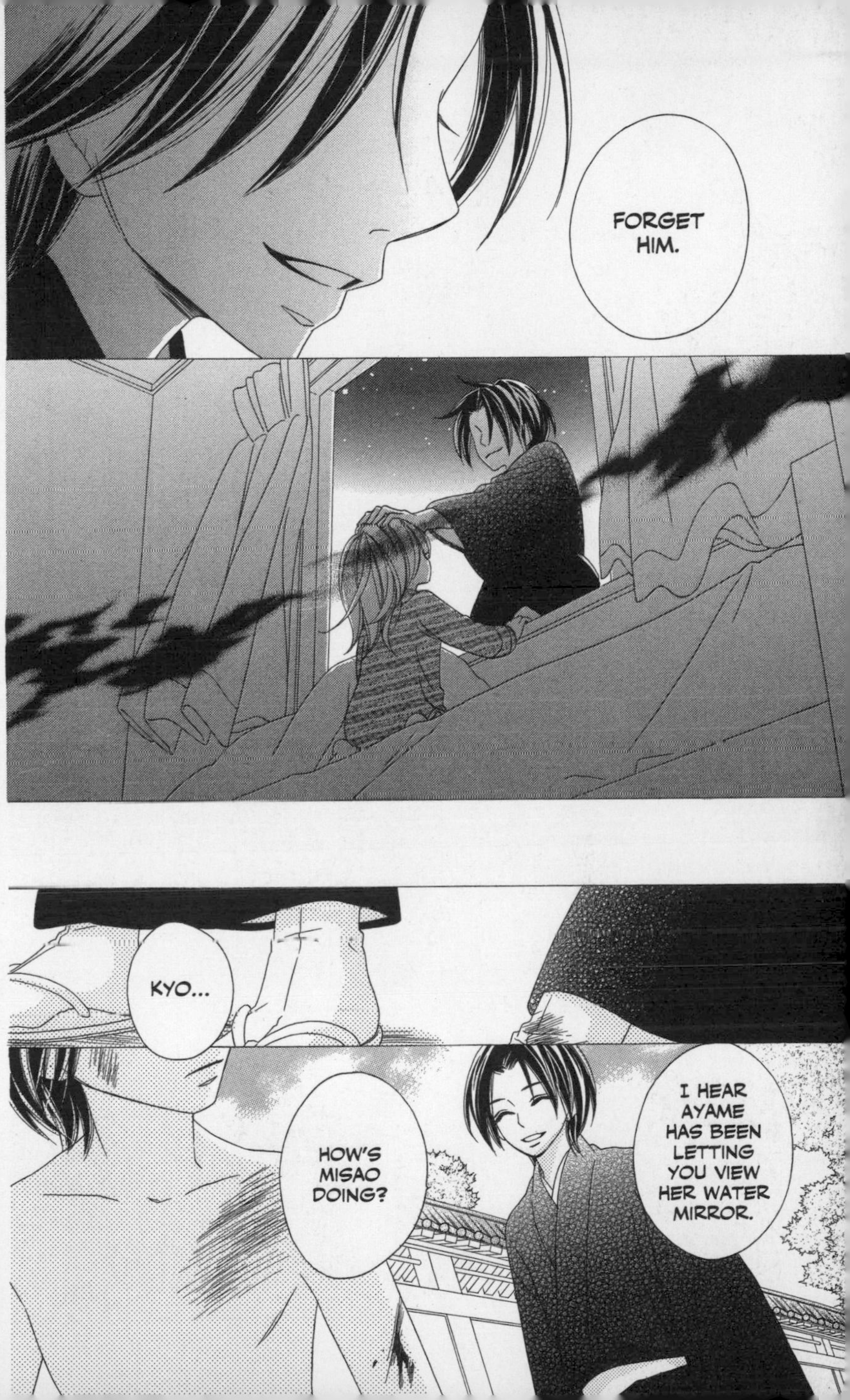
FORGET HIM.
KYO...
I HEAR AYAME HAS BEEN LETTING YOU VIEW HER WATER MIRROR.
HOW'S MISAO DOING?

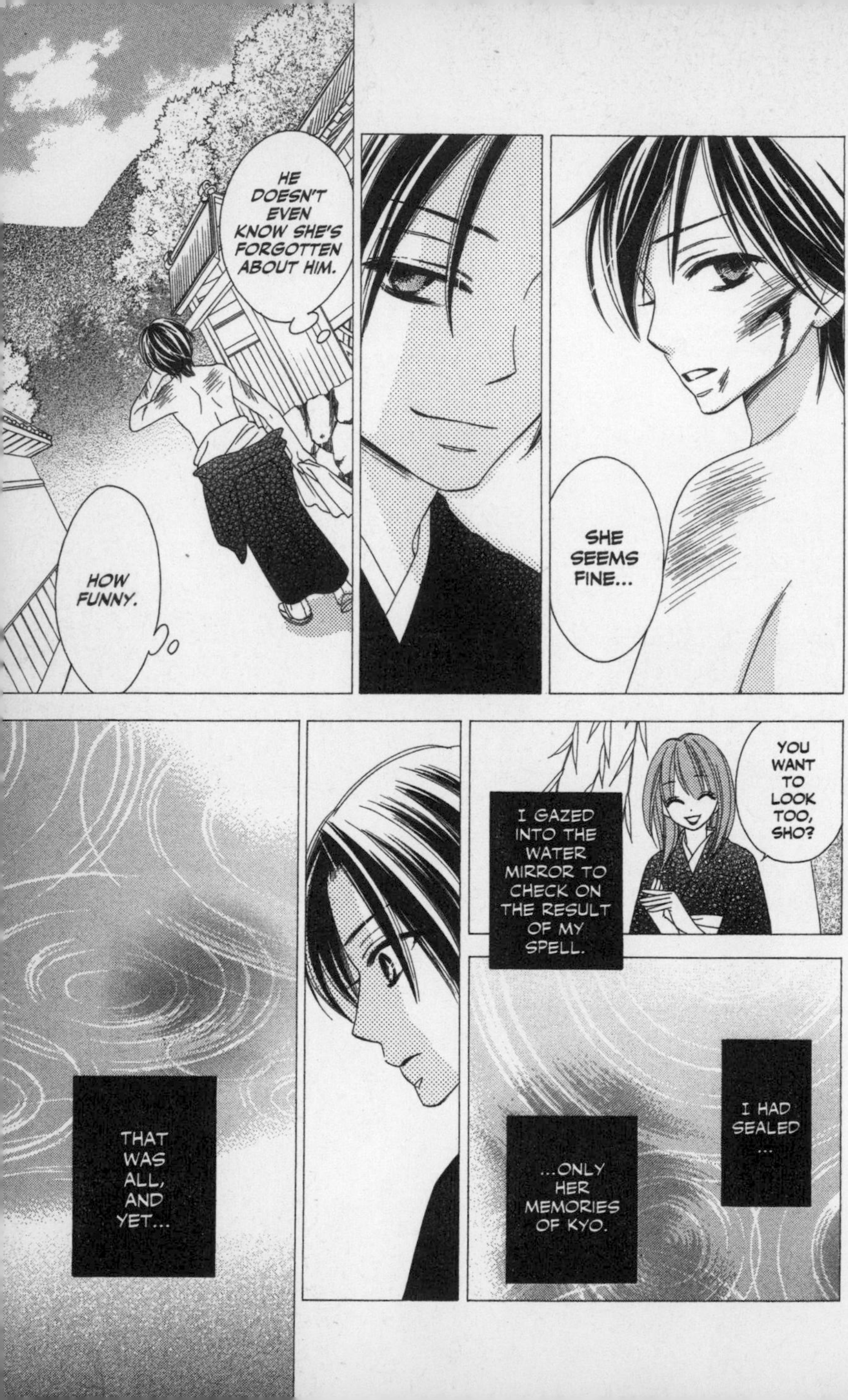
SHE SEEMS FINE...
HE DOESN'T EVEN KNOW SHE'S FORGOTTEN ABOUT HIM.
HOW FUNNY.
YOU WANT TO LOOK TOO, SHO?
I GAZED INTO THE WATER MIRROR TO CHECK ON THE RESULT OF MY SPELL.
I HAD SEALED...
...ONLY HER MEMORIES OF KYO.
THAT WAS ALL, AND YET...

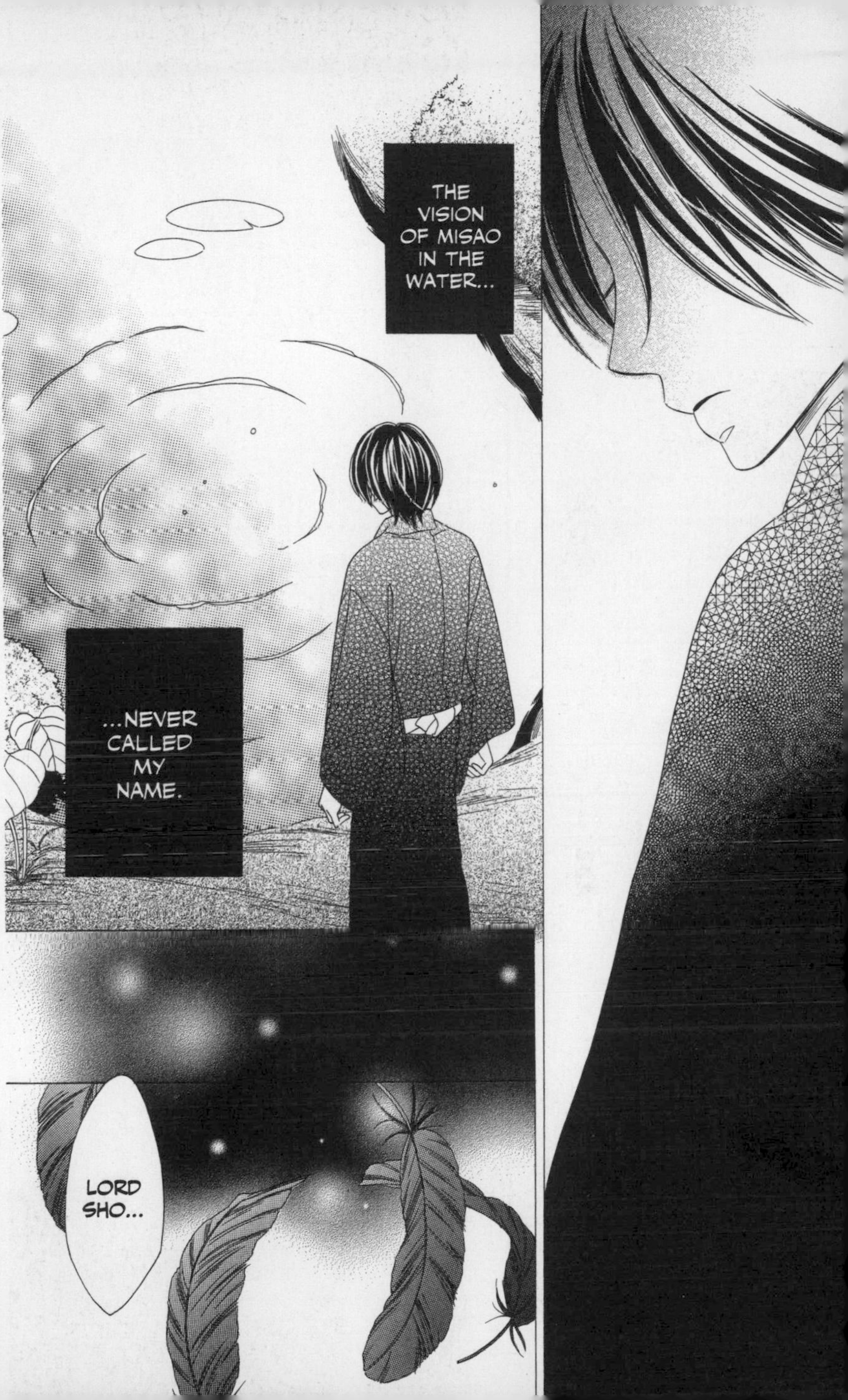
THE VISION OF MISAO IN THE WATER...
...NEVER CALLED MY NAME.
LORD SHO...

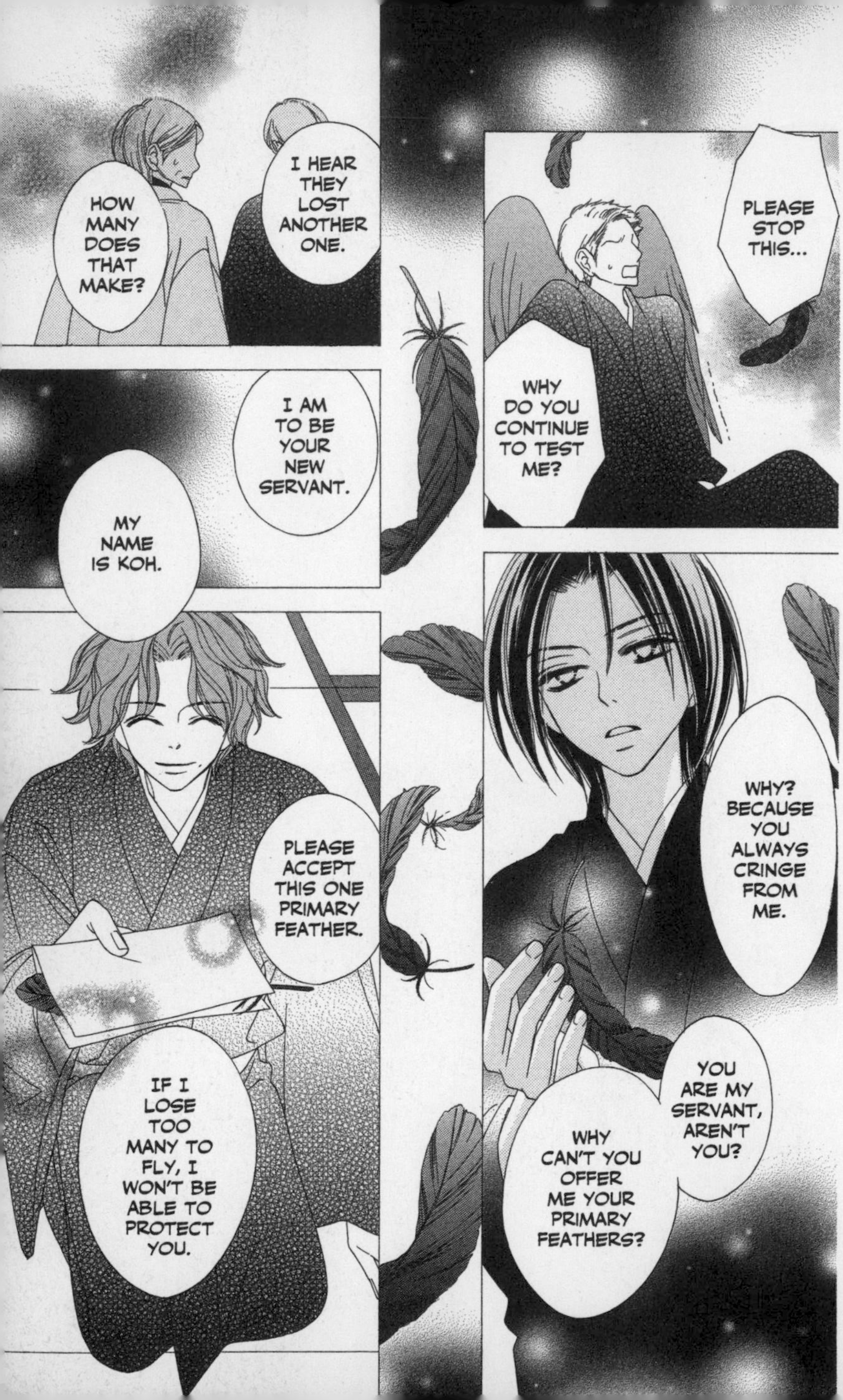
PLEASE STOP THIS...
WHY DO YOU CONTINUE TO TEST ME?
WHY? BECAUSE YOU ALWAYS CRINGE FROM ME.
YOU ARE MY SERVANT, AREN'T YOU?
WHY CAN'T YOU OFFER ME YOUR PRIMARY FEATHERS?
I HEAR THEY LOST ANOTHER ONE.
HOW MANY DOES THAT MAKE?
I AM TO BE YOUR NEW SERVANT.
MY NAME IS KOH.
PLEASE ACCEPT THIS ONE PRIMARY FEATHER.
IF I LOSE TOO MANY TO FLY, I WON'T BE ABLE TO PROTECT YOU.

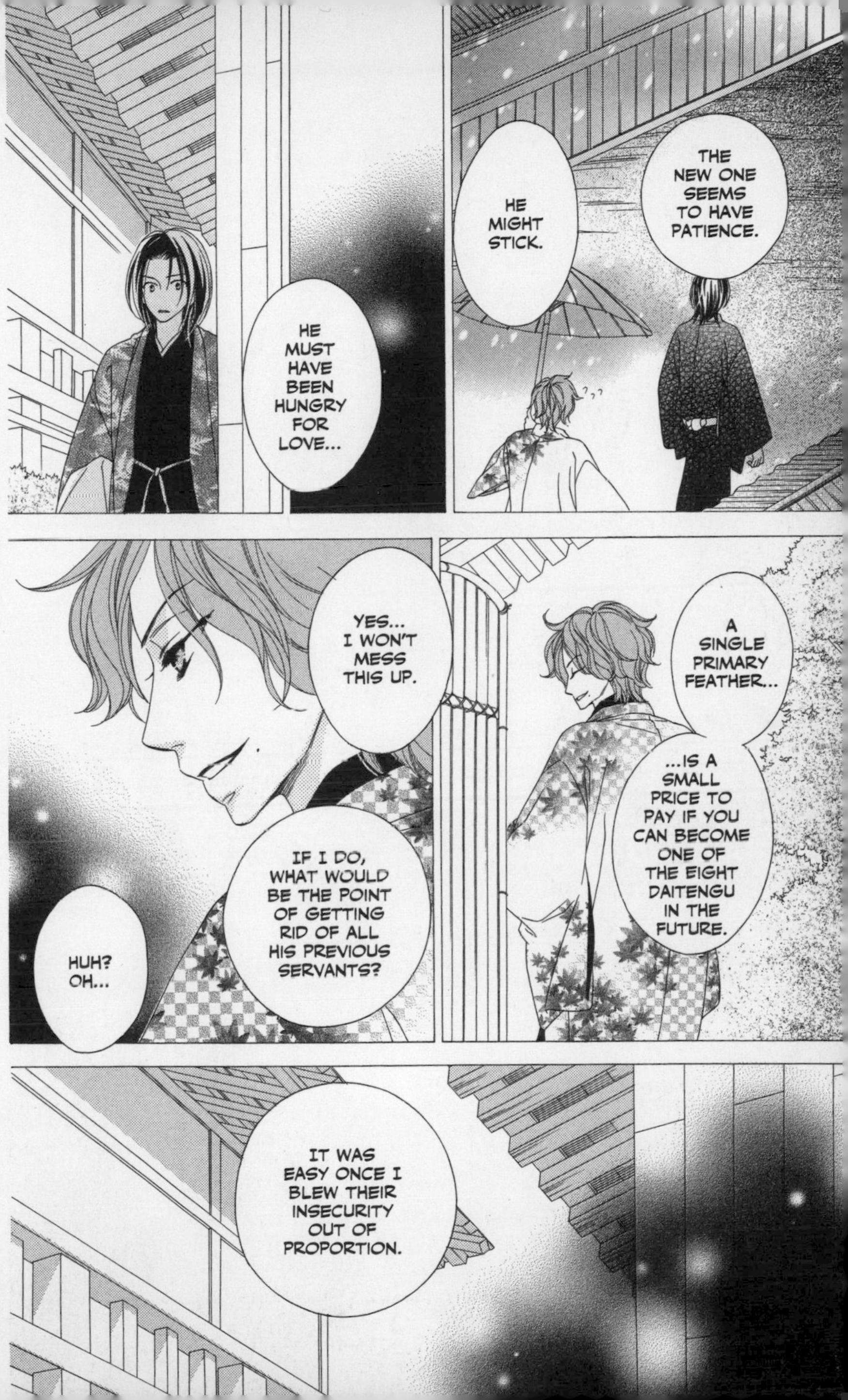
THE NEW ONE SEEMS TO HAVE PATIENCE.
HE MIGHT STICK.
HE MUST HAVE BEEN HUNGRY FOR LOVE...
A SINGLE PRIMARY FEATHER...
...IS A SMALL PRICE TO PAY IF YOU CAN BECOME ONE OF THE EIGHT DAITENGU IN THE FUTURE.
YES... I WON'T MESS THIS UP.
IF I DO, WHAT WOULD BE THE POINT OF GETTING RID OF ALL HIS PREVIOUS SERVANTS?
HUH? OH...
IT WAS EASY ONCE I BLEW THEIR INSECURITY OUT OF PROPORTION.

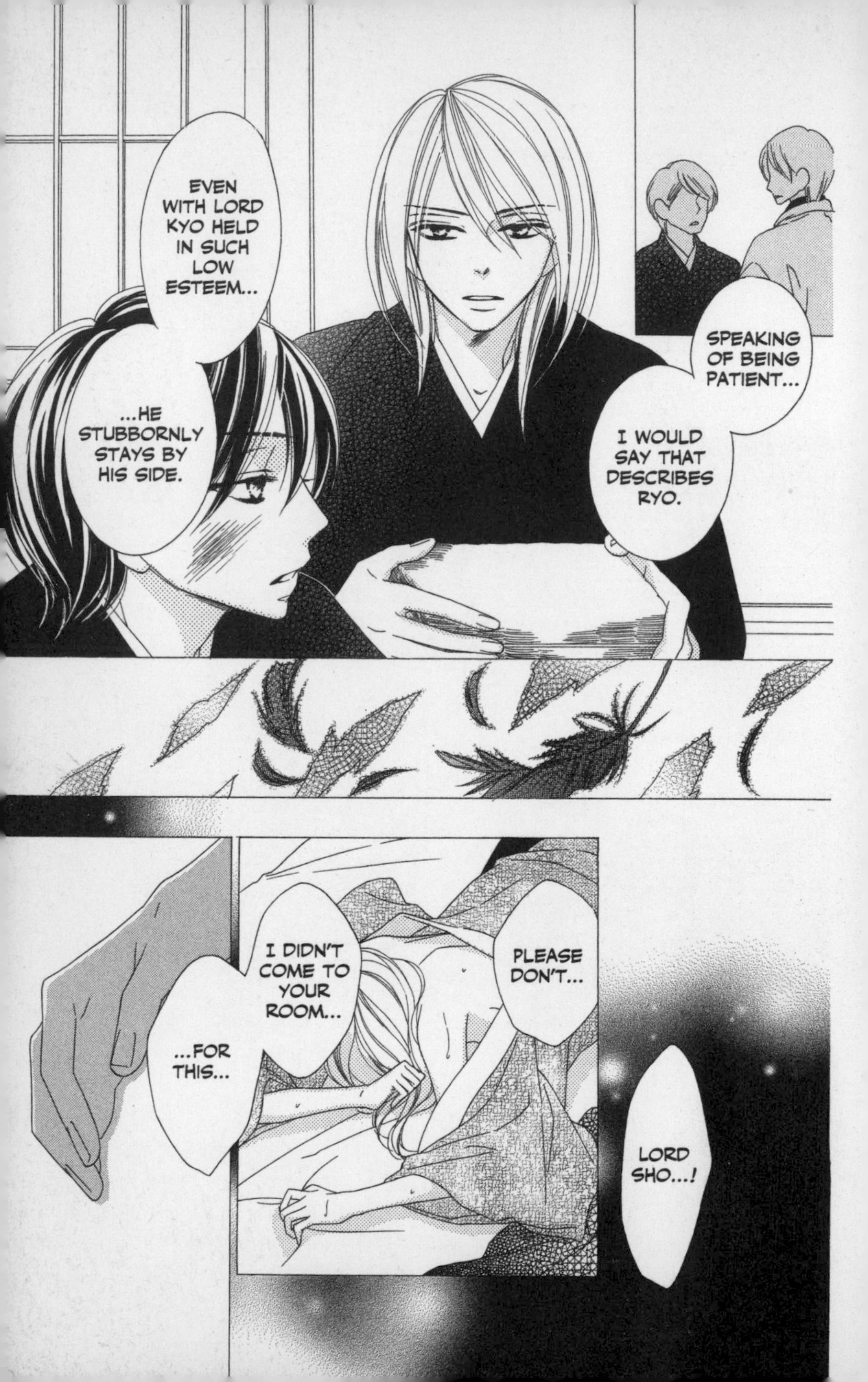
EVEN WITH LORD KYO HELD IN SUCH LOW ESTEEM...
...HE STUBBORNLY STAYS BY HIS SIDE.
SPEAKING OF BEING PATIENT...
I WOULD SAY THAT DESCRIBES RYO.
PLEASE DON'T...
I DIDN'T COME TO YOUR ROOM...
...FOR THIS...
LORD SHO...!

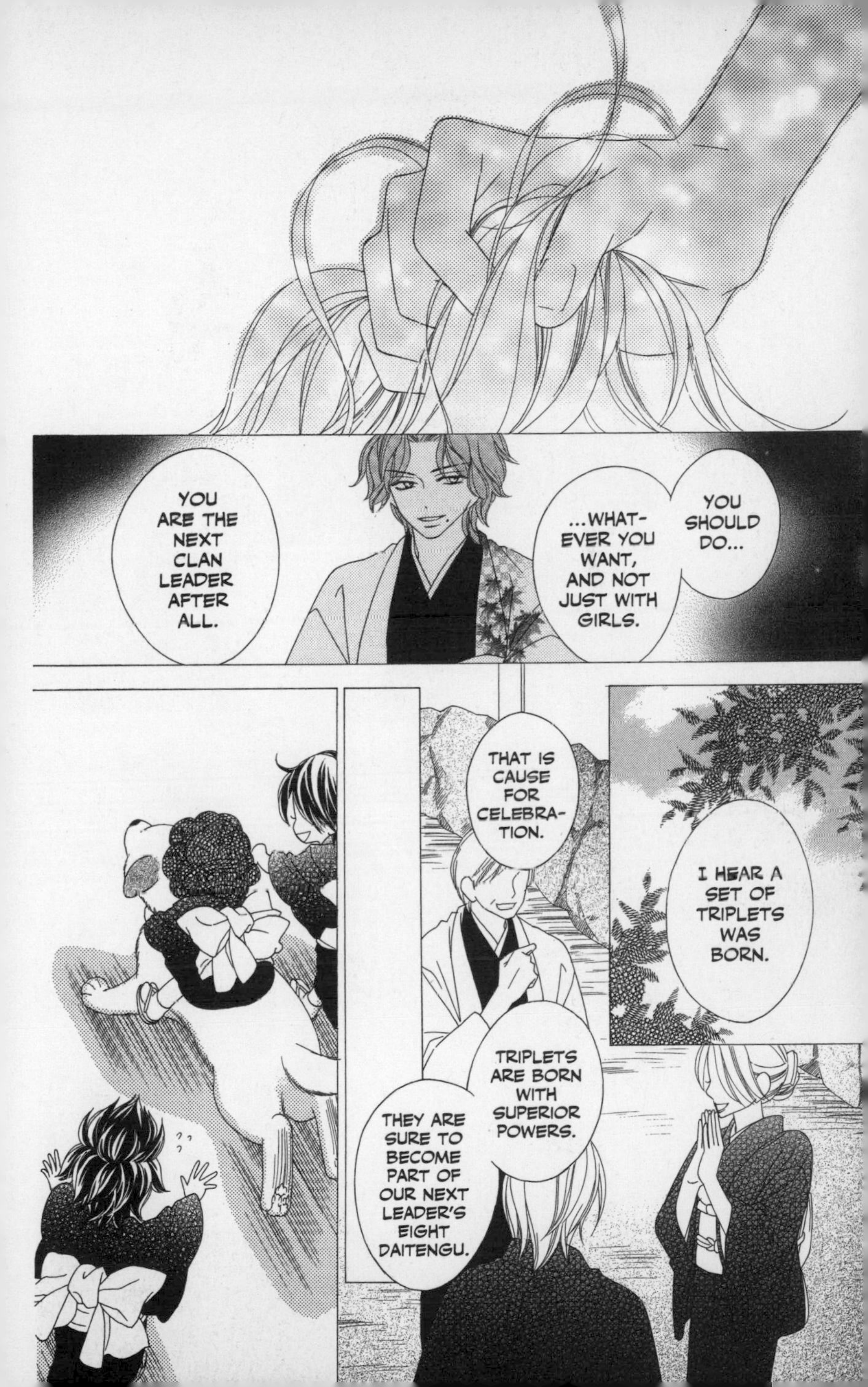
YOU SHOULD DO...
...WHAT-EVER YOU WANT, AND NOT JUST WITH GIRLS.
YOU ARE THE NEXT CLAN LEADER AFTER ALL.
I HEAR A SET OF TRIPLETS WAS BORN.
THAT IS CAUSE FOR CELEBRATION.
TRIPLETS ARE BORN WITH SUPERIOR POWERS.
THEY ARE SURE TO BECOME PART OF OUR NEXT LEADER'S EIGHT DAITENGU.

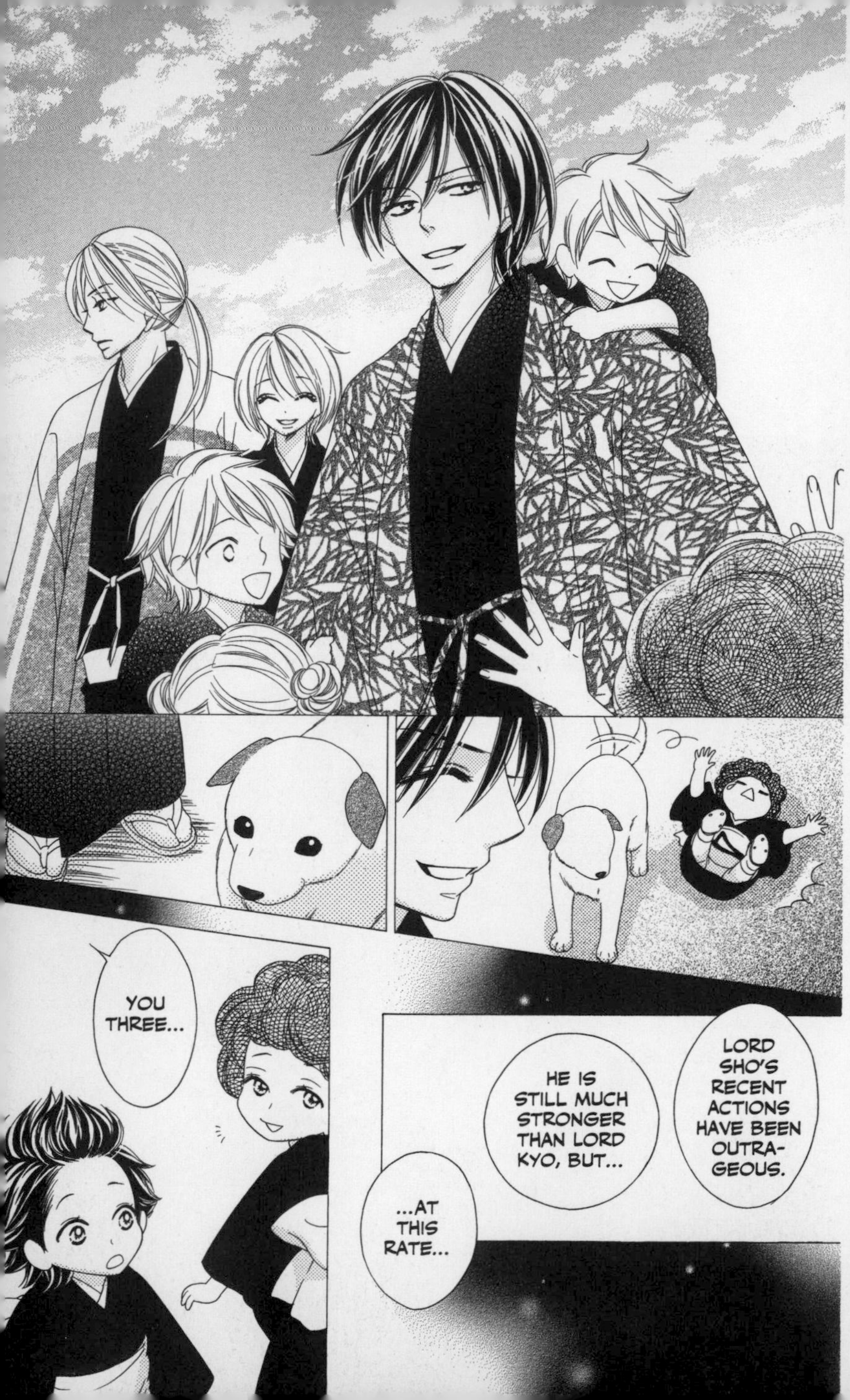
LORD SHO'S RECENT ACTIONS HAVE BEEN OUTRAGEOUS.
HE IS STILL MUCH STRONGER THAN LORD KYO, BUT...
...AT THIS RATE...
YOU THREE...

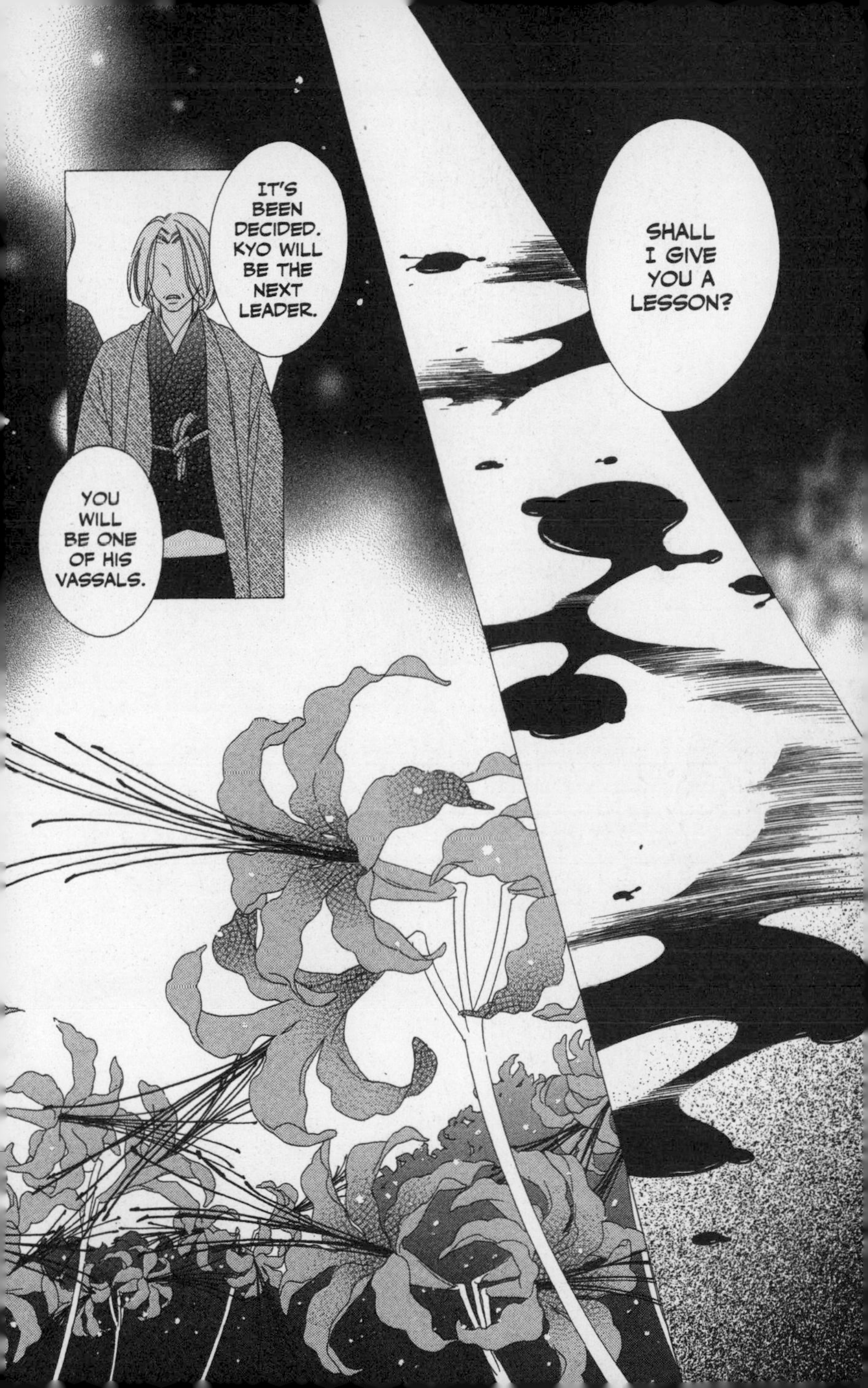
SHALL I GIVE YOU A LESSON?
IT'S BEEN DECIDED. KYO WILL BE THE NEXT LEADER.
YOU WILL BE ONE OF HIS VASSALS.

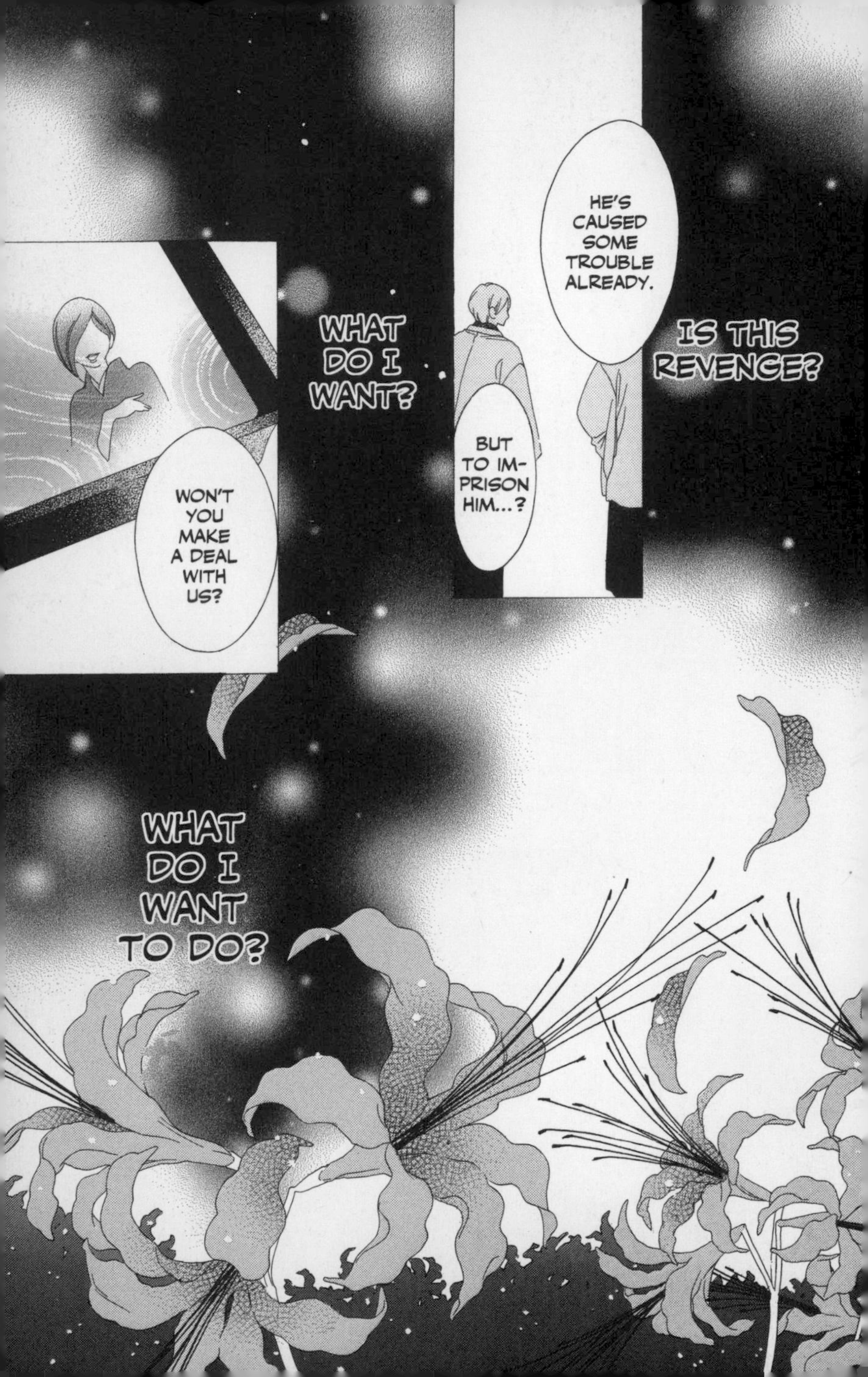
IS THIS REVENGE?
HE'S CAUSED SOME TROUBLE ALREADY.
BUT TO IM-PRISON HIM...?
WHAT DO I WANT?
WON'T YOU MAKE A DEAL WITH US?
WHAT DO I WANT TO DO?

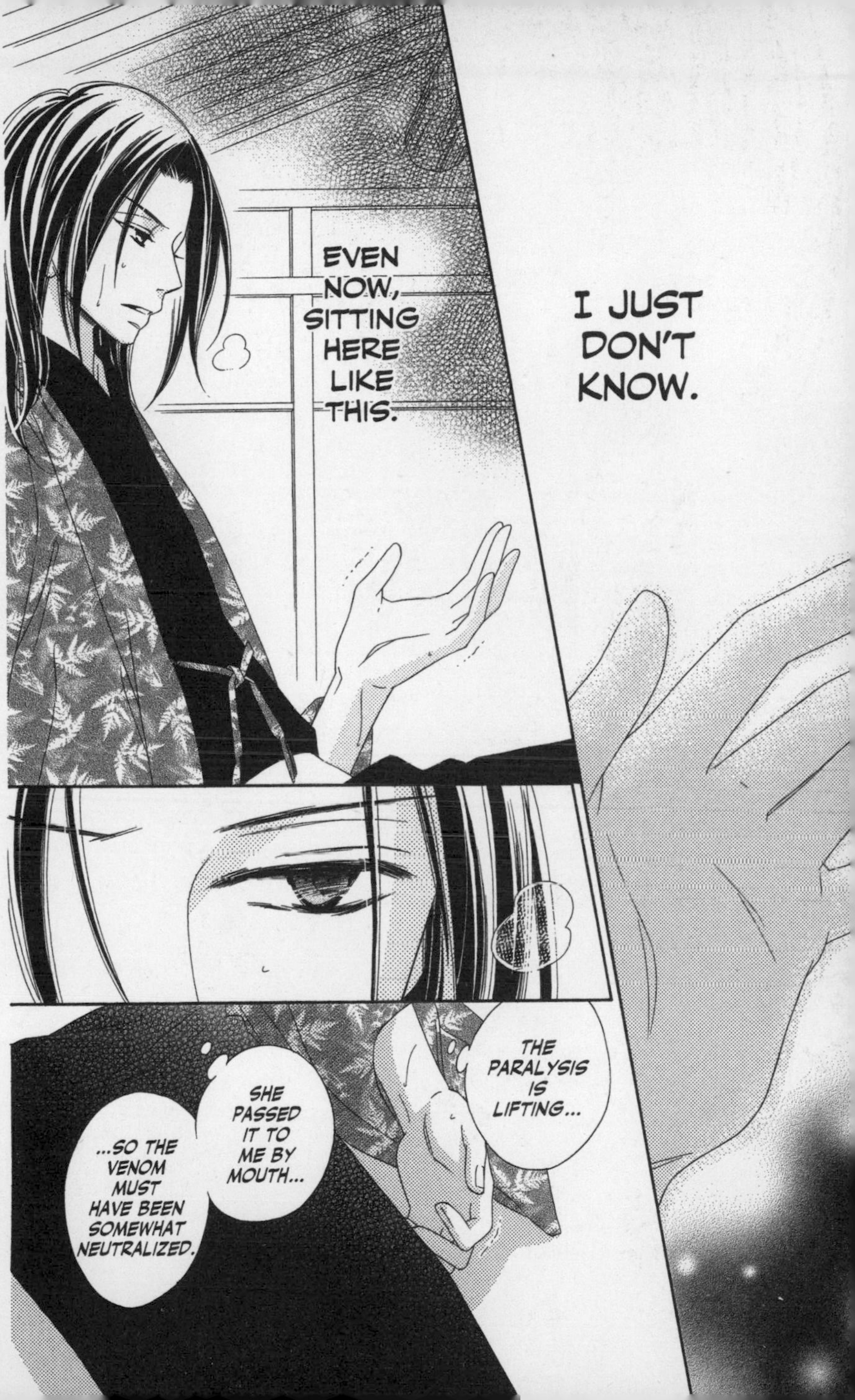
I JUST DON'T KNOW.
EVEN NOW, SITTING HERE LIKE THIS.
THE PARALYSIS IS LIFTING...
SHE PASSED IT TO ME BY MOUTH...
...SO THE VENOM MUST HAVE BEEN SOMEWHAT NEUTRALIZED.

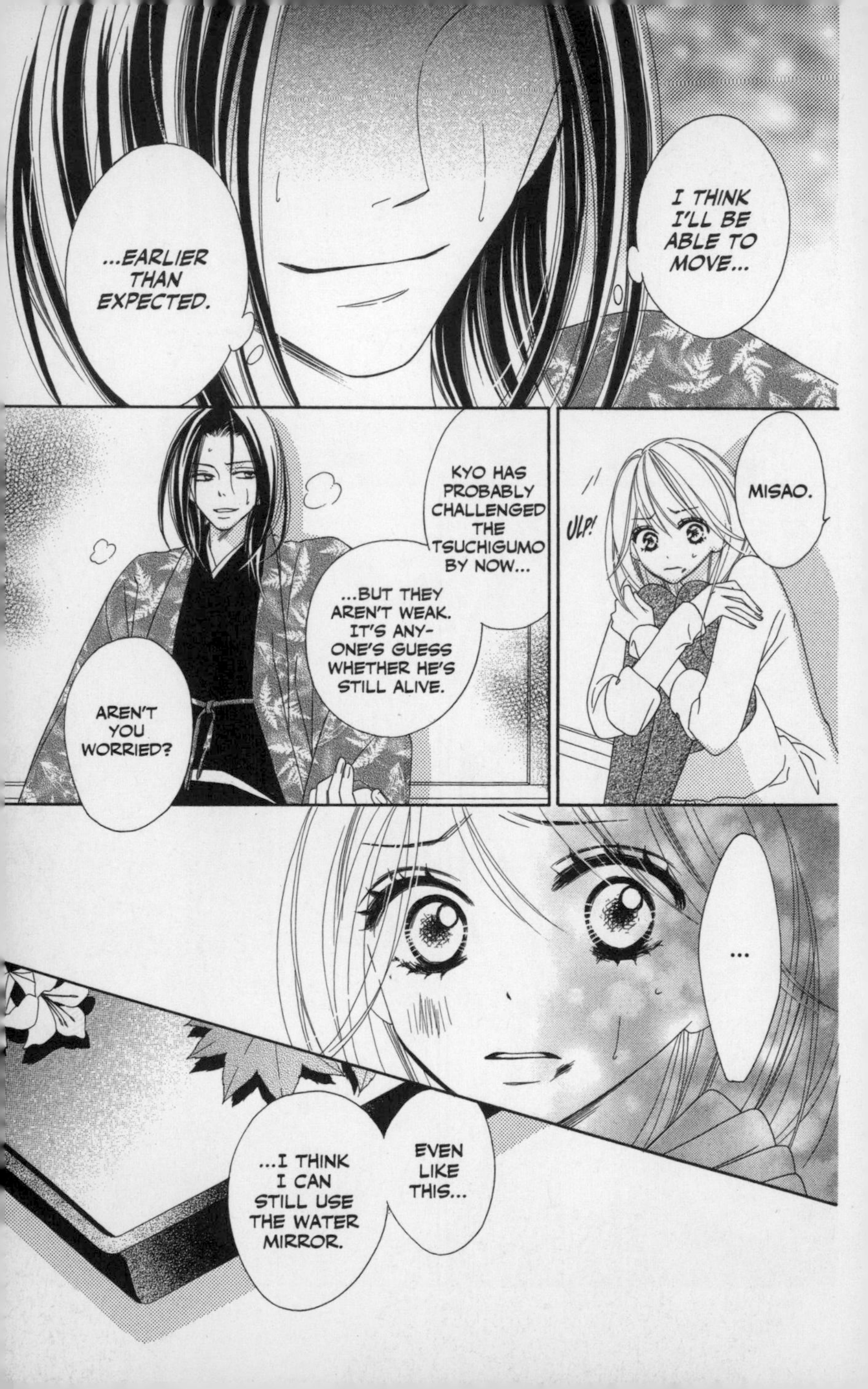
I THINK I'LL BE ABLE TO MOVE...
...EARLIER THAN EXPECTED.
MISAO.
ULP!
KYO HAS PROBABLY CHALLENGED THE TSUCHIGUMO BY NOW...
...BUT THEY AREN'T WEAK. IT'S ANY-ONE'S GUESS WHETHER HE'S STILL ALIVE.
AREN'T YOU WORRIED?
...
EVEN LIKE THIS...
...I THINK I CAN STILL USE THE WATER MIRROR.

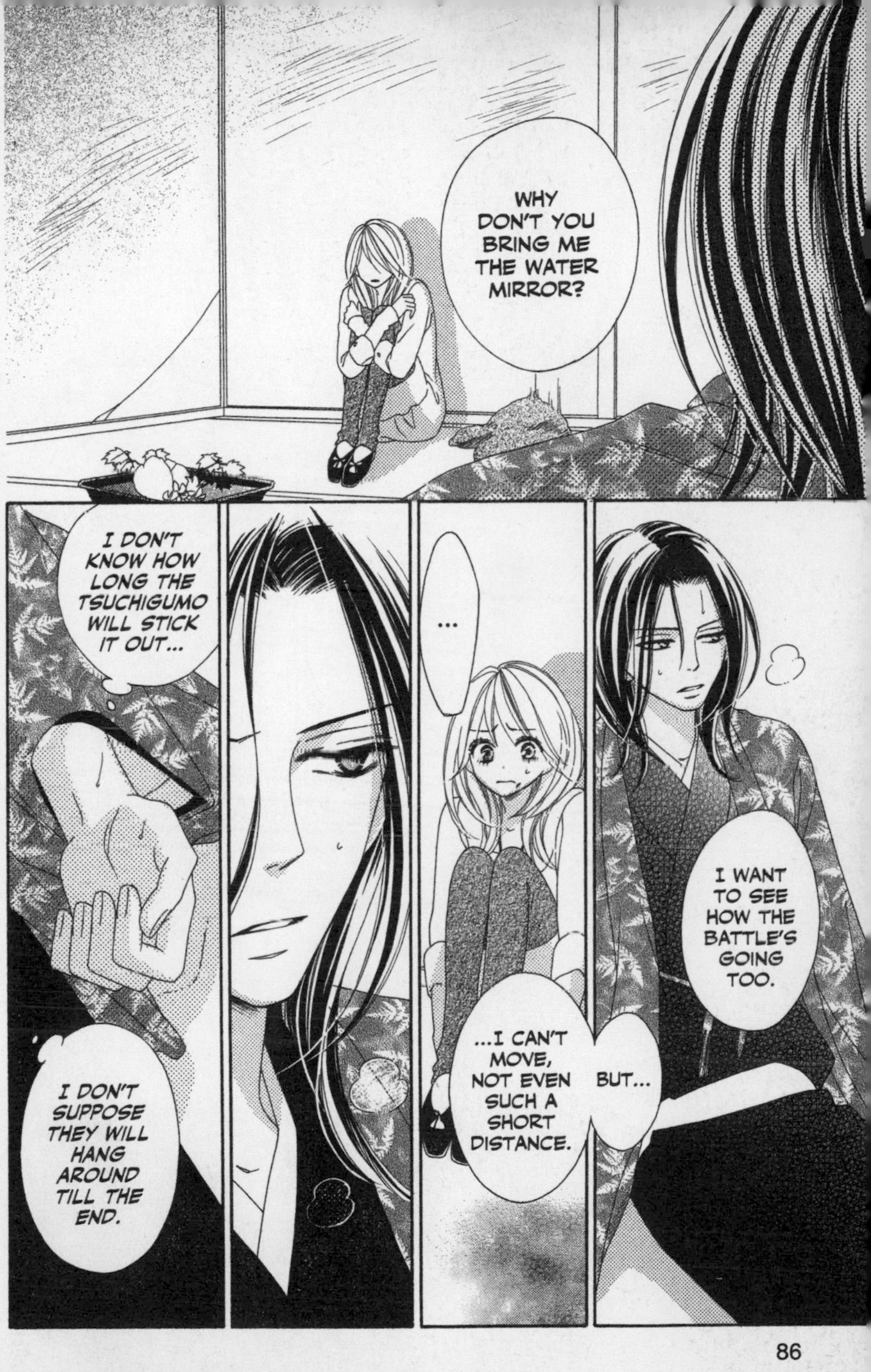
WHY DON'T YOU BRING ME THE WATER MIRROR?
I WANT TO SEE HOW THE BATTLE'S GOING TOO.
BUT...
...
...I CAN'T MOVE, NOT EVEN SUCH A SHORT DISTANCE.
I DON'T KNOW HOW LONG THE TSUCHIGUMO WILL STICK IT OUT...
I DON'T SUPPOSE THEY WILL HANG AROUND TILL THE END.

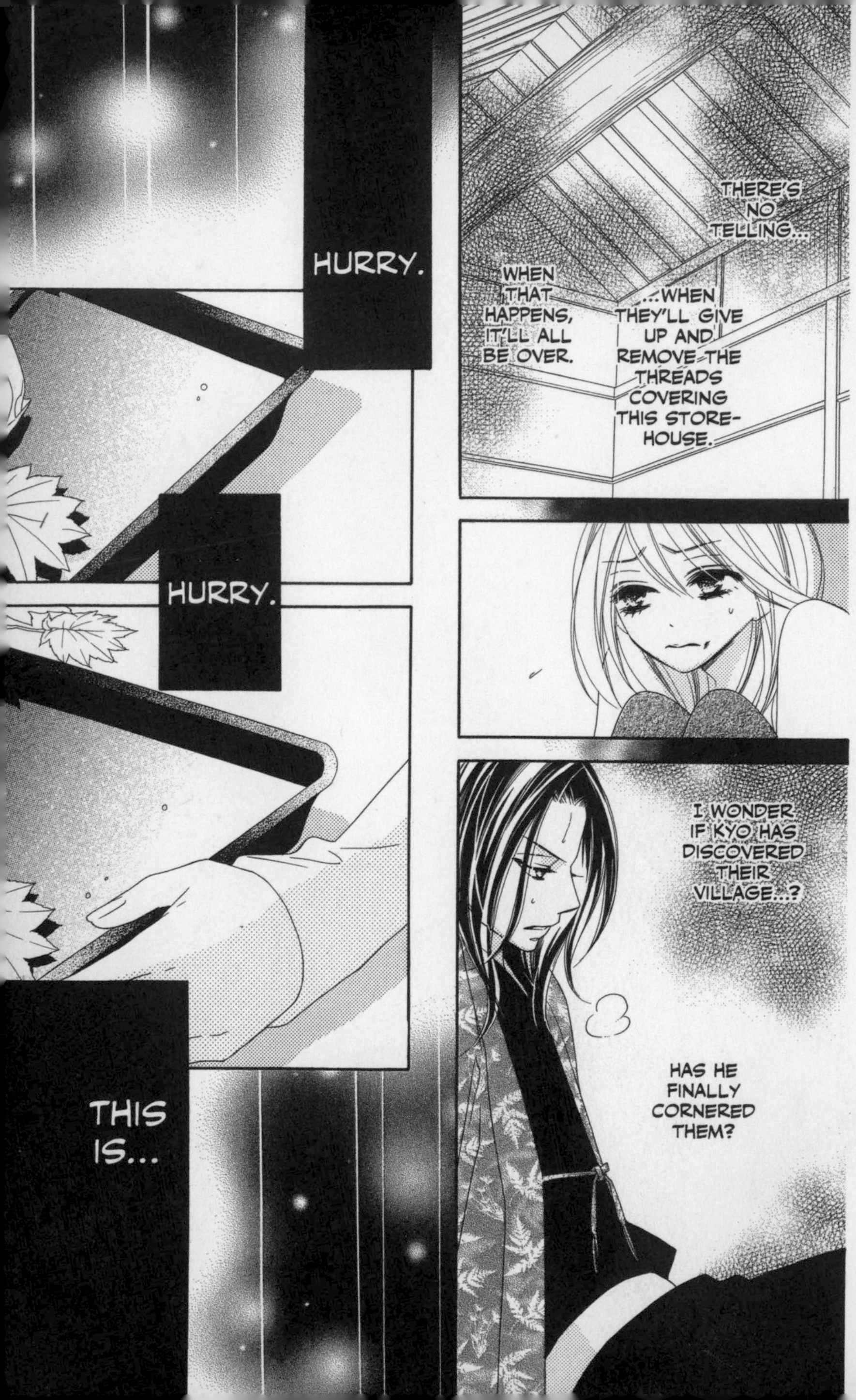
THERE'S NO TELLING...
...WHEN THEY'LL GIVE UP AND REMOVE THE THREADS COVERING THIS STORE-HOUSE.
WHEN THAT HAPPENS, IT'LL ALL BE OVER.
I WONDER IF KYO HAS DISCOVERED THEIR VILLAGE...?
HAS HE FINALLY CORNERED THEM?
HURRY.
HURRY.
THIS IS...

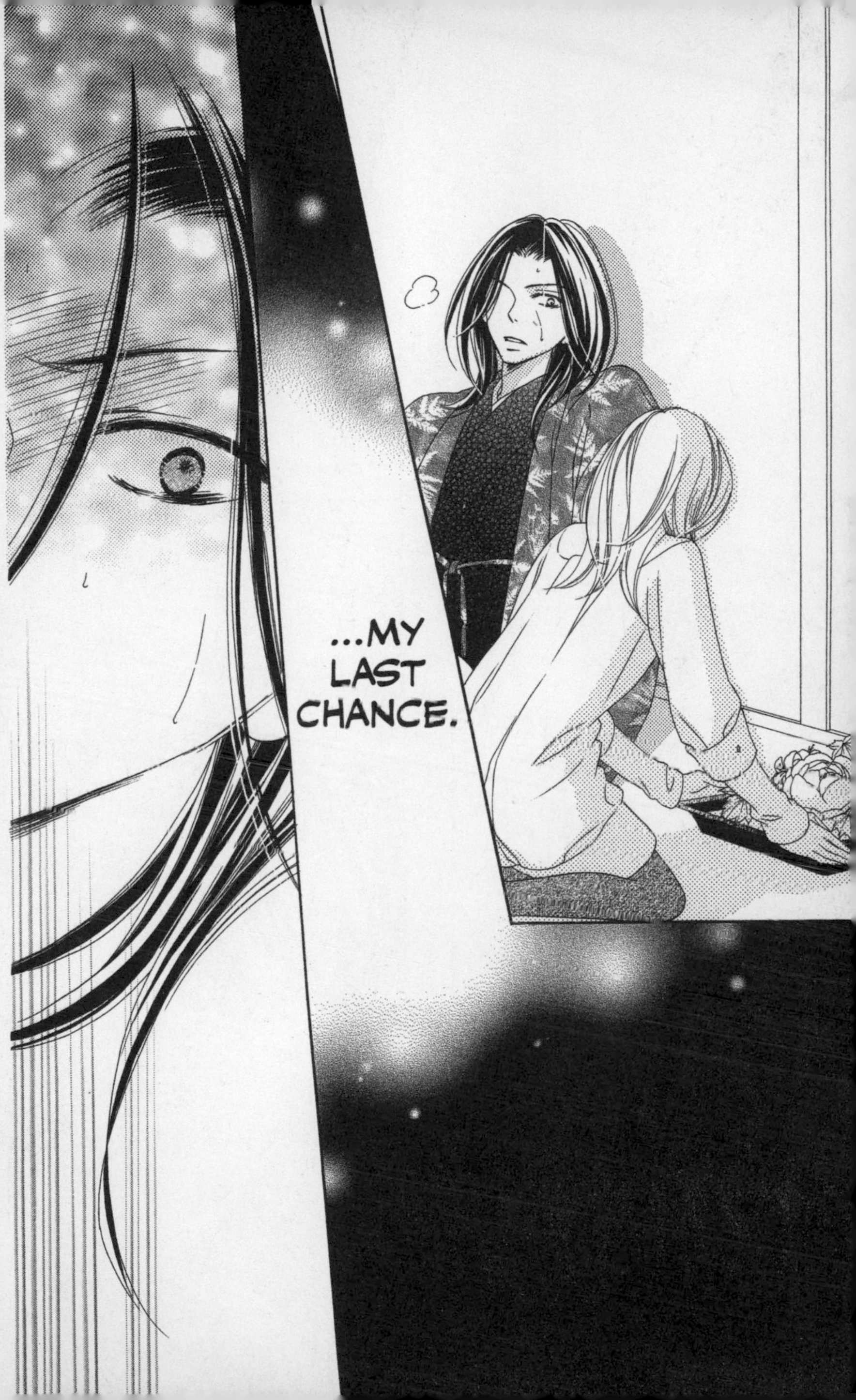
...MY LAST CHANCE.

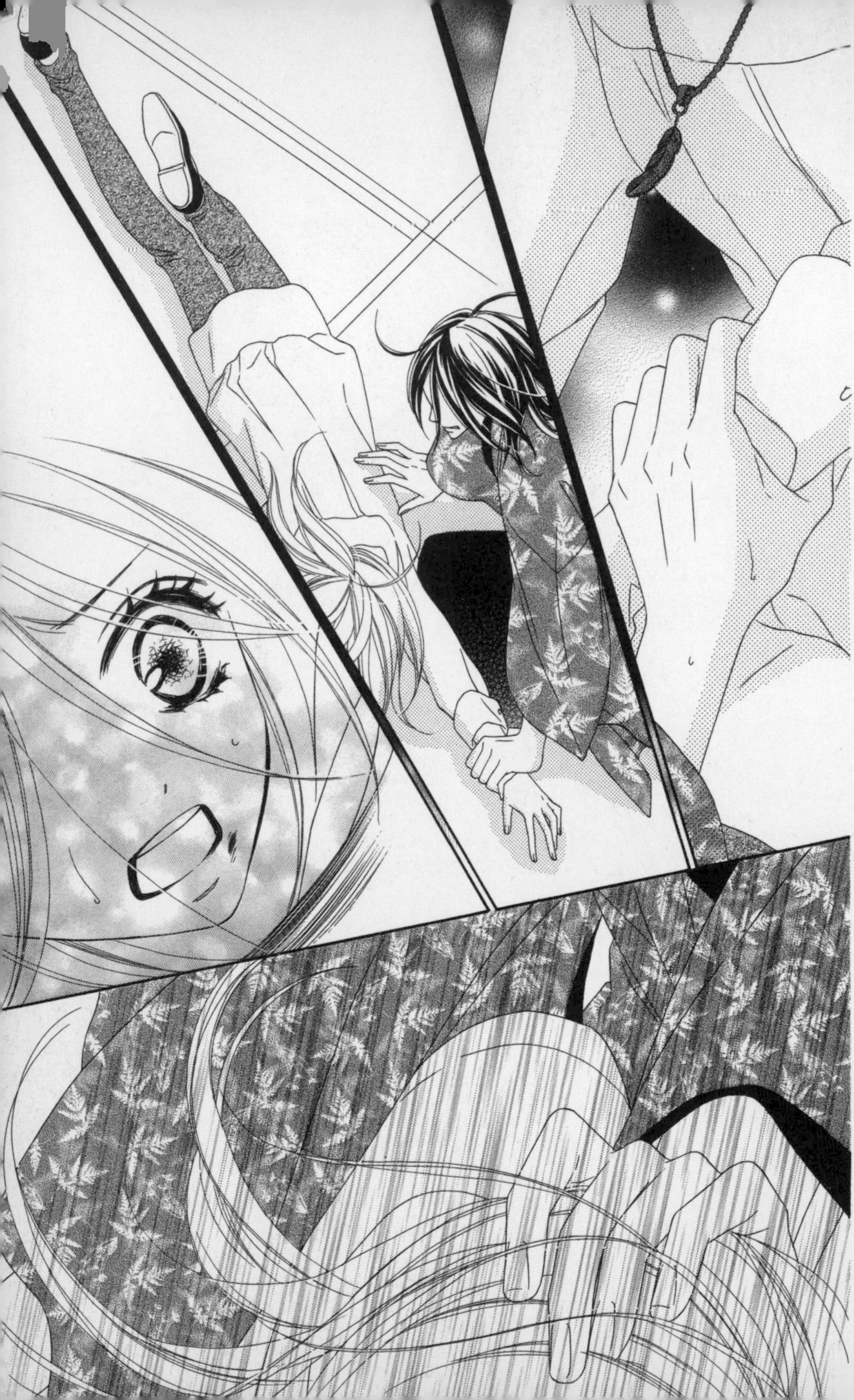

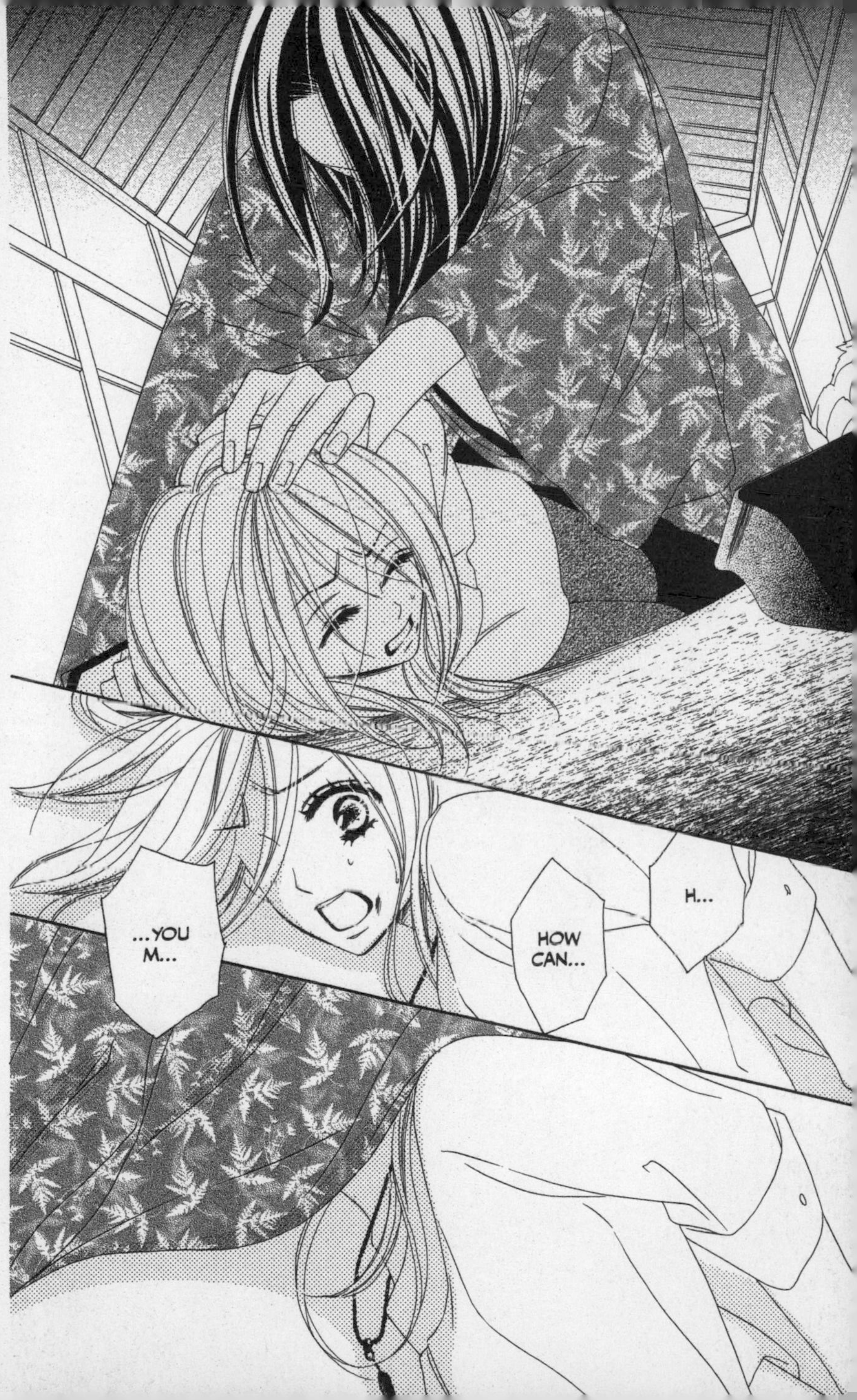
H...
HOW CAN...
...YOU M...

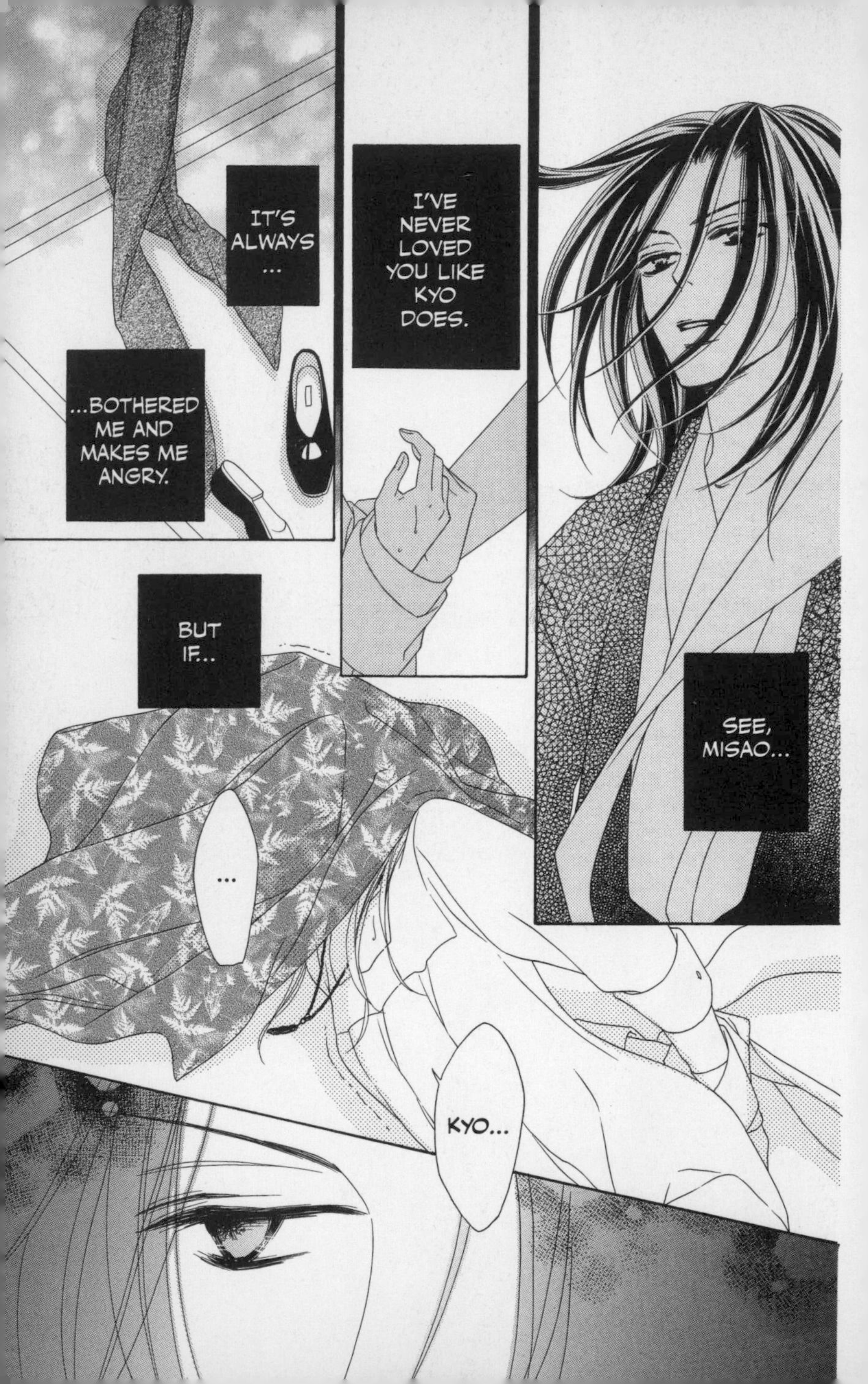
SEE, MISAO...
I'VE NEVER LOVED YOU LIKE KYO DOES.
IT'S ALWAYS...
...BOTHERED ME AND MAKES ME ANGRY.
BUT IF...
...
KYO...

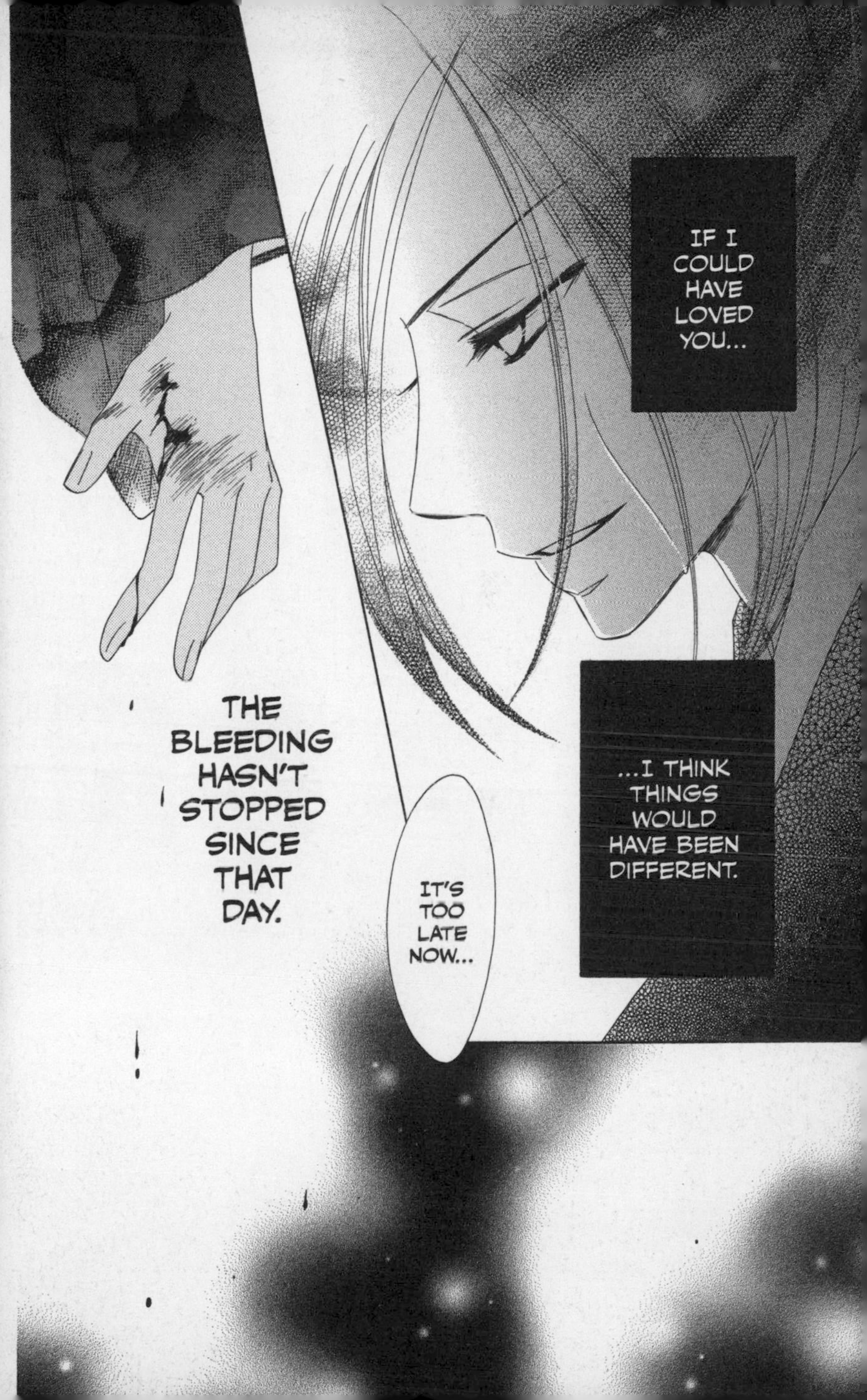
IF I COULD HAVE LOVED YOU...
...I THINK THINGS WOULD HAVE BEEN DIFFERENT.
IT'S TOO LATE NOW...
THE BLEEDING HASN'T STOPPED SINCE THAT DAY.

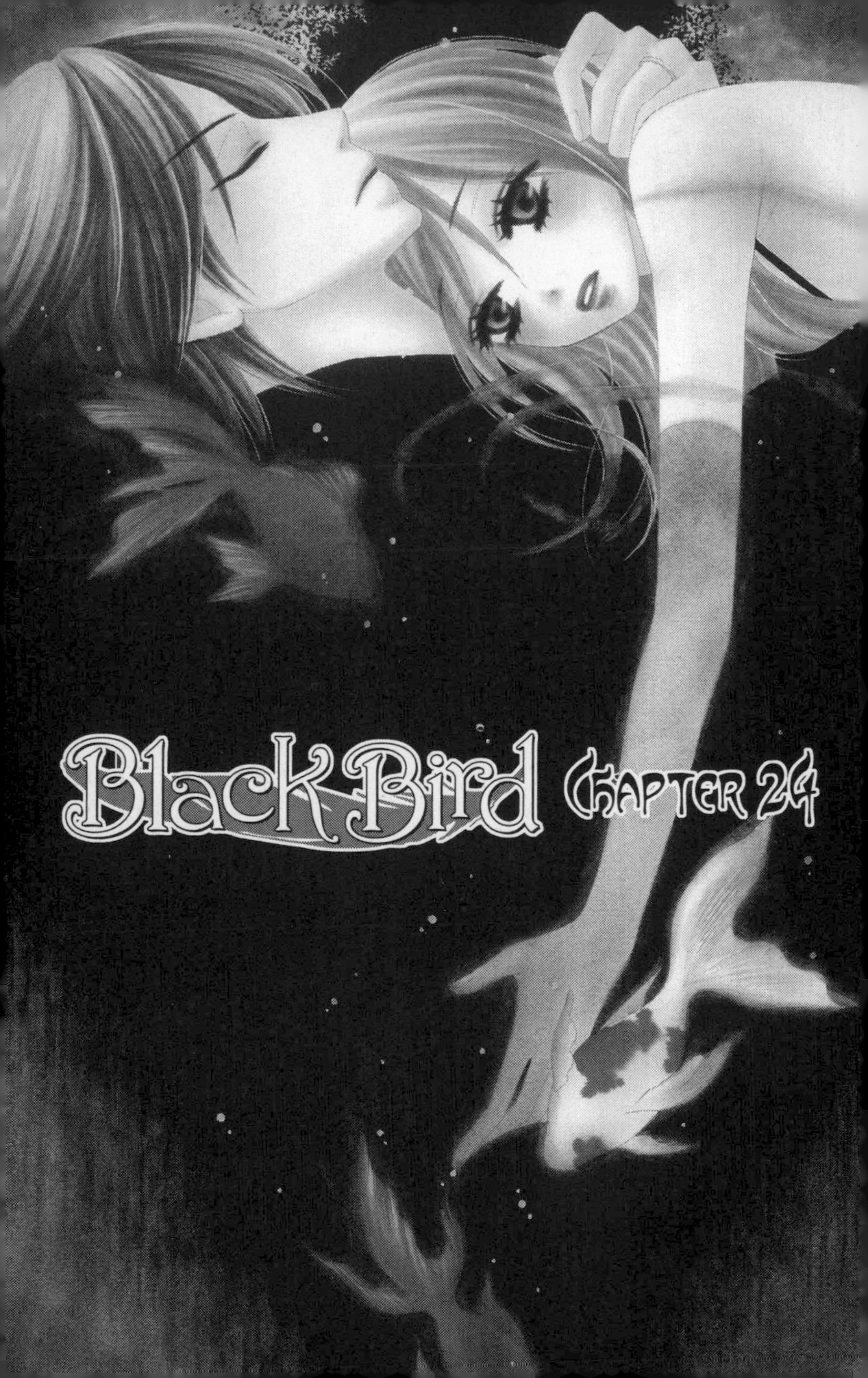
Black Bird
Chapter 24

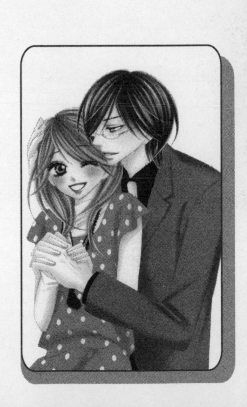

I WASN'T LYING...
...WHEN I TOLD KYO I WOULD BECOME HIS PARTNER...
...BUT I WONDER HOW FAR I CAN GO.

At the end of this volume I have included some "A Little Extra" manga essays I've been drawing for *Deluxe Betsucomi*. I hope this gives you a hint of the passion I put into filling these empty spaces.

Ahh...
Anything more than this I save for my wife...
Come on, give them a little more.

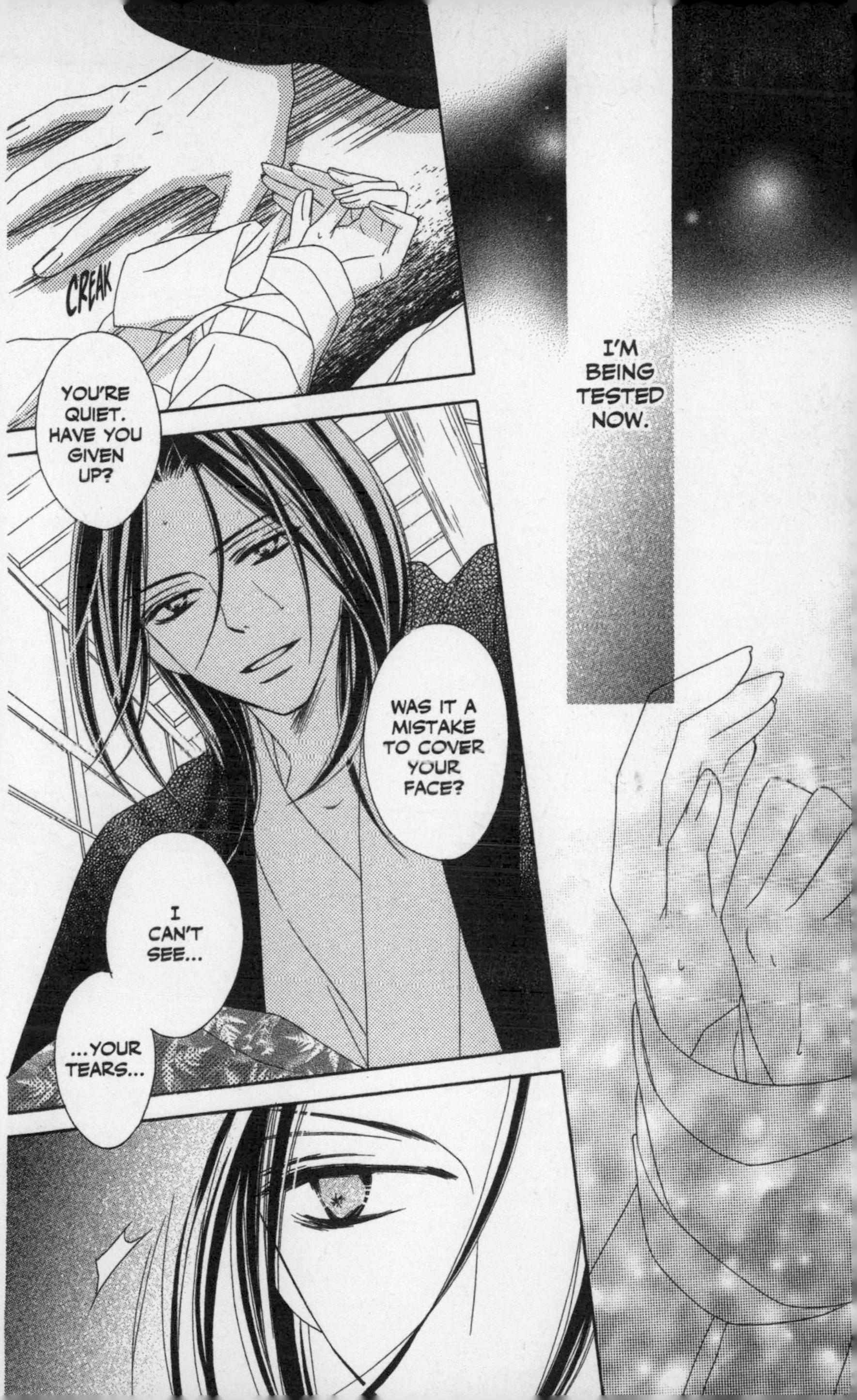
I'M BEING TESTED NOW.
CREAK
YOU'RE QUIET. HAVE YOU GIVEN UP?
WAS IT A MISTAKE TO COVER YOUR FACE?
I CAN'T SEE...
...YOUR TEARS...

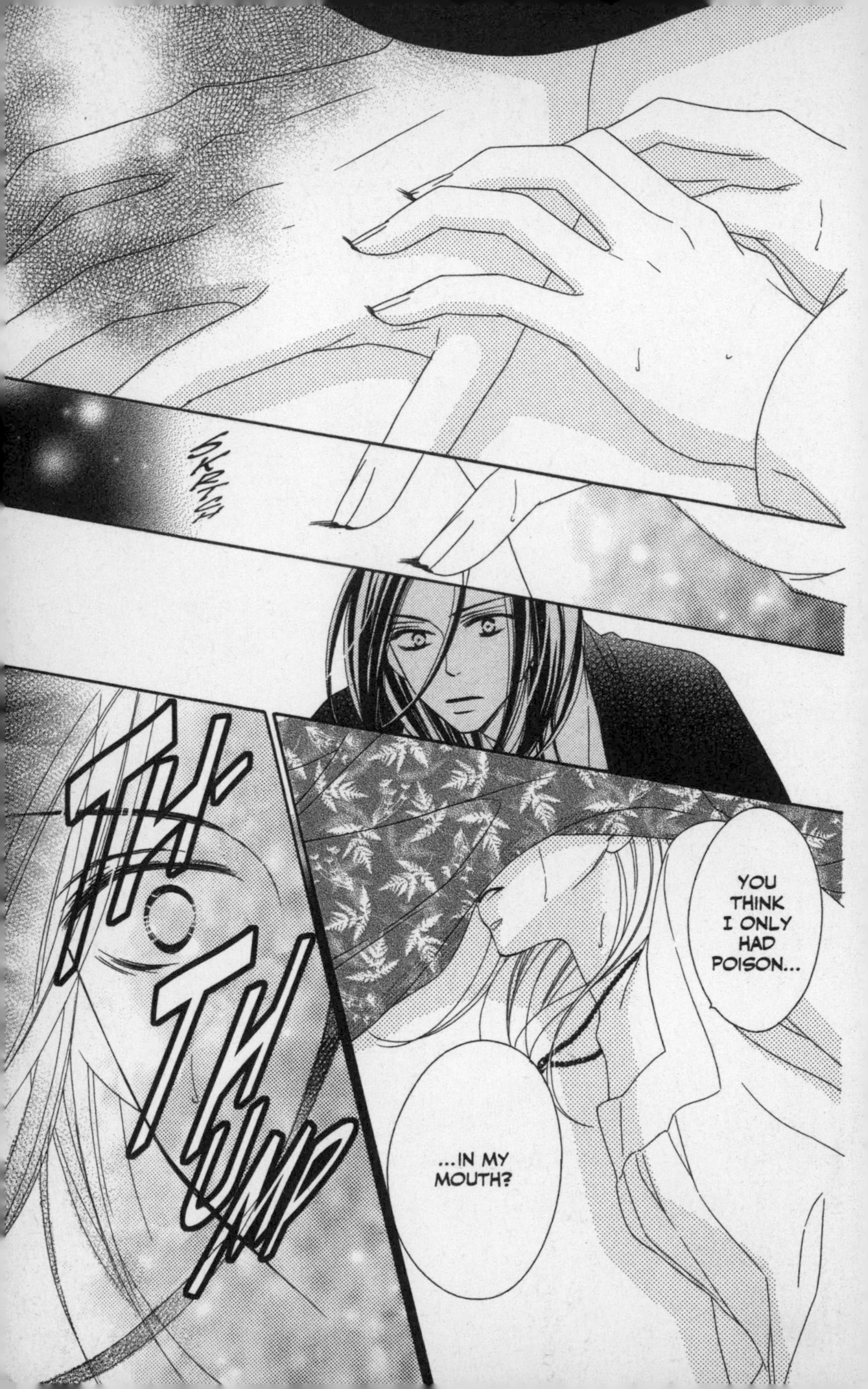
YOU THINK I ONLY HAD POISON...
...IN MY MOUTH?

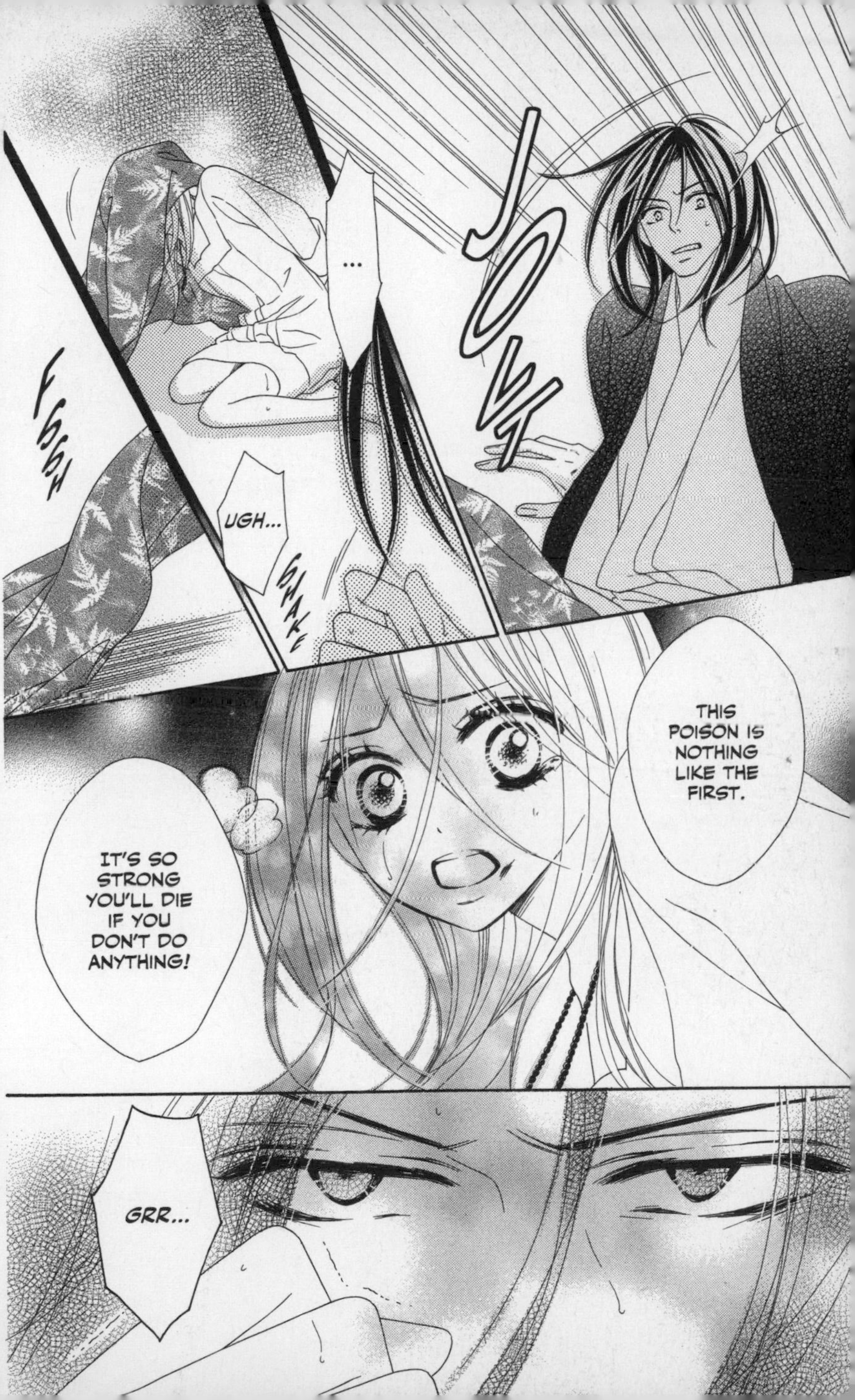
JOLT
...
UGH...
SHAKE
FSSH
THIS POISON IS NOTHING LIKE THE FIRST.
IT'S SO STRONG YOU'LL DIE IF YOU DON'T DO ANYTHING!
GRR...

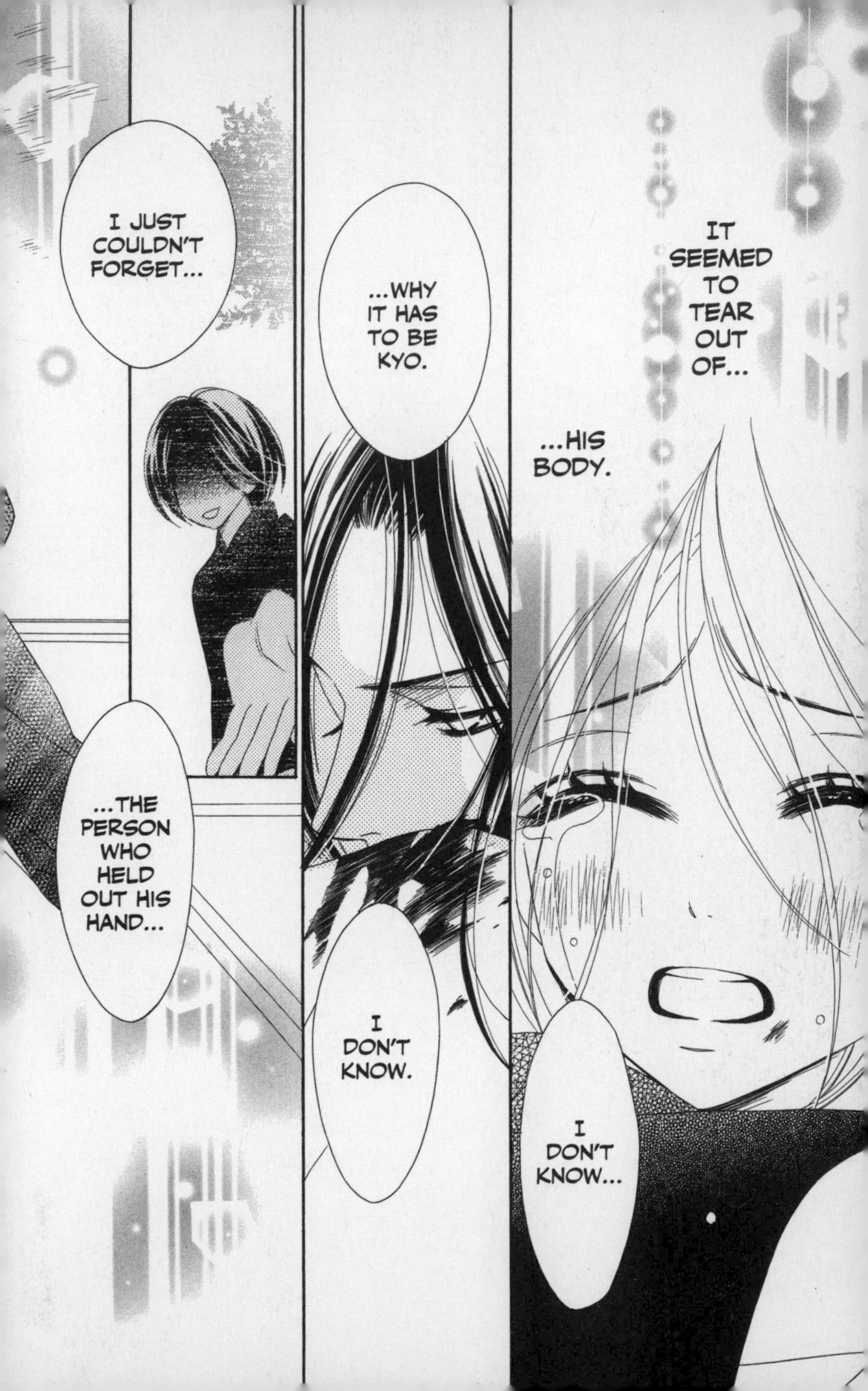
IT SEEMED TO TEAR OUT OF...
...HIS BODY.
I DON'T KNOW...
...WHY IT HAS TO BE KYO.
I DON'T KNOW.
I JUST COULDN'T FORGET...
...THE PERSON WHO HELD OUT HIS HAND...

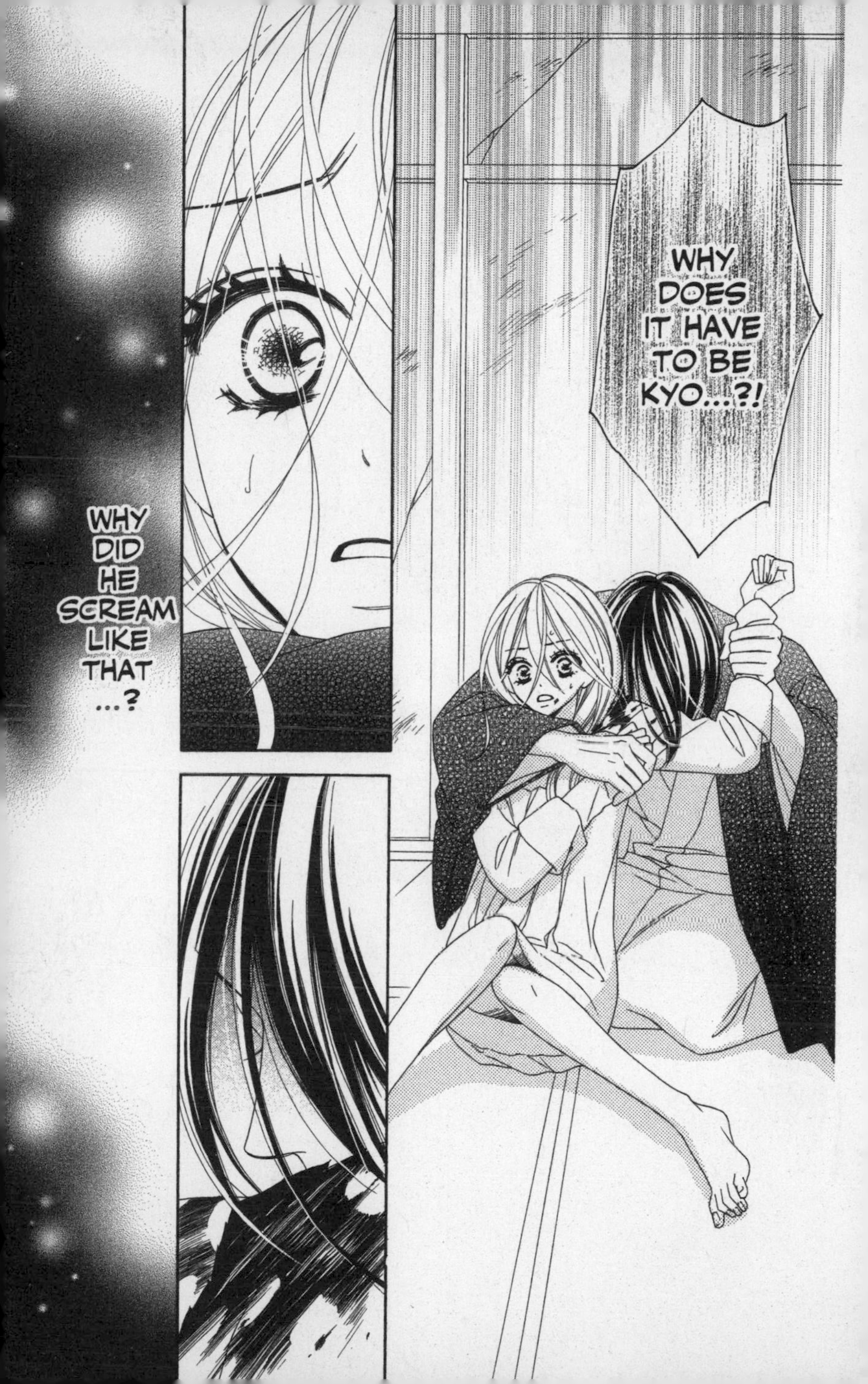
WHY DOES IT HAVE TO BE KYO...?!
WHY DID HE SCREAM LIKE THAT ...?

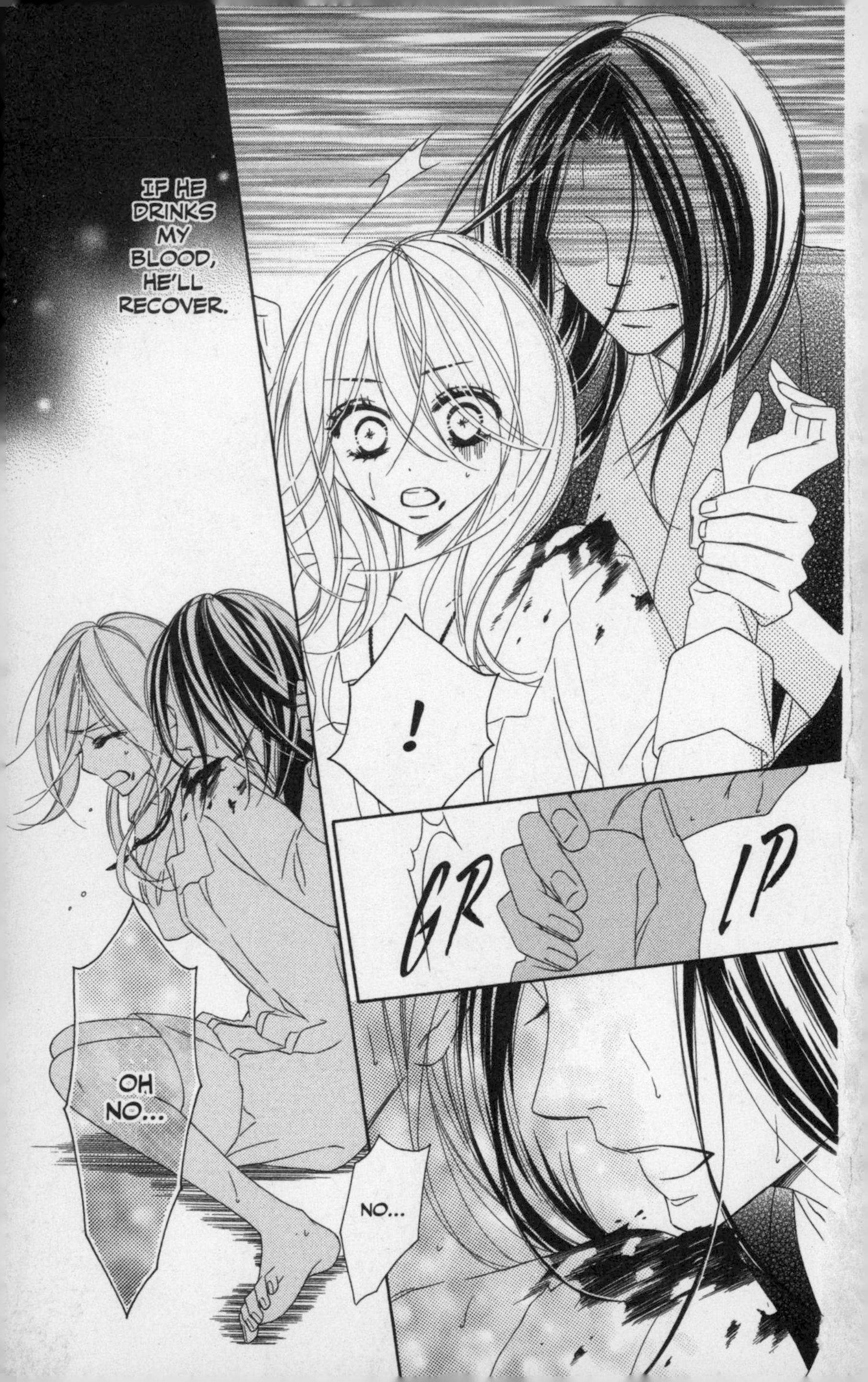
!
GRIP
NO...
IF HE DRINKS MY BLOOD, HE'LL RECOVER.
OH NO...

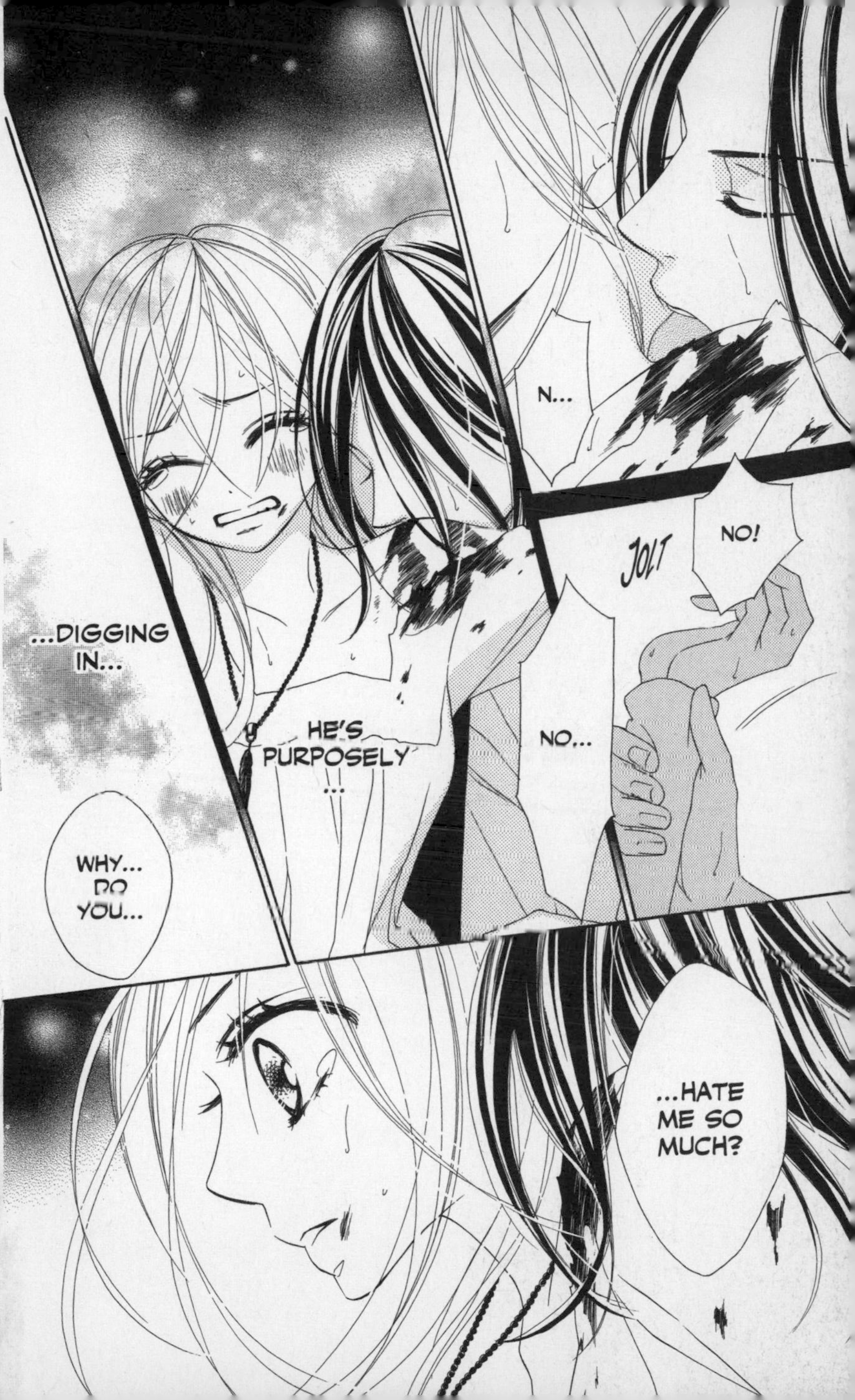
N...
NO!
JOLT
NO...
HE'S PURPOSELY ...
...DIGGING IN...
WHY... DO YOU...
...HATE ME SO MUCH?

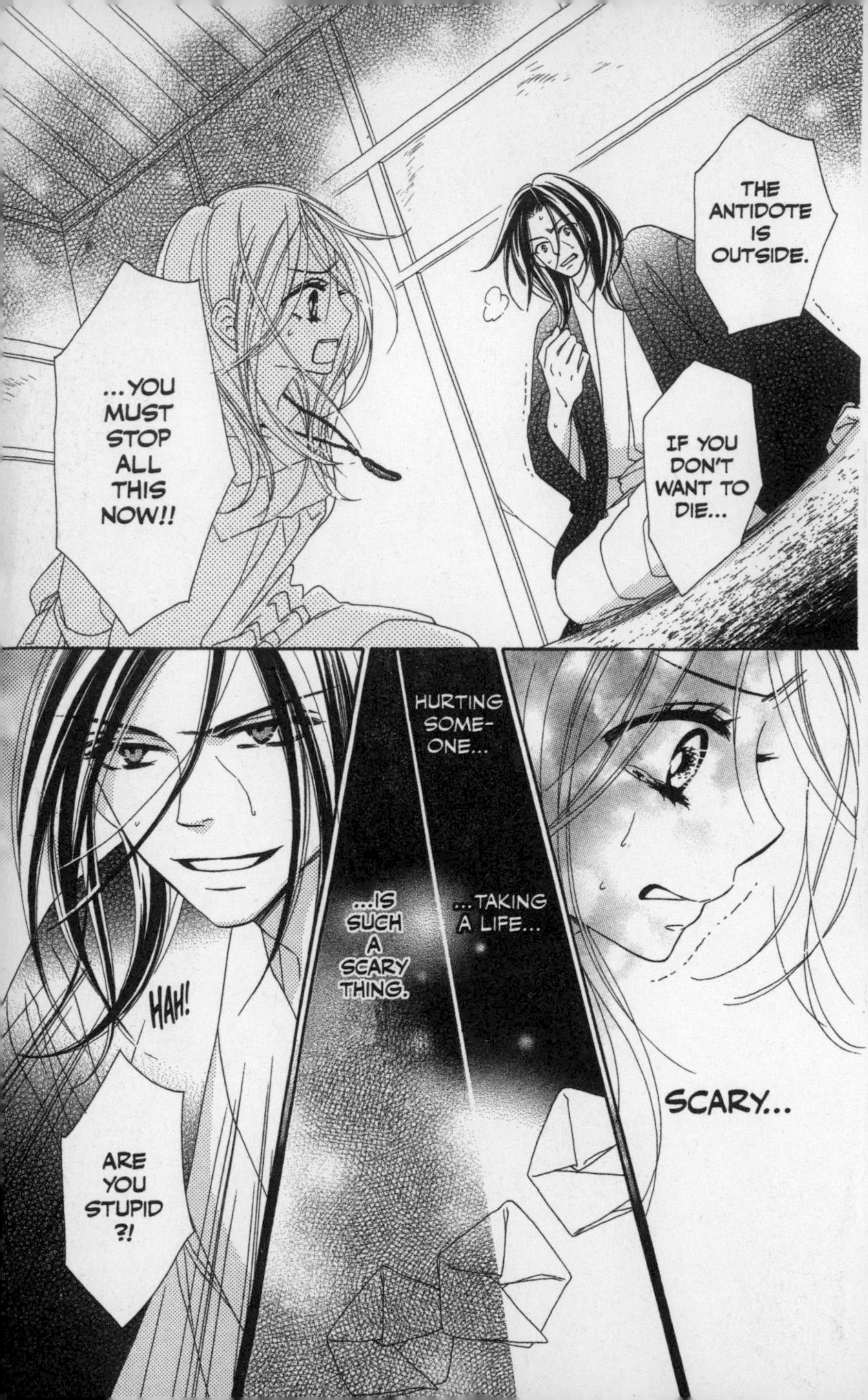
THE ANTIDOTE IS OUTSIDE.
IF YOU DON'T WANT TO DIE...
...YOU MUST STOP ALL THIS NOW!!
SCARY...
HURTING SOME-ONE...
...TAKING A LIFE...
...IS SUCH A SCARY THING.
HAH!
ARE YOU STUPID ?!

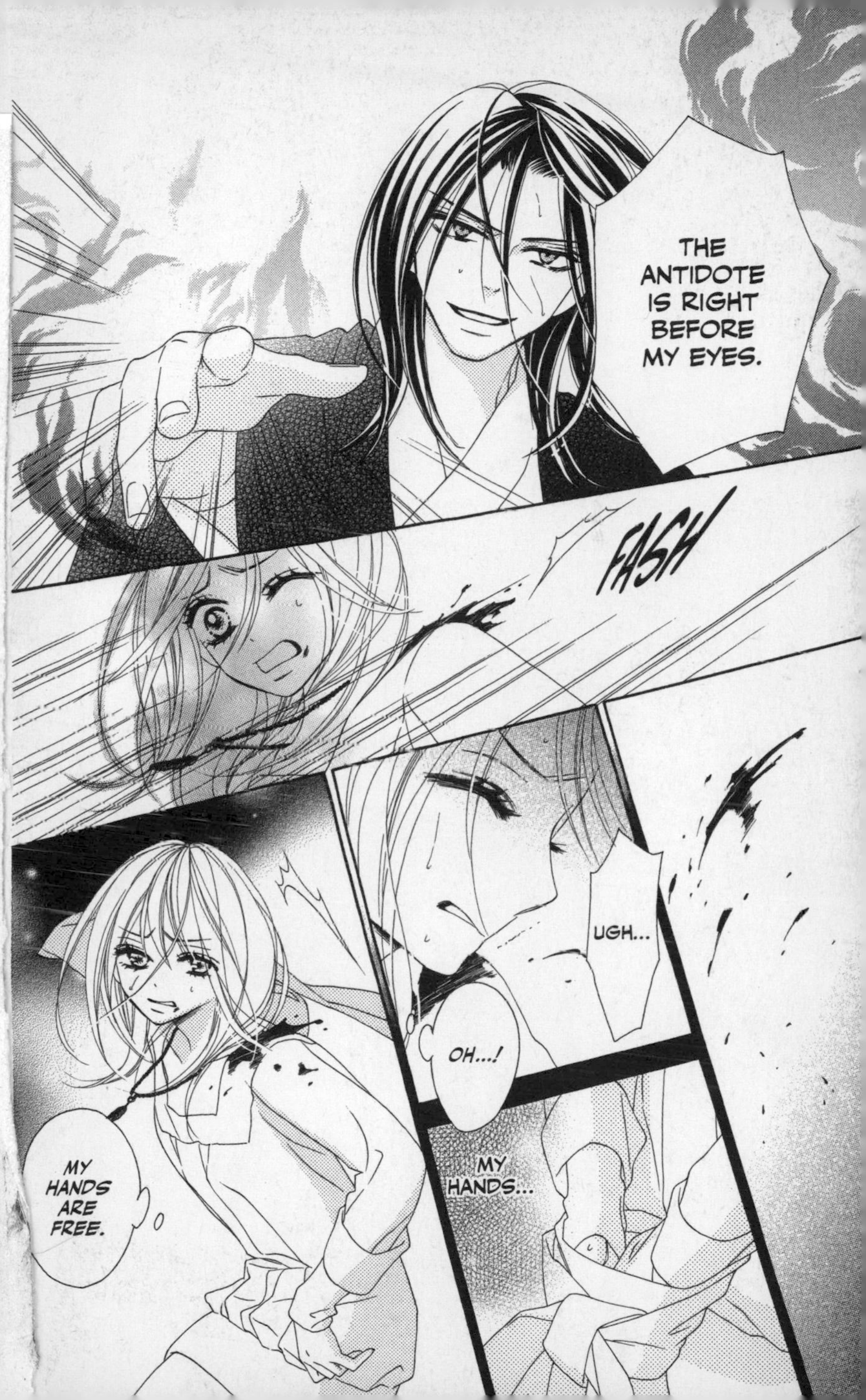
THE ANTIDOTE IS RIGHT BEFORE MY EYES.
FASH
UGH...
OH...!
MY HANDS...
MY HANDS ARE FREE.

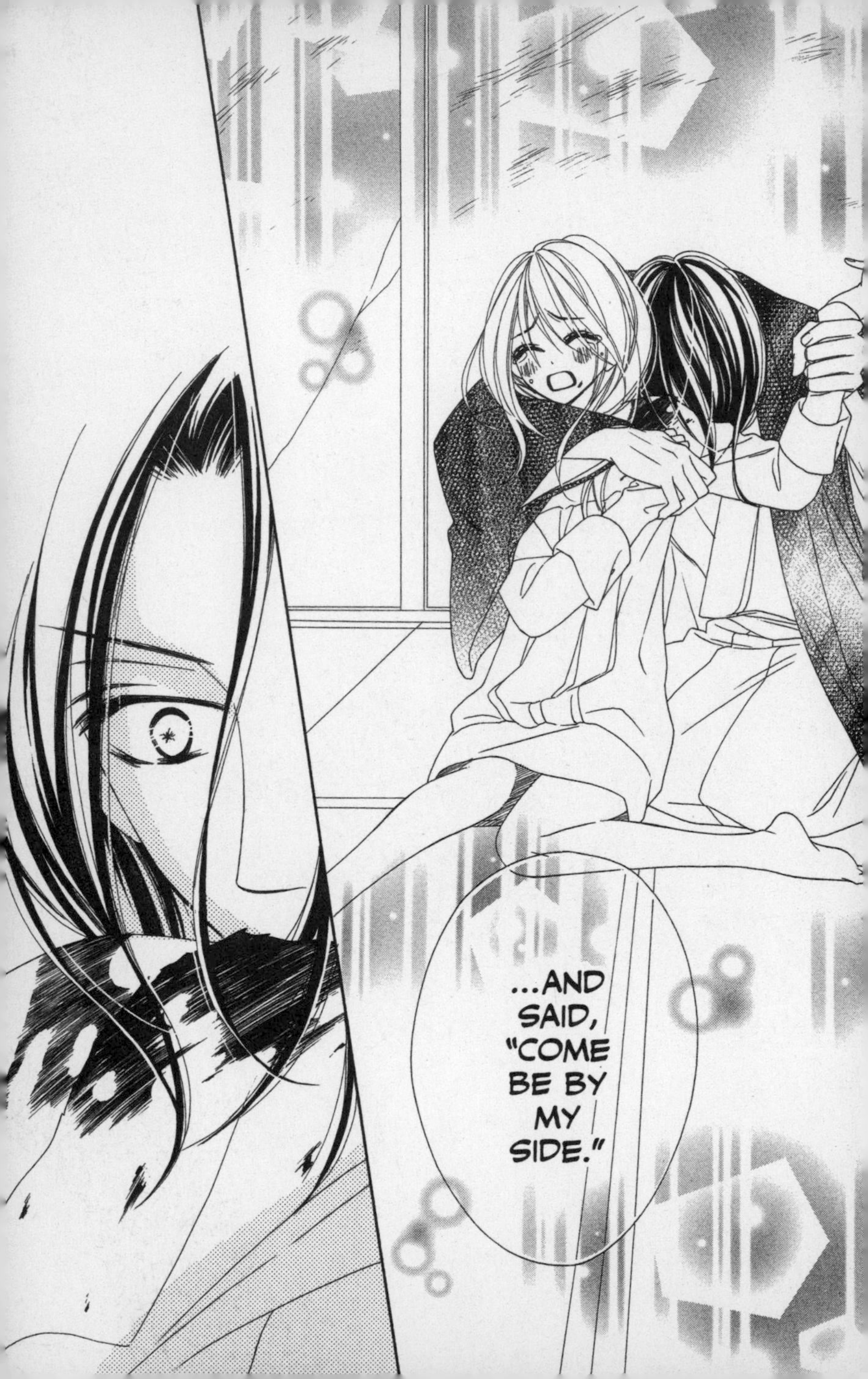
...AND SAID, "COME BE BY MY SIDE."

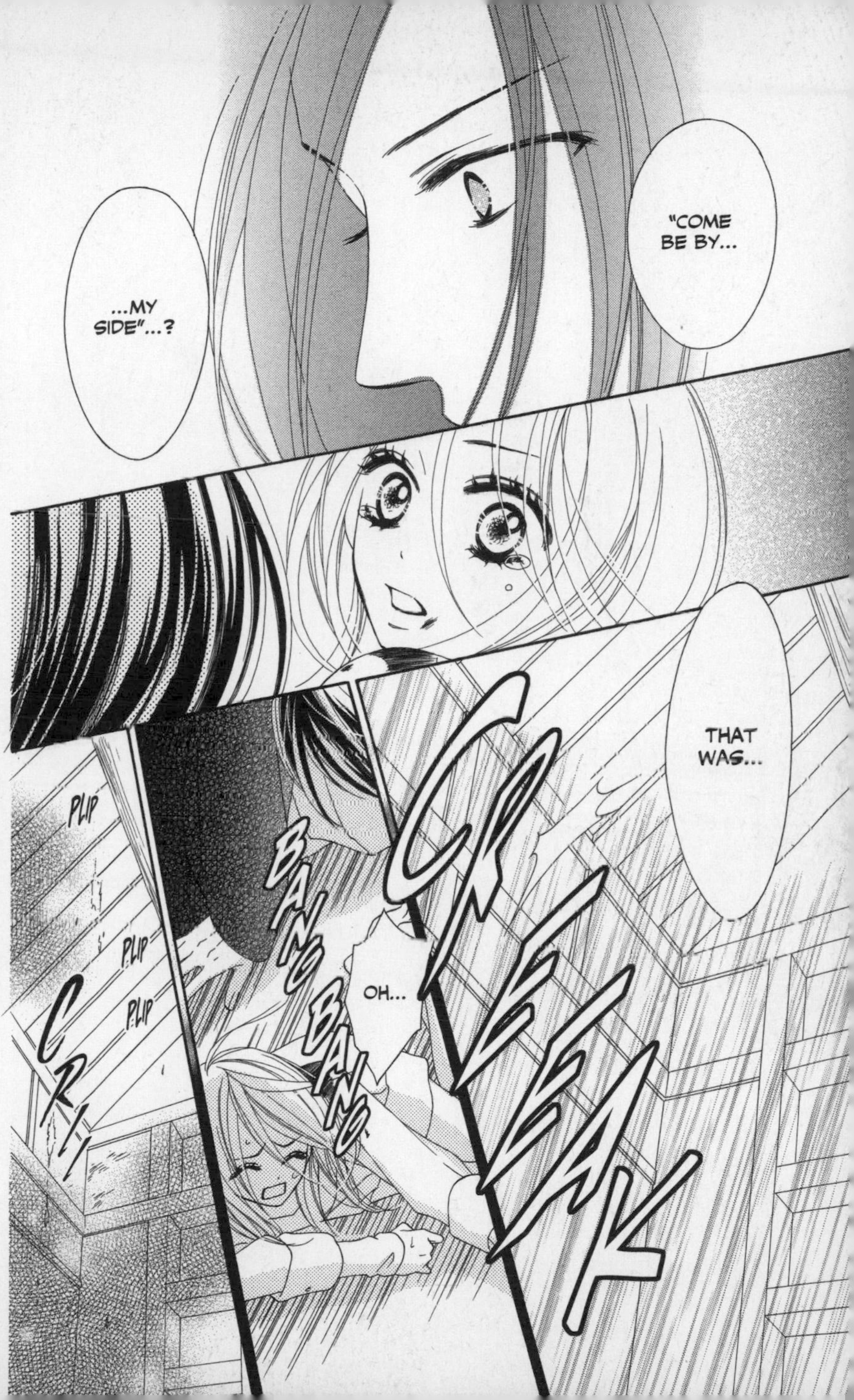
"COME BE BY...
...MY SIDE"...?
THAT WAS...
CREEEAK
BANG BANG
OH...
PLIP
PLIP
PLIP
CRI

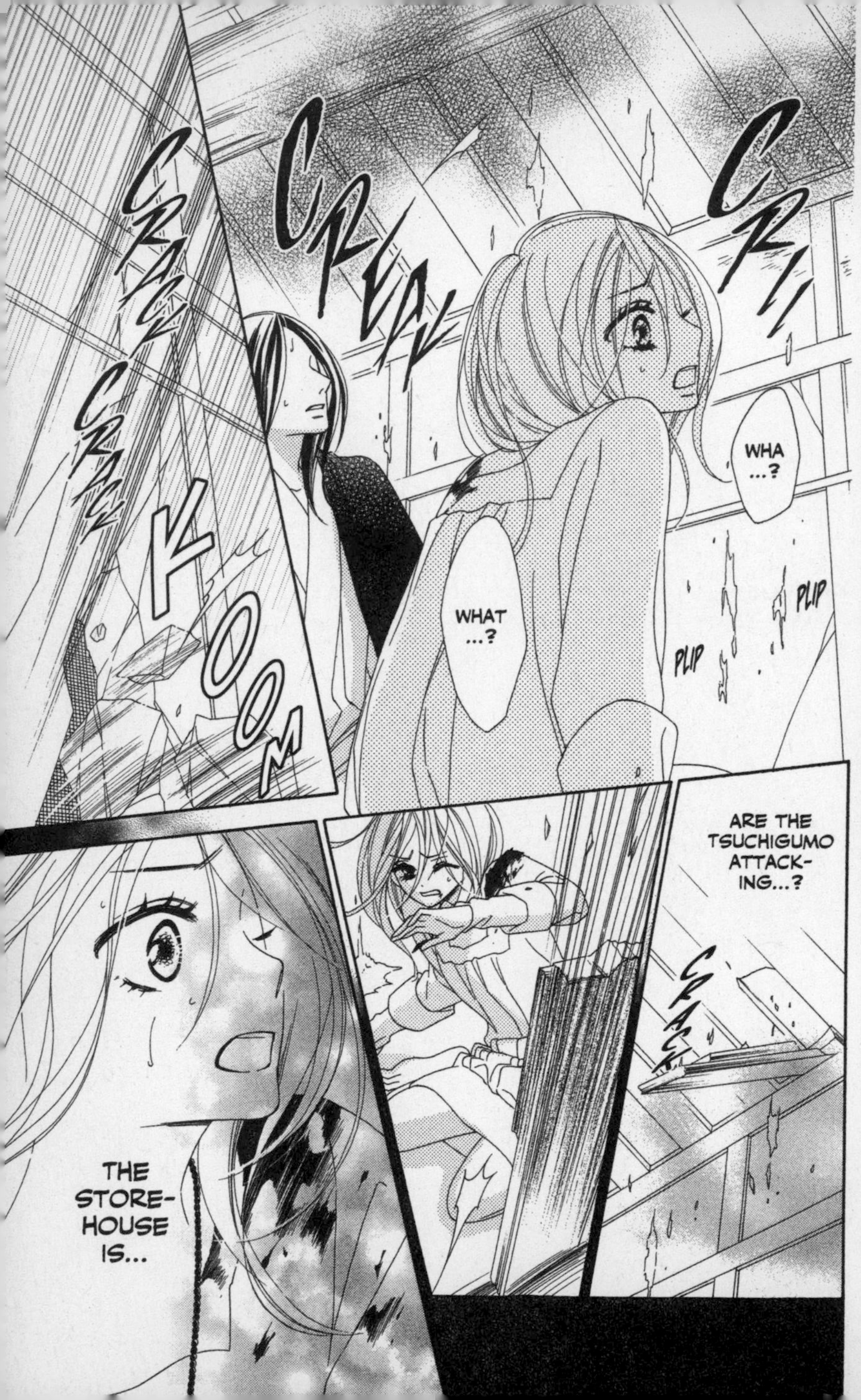
CRII
CREAK
WHA ...?
PLIP
PLIP
WHAT ...?
CRACK CRACK
KOOM
ARE THE TSUCHIGUMO ATTACKING...?
CRACK
THE STOREHOUSE IS...

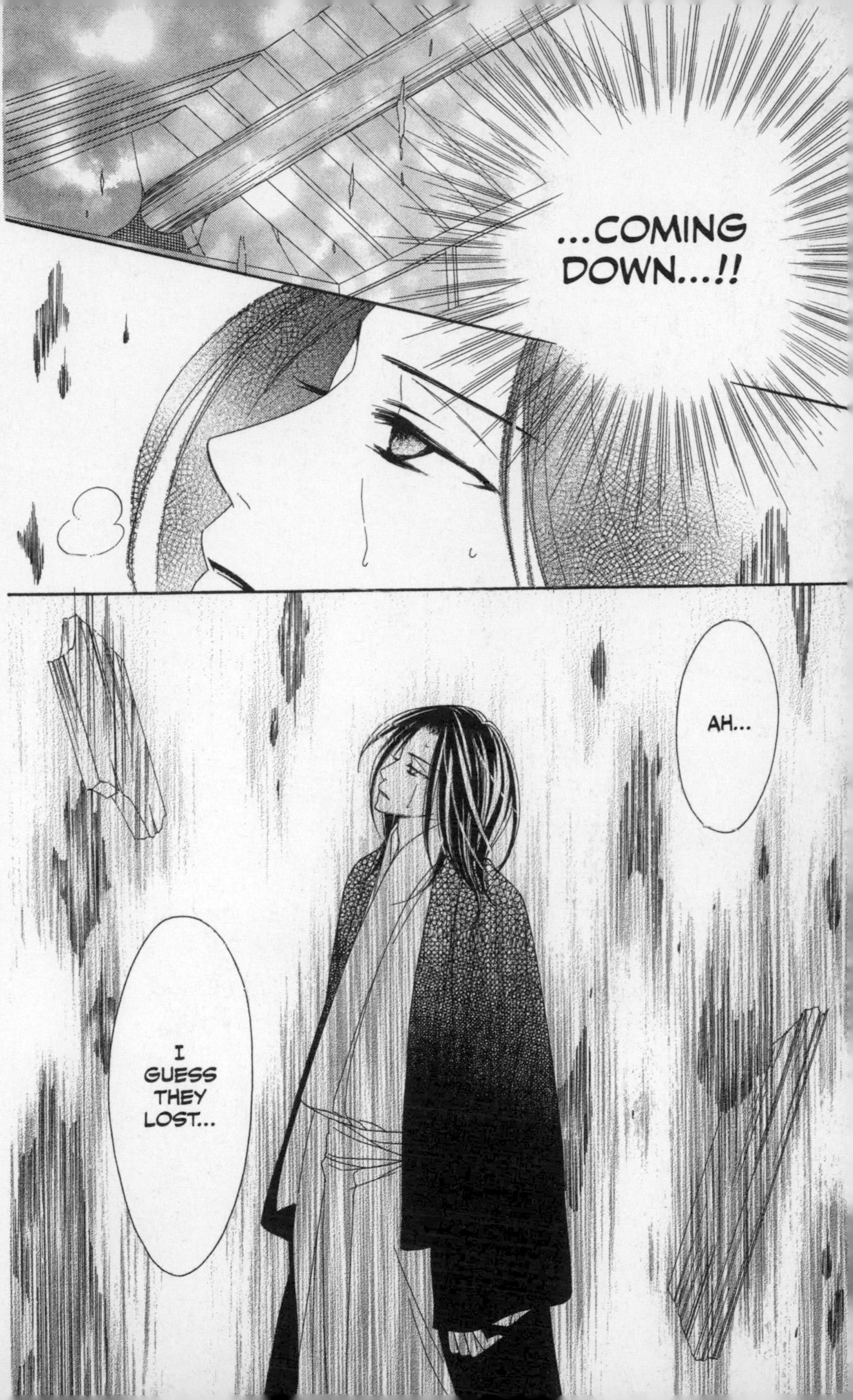
...COMING DOWN...!!
AH...
I GUESS THEY LOST...

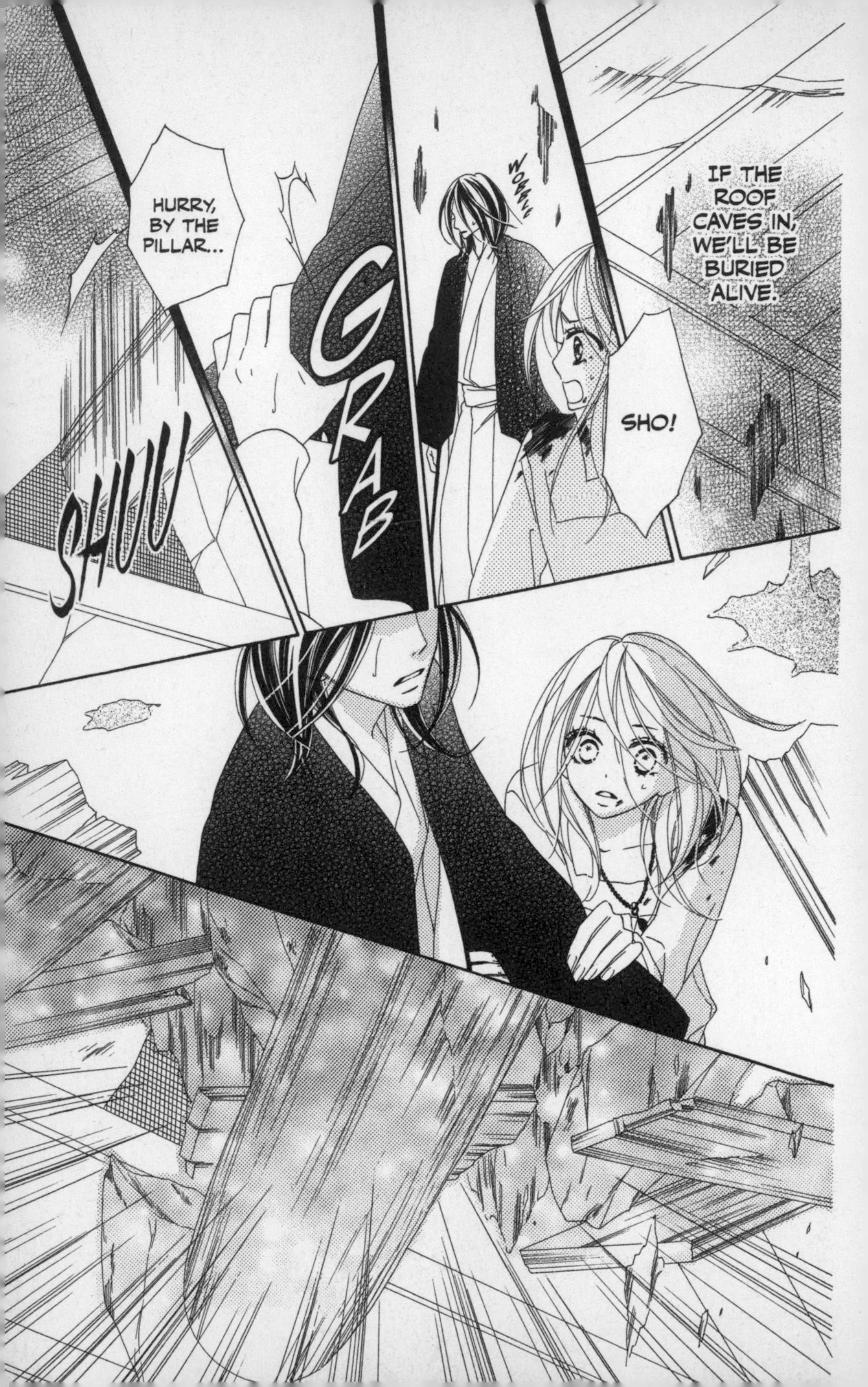
IF THE ROOF CAVES IN, WE'LL BE BURIED ALIVE.
SHO!
GRAB
HURRY, BY THE PILLAR...
SHUU

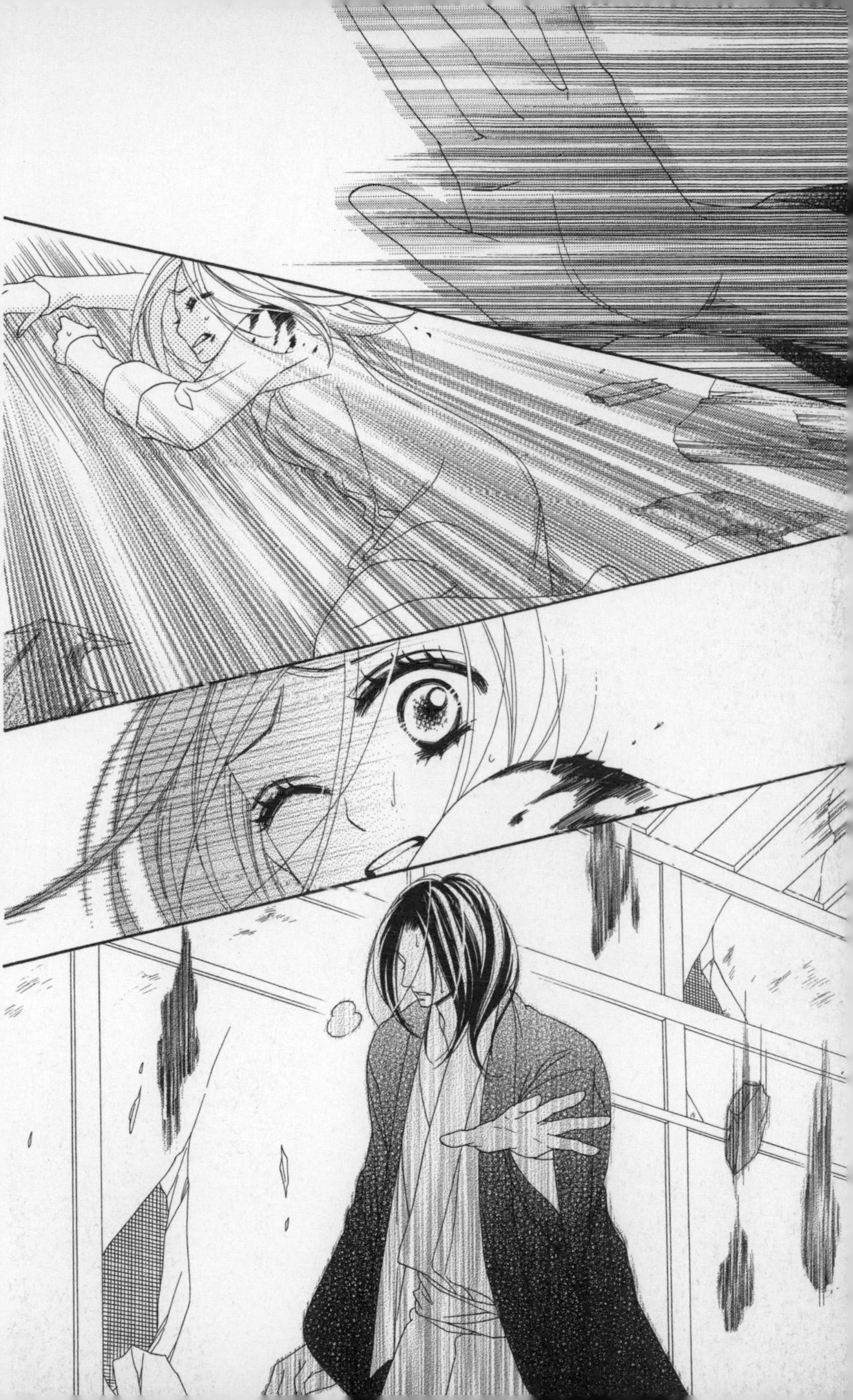

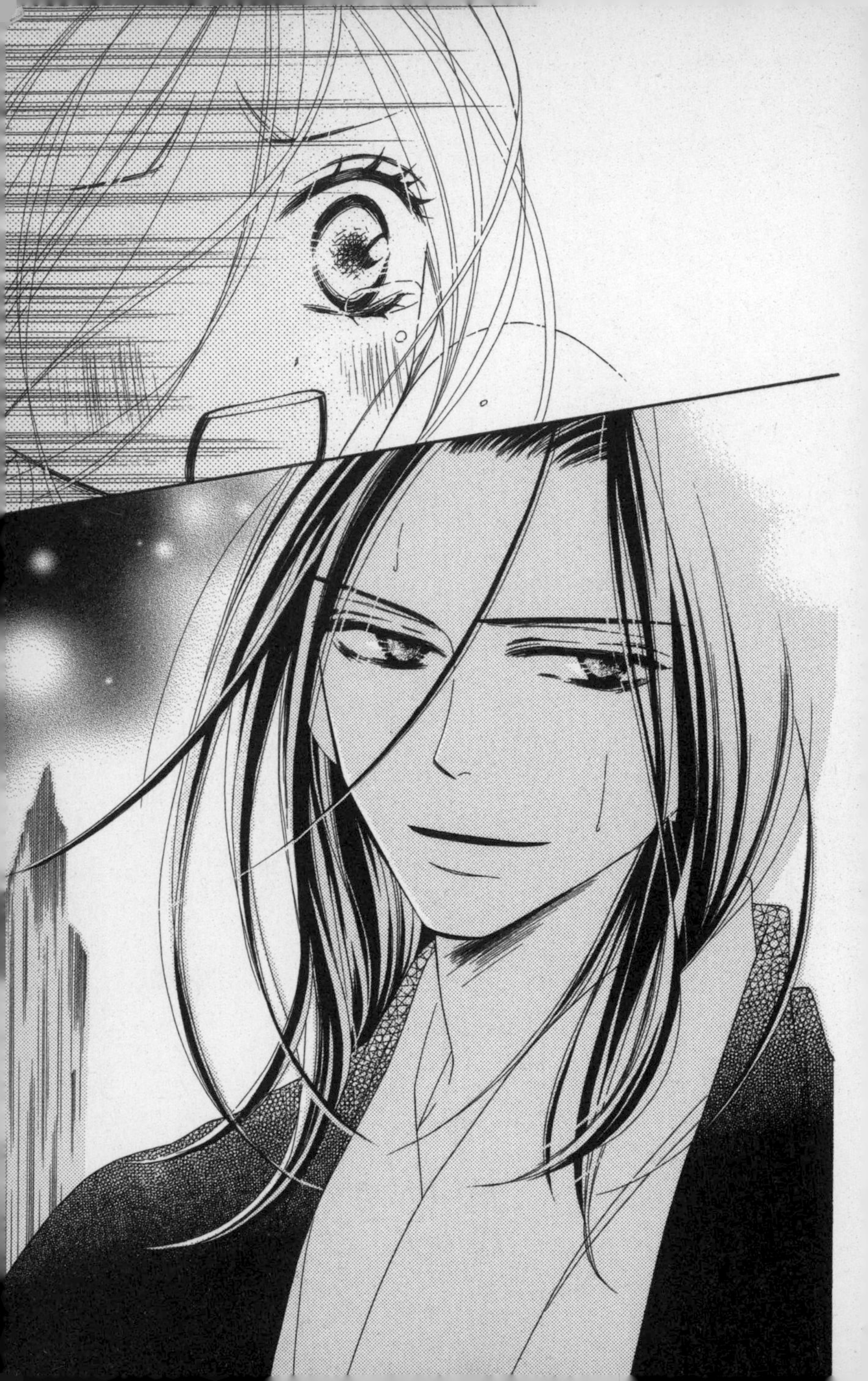

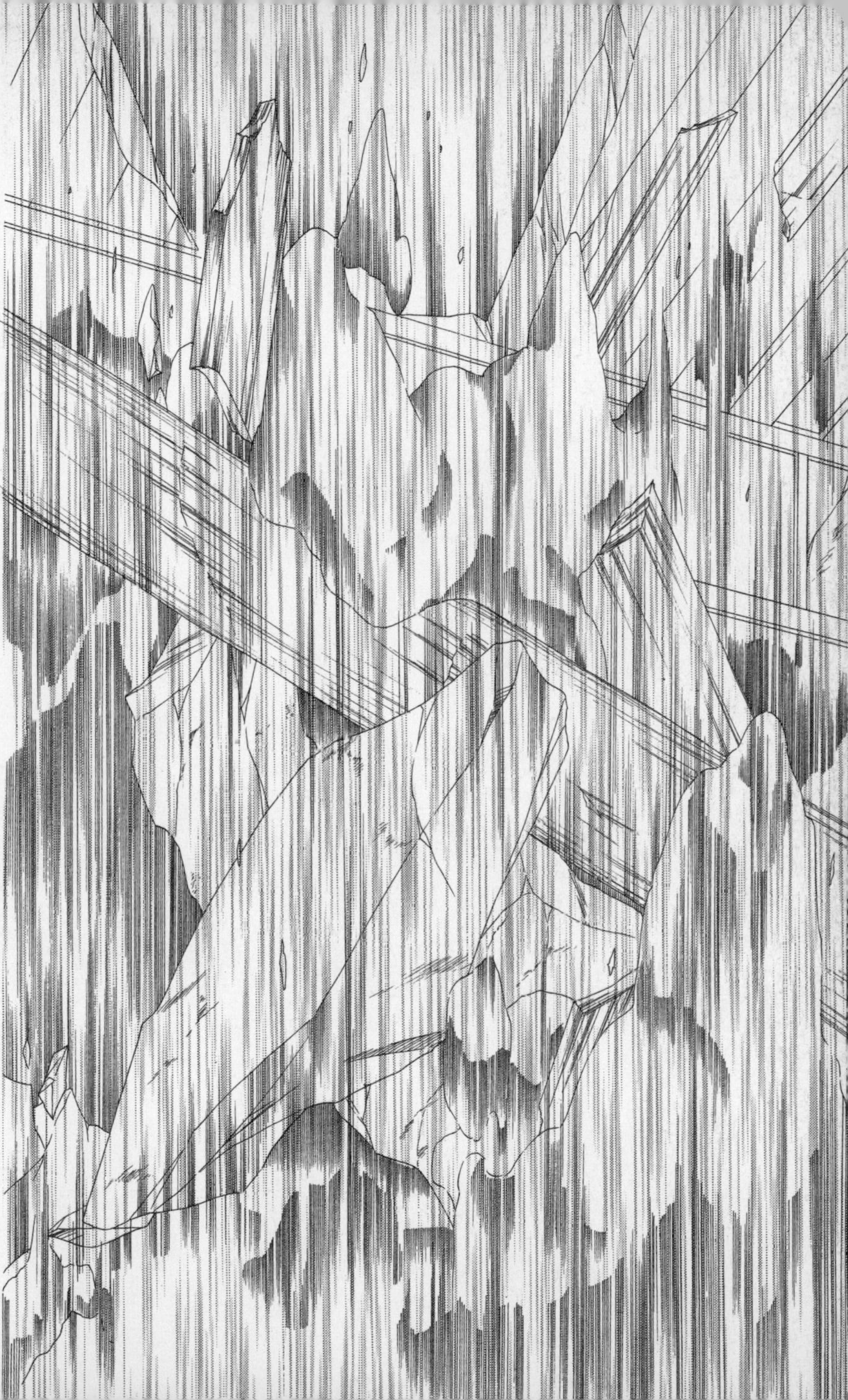

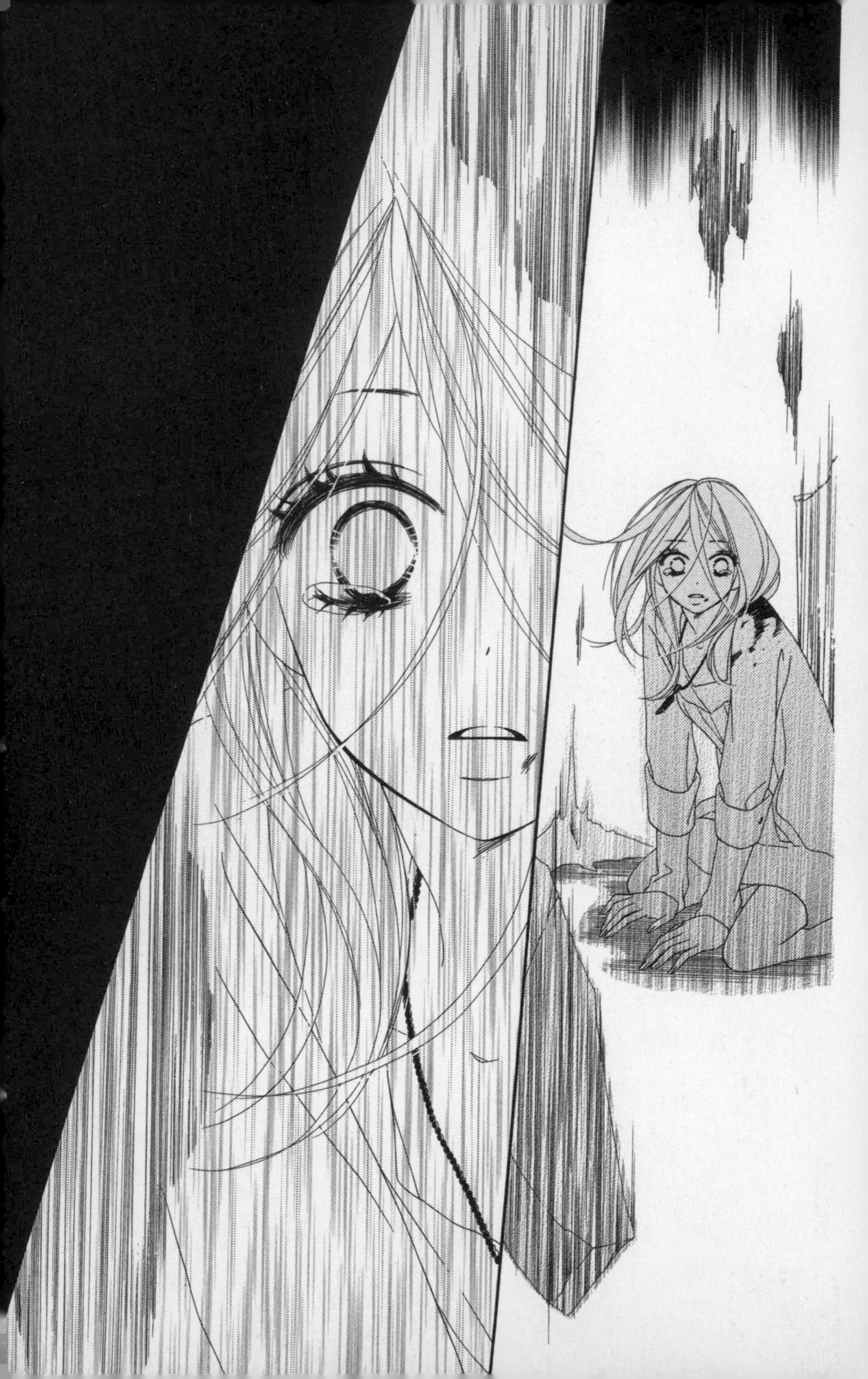

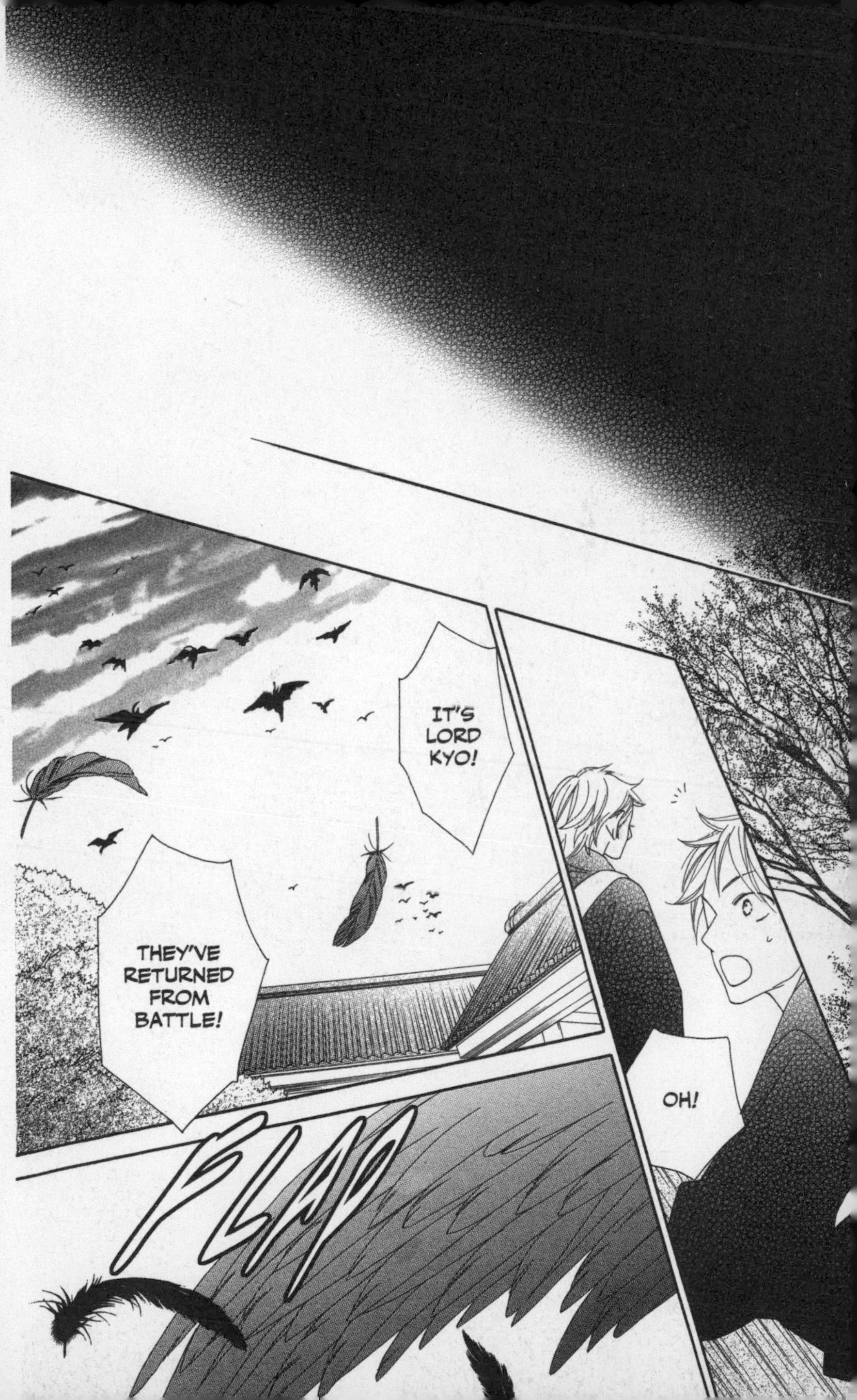
OH!
IT'S LORD KYO!
THEY'VE RETURNED FROM BATTLE!
PLAP

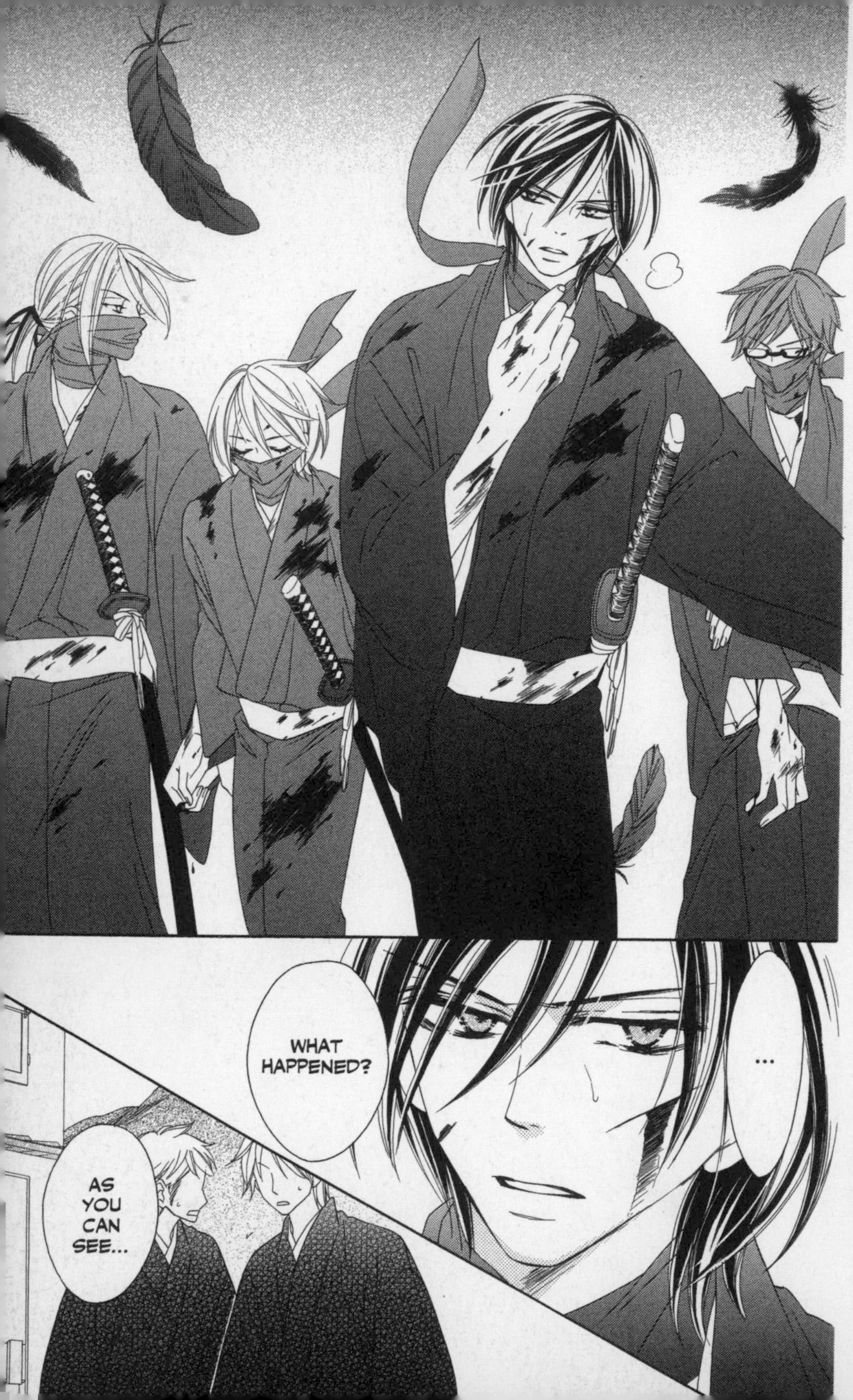
...
WHAT HAPPENED?
AS YOU CAN SEE...

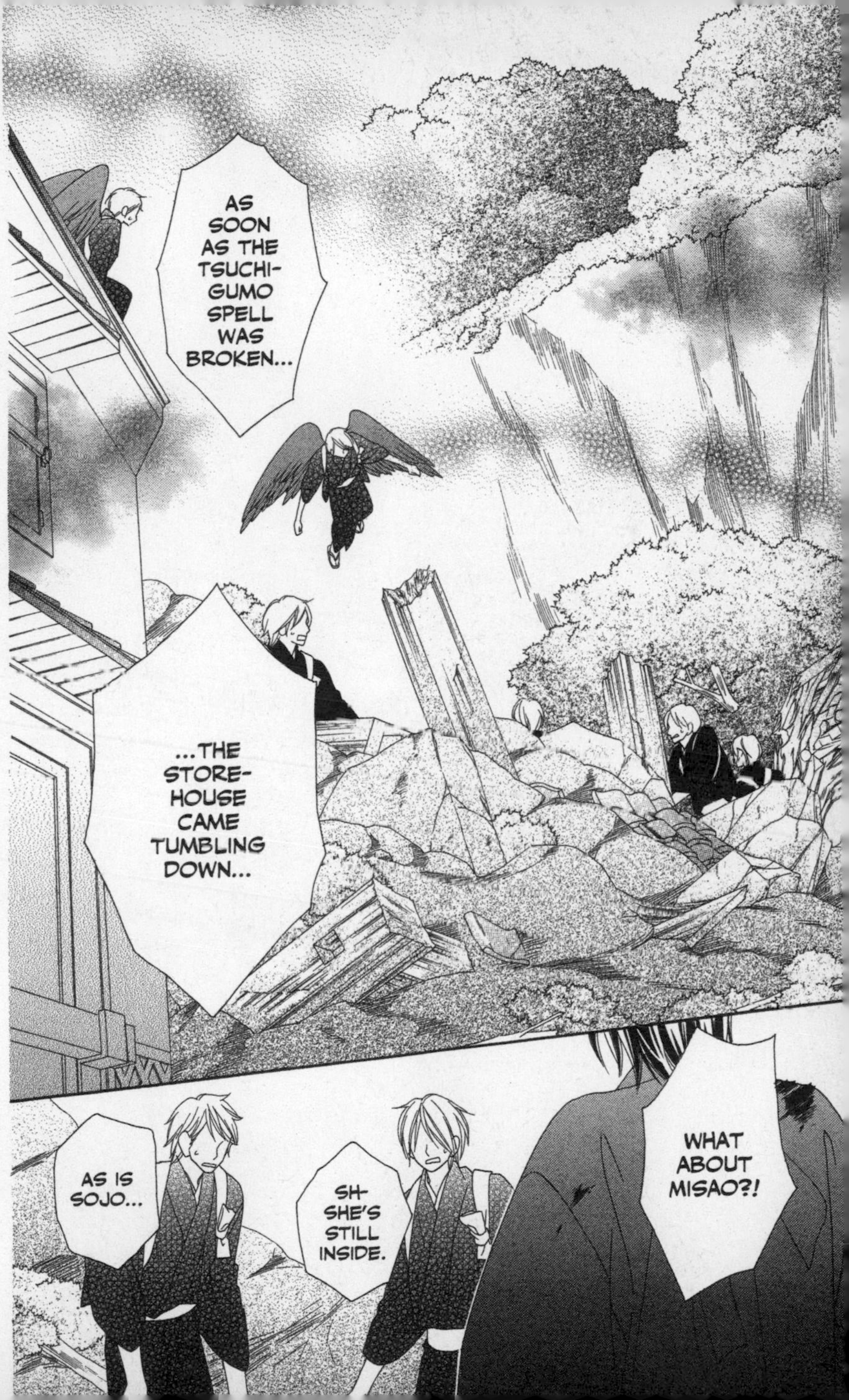
AS SOON AS THE TSUCHI-GUMO SPELL WAS BROKEN...
...THE STORE-HOUSE CAME TUMBLING DOWN...
WHAT ABOUT MISAO?!
SH-SHE'S STILL INSIDE.
AS IS SOJO...

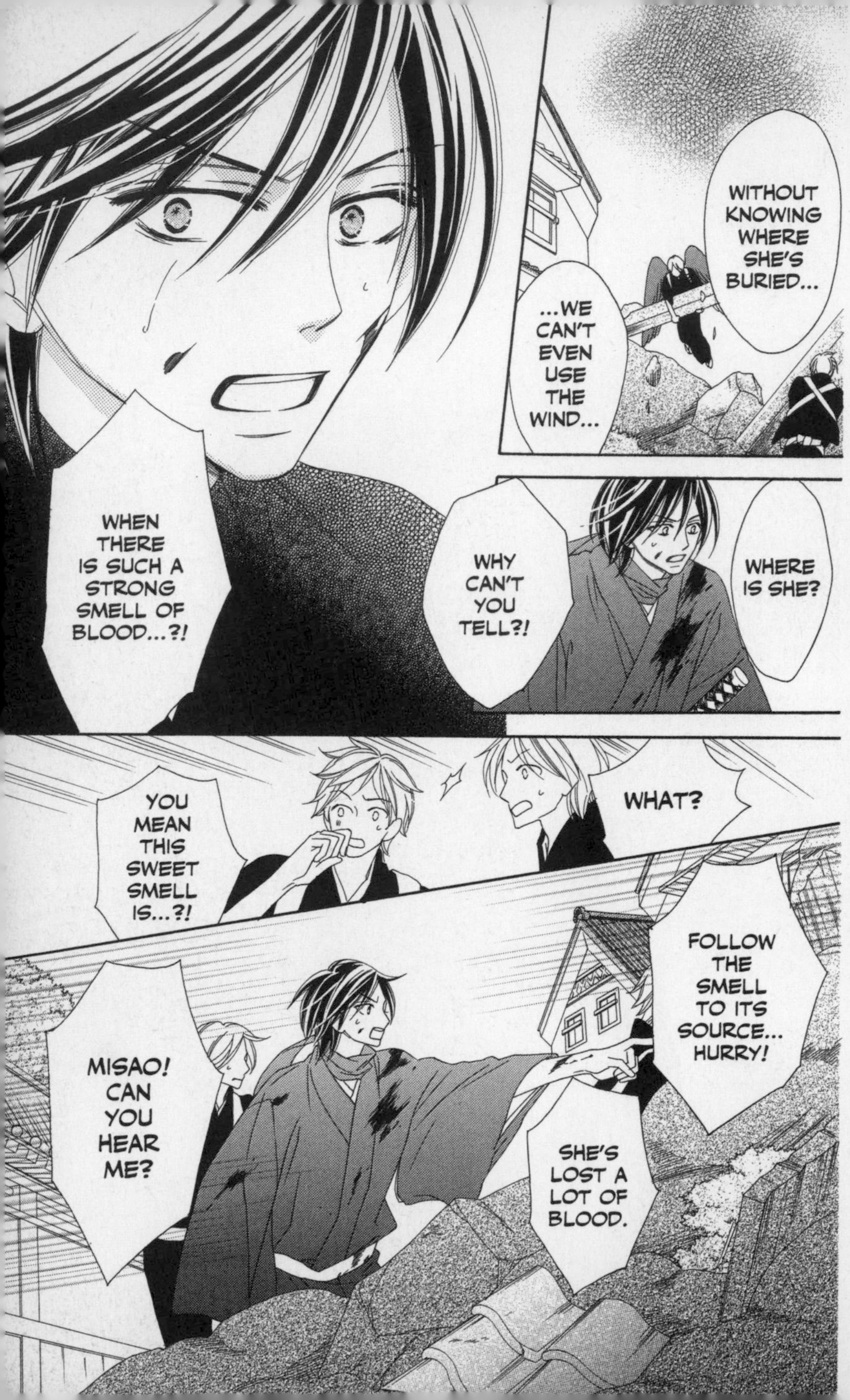
WITHOUT KNOWING WHERE SHE'S BURIED...
...WE CAN'T EVEN USE THE WIND...
WHERE IS SHE?
WHY CAN'T YOU TELL?!
WHEN THERE IS SUCH A STRONG SMELL OF BLOOD...?!
WHAT?
YOU MEAN THIS SWEET SMELL IS...?!
FOLLOW THE SMELL TO ITS SOURCE... HURRY!
SHE'S LOST A LOT OF BLOOD.
MISAO! CAN YOU HEAR ME?

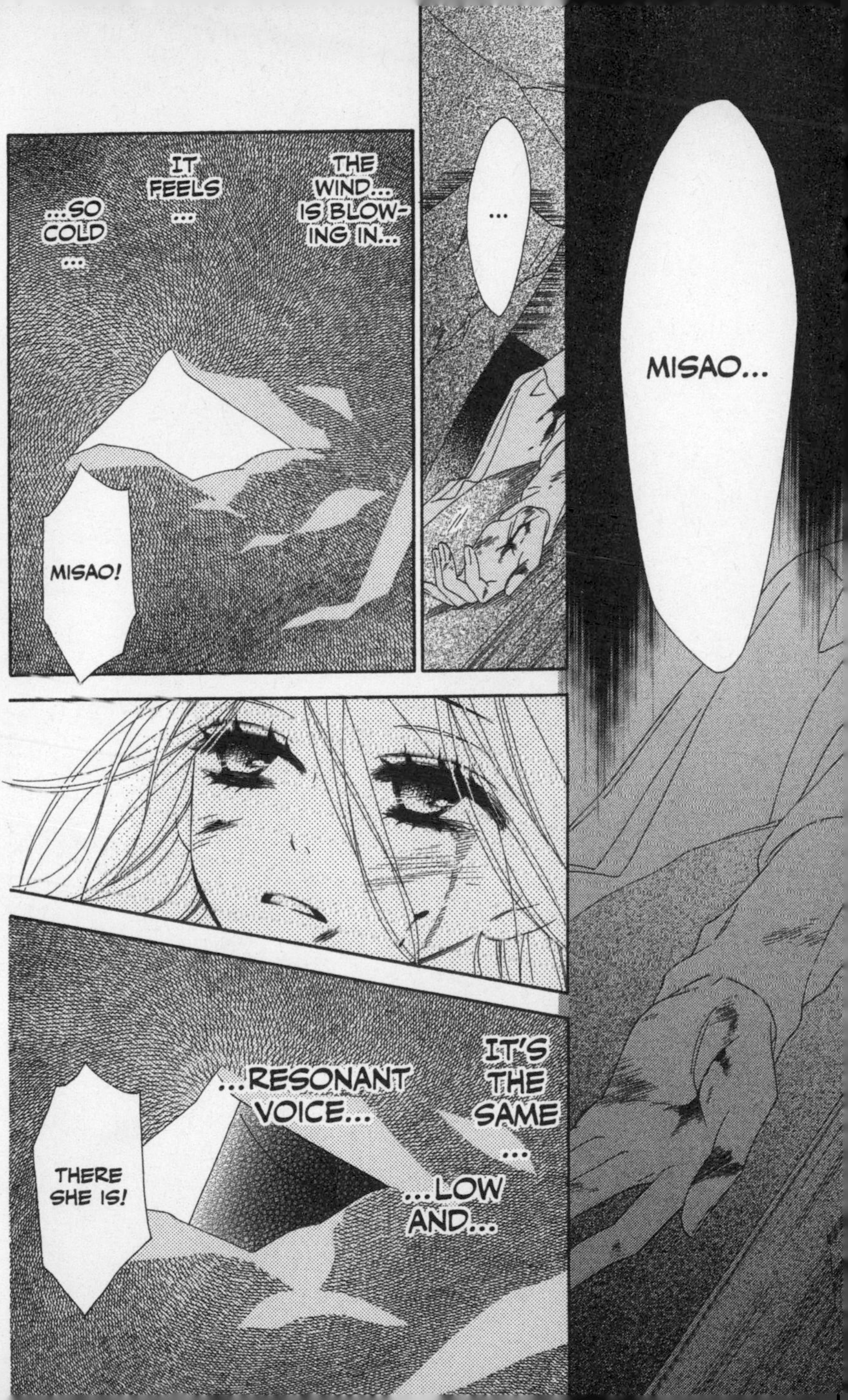
MISAO...
...
THE WIND... IS BLOW-ING IN...
IT FEELS...
...SO COLD...
MISAO!
IT'S THE SAME...
...LOW AND...
...RESONANT VOICE...
THERE SHE IS!

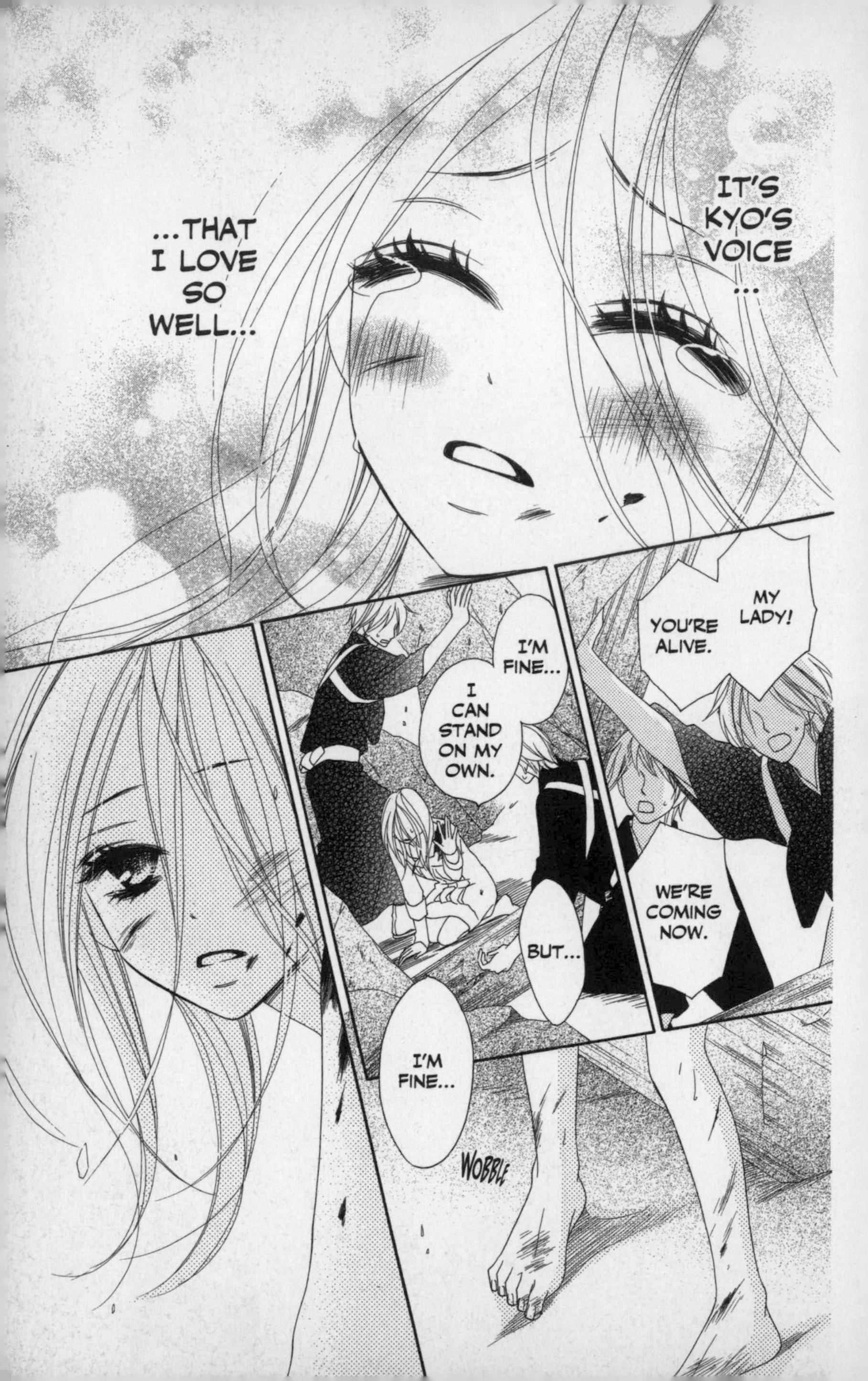
IT'S KYO'S VOICE ...
...THAT I LOVE SO WELL...
MY LADY!
YOU'RE ALIVE.
WE'RE COMING NOW.
I'M FINE...
I CAN STAND ON MY OWN.
BUT...
I'M FINE...
WOBBLE

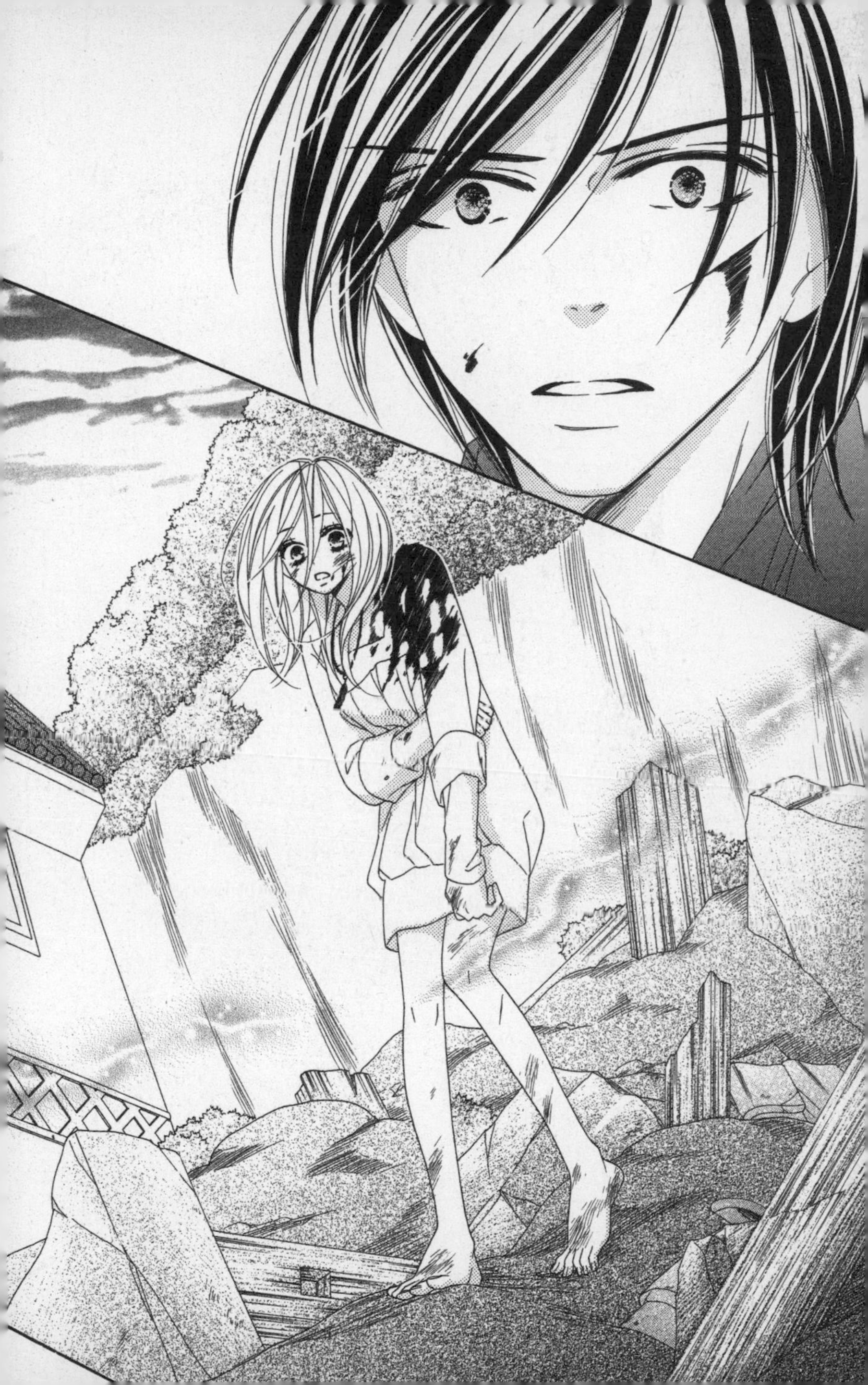

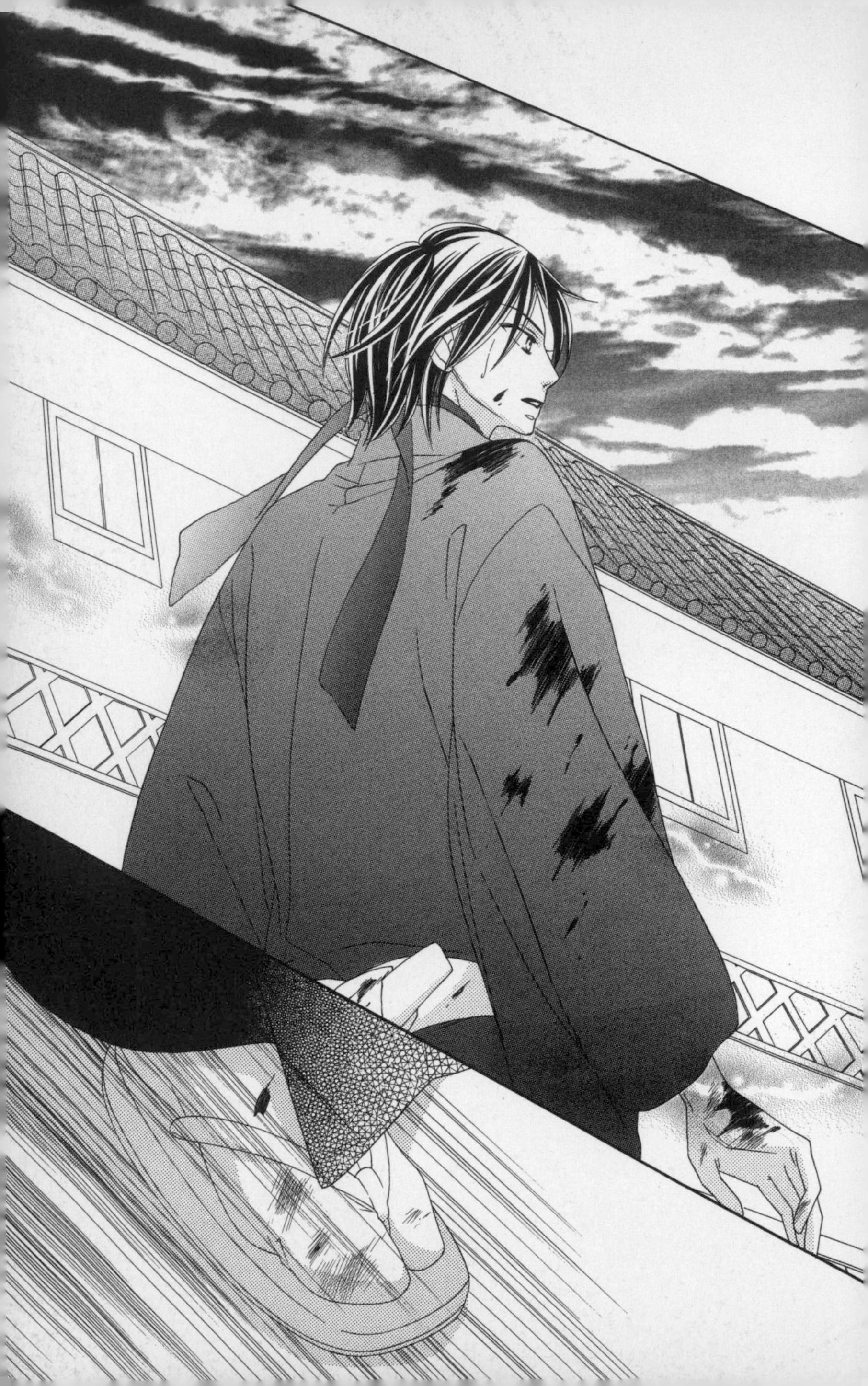

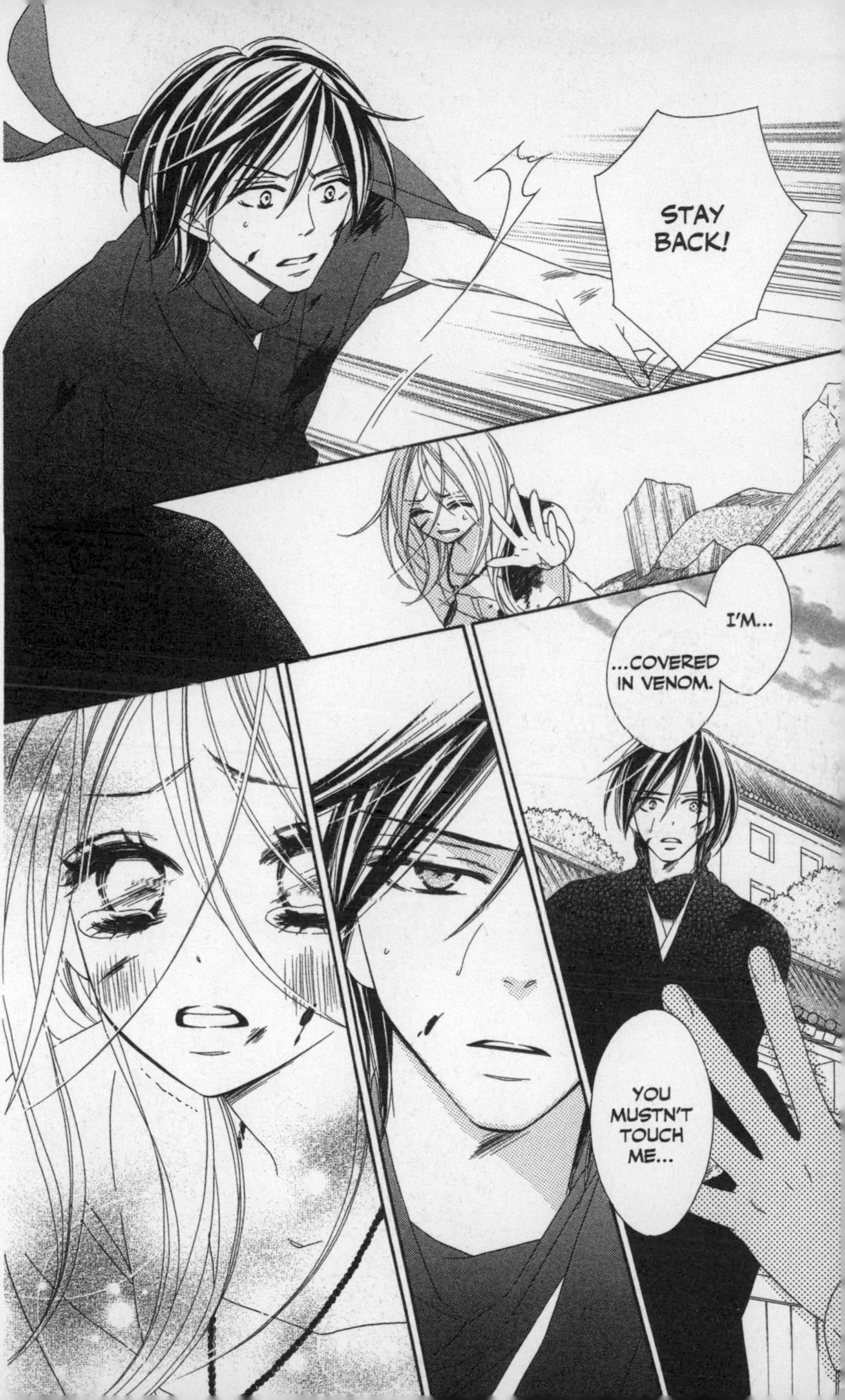
STAY BACK!
I'M...
...COVERED IN VENOM.
YOU MUSTN'T TOUCH ME...

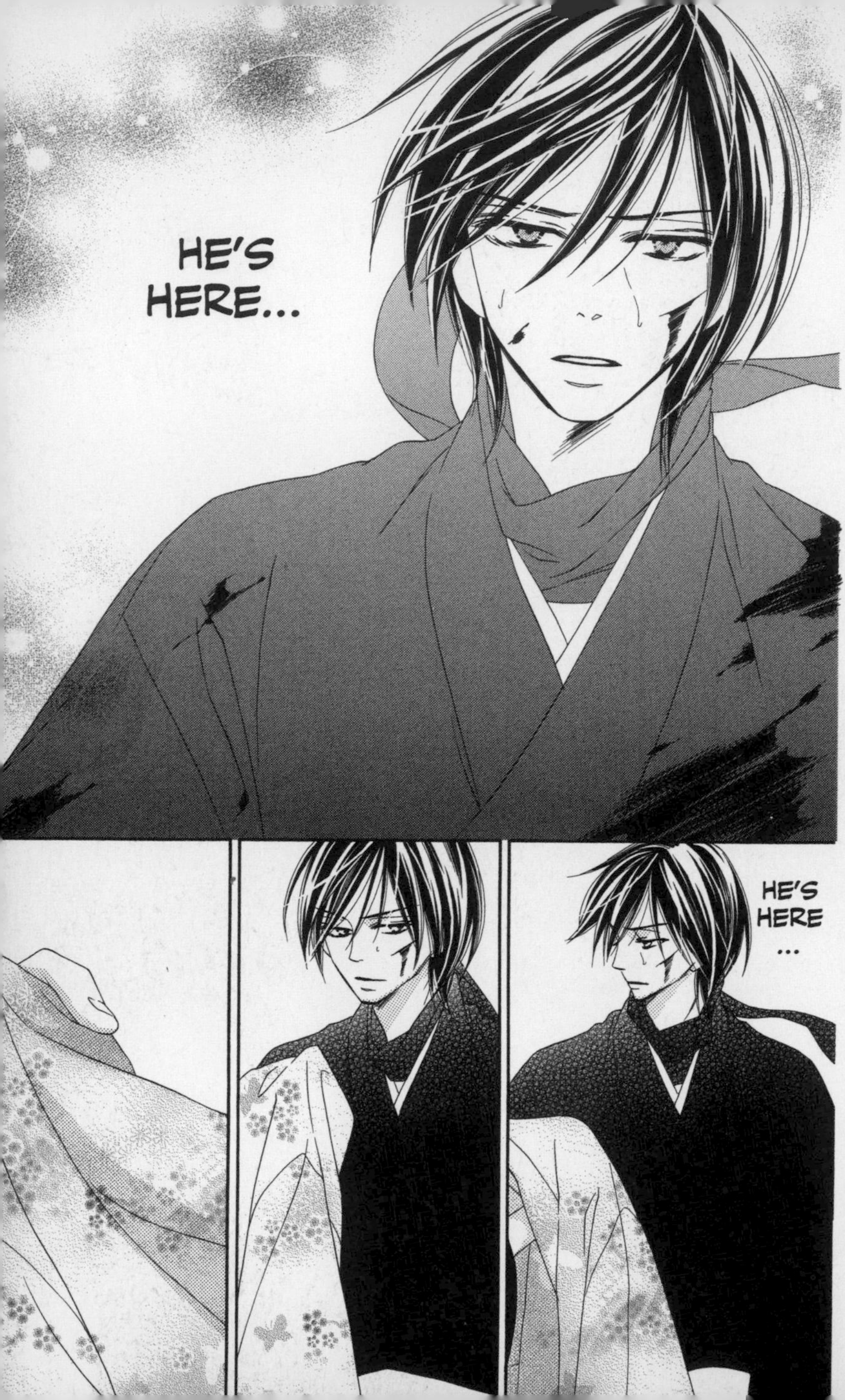
HE'S HERE...
HE'S HERE ...

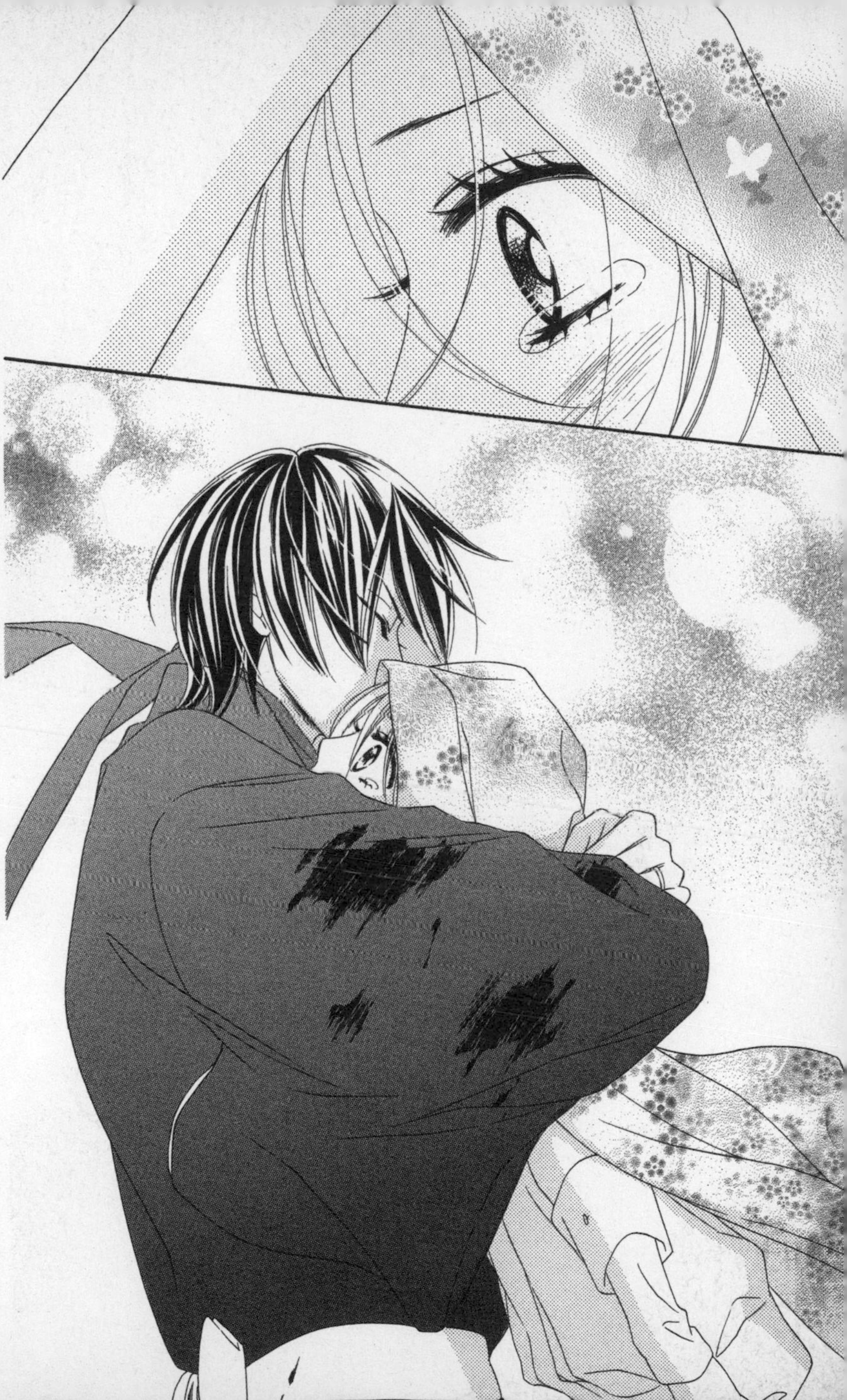

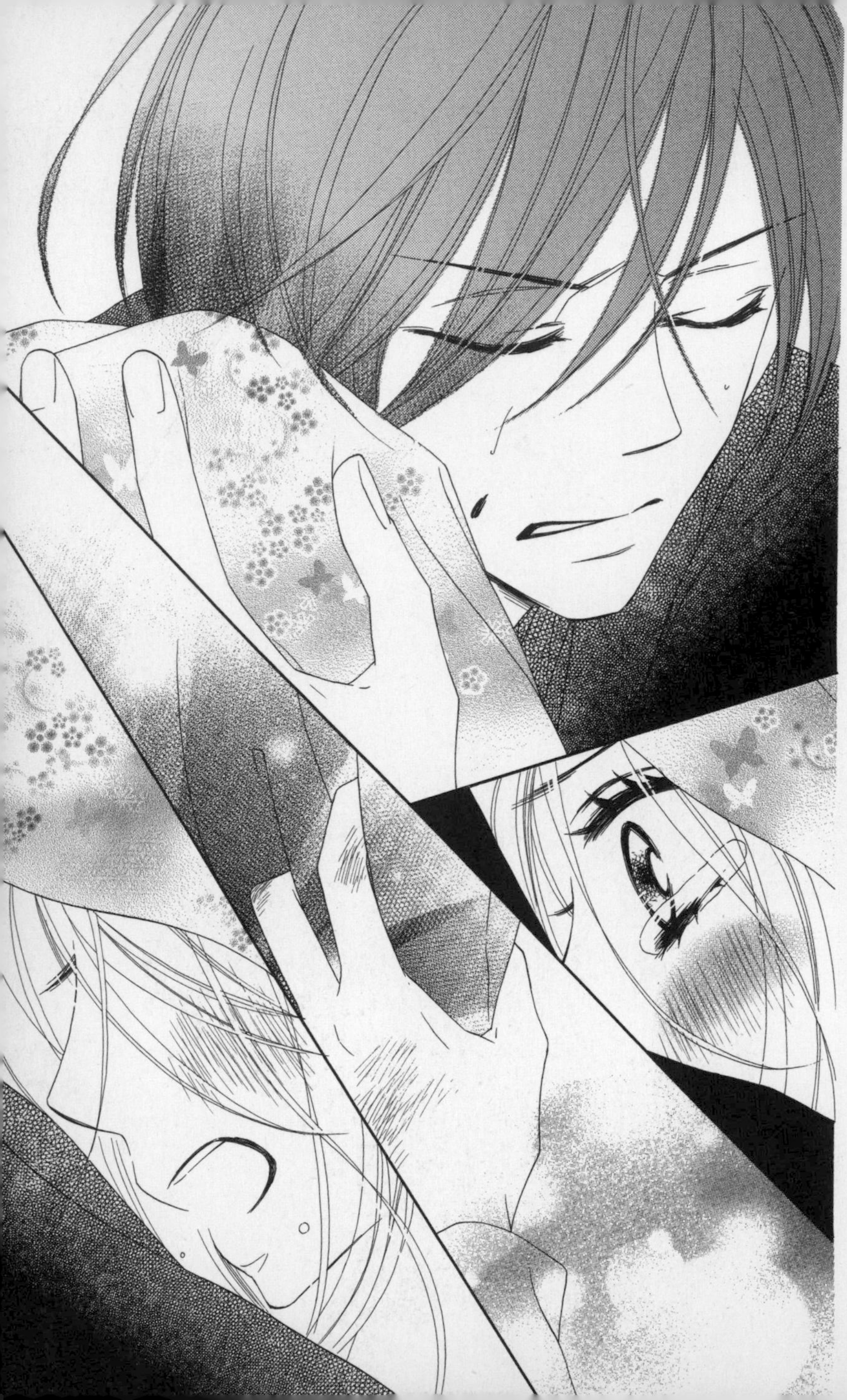

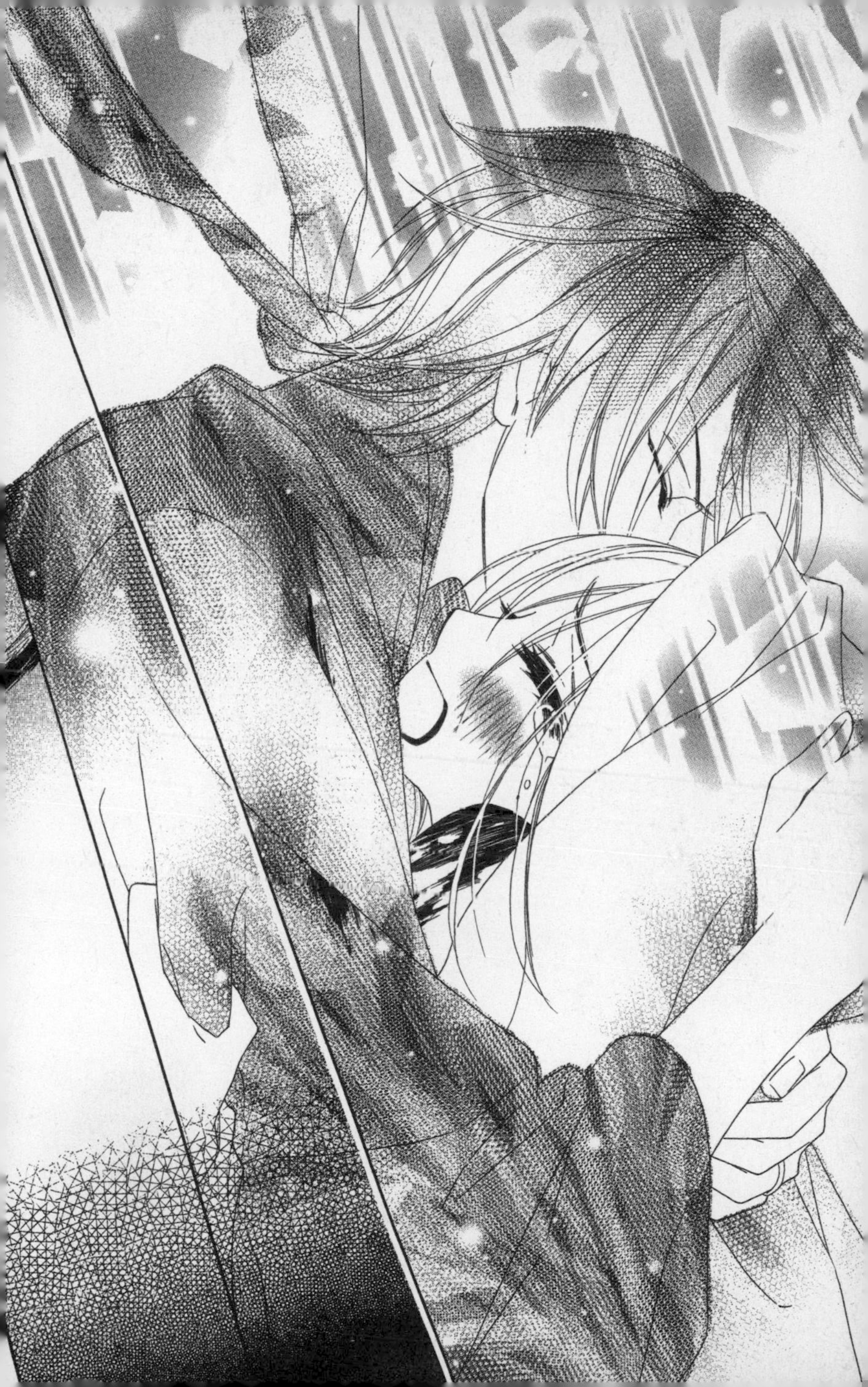

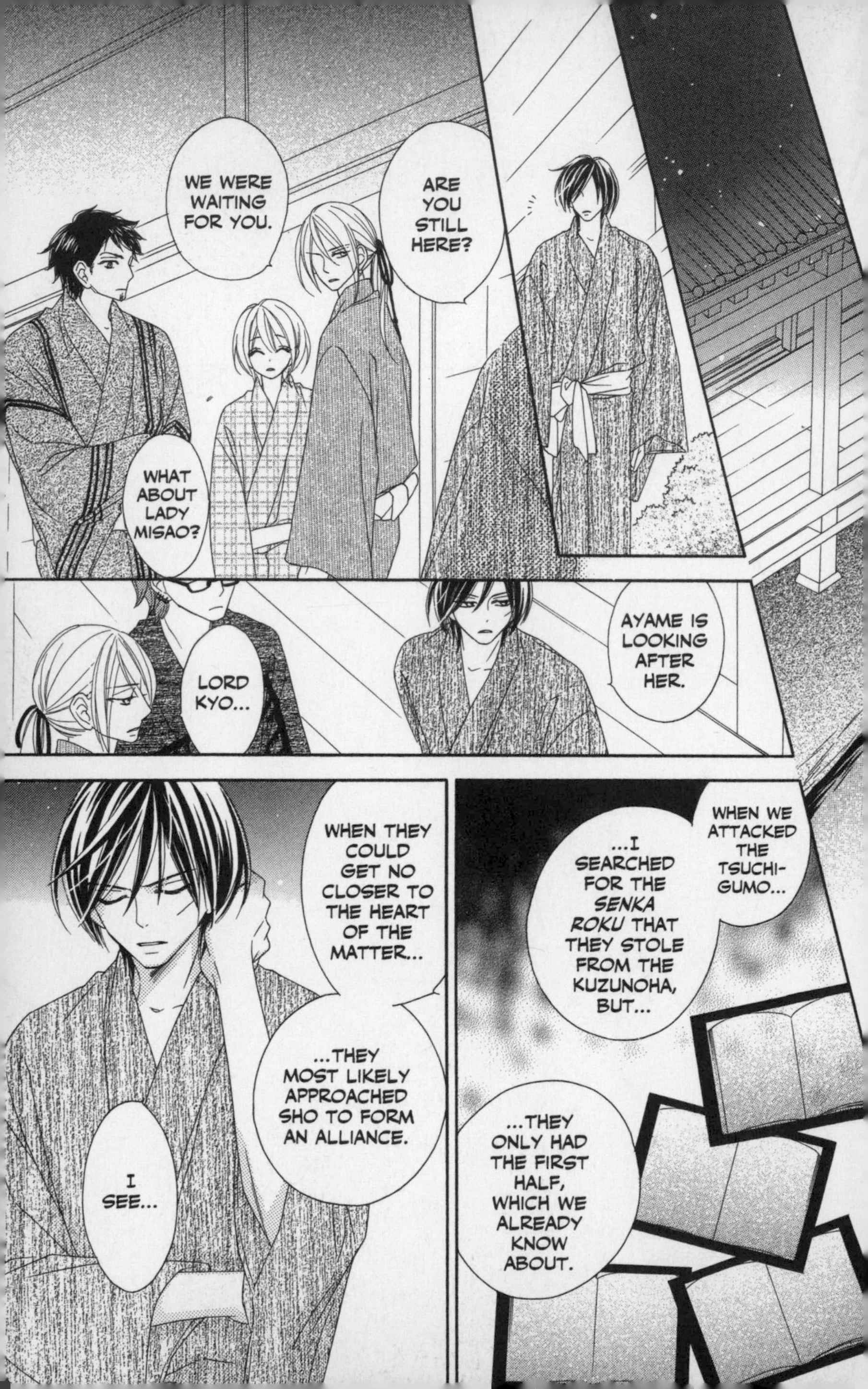
ARE YOU STILL HERE?
WE WERE WAITING FOR YOU.
WHAT ABOUT LADY MISAO?
AYAME IS LOOKING AFTER HER.
LORD KYO...
WHEN WE ATTACKED THE TSUCHI-GUMO...
...I SEARCHED FOR THE *SENKA ROKU* THAT THEY STOLE FROM THE KUZUNOHA, BUT...
...THEY ONLY HAD THE FIRST HALF, WHICH WE ALREADY KNOW ABOUT.
WHEN THEY COULD GET NO CLOSER TO THE HEART OF THE MATTER...
...THEY MOST LIKELY APPROACHED SHO TO FORM AN ALLIANCE.
I SEE...

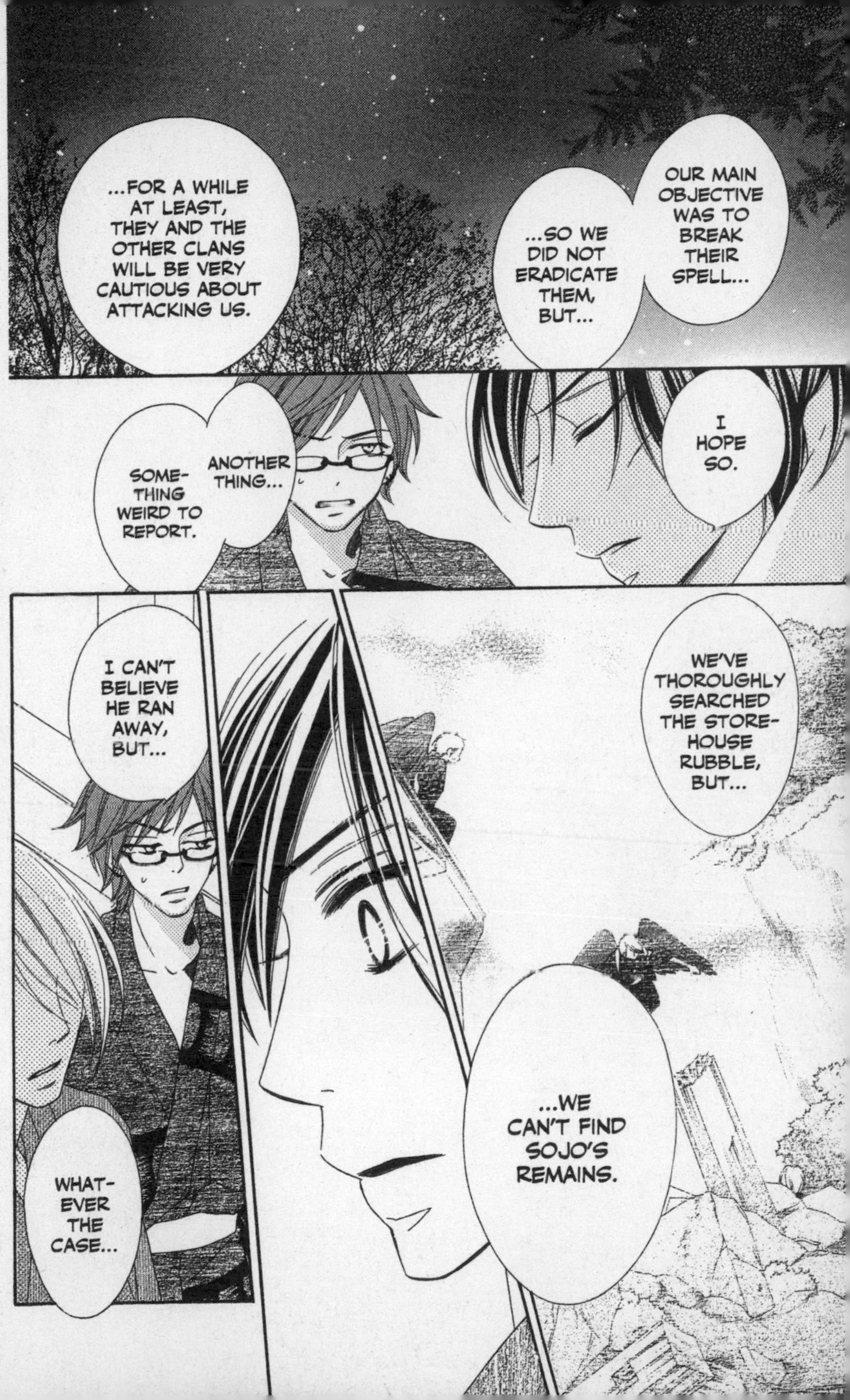
OUR MAIN OBJECTIVE WAS TO BREAK THEIR SPELL...
...SO WE DID NOT ERADICATE THEM, BUT...
...FOR A WHILE AT LEAST, THEY AND THE OTHER CLANS WILL BE VERY CAUTIOUS ABOUT ATTACKING US.
I HOPE SO.
ANOTHER THING...
SOME-THING WEIRD TO REPORT.
WE'VE THOROUGHLY SEARCHED THE STORE-HOUSE RUBBLE, BUT...
...WE CAN'T FIND SOJO'S REMAINS.
I CAN'T BELIEVE HE RAN AWAY, BUT...
WHAT-EVER THE CASE...

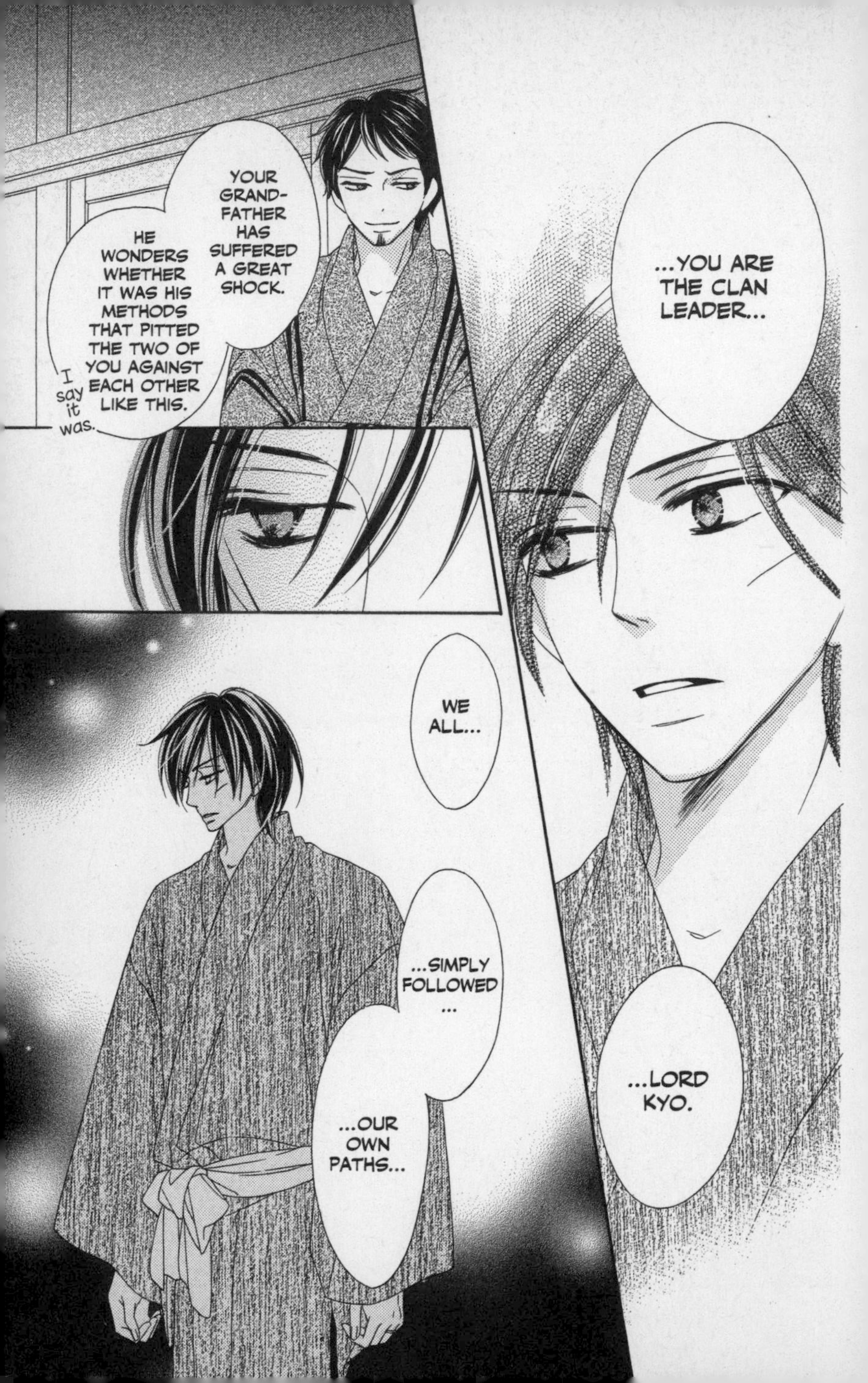
...YOU ARE THE CLAN LEADER...
...LORD KYO.
YOUR GRAND-FATHER HAS SUFFERED A GREAT SHOCK.
HE WONDERS WHETHER IT WAS HIS METHODS THAT PITTED THE TWO OF YOU AGAINST EACH OTHER LIKE THIS.
I say it was.
WE ALL...
...SIMPLY FOLLOWED...
...OUR OWN PATHS...

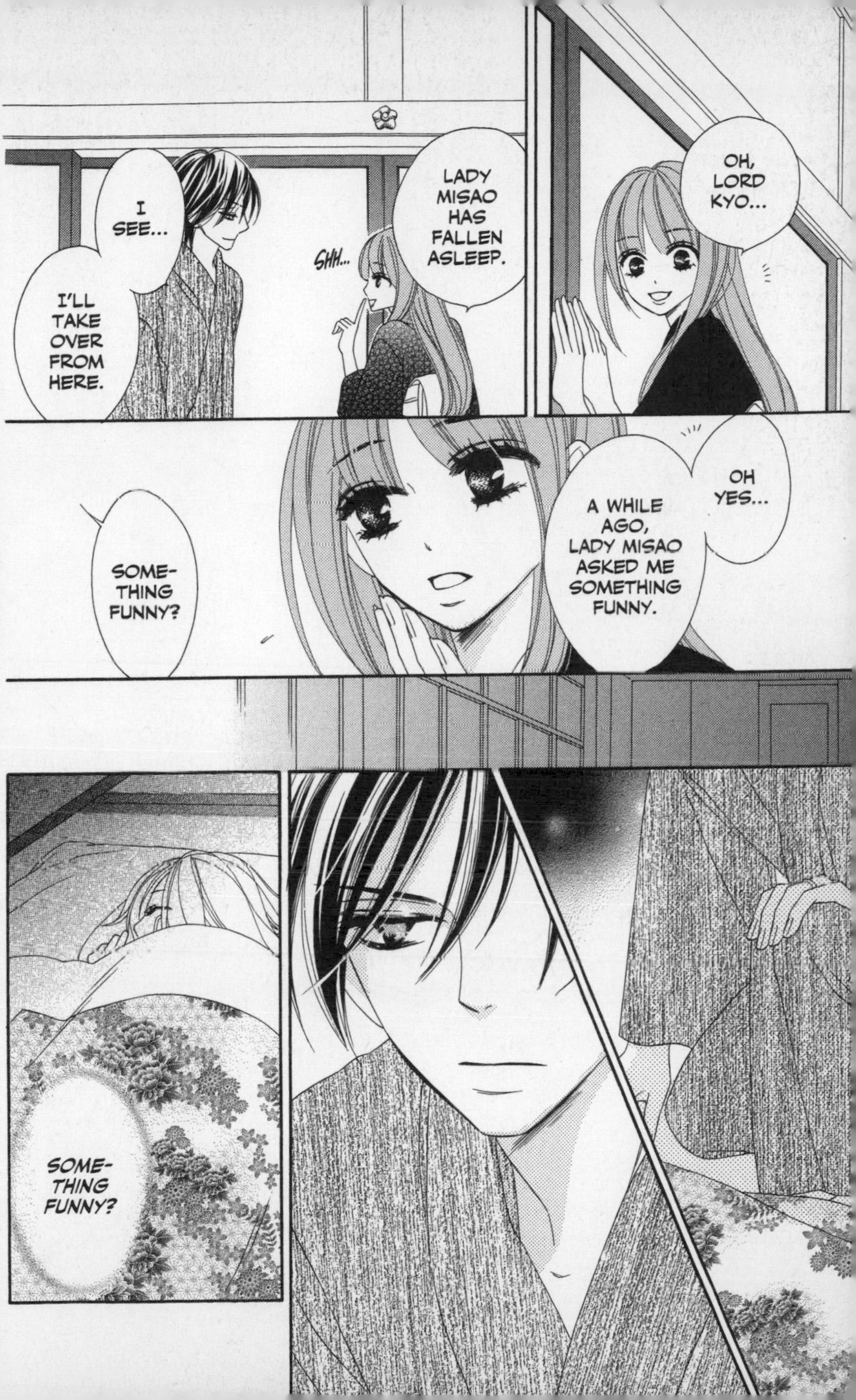
OH, LORD KYO...
LADY MISAO HAS FALLEN ASLEEP.
SHH...
I SEE...
I'LL TAKE OVER FROM HERE.
OH YES...
A WHILE AGO, LADY MISAO ASKED ME SOMETHING FUNNY.
SOME-THING FUNNY?
SOME-THING FUNNY?

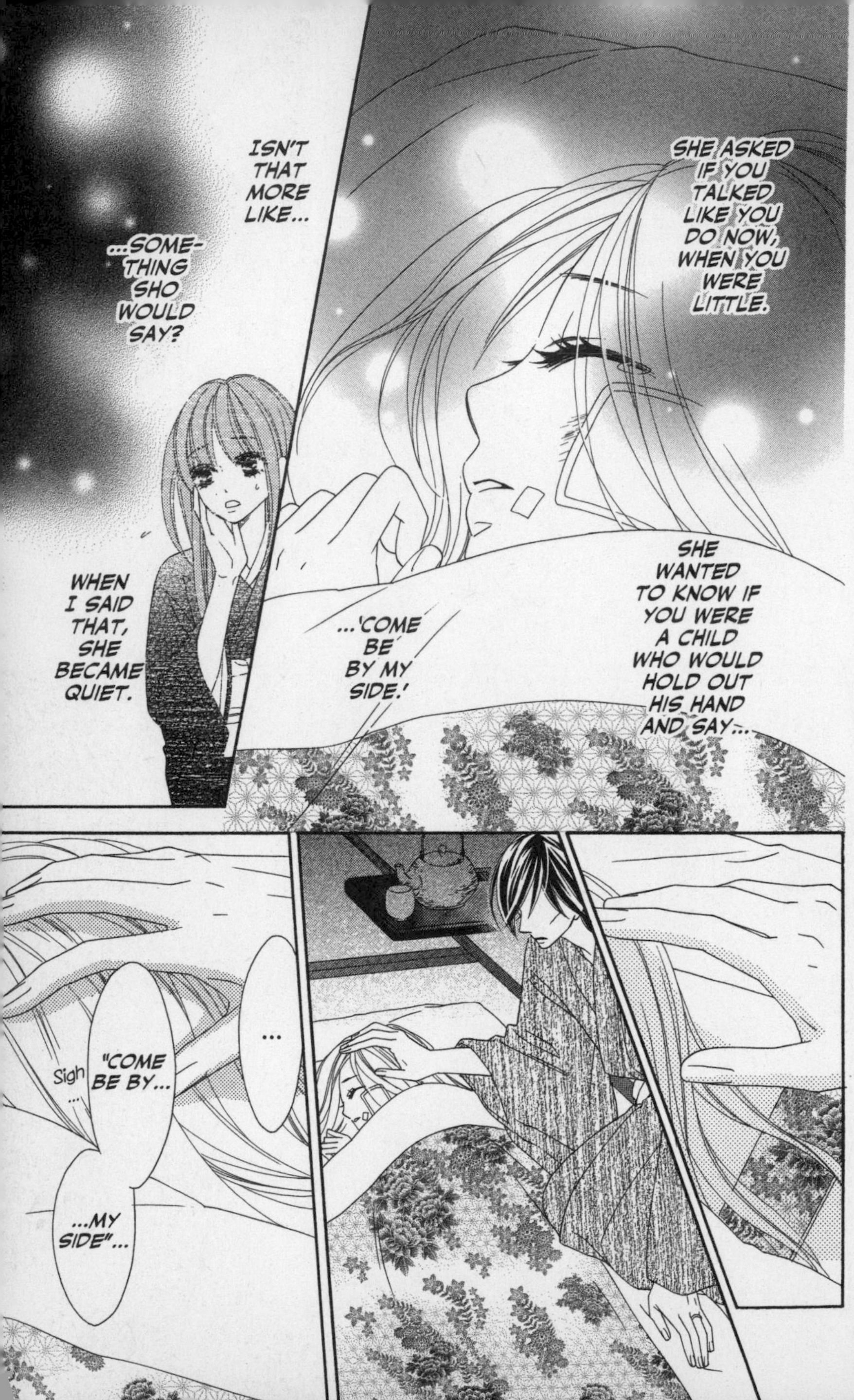
SHE ASKED IF YOU TALKED LIKE YOU DO NOW, WHEN YOU WERE LITTLE.
SHE WANTED TO KNOW IF YOU WERE A CHILD WHO WOULD HOLD OUT HIS HAND AND SAY...
...'COME BE BY MY SIDE.'
ISN'T THAT MORE LIKE...
...SOME-THING SHO WOULD SAY?
WHEN I SAID THAT, SHE BECAME QUIET.
...
"COME BE BY...
Sigh...
...MY SIDE"...

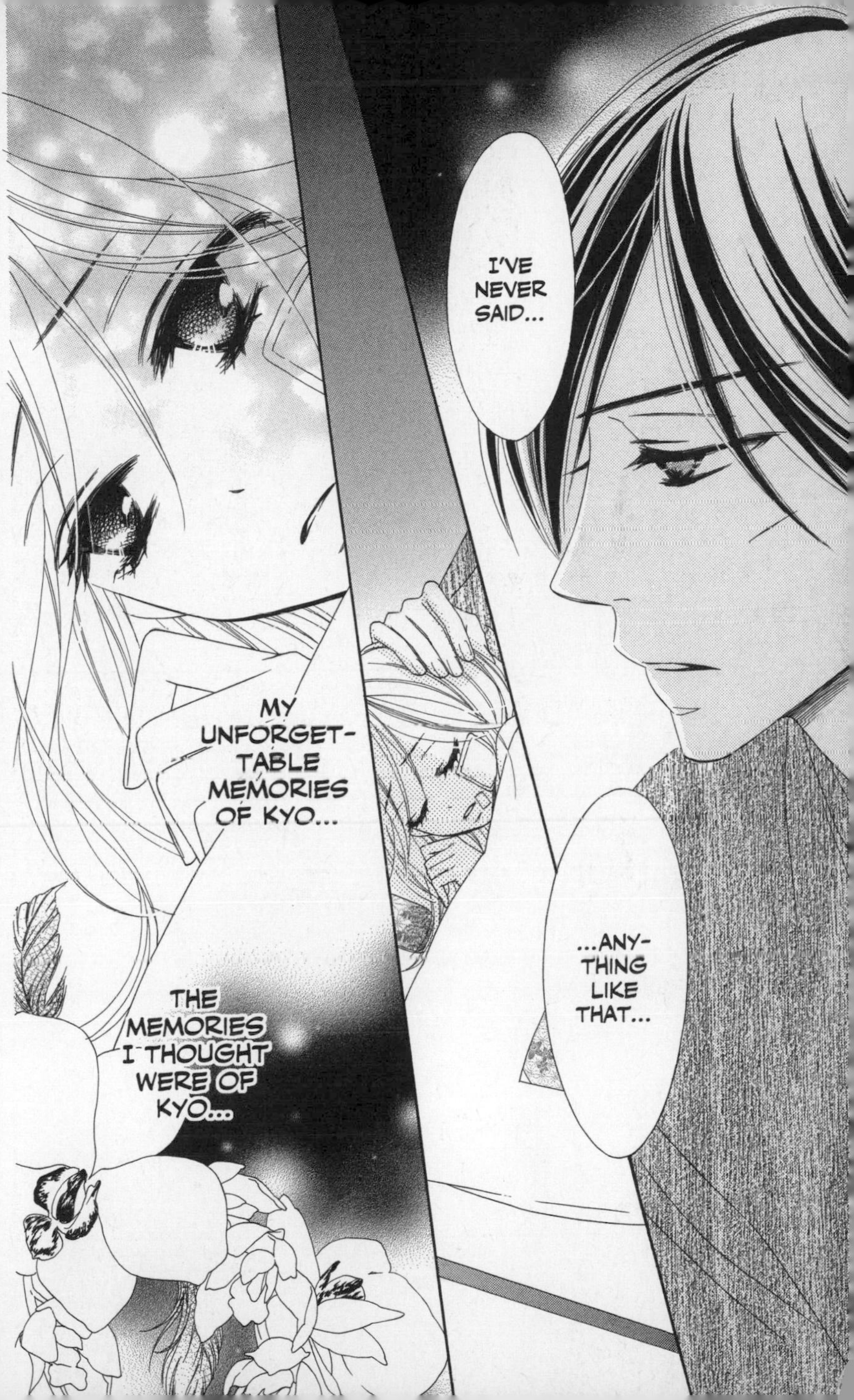
I'VE NEVER SAID...
...ANY-THING LIKE THAT...
MY UNFORGET-TABLE MEMORIES OF KYO...
THE MEMORIES I THOUGHT WERE OF KYO...

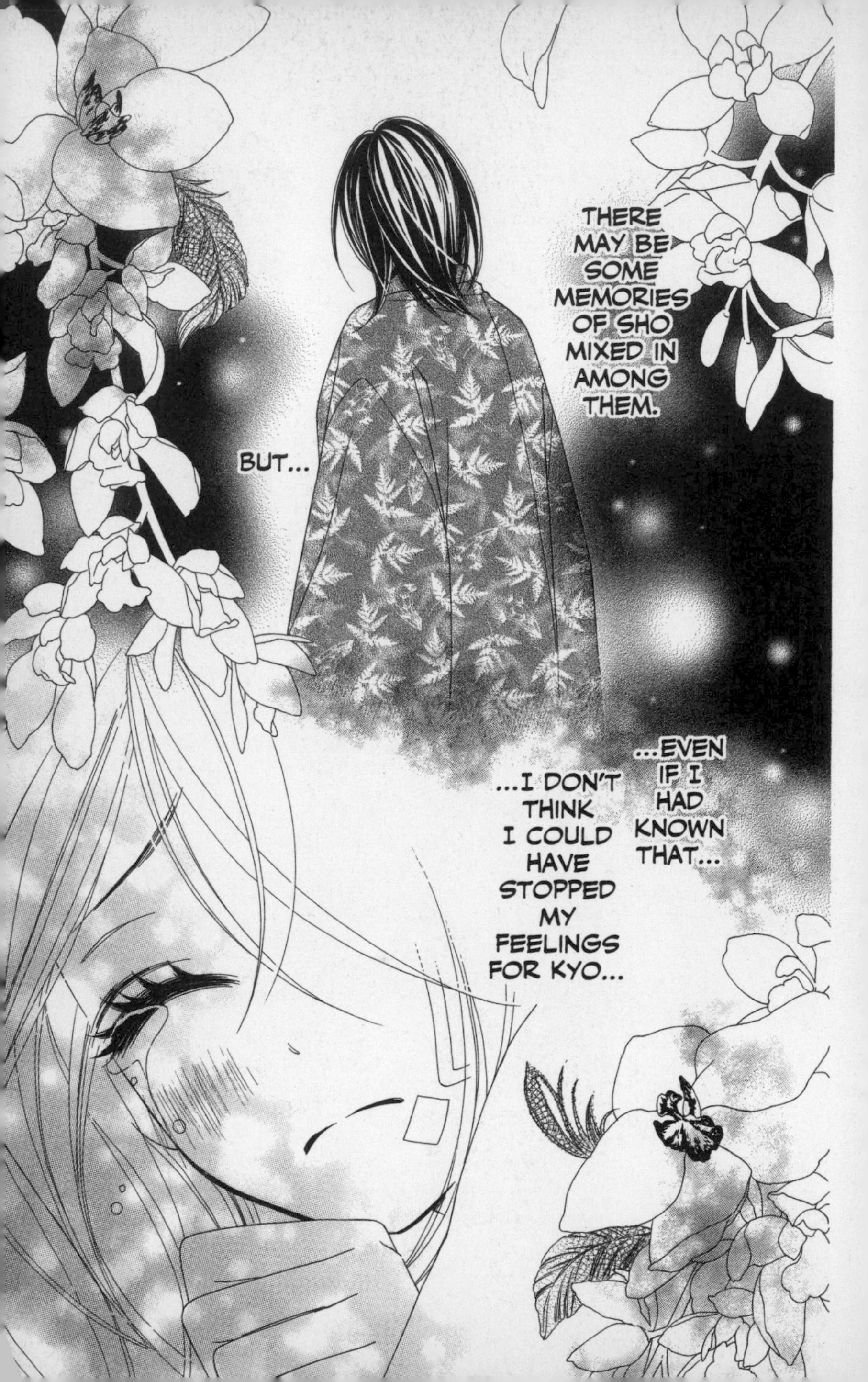
THERE MAY BE SOME MEMORIES OF SHO MIXED IN AMONG THEM.
BUT...
...EVEN IF I HAD KNOWN THAT...
...I DON'T THINK I COULD HAVE STOPPED MY FEELINGS FOR KYO...

Illustration Request Number Nine

"Athletes"

This coincided with the Beijing Olympics.
Jiro is supposed to be on the pommel horse,
but there's something wrong.
Hoki was holding a pole at first...

This is what happens when I draw without all my
reference materials on hand!

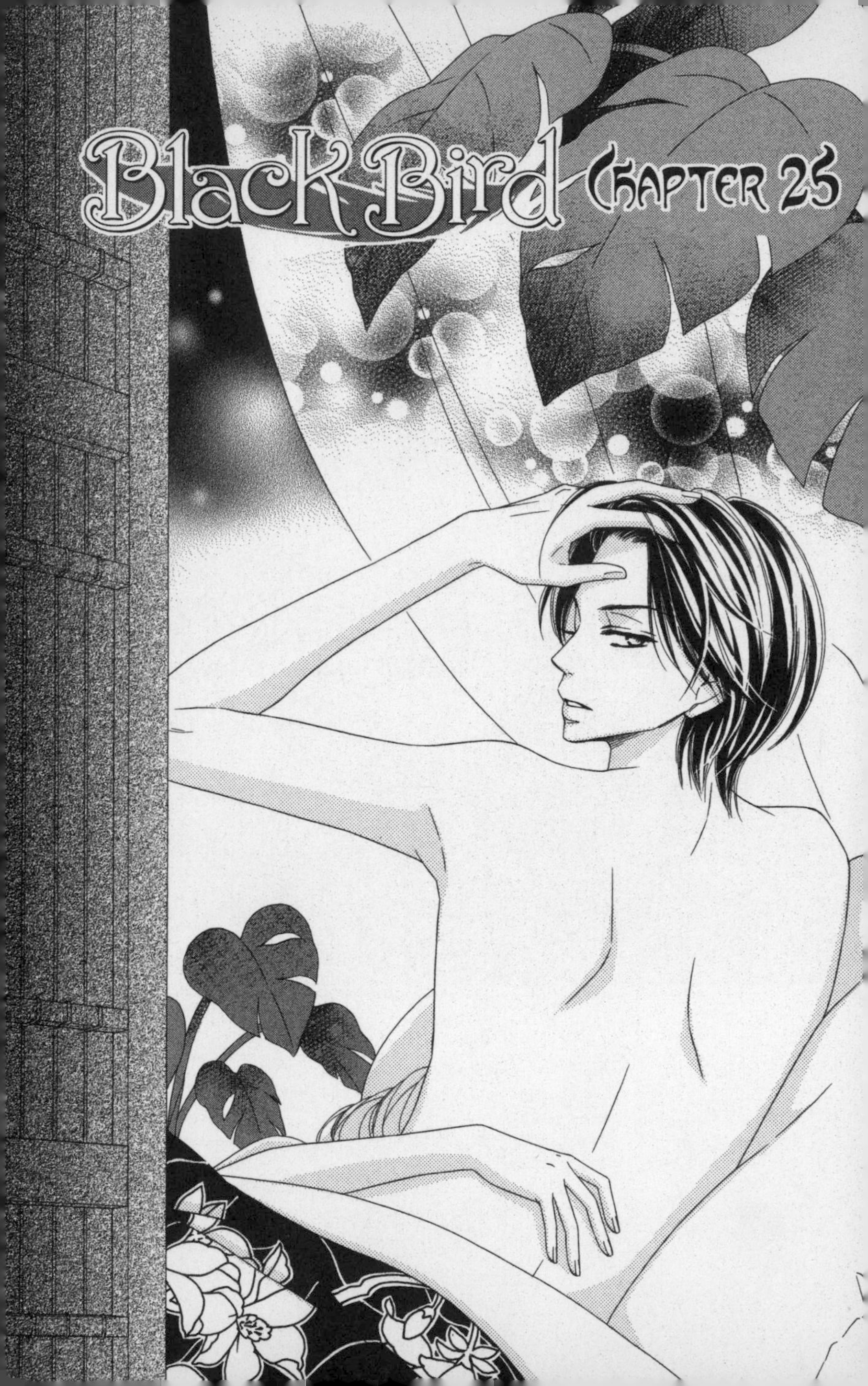
Black Bird
Chapter 25

IS IT TRUE THAT LADY MISAO IS IN BED WITH A FEVER?
YES.
BUT LORD KYO HAS BEEN SITTING WITH HER...
MISAO...
SHHH
I LET YOUR PARENTS KNOW THAT YOU'D BE STAYING HERE UNTIL YOU'RE BETTER.
UH...

• Character Introduction • Koh

age: 24
height: 186 cm

Hee...

I also had a version where he shines as a much cooler character. (What's more, I had planned to have one of the Eight Daitengu take this role.) But I changed my mind.

His manner of speaking is supposed to be reminiscent of an old Edo retiree. Not fey.

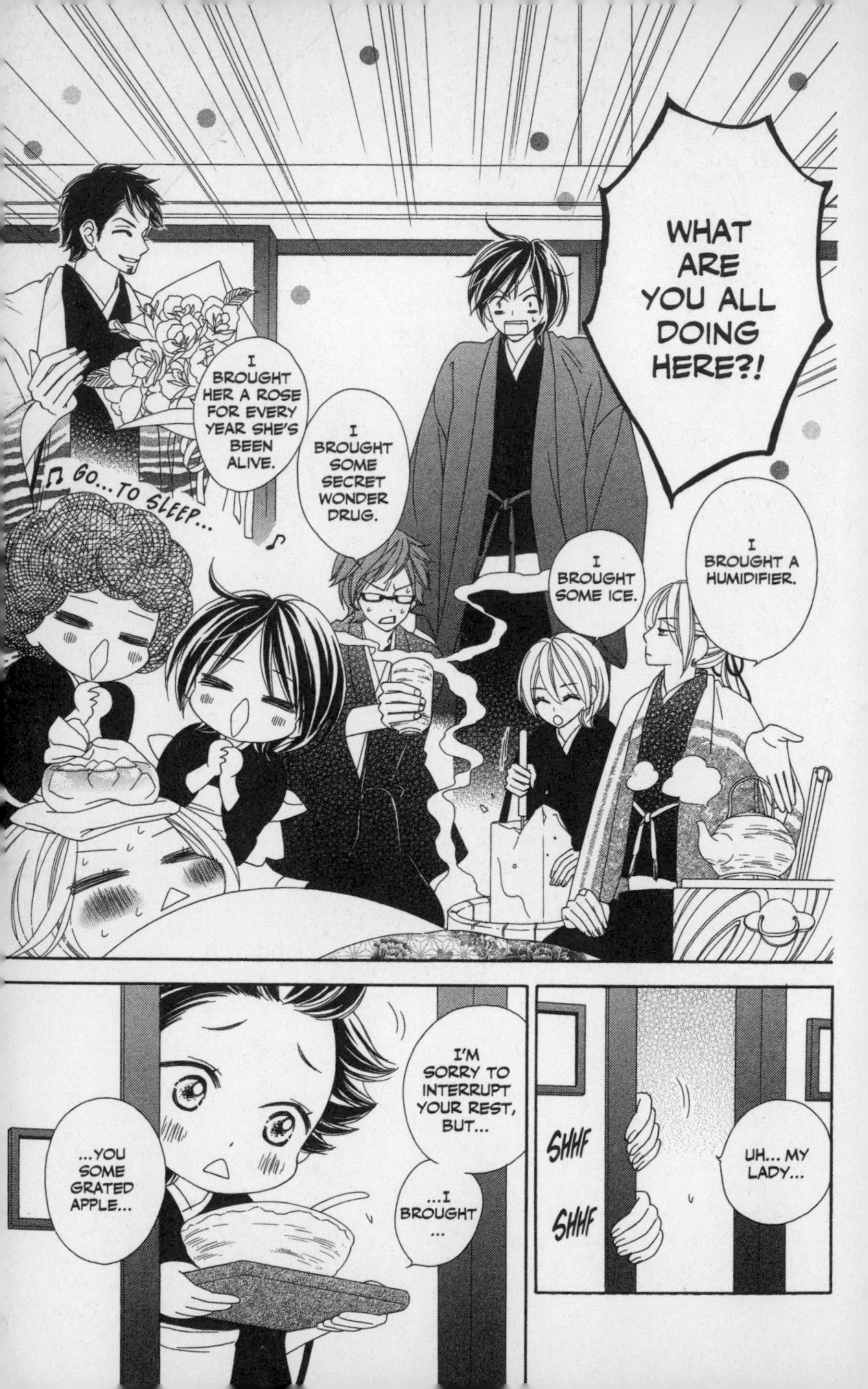
WHAT ARE YOU ALL DOING HERE?!
I BROUGHT A HUMIDIFIER.
I BROUGHT SOME ICE.
I BROUGHT SOME SECRET WONDER DRUG.
I BROUGHT HER A ROSE FOR EVERY YEAR SHE'S BEEN ALIVE.
♫ GO...TO SLEEP... ♪
UH... MY LADY...
SHHF
SHHF
I'M SORRY TO INTERRUPT YOUR REST, BUT...
...I BROUGHT ...
...YOU SOME GRATED APPLE...

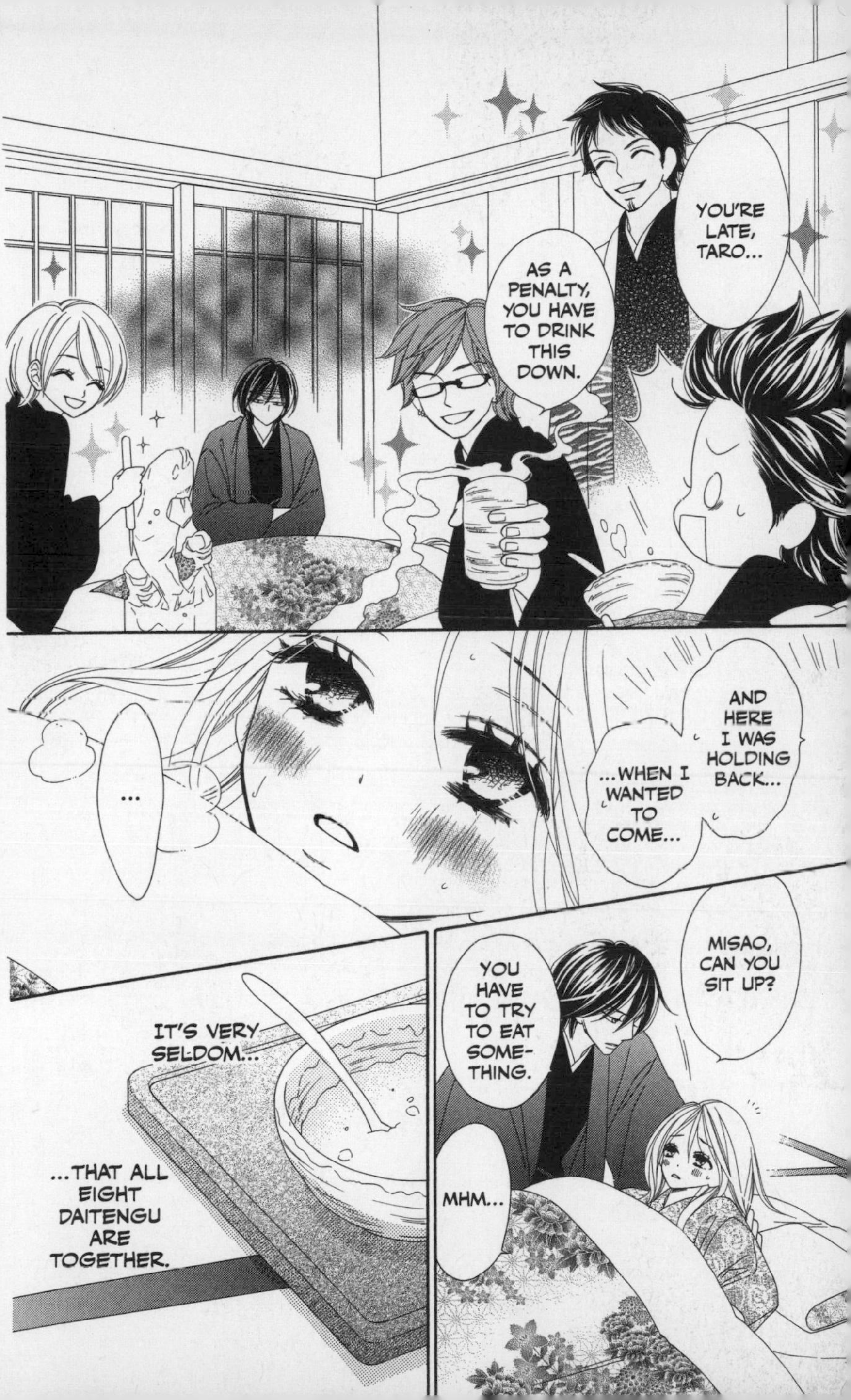
YOU'RE LATE, TARO...
AS A PENALTY, YOU HAVE TO DRINK THIS DOWN.
AND HERE I WAS HOLDING BACK...
...WHEN I WANTED TO COME...
...
MISAO, CAN YOU SIT UP?
YOU HAVE TO TRY TO EAT SOME-THING.
MHM...
IT'S VERY SELDOM...
...THAT ALL EIGHT DAITENGU ARE TOGETHER.

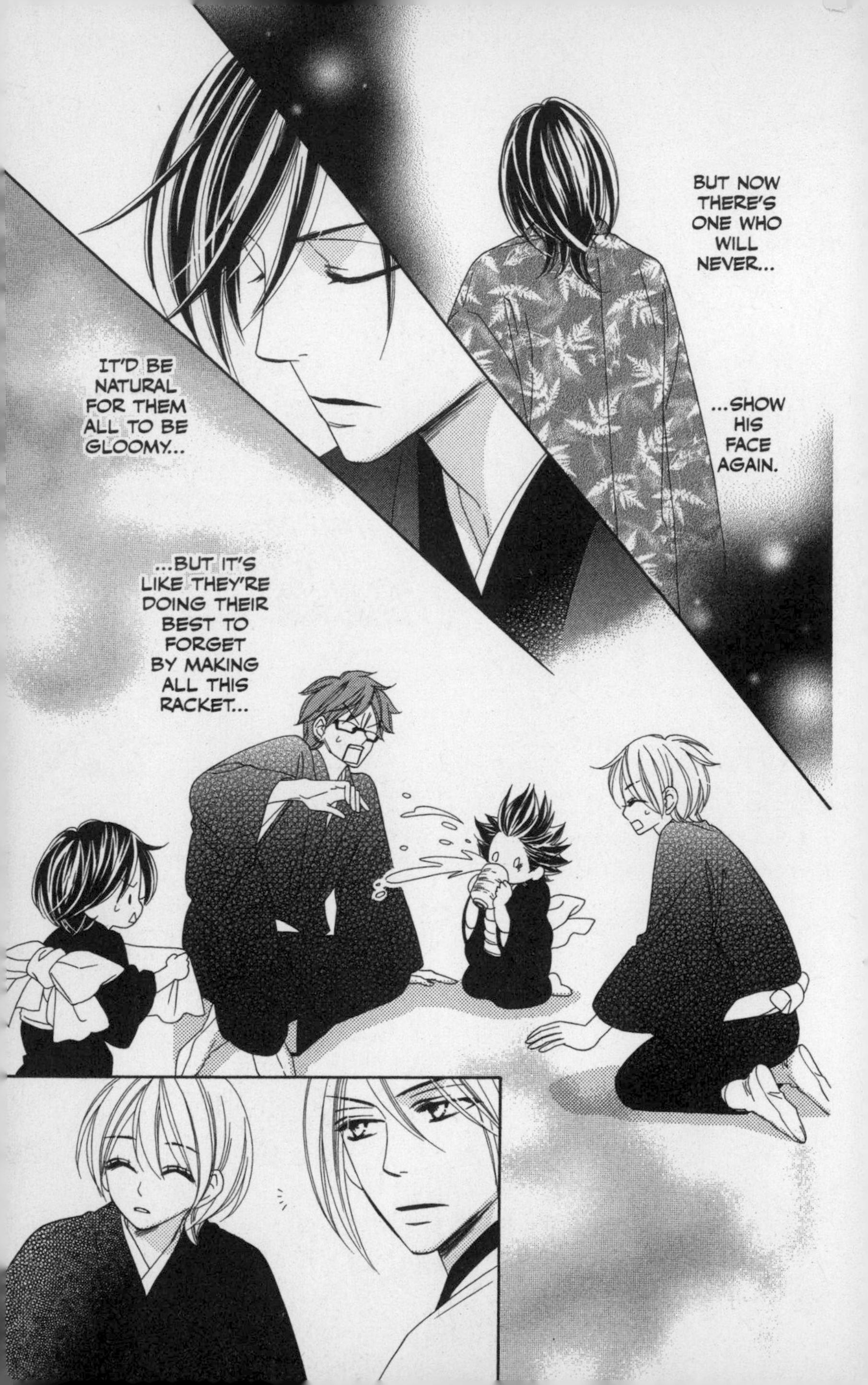
BUT NOW THERE'S ONE WHO WILL NEVER...
...SHOW HIS FACE AGAIN.
IT'D BE NATURAL FOR THEM ALL TO BE GLOOMY...
...BUT IT'S LIKE THEY'RE DOING THEIR BEST TO FORGET BY MAKING ALL THIS RACKET...

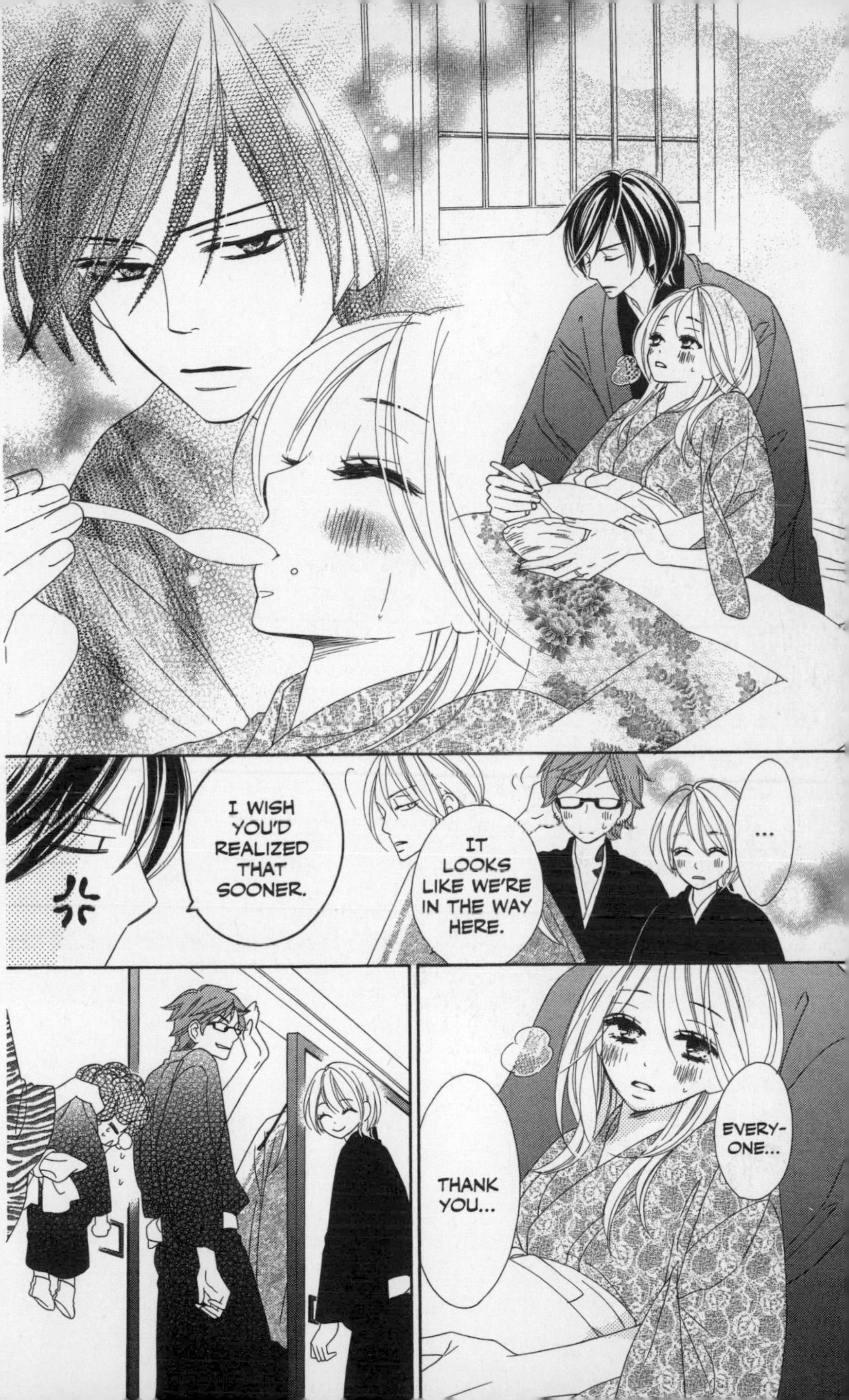
...
IT LOOKS LIKE WE'RE IN THE WAY HERE.
I WISH YOU'D REALIZED THAT SOONER.
EVERY-ONE...
THANK YOU...

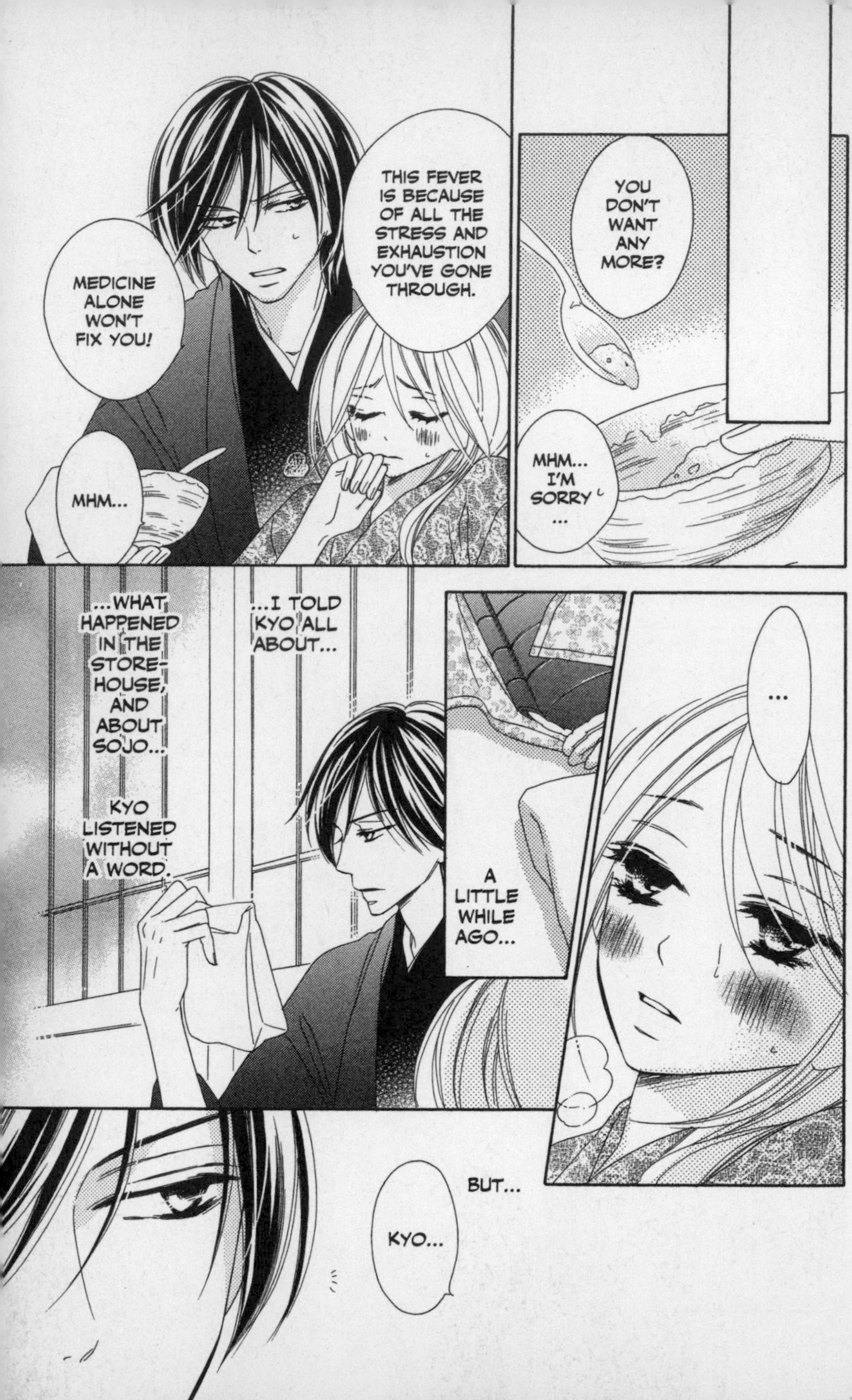
YOU DON'T WANT ANY MORE?
MHM... I'M SORRY ...
THIS FEVER IS BECAUSE OF ALL THE STRESS AND EXHAUSTION YOU'VE GONE THROUGH.
MEDICINE ALONE WON'T FIX YOU!
MHM...
...
A LITTLE WHILE AGO...
...I TOLD KYO ALL ABOUT...
...WHAT HAPPENED IN THE STORE-HOUSE, AND ABOUT SOJO...
KYO LISTENED WITHOUT A WORD.
BUT...
KYO...

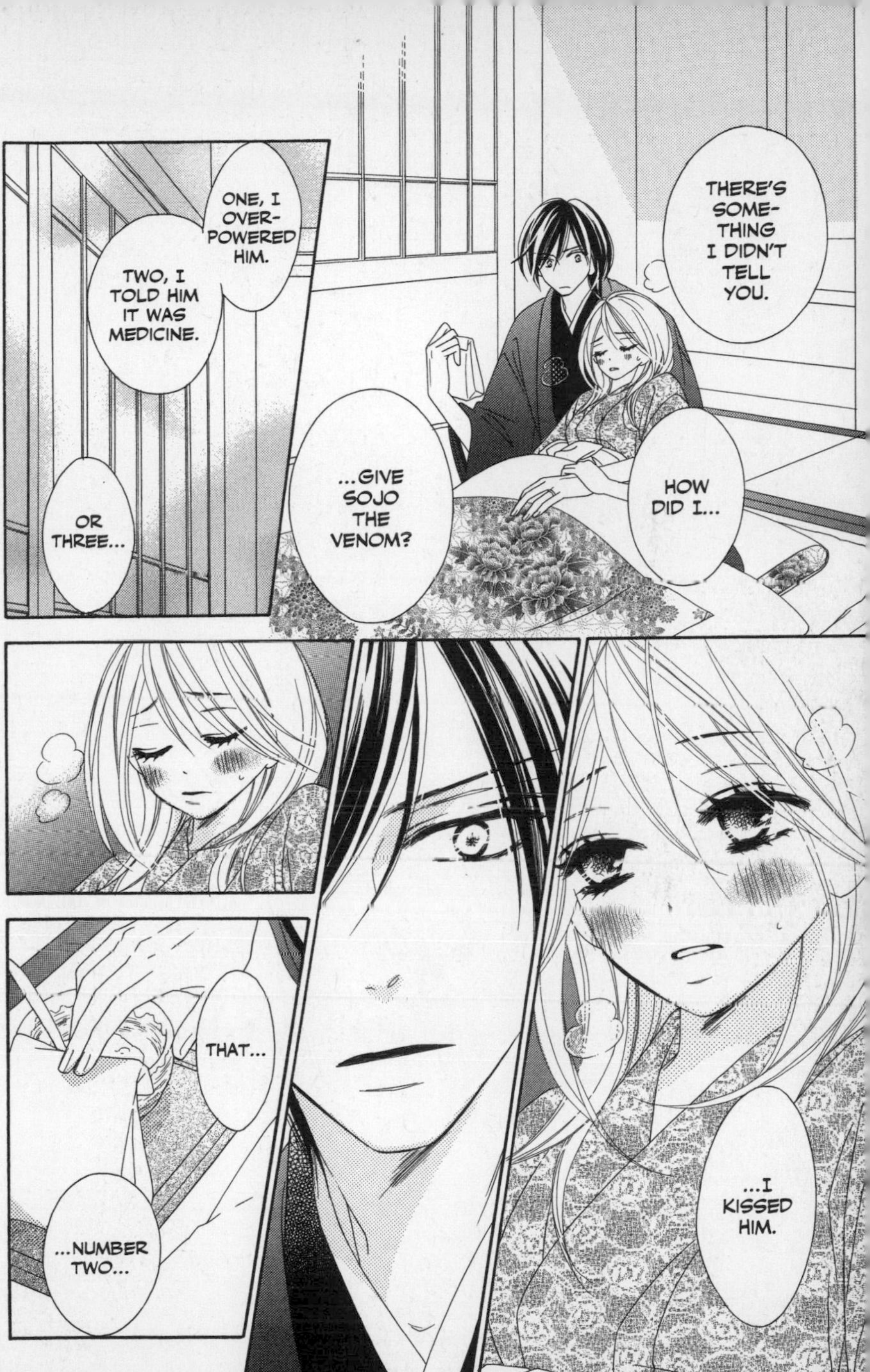
THERE'S SOME-THING I DIDN'T TELL YOU.
HOW DID I...
...GIVE SOJO THE VENOM?
ONE, I OVER-POWERED HIM.
TWO, I TOLD HIM IT WAS MEDICINE.
OR THREE...
...I KISSED HIM.
THAT...
...NUMBER TWO...

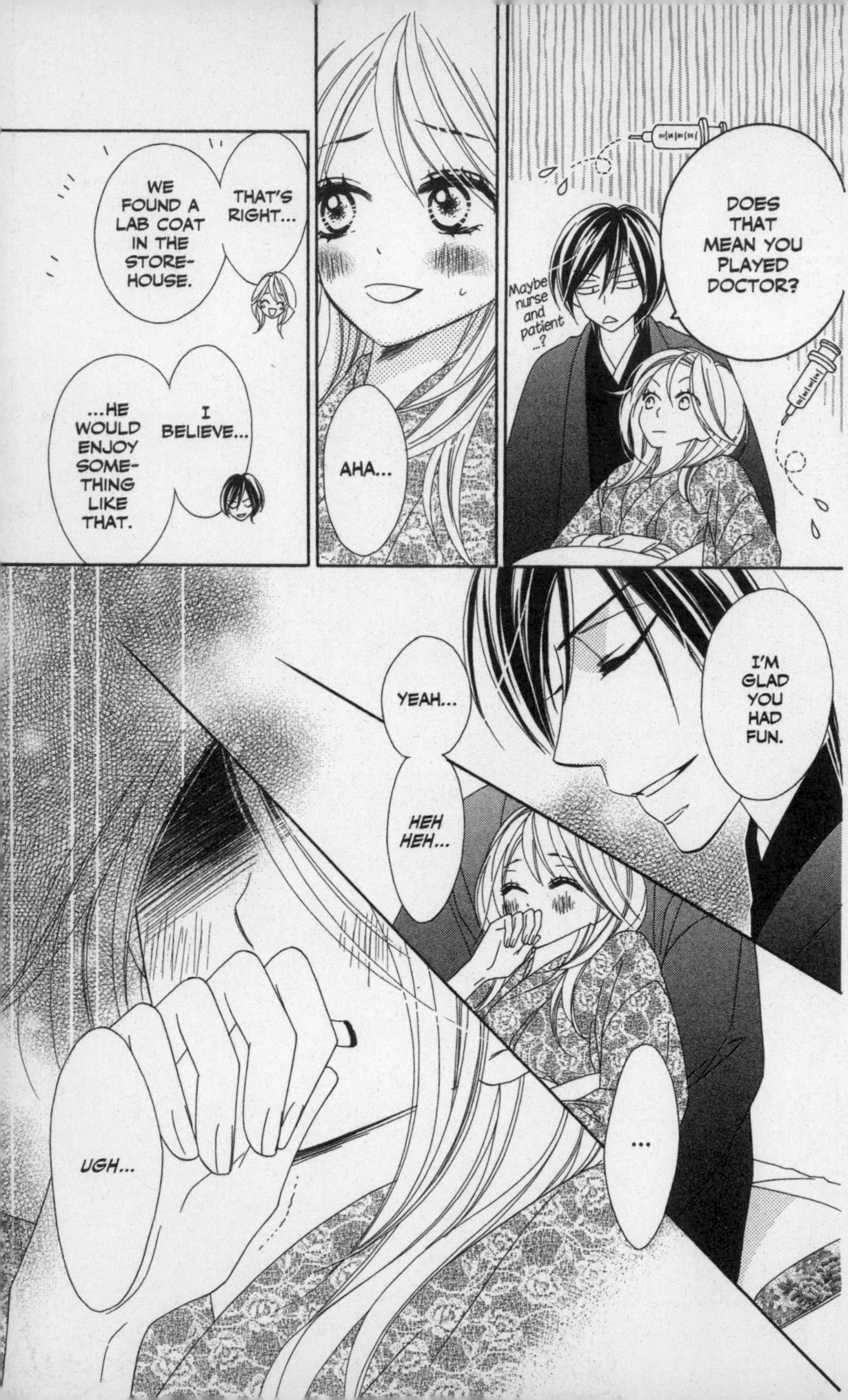
DOES THAT MEAN YOU PLAYED DOCTOR?
Maybe nurse and patient ...?
AHA...
THAT'S RIGHT...
WE FOUND A LAB COAT IN THE STORE-HOUSE.
I BELIEVE...
...HE WOULD ENJOY SOME-THING LIKE THAT.
I'M GLAD YOU HAD FUN.
YEAH...
HEH HEH...
...
UGH...

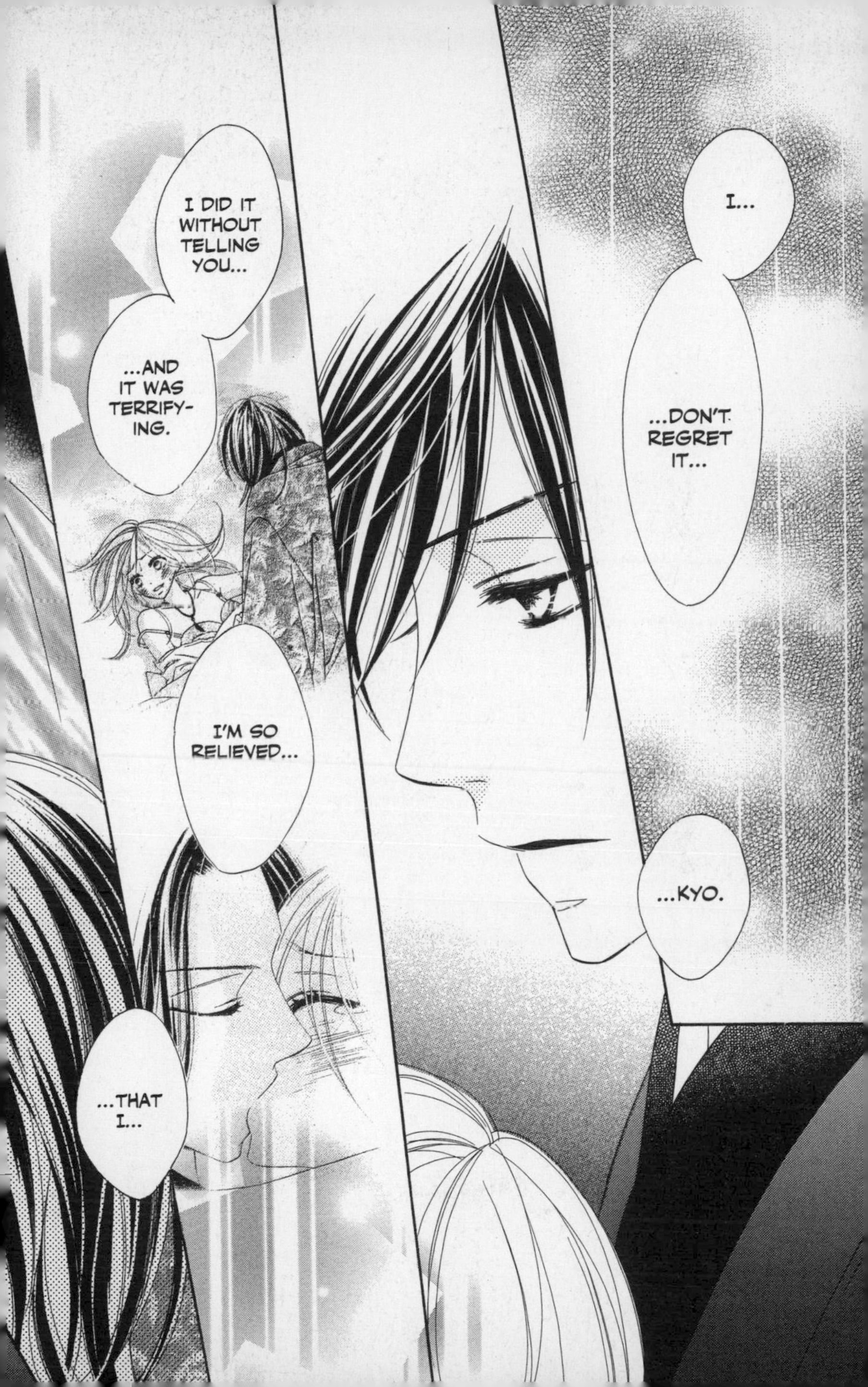
I...
...DON'T REGRET IT...
...KYO.
I DID IT WITHOUT TELLING YOU...
...AND IT WAS TERRIFY-ING.
I'M SO RELIEVED...
...THAT I...

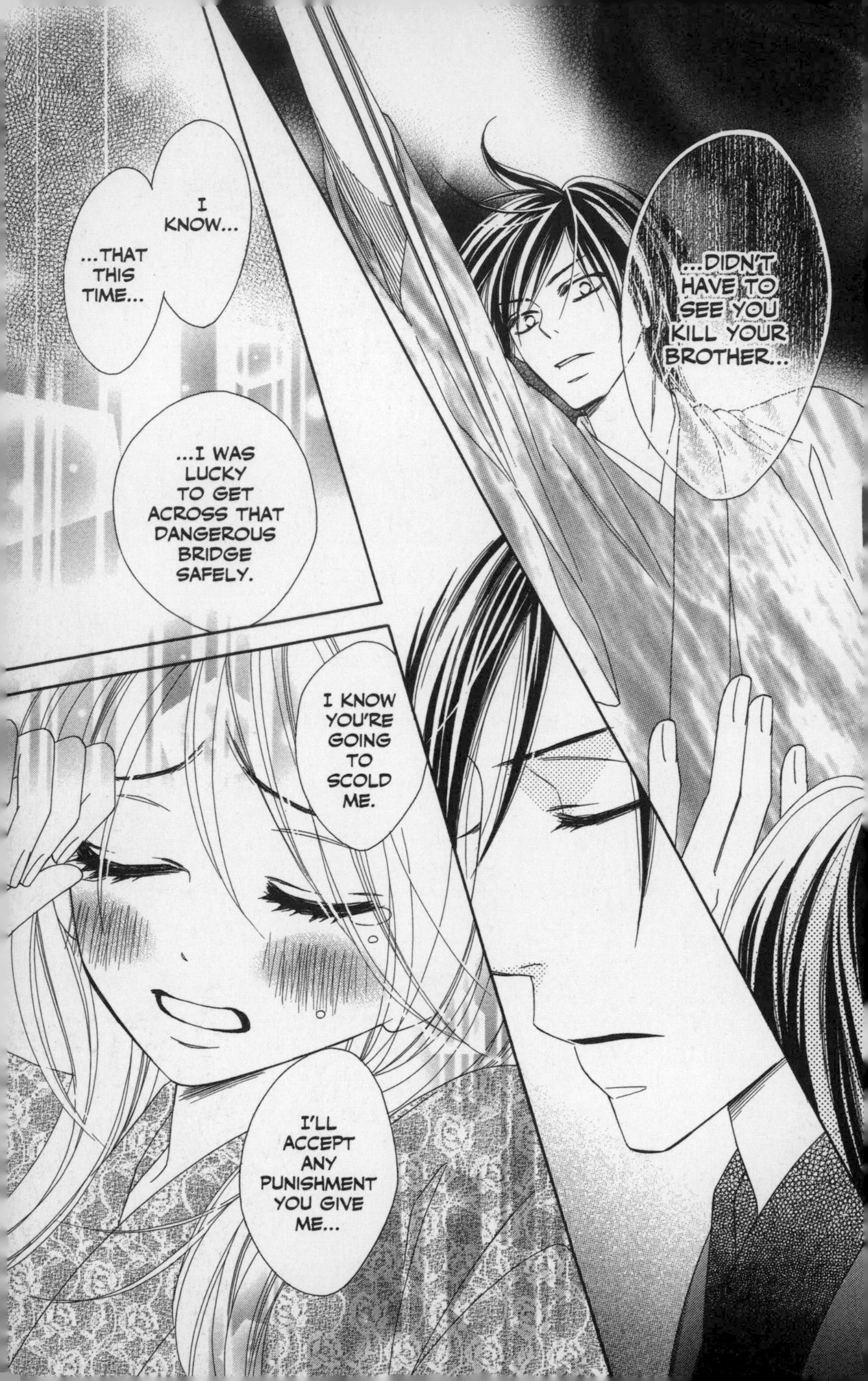
...DIDN'T HAVE TO SEE YOU KILL YOUR BROTHER...
I KNOW...
...THAT THIS TIME...
...I WAS LUCKY TO GET ACROSS THAT DANGEROUS BRIDGE SAFELY.
I KNOW YOU'RE GOING TO SCOLD ME.
I'LL ACCEPT ANY PUNISHMENT YOU GIVE ME...

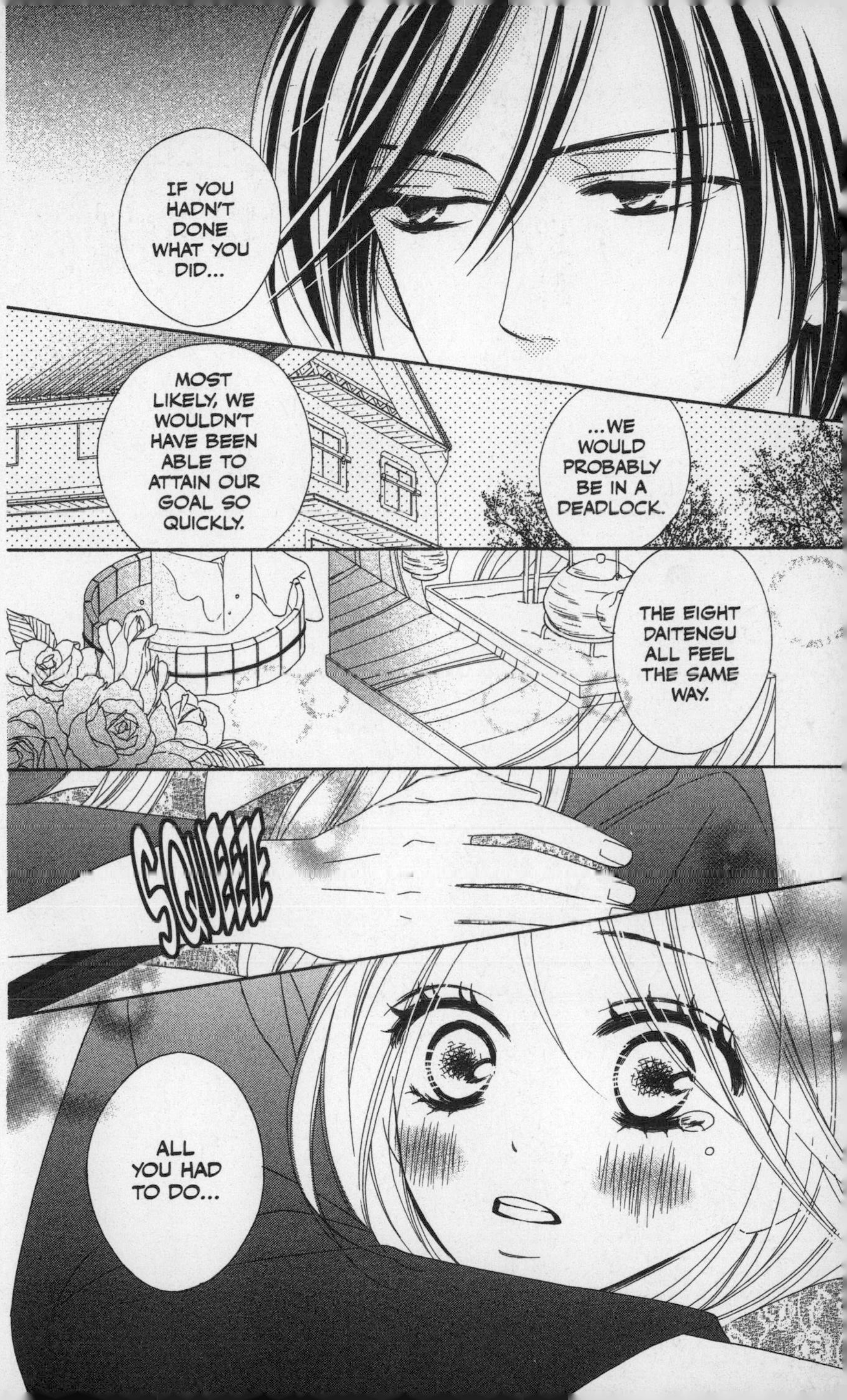
IF YOU HADN'T DONE WHAT YOU DID...
...WE WOULD PROBABLY BE IN A DEADLOCK.
MOST LIKELY, WE WOULDN'T HAVE BEEN ABLE TO ATTAIN OUR GOAL SO QUICKLY.
THE EIGHT DAITENGU ALL FEEL THE SAME WAY.
SQUEEZE
ALL YOU HAD TO DO...

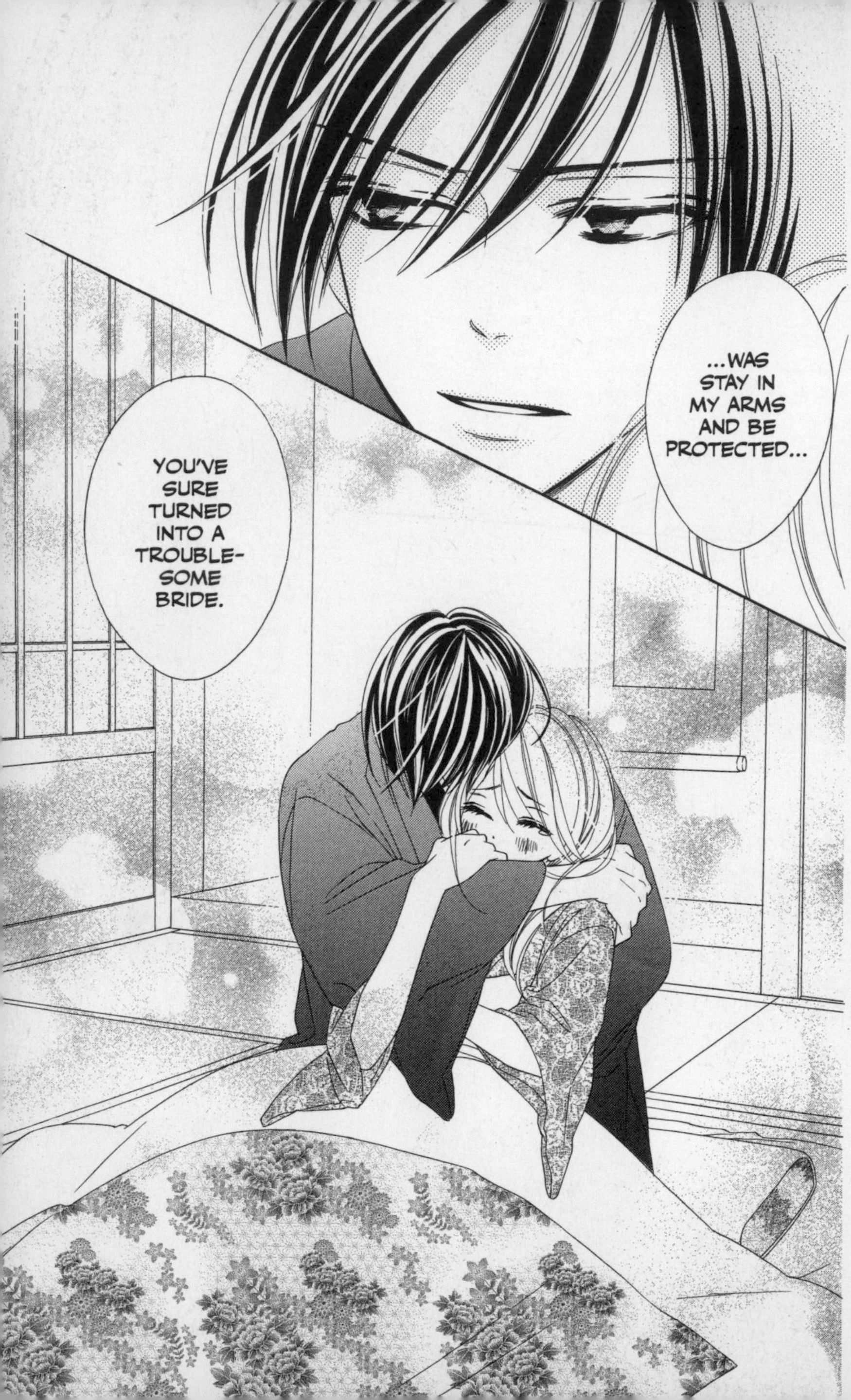
...WAS STAY IN MY ARMS AND BE PROTECTED...
YOU'VE SURE TURNED INTO A TROUBLE-SOME BRIDE.

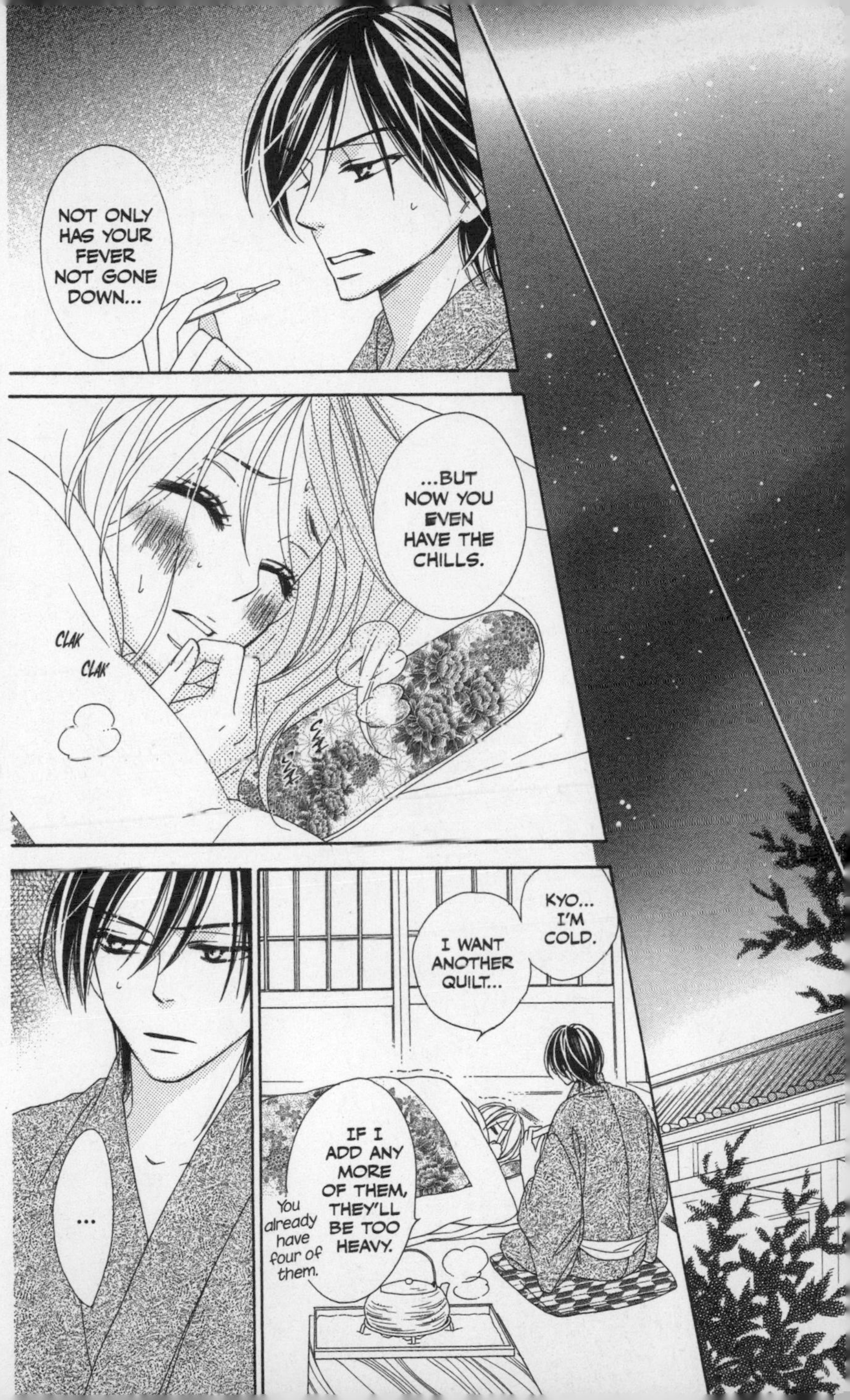
NOT ONLY HAS YOUR FEVER NOT GONE DOWN...
...BUT NOW YOU EVEN HAVE THE CHILLS.
CLAK
CLAK
KYO... I'M COLD.
I WANT ANOTHER QUILT...
IF I ADD ANY MORE OF THEM, THEY'LL BE TOO HEAVY.
You already have four of them.
...

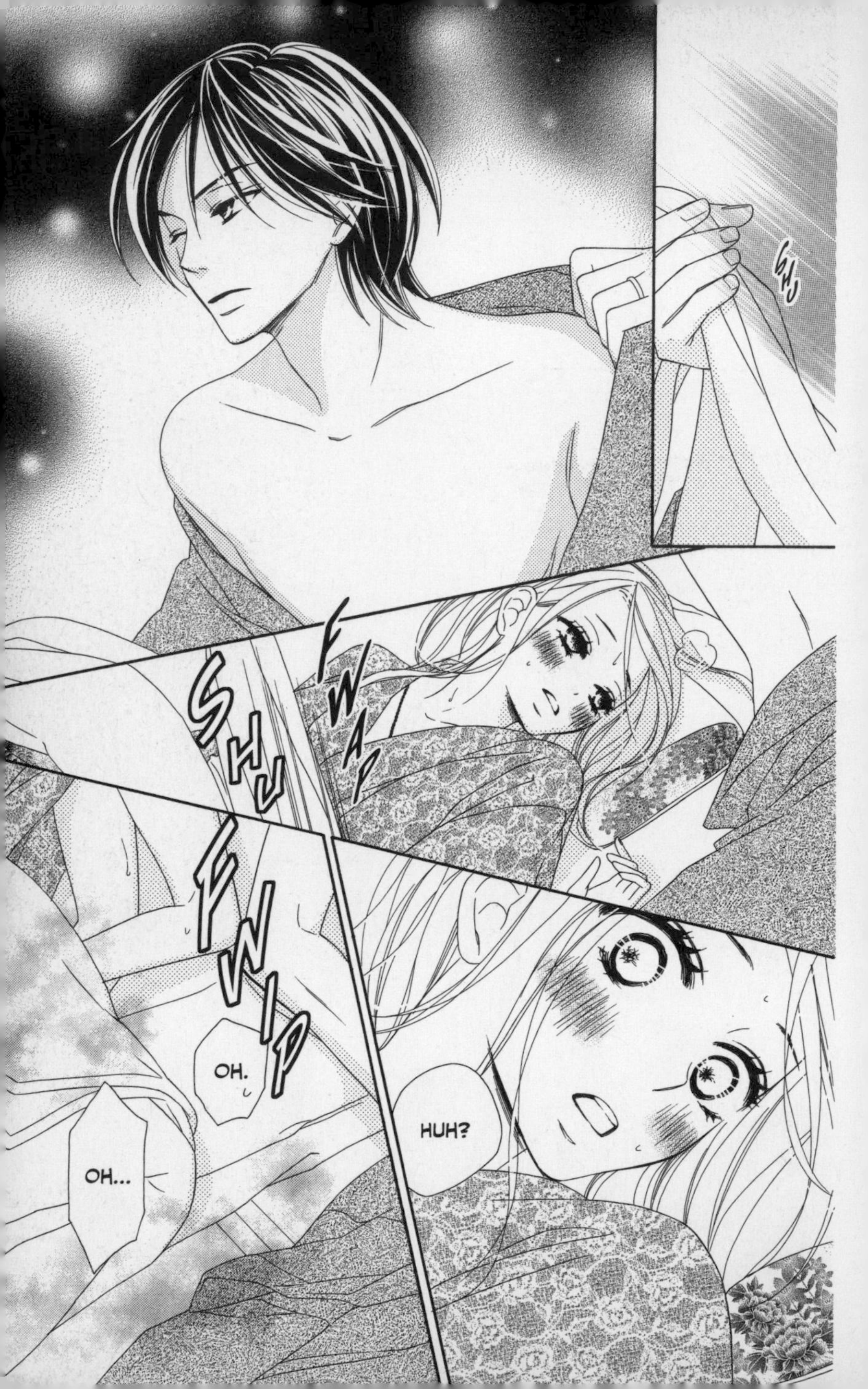
SHU
FWAP
SHU
FWIP
HUH?
OH.
OH...

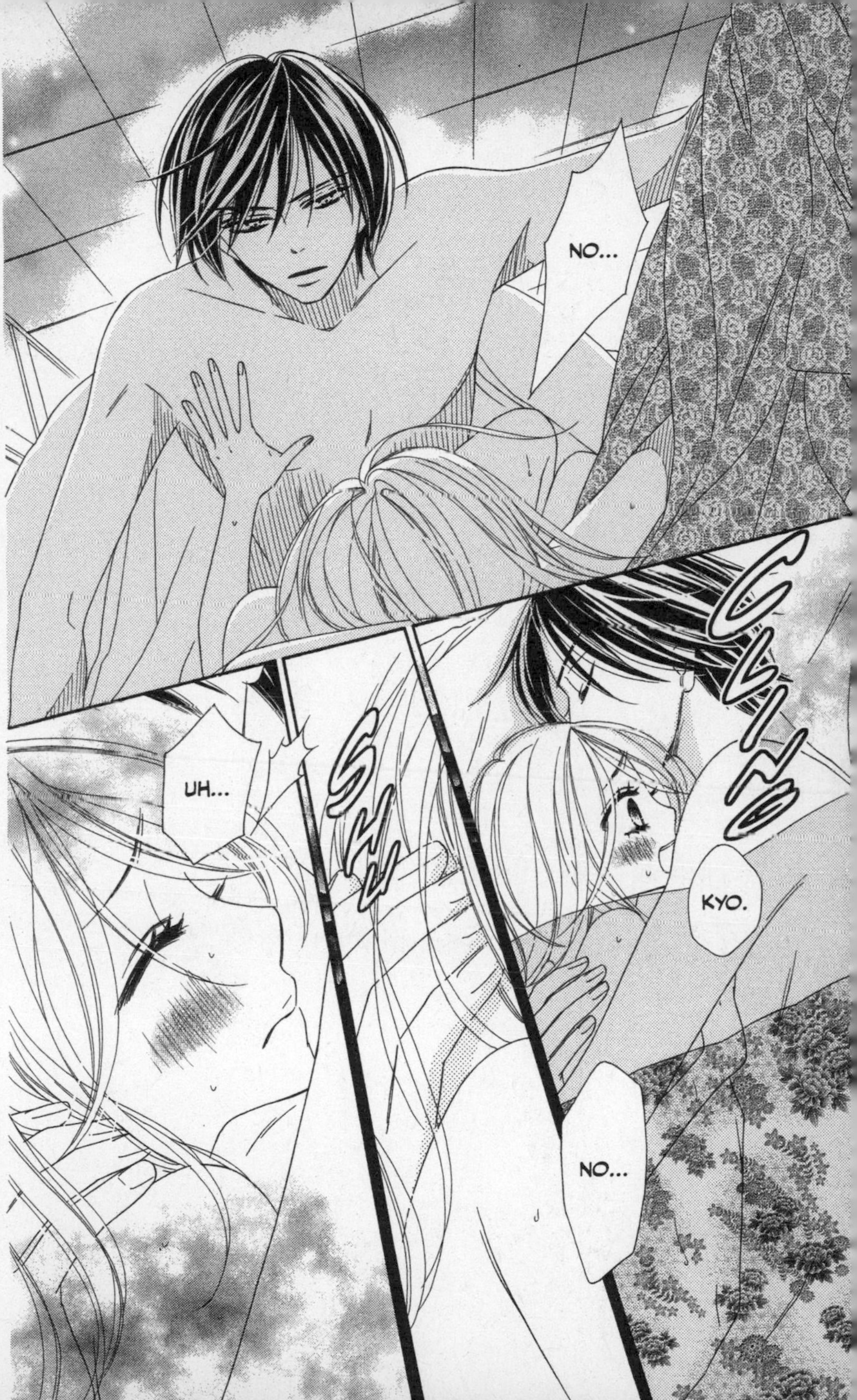
NO...
CLING
KYO.
NO...
UH...

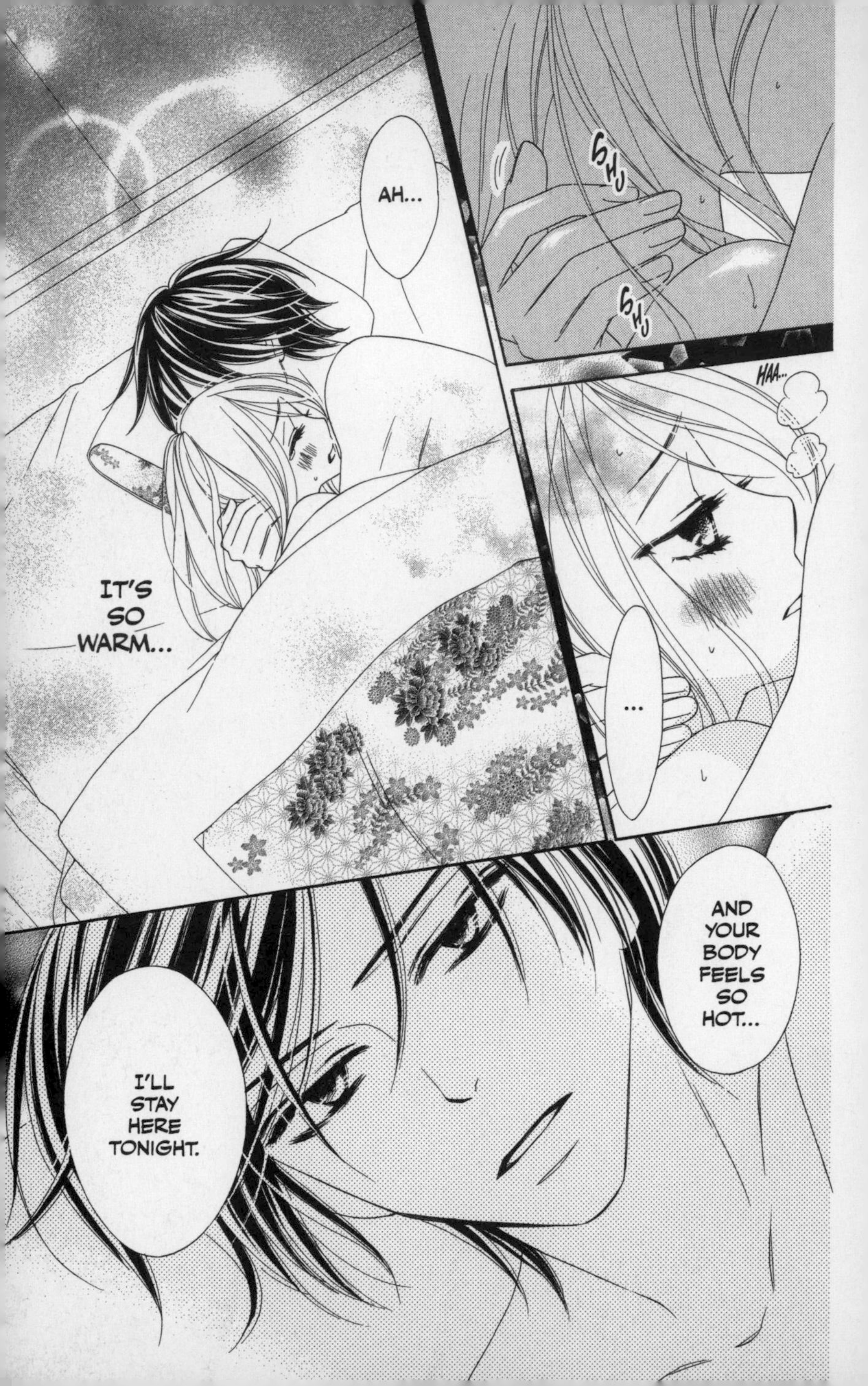
SHU
SHU
HAA...
...
AH...
IT'S SO WARM...
AND YOUR BODY FEELS SO HOT...
I'LL STAY HERE TONIGHT.

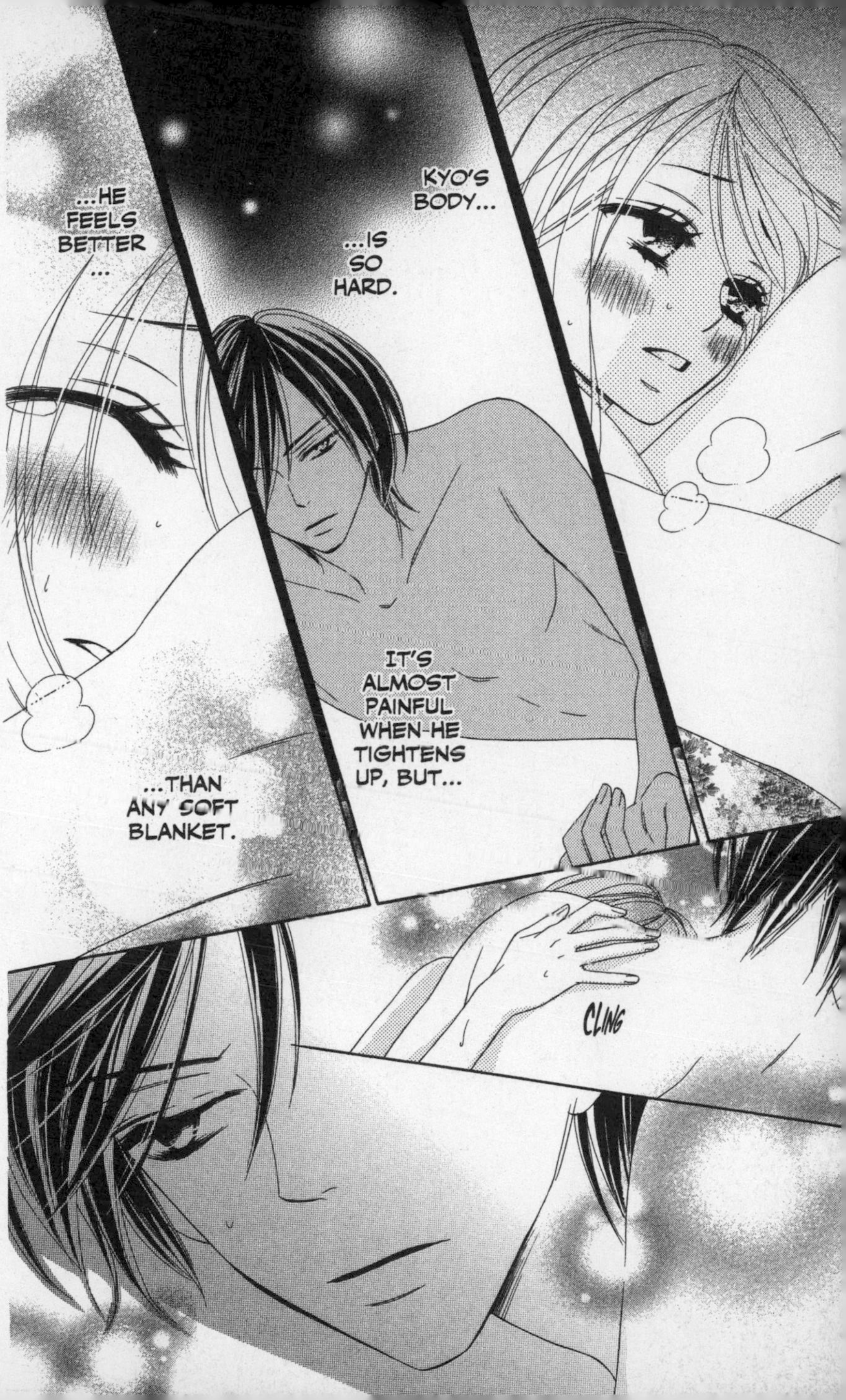
KYO'S BODY...
...IS SO HARD.
...HE FEELS BETTER ...
IT'S ALMOST PAINFUL WHEN HE TIGHTENS UP, BUT...
...THAN ANY SOFT BLANKET.
CLING

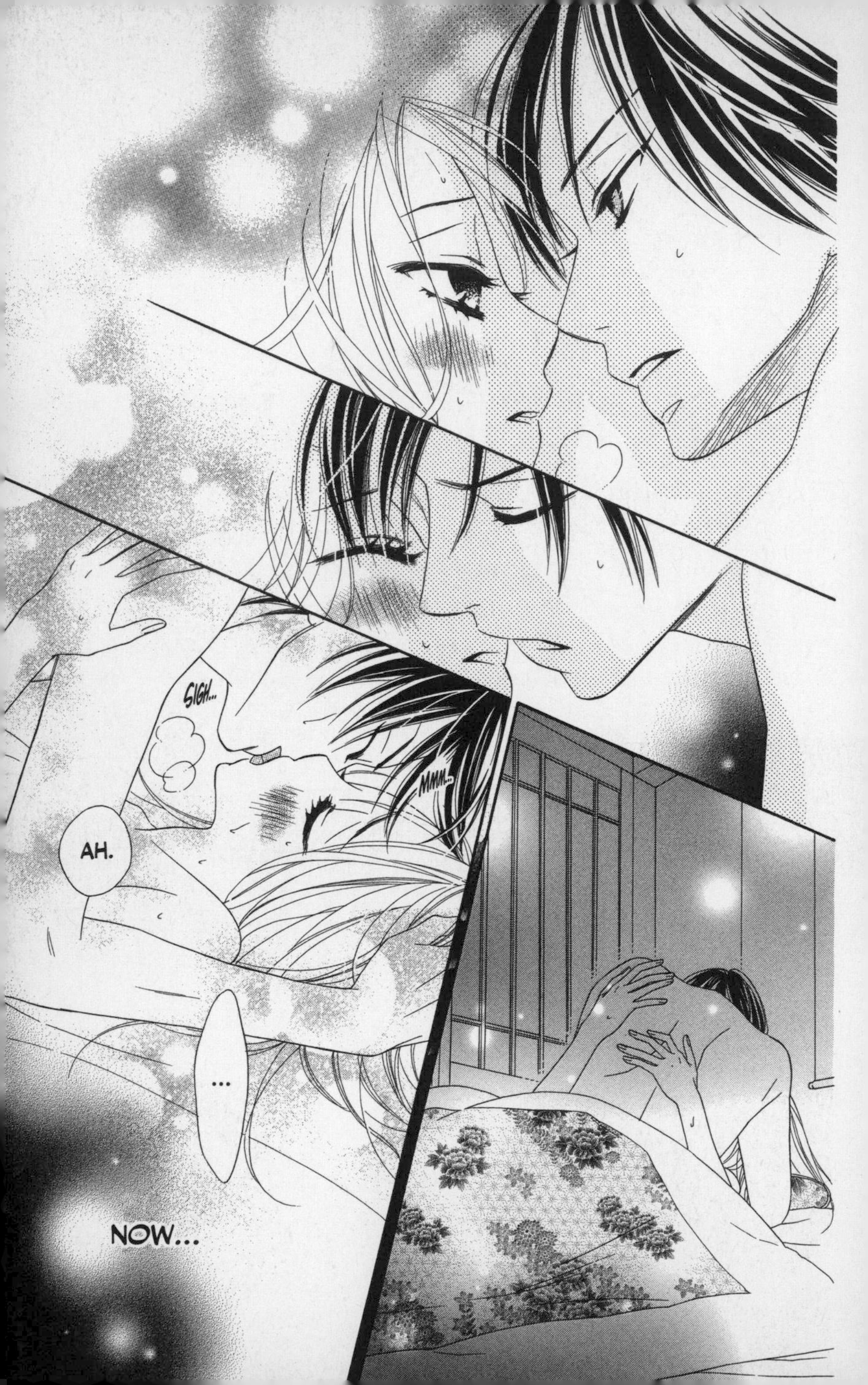
MMM...
SIGH...
AH.
...
NOW...

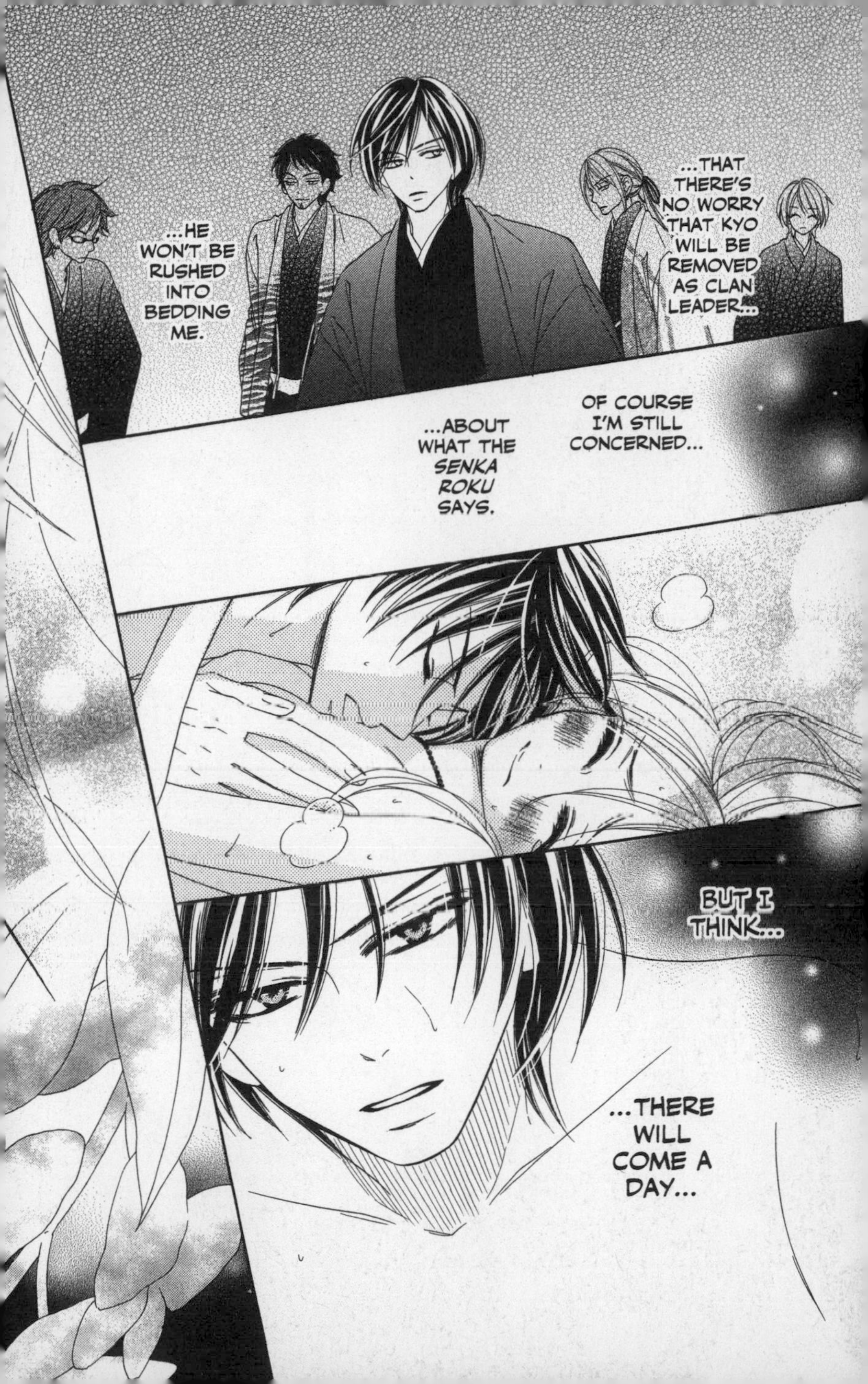
...THAT THERE'S NO WORRY THAT KYO WILL BE REMOVED AS CLAN LEADER...
...HE WON'T BE RUSHED INTO BEDDING ME.
OF COURSE I'M STILL CONCERNED...
...ABOUT WHAT THE SENKA ROKU SAYS.
BUT I THINK...
...THERE WILL COME A DAY...

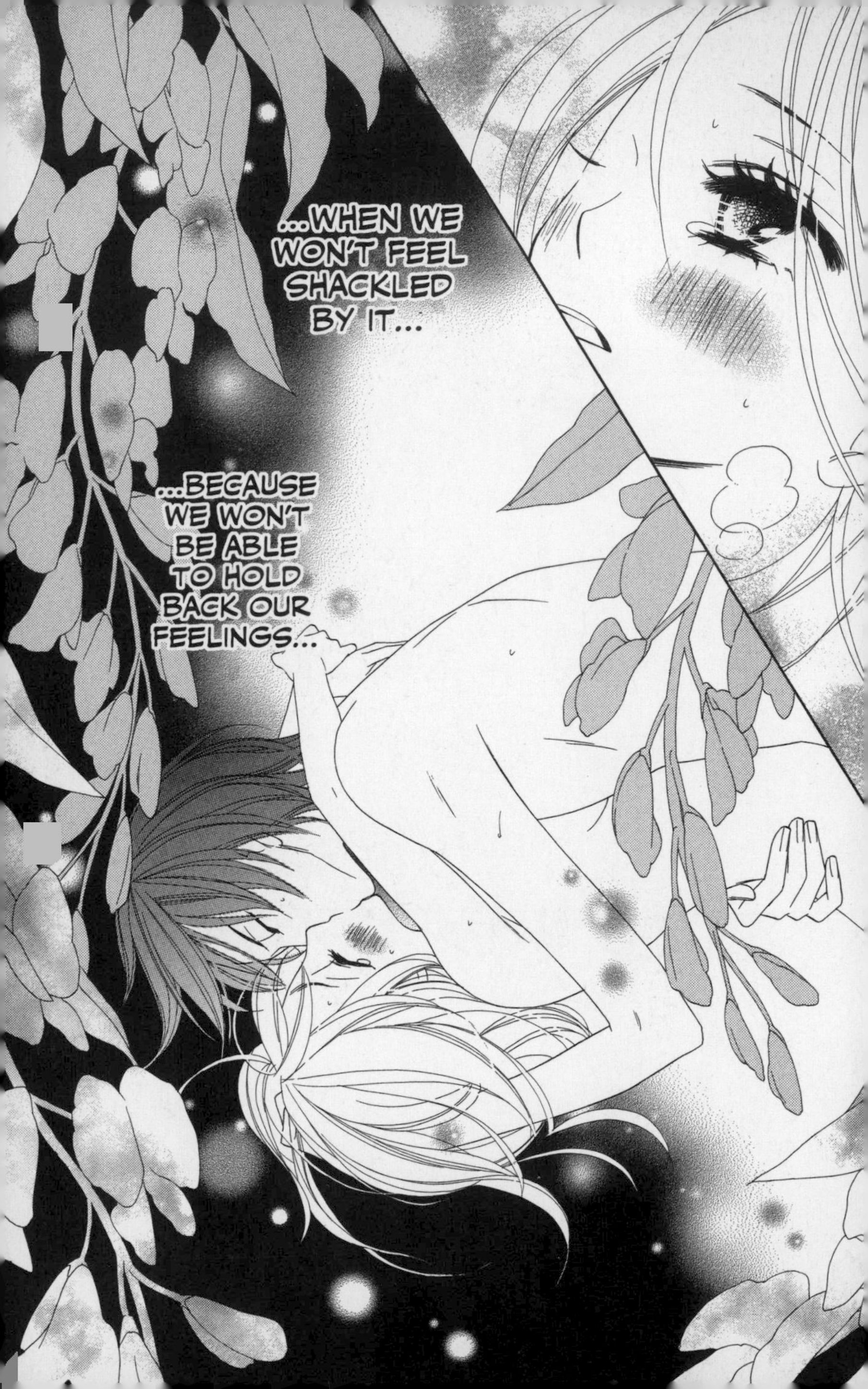
...WHEN WE WON'T FEEL SHACKLED BY IT...
...BECAUSE WE WON'T BE ABLE TO HOLD BACK OUR FEELINGS...

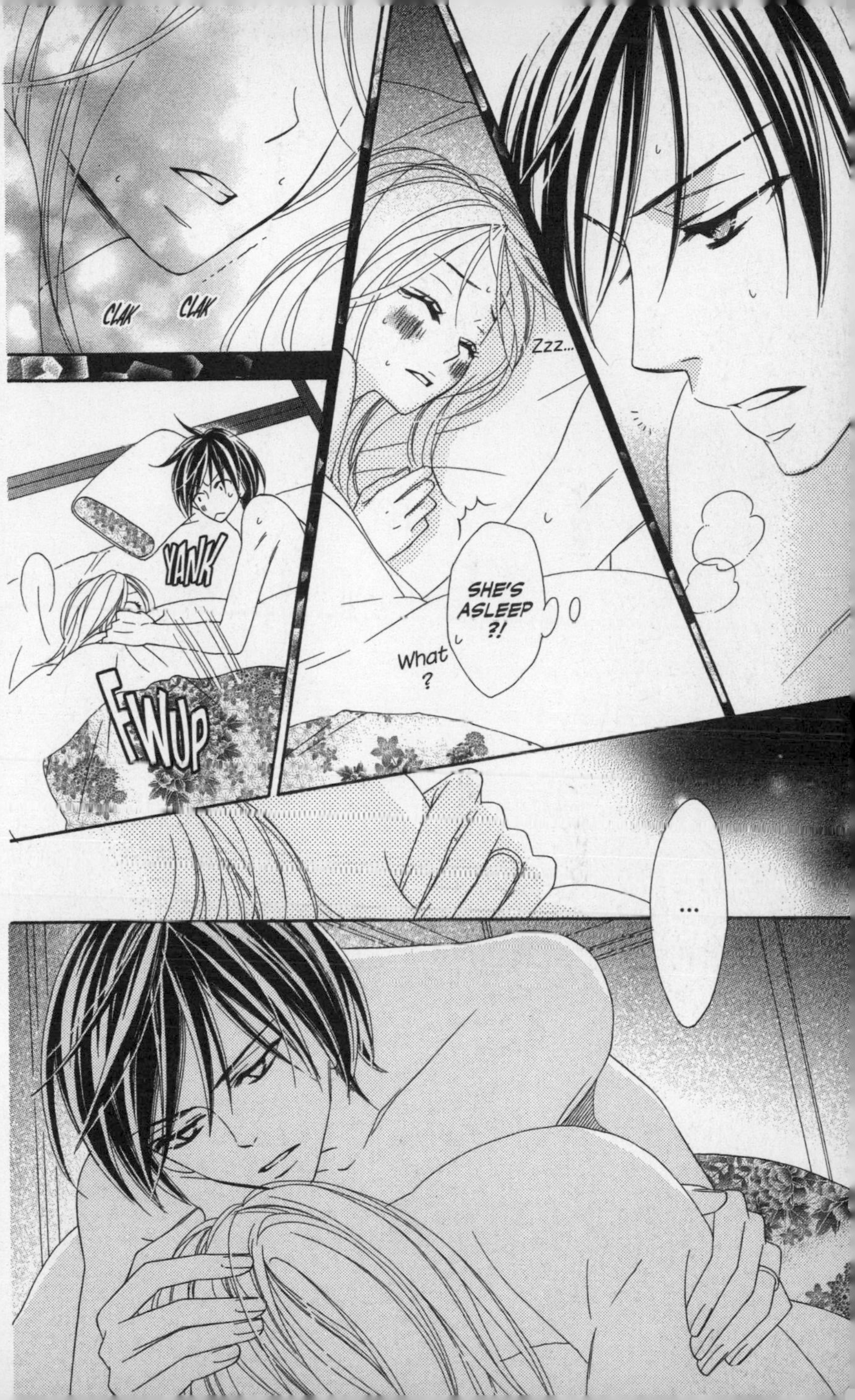
Zzz...
SHE'S ASLEEP ?!
What ?
CLAK
CLAK
YANK!
FWUP
...

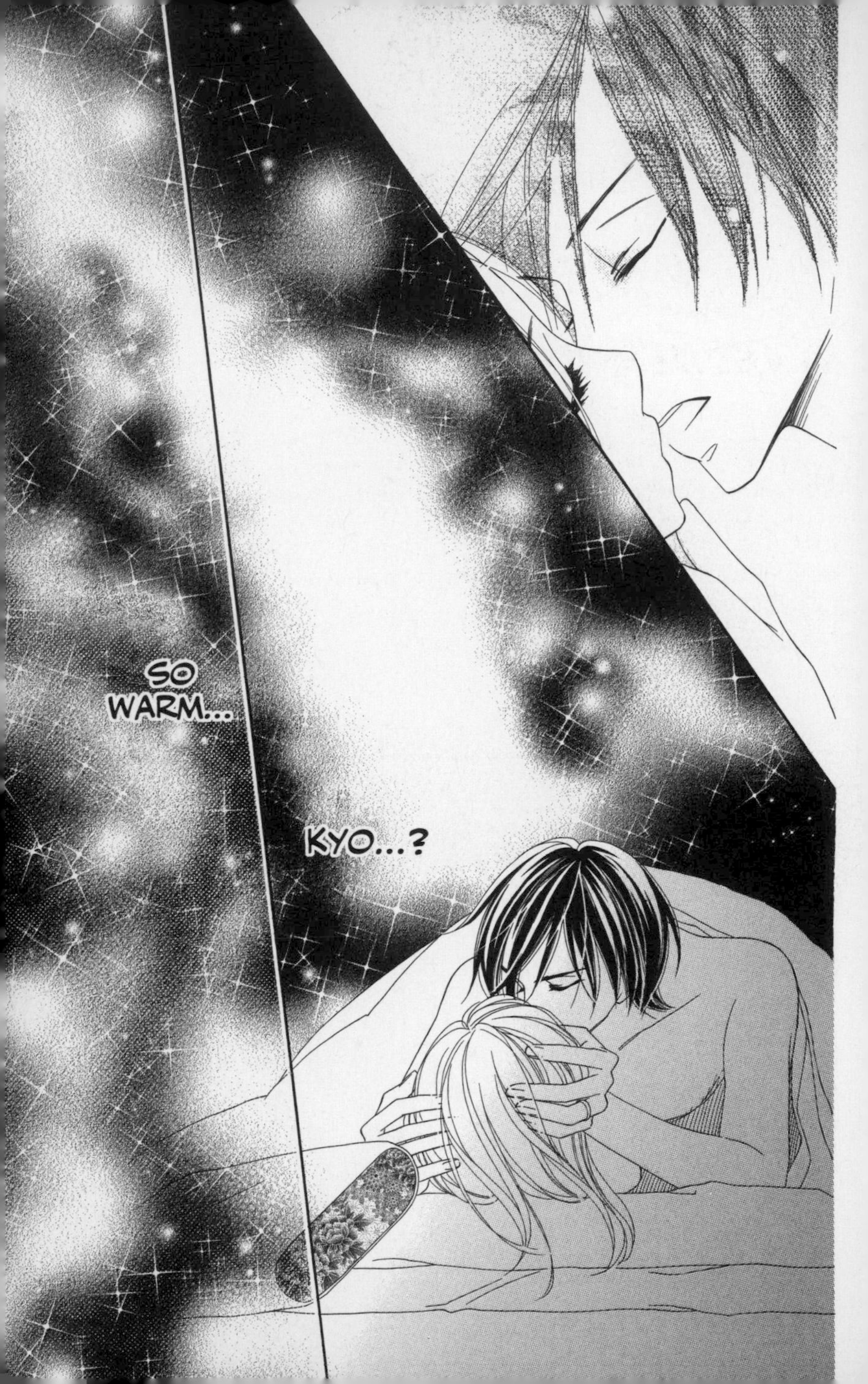
KYO...?
SO WARM...

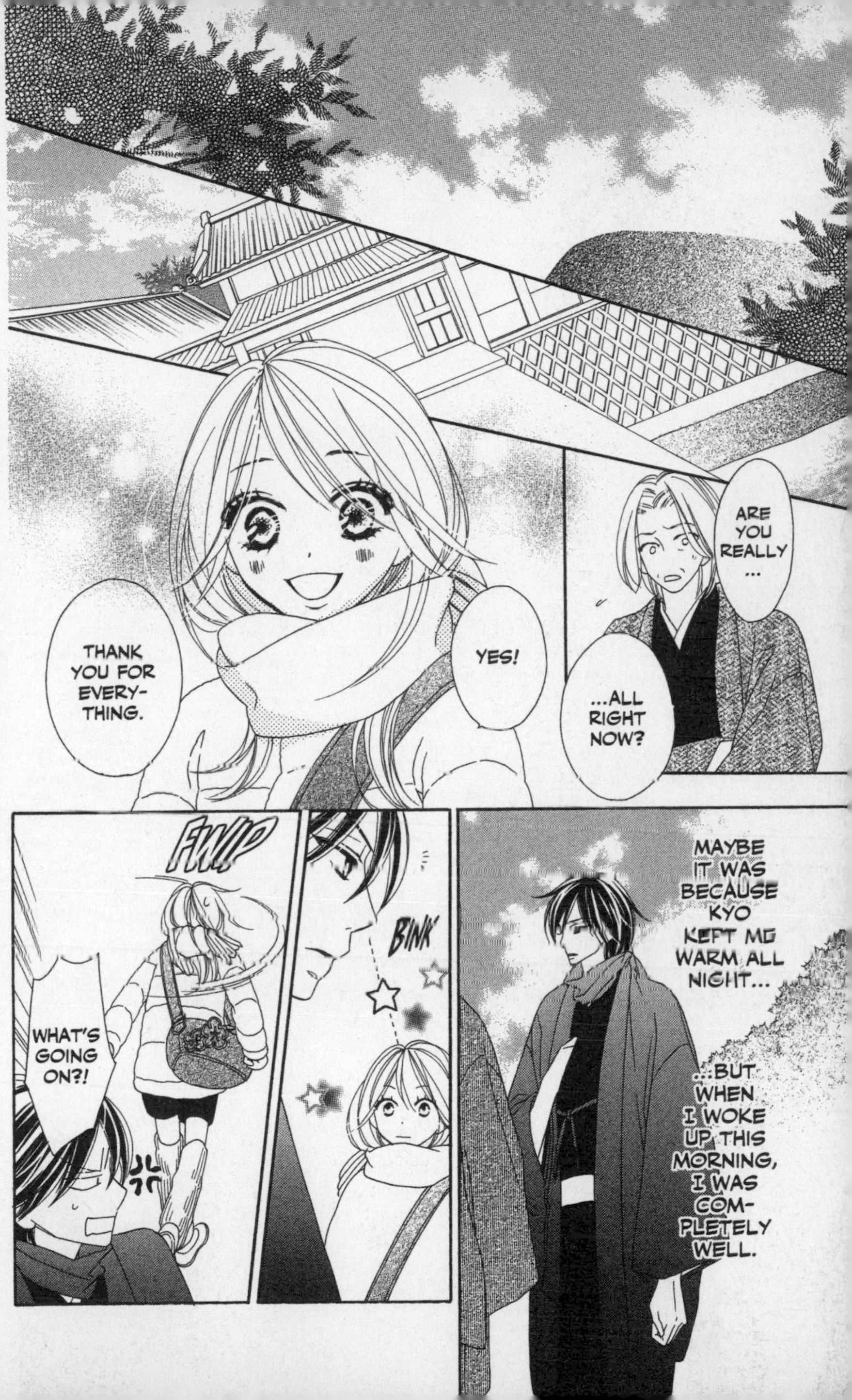
ARE YOU REALLY...
...ALL RIGHT NOW?
YES!
THANK YOU FOR EVERY-THING.
MAYBE IT WAS BECAUSE KYO KEPT ME WARM ALL NIGHT...
...BUT WHEN I WOKE UP THIS MORNING, I WAS COM-PLETELY WELL.
BINK
FWIP
WHAT'S GOING ON?!

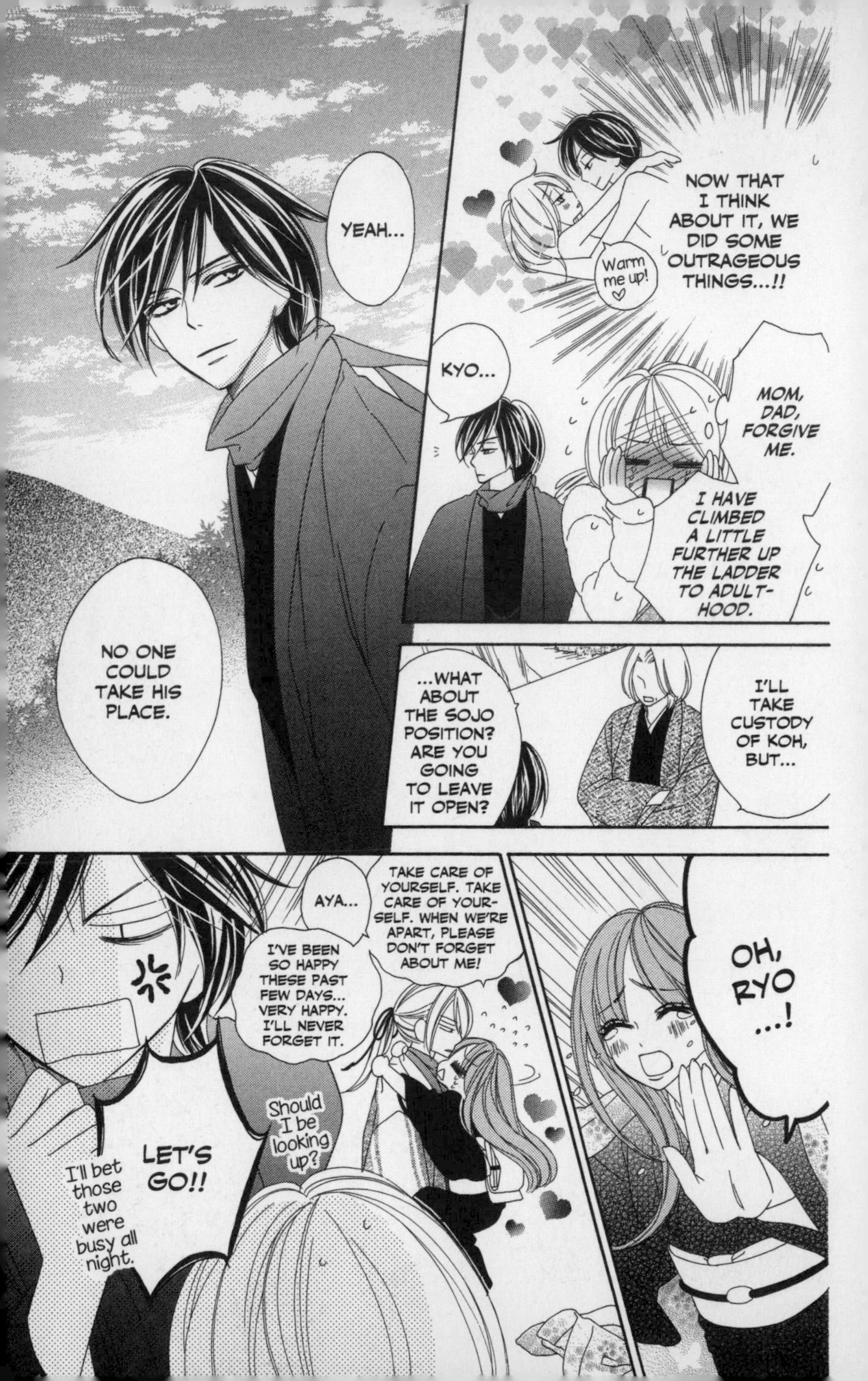
NOW THAT I THINK ABOUT IT, WE DID SOME OUTRAGEOUS THINGS...!!
Warm me up! ♡
MOM, DAD, FORGIVE ME.
I HAVE CLIMBED A LITTLE FURTHER UP THE LADDER TO ADULT-HOOD.
KYO...
I'LL TAKE CUSTODY OF KOH, BUT...
...WHAT ABOUT THE SOJO POSITION? ARE YOU GOING TO LEAVE IT OPEN?
YEAH...
NO ONE COULD TAKE HIS PLACE.
OH, RYO ...!
TAKE CARE OF YOURSELF. TAKE CARE OF YOUR-SELF. WHEN WE'RE APART, PLEASE DON'T FORGET ABOUT ME!
AYA...
I'VE BEEN SO HAPPY THESE PAST FEW DAYS... VERY HAPPY. I'LL NEVER FORGET IT.
Should I be looking up?
LET'S GO!!
I'll bet those two were busy all night.

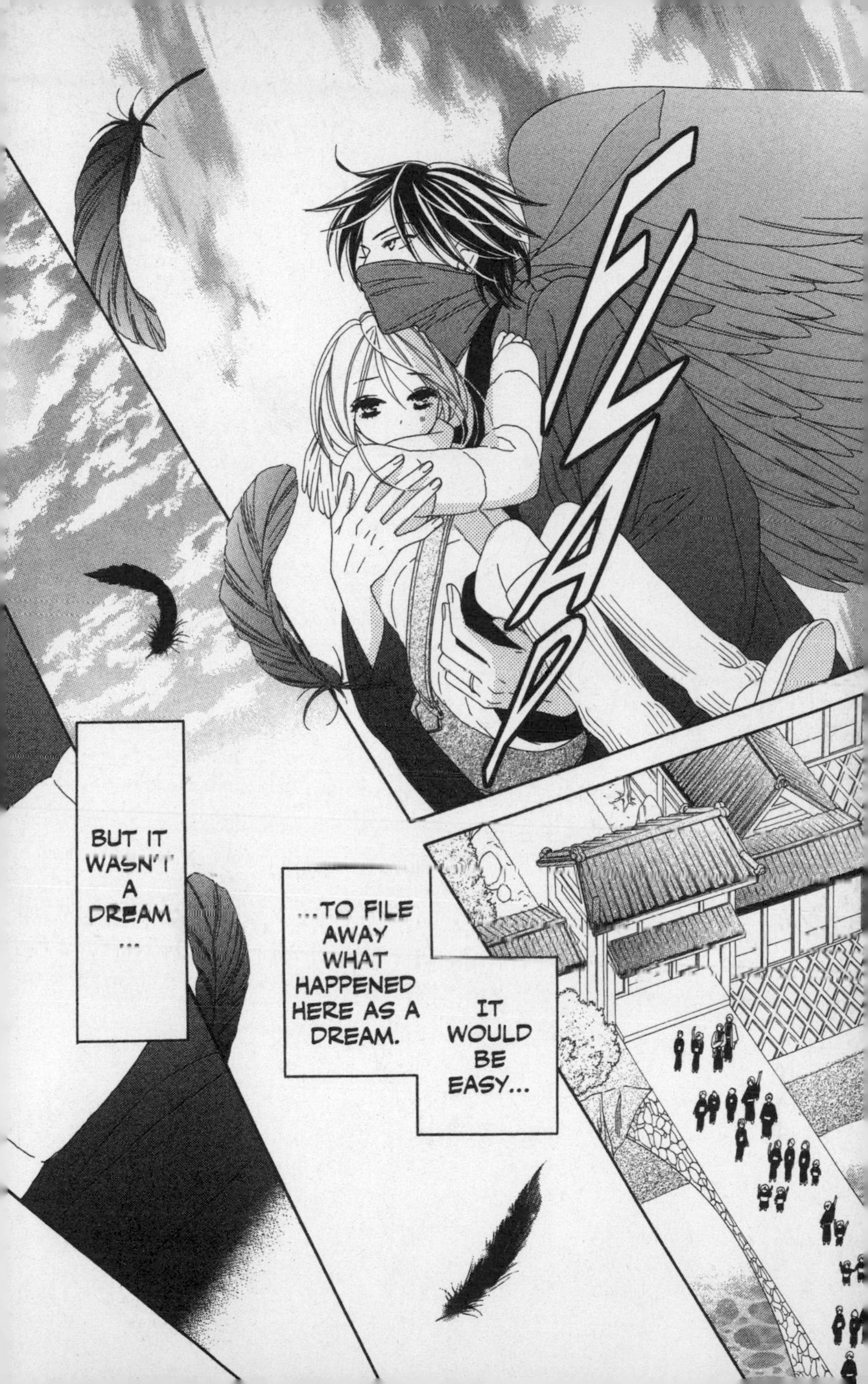
FLAP
IT WOULD BE EASY...
...TO FILE AWAY WHAT HAPPENED HERE AS A DREAM.
BUT IT WASN'T A DREAM...

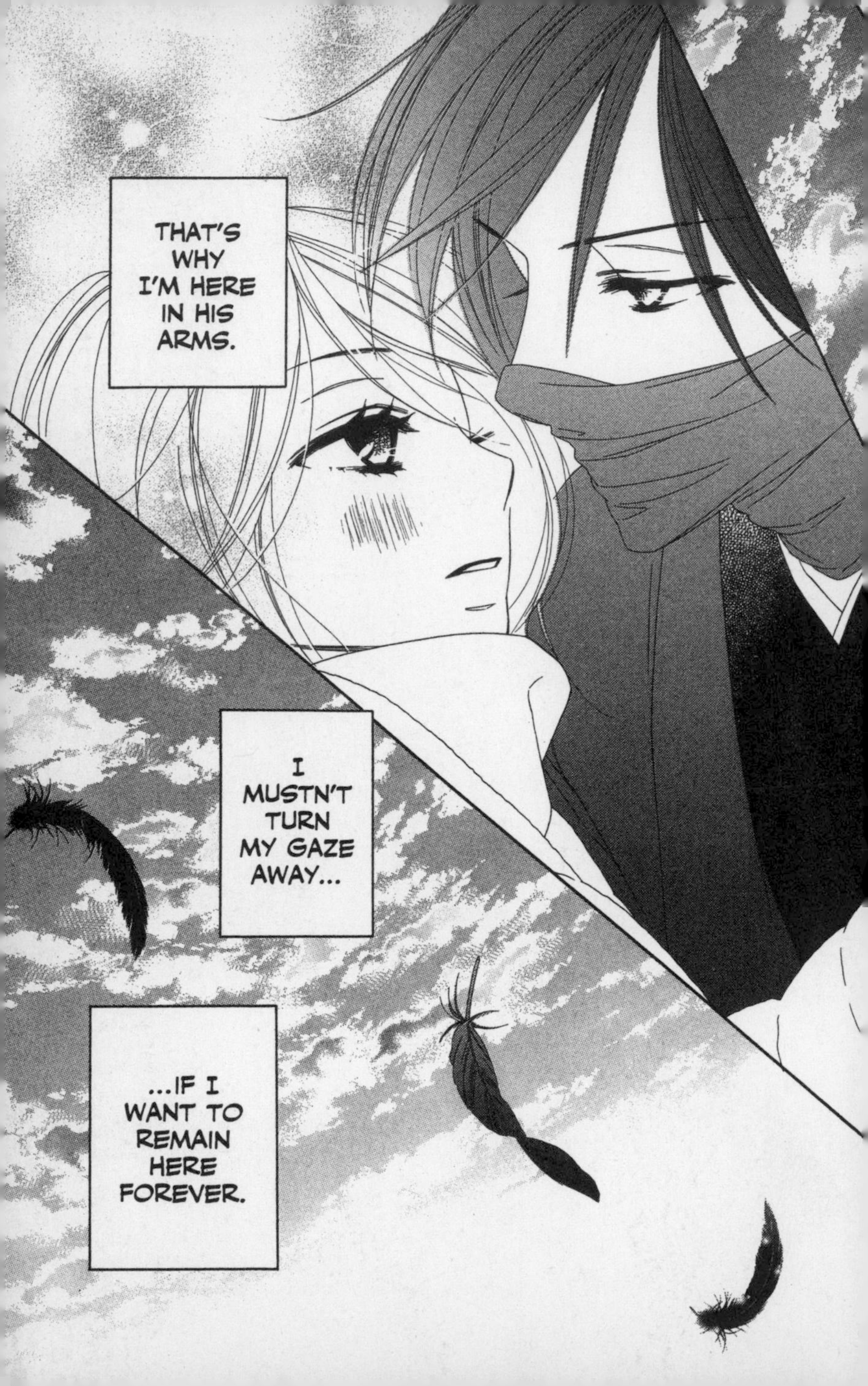
THAT'S WHY I'M HERE IN HIS ARMS.
I MUSTN'T TURN MY GAZE AWAY...
...IF I WANT TO REMAIN HERE FOREVER.

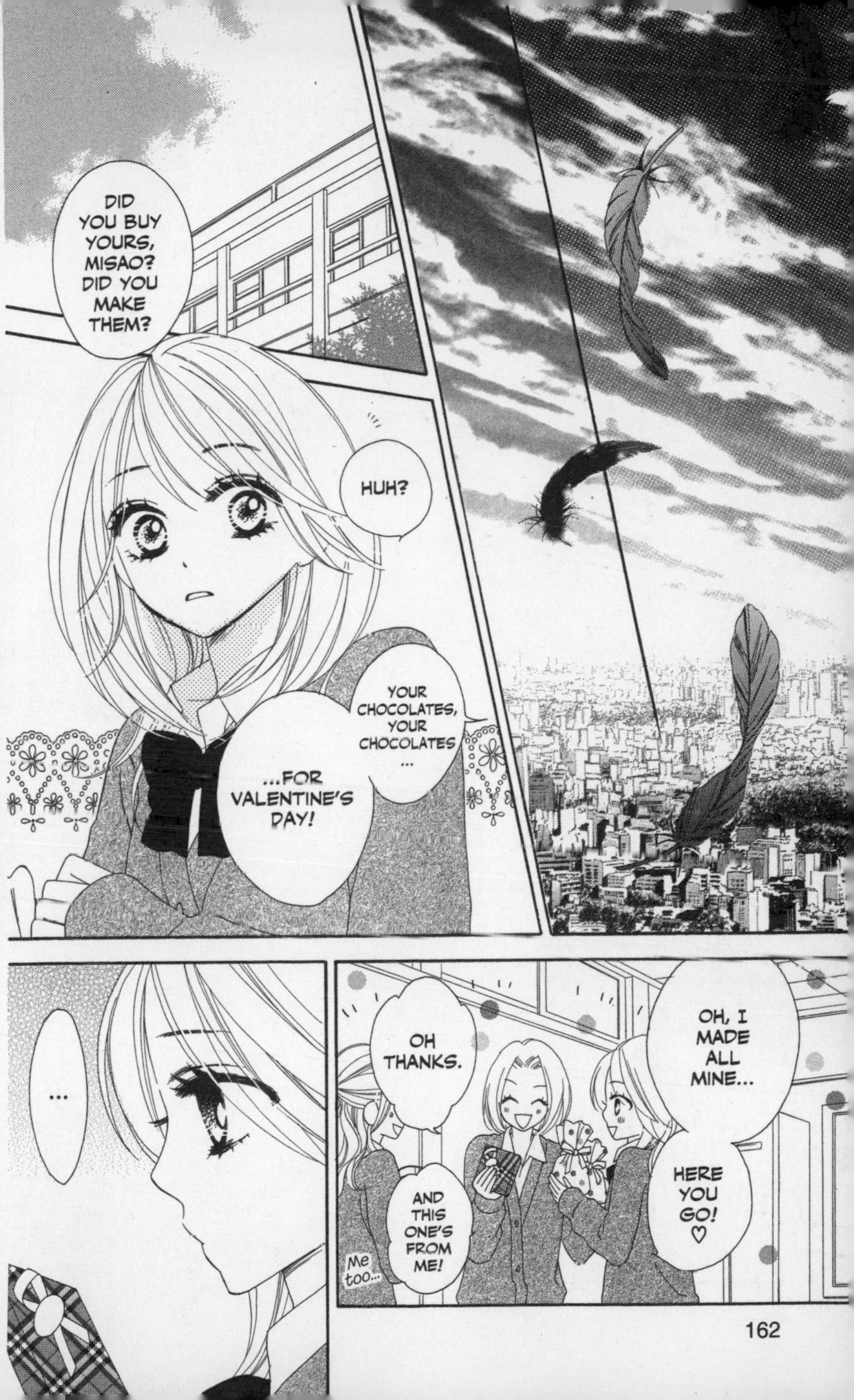
DID YOU BUY YOURS, MISAO? DID YOU MAKE THEM?
HUH?
YOUR CHOCOLATES, YOUR CHOCOLATES ...
...FOR VALENTINE'S DAY!
OH, I MADE ALL MINE...
HERE YOU GO! ♡
OH THANKS.
AND THIS ONE'S FROM ME!
Me too...
...

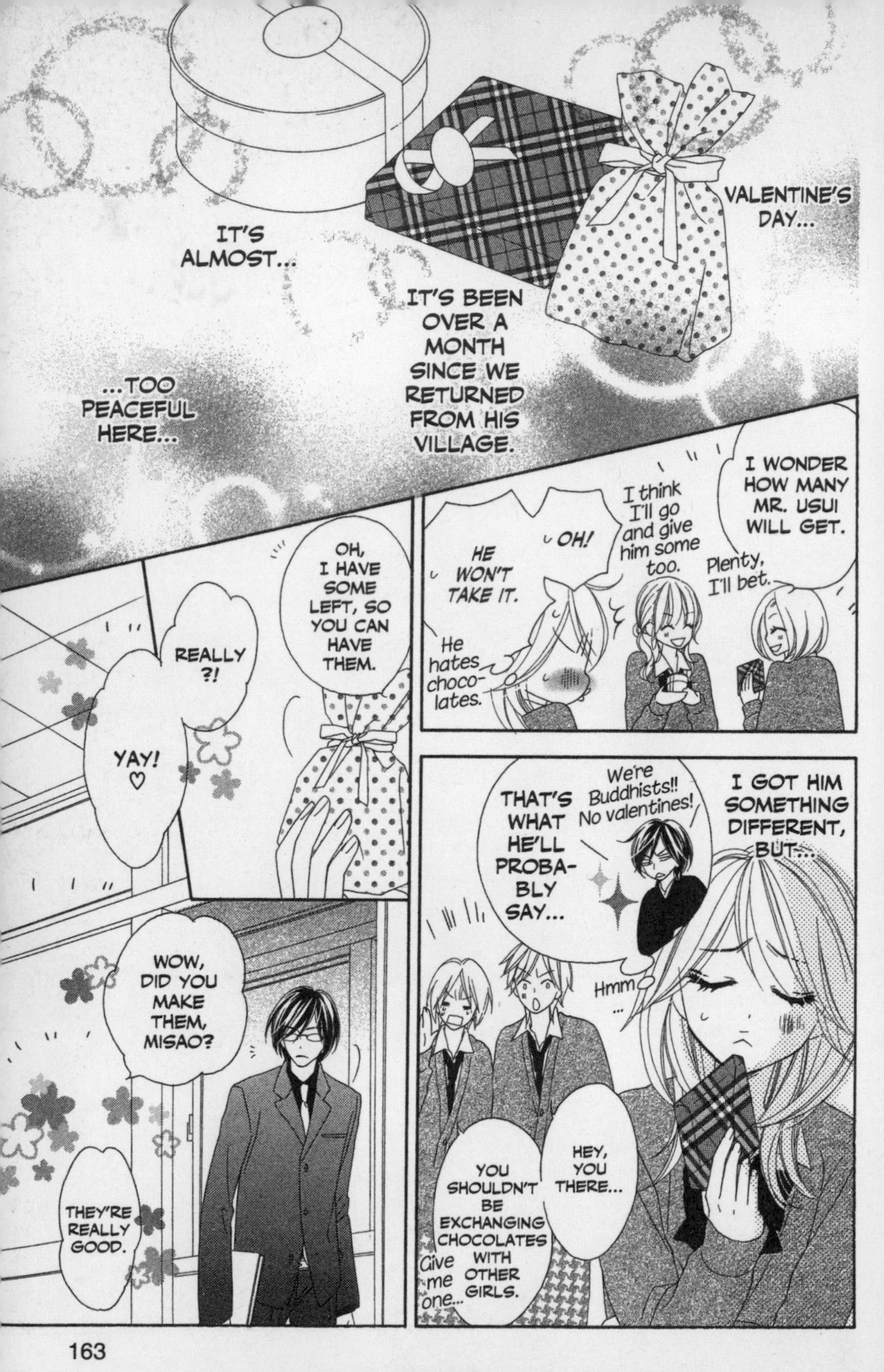
IT'S ALMOST...
VALENTINE'S DAY...
IT'S BEEN OVER A MONTH SINCE WE RETURNED FROM HIS VILLAGE.
...TOO PEACEFUL HERE...
I WONDER HOW MANY MR. USUI WILL GET.
Plenty, I'll bet.
I think I'll go and give him some too.
OH!
HE WON'T TAKE IT.
He hates chocolates.
OH, I HAVE SOME LEFT, SO YOU CAN HAVE THEM.
REALLY ?!
YAY! ♡
I GOT HIM SOMETHING DIFFERENT, BUT...
We're Buddhists!! No valentines!
THAT'S WHAT HE'LL PROBABLY SAY...
Hmm...
HEY, YOU THERE...
YOU SHOULDN'T BE EXCHANGING CHOCOLATES WITH OTHER GIRLS.
Give me one...
WOW, DID YOU MAKE THEM, MISAO?
THEY'RE REALLY GOOD.

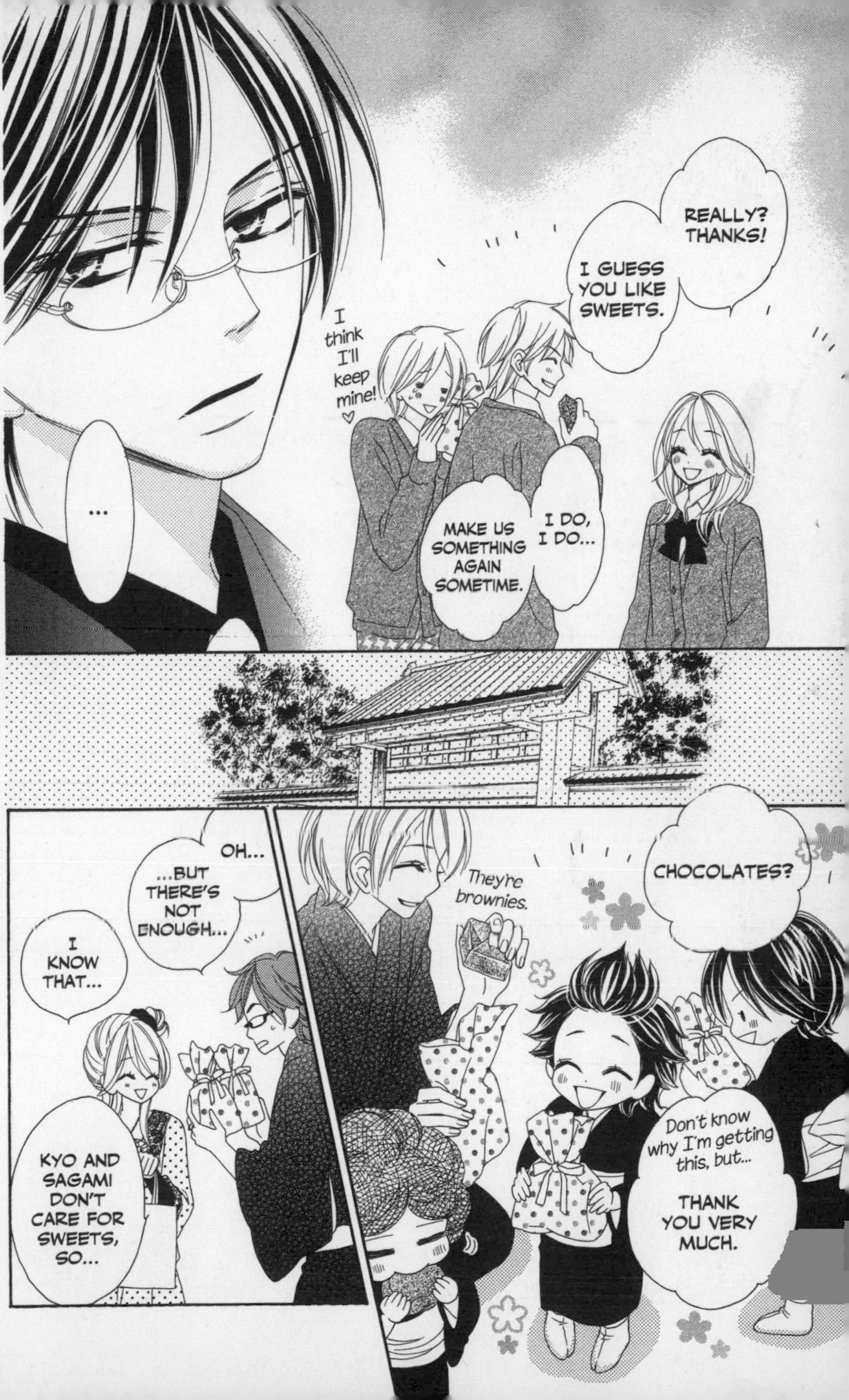
REALLY? THANKS!
I GUESS YOU LIKE SWEETS.
I think I'll keep mine! ♡
I DO, I DO...
MAKE US SOMETHING AGAIN SOMETIME.
...
CHOCOLATES?
They're brownies.
Don't know why I'm getting this, but...
THANK YOU VERY MUCH.
OH...
...BUT THERE'S NOT ENOUGH...
I KNOW THAT...
KYO AND SAGAMI DON'T CARE FOR SWEETS, SO...

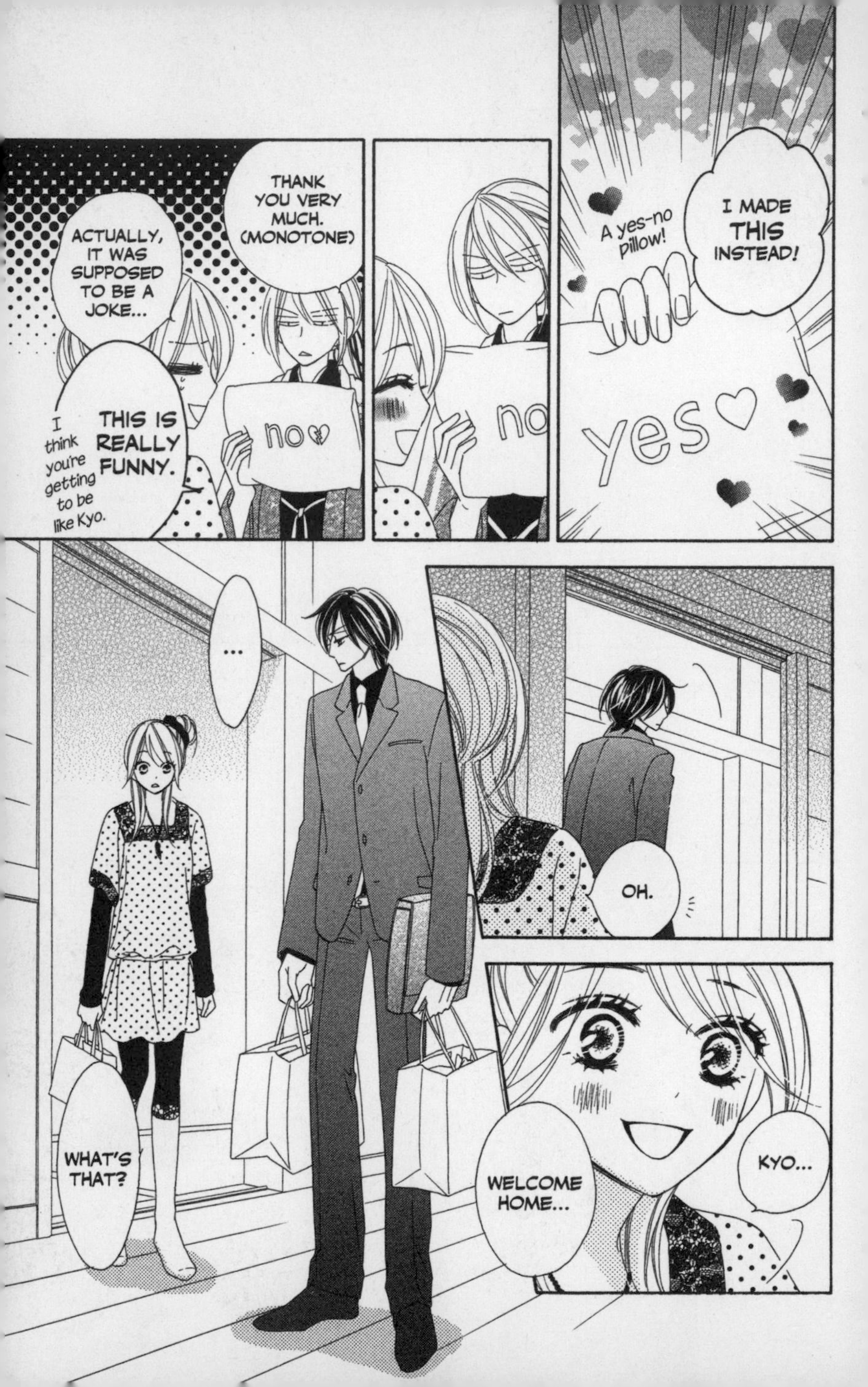
I MADE THIS INSTEAD!
A yes-no pillow!
yes
no
THANK YOU VERY MUCH. (MONOTONE)
ACTUALLY, IT WAS SUPPOSED TO BE A JOKE...
no
THIS IS REALLY FUNNY.
I think you're getting to be like Kyo.
OH.
KYO...
WELCOME HOME...
...
WHAT'S THAT?

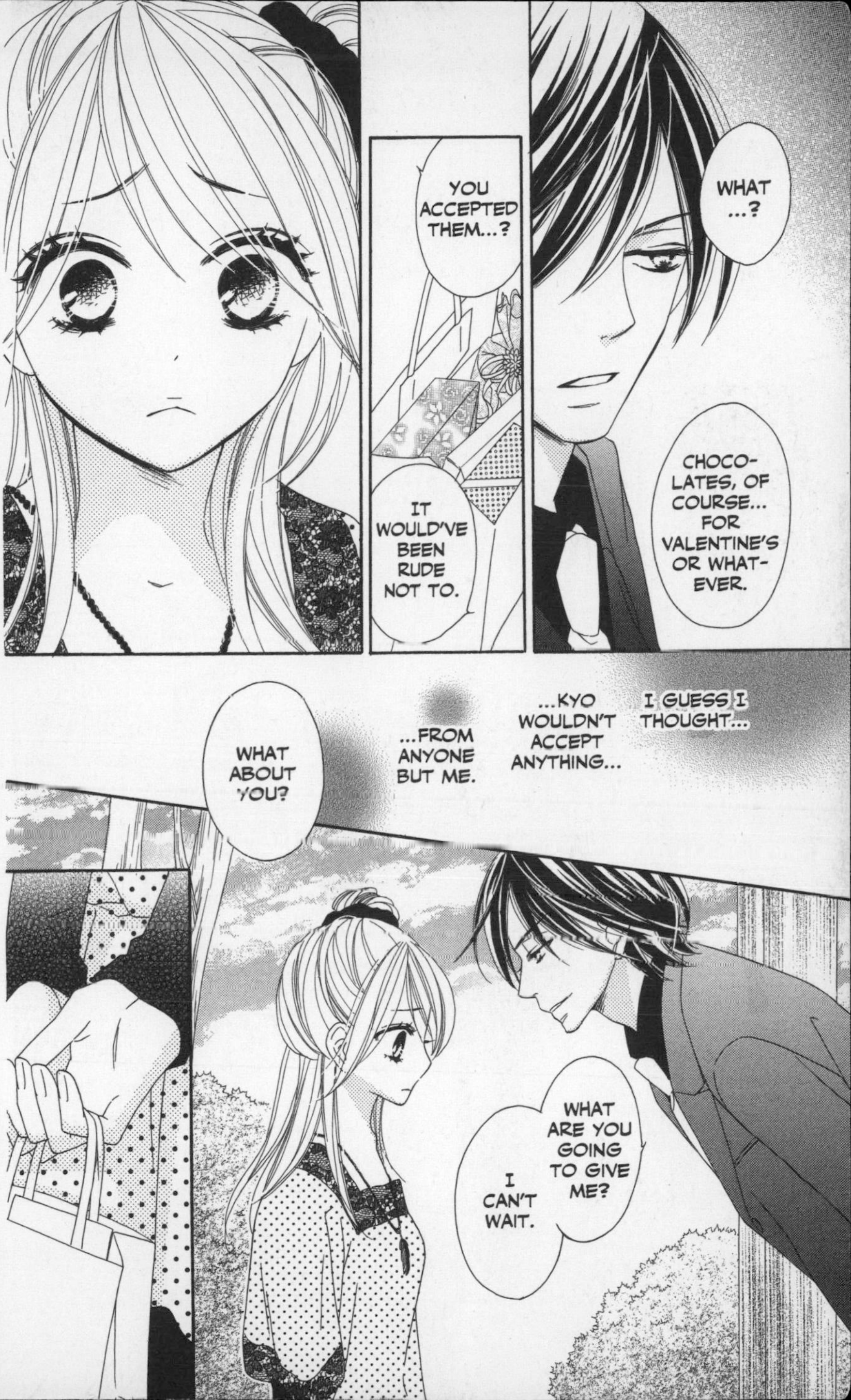
WHAT ...?
CHOCO-LATES, OF COURSE... FOR VALENTINE'S OR WHAT-EVER.
YOU ACCEPTED THEM...?
IT WOULD'VE BEEN RUDE NOT TO.
I GUESS I THOUGHT...
...KYO WOULDN'T ACCEPT ANYTHING...
...FROM ANYONE BUT ME.
WHAT ABOUT YOU?
WHAT ARE YOU GOING TO GIVE ME?
I CAN'T WAIT.

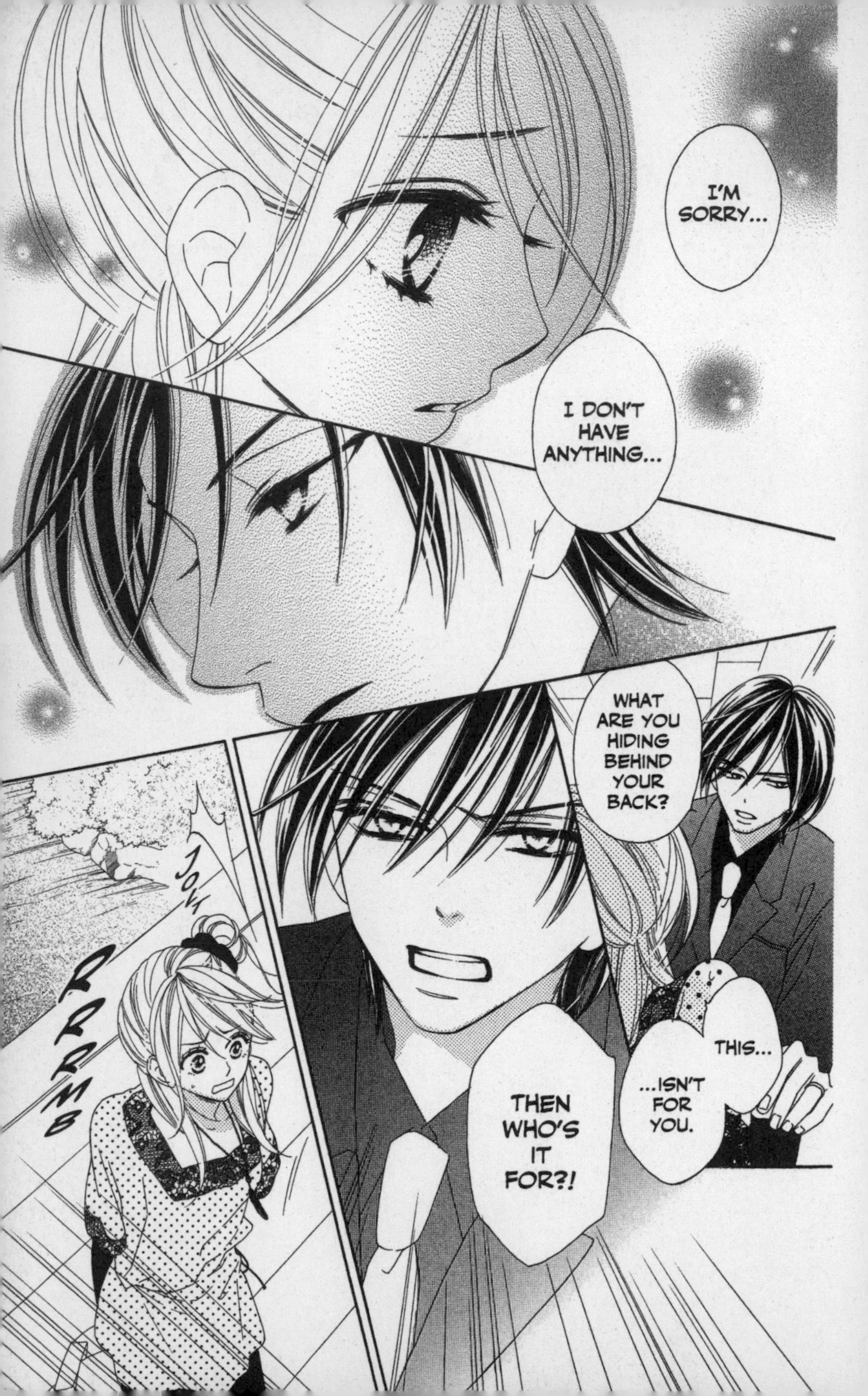
I'M SORRY...
I DON'T HAVE ANYTHING...
WHAT ARE YOU HIDING BEHIND YOUR BACK?
THIS...
...ISN'T FOR YOU.
THEN WHO'S IT FOR?!
JOLT
RRRMB

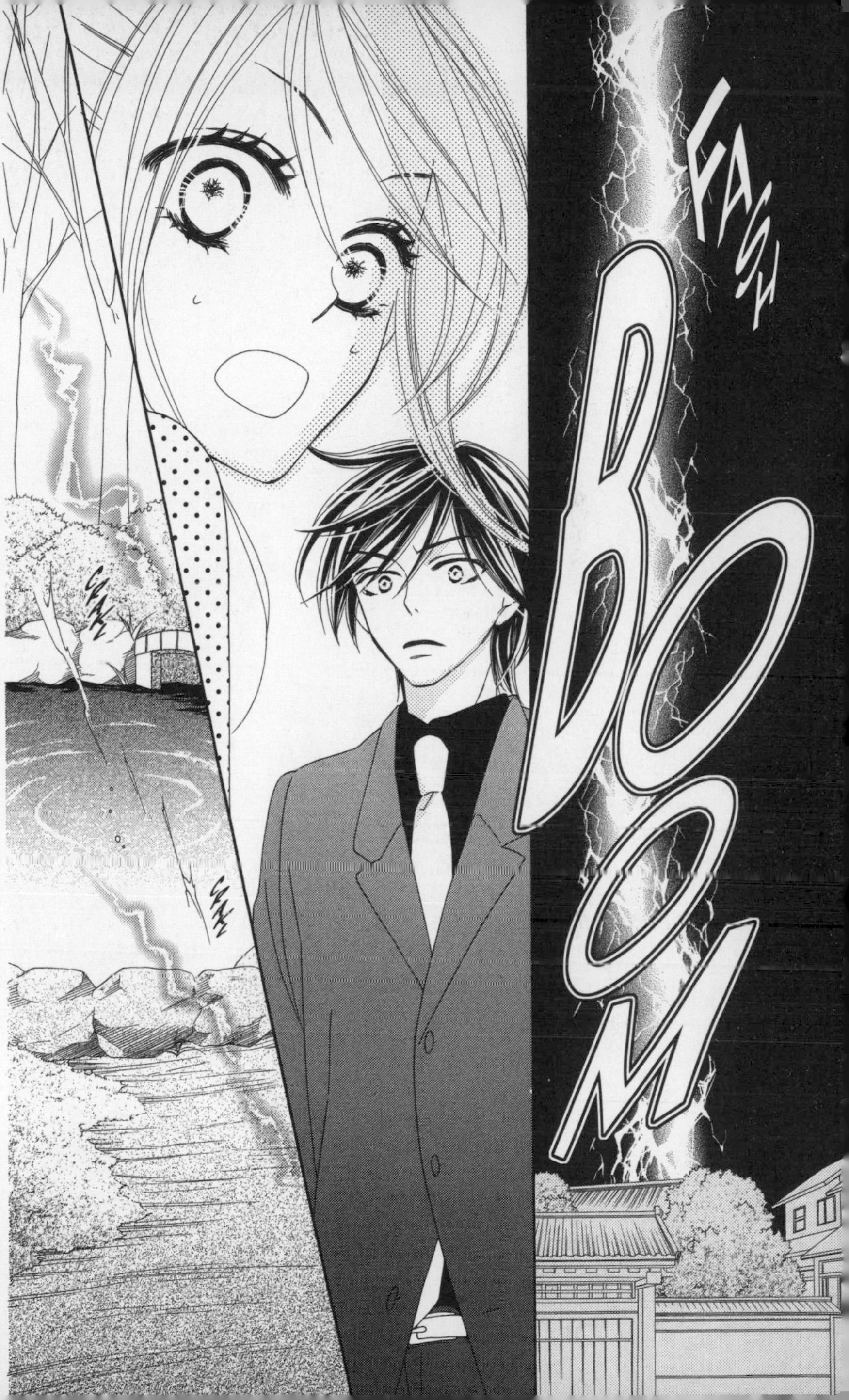
FLASH
BOOOM

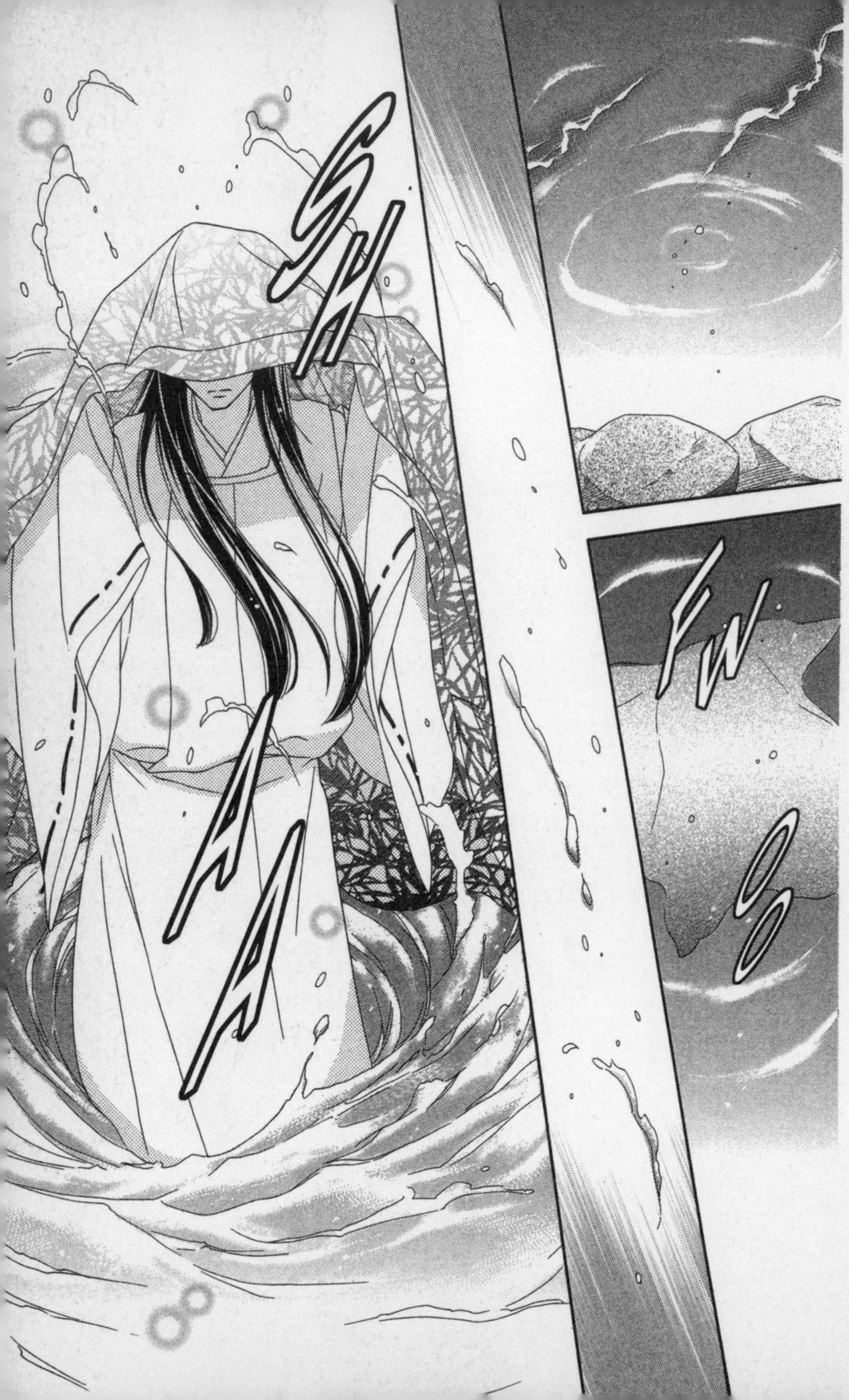
FWOO
SHAA

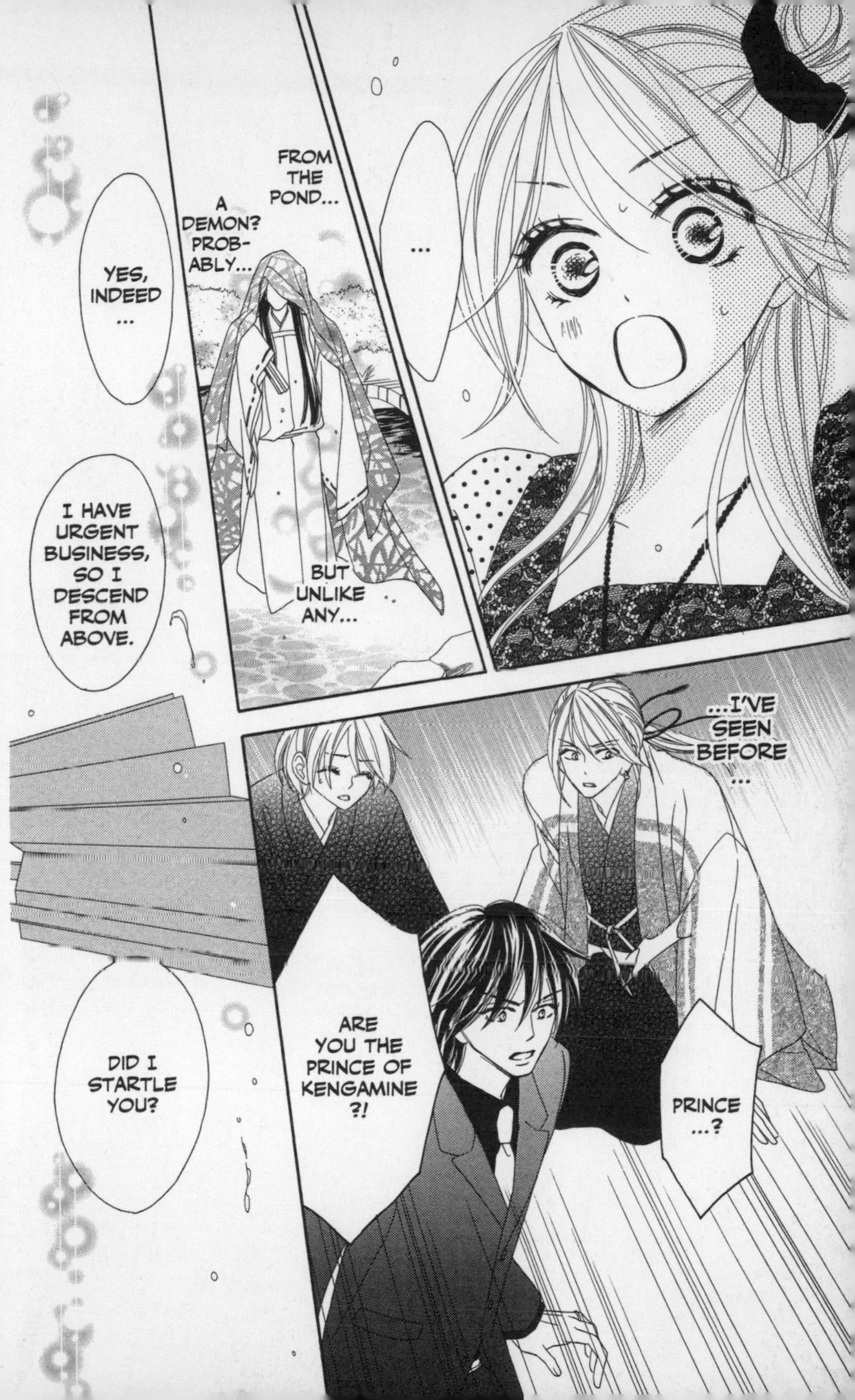
...
FROM THE POND...
A DEMON? PROBABLY...
BUT UNLIKE ANY...
YES, INDEED ...
I HAVE URGENT BUSINESS, SO I DESCEND FROM ABOVE.
...I'VE SEEN BEFORE ...
PRINCE ...?
ARE YOU THE PRINCE OF KENGAMINE ?!
DID I STARTLE YOU?

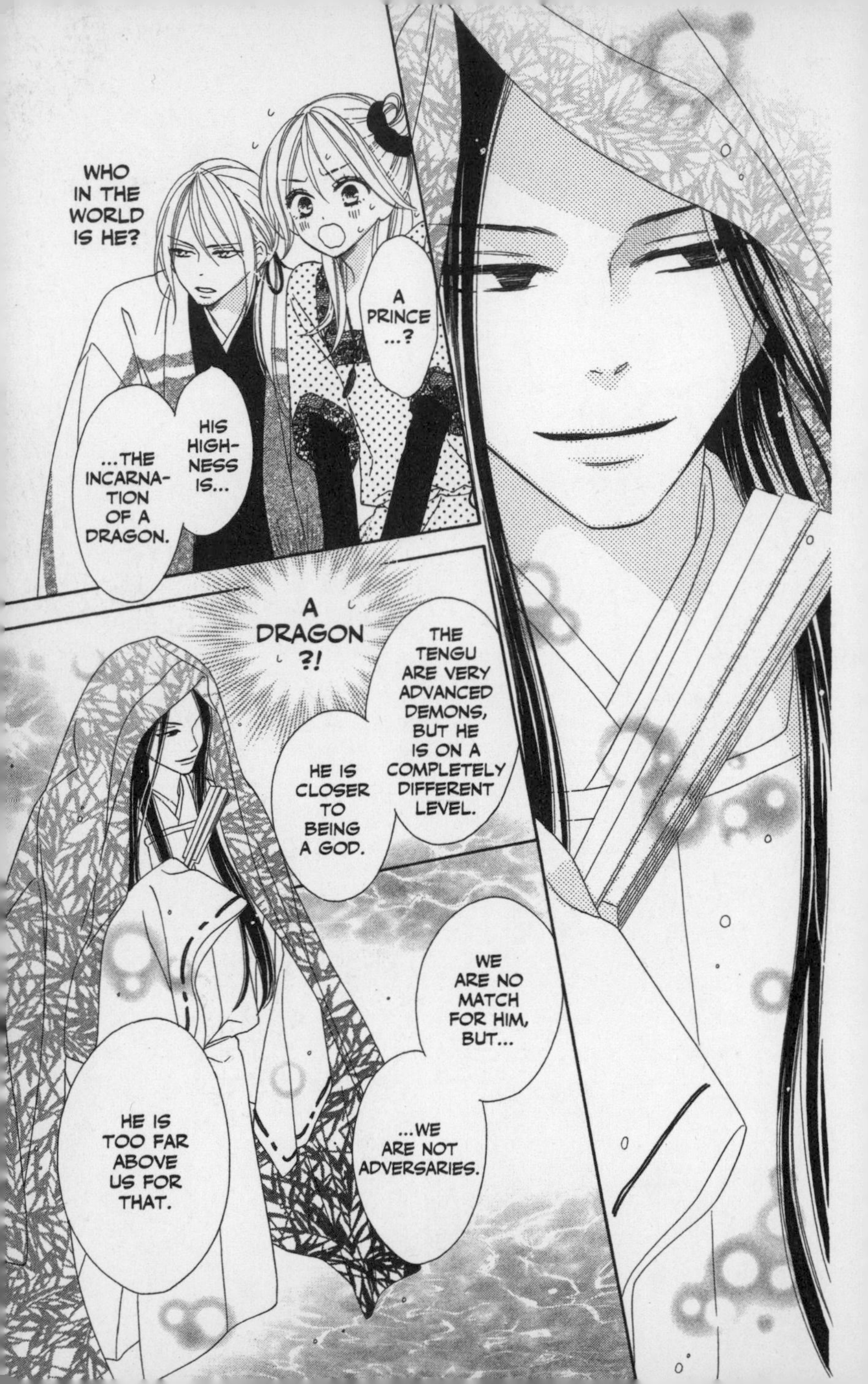
A PRINCE ...?
WHO IN THE WORLD IS HE?
HIS HIGHNESS IS...
...THE INCARNATION OF A DRAGON.
A DRAGON ?!
THE TENGU ARE VERY ADVANCED DEMONS, BUT HE IS ON A COMPLETELY DIFFERENT LEVEL.
HE IS CLOSER TO BEING A GOD.
WE ARE NO MATCH FOR HIM, BUT...
...WE ARE NOT ADVERSARIES.
HE IS TOO FAR ABOVE US FOR THAT.

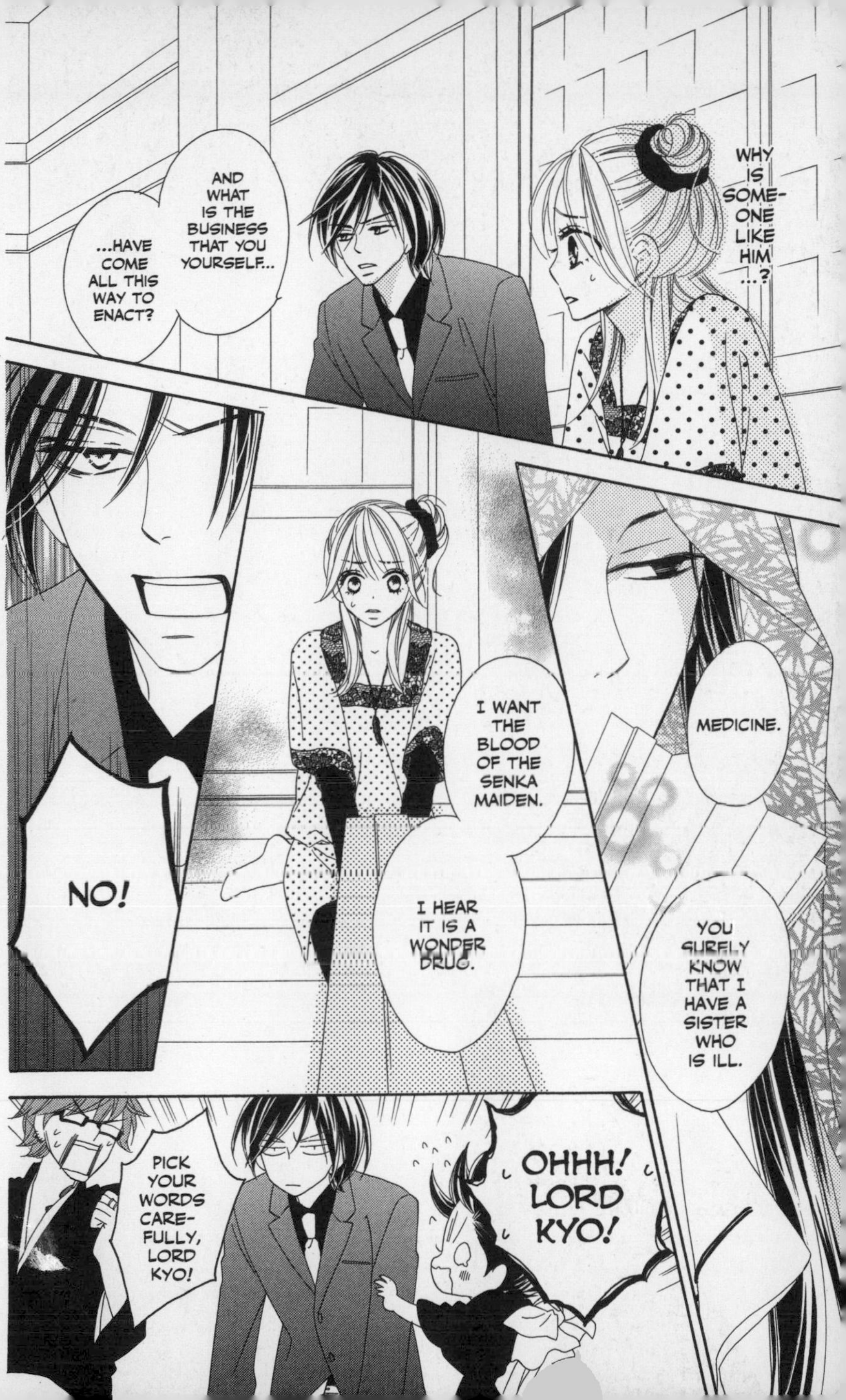
WHY IS SOMEONE LIKE HIM...?
AND WHAT IS THE BUSINESS THAT YOU YOURSELF...
...HAVE COME ALL THIS WAY TO ENACT?
MEDICINE.
YOU SURELY KNOW THAT I HAVE A SISTER WHO IS ILL.
I WANT THE BLOOD OF THE SENKA MAIDEN.
I HEAR IT IS A WONDER DRUG.
NO!
OHHH! LORD KYO!
PICK YOUR WORDS CAREFULLY, LORD KYO!

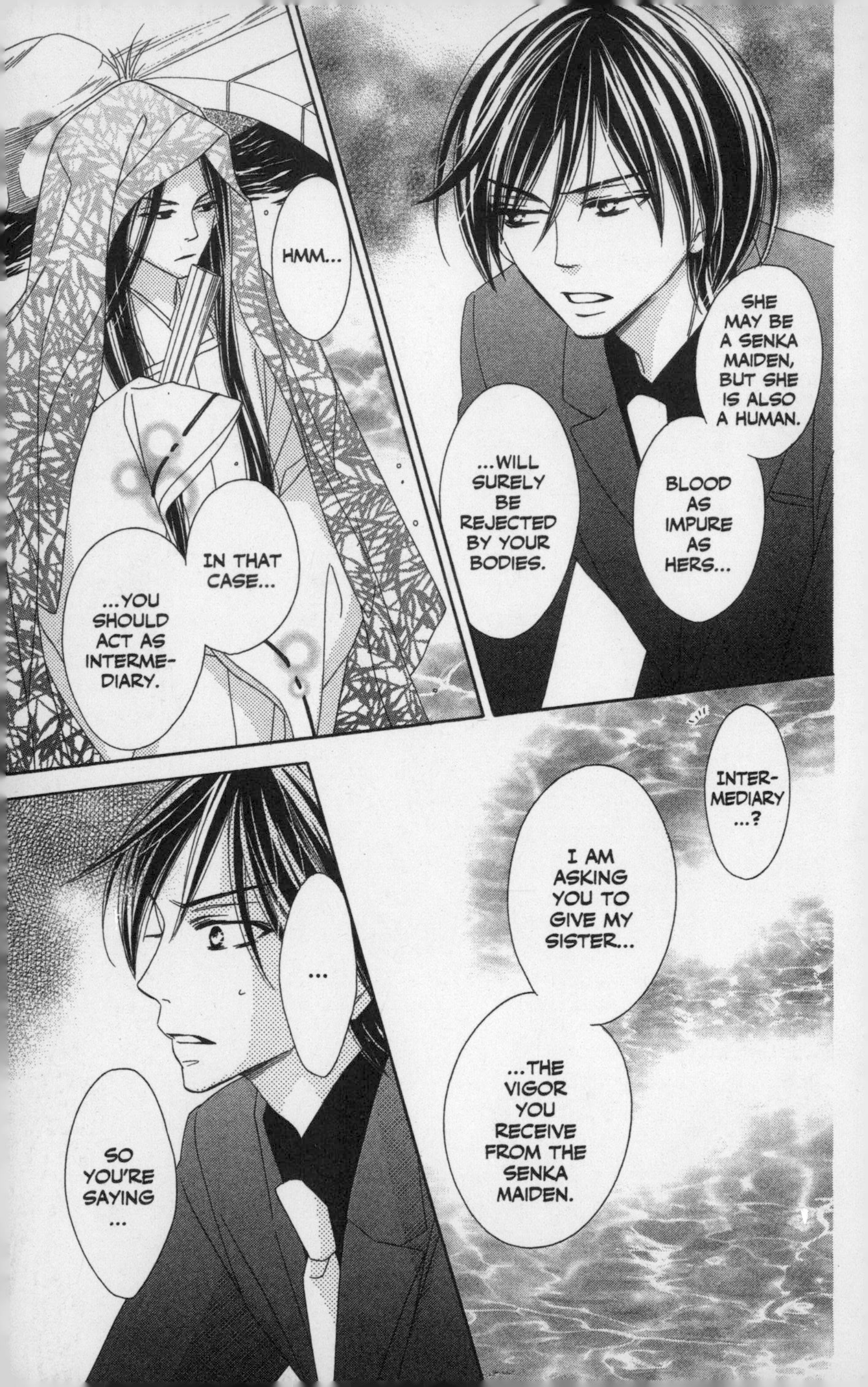
SHE MAY BE A SENKA MAIDEN, BUT SHE IS ALSO A HUMAN.
BLOOD AS IMPURE AS HERS...
...WILL SURELY BE REJECTED BY YOUR BODIES.
HMM...
IN THAT CASE...
...YOU SHOULD ACT AS INTERME-DIARY.
INTER-MEDIARY ...?
I AM ASKING YOU TO GIVE MY SISTER...
...THE VIGOR YOU RECEIVE FROM THE SENKA MAIDEN.
...
SO YOU'RE SAYING ...

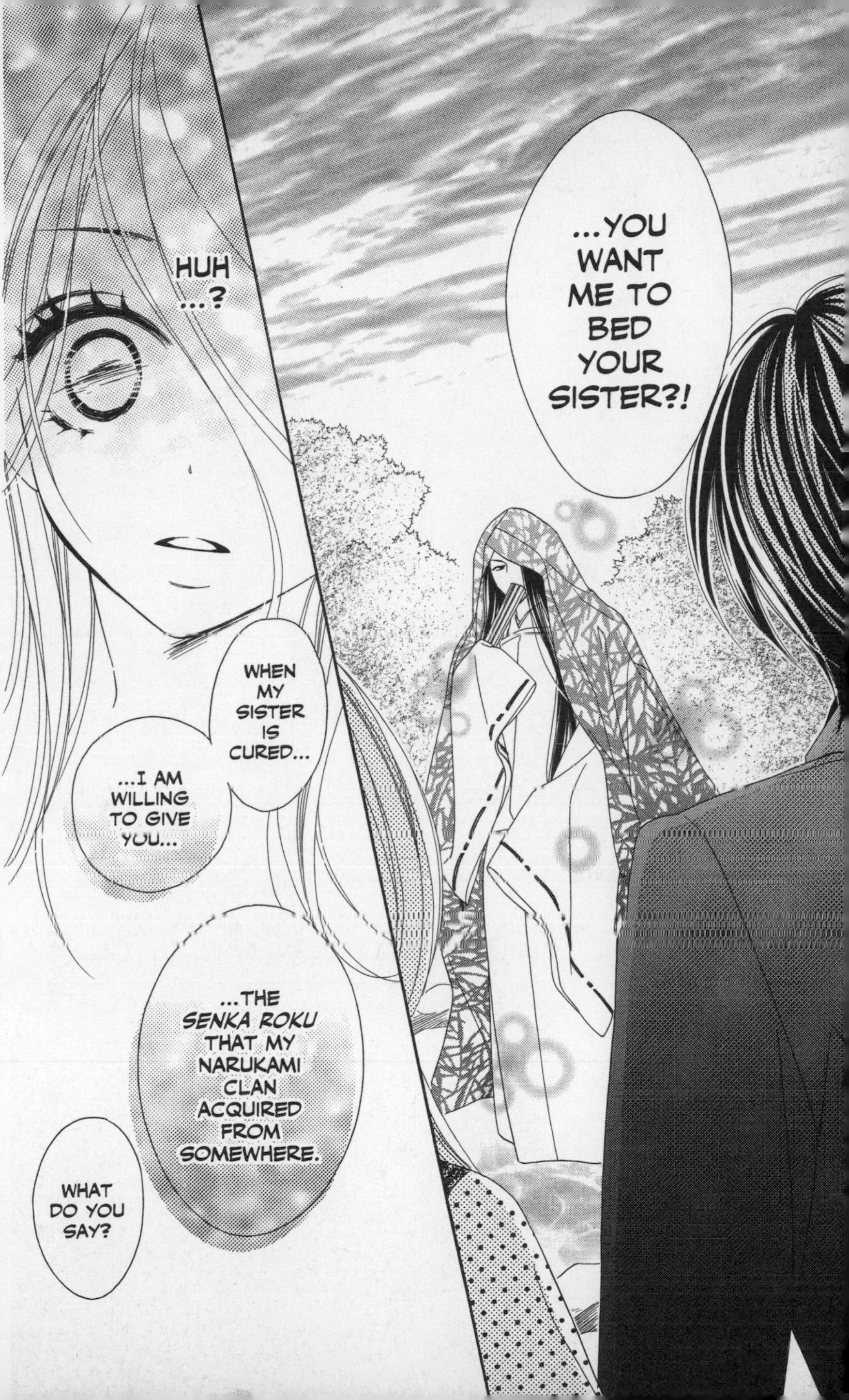
...YOU WANT ME TO BED YOUR SISTER?!
HUH ...?
WHEN MY SISTER IS CURED...
...I AM WILLING TO GIVE YOU...
...THE *SENKA ROKU* THAT MY NARUKAMI CLAN ACQUIRED FROM SOMEWHERE.
WHAT DO YOU SAY?

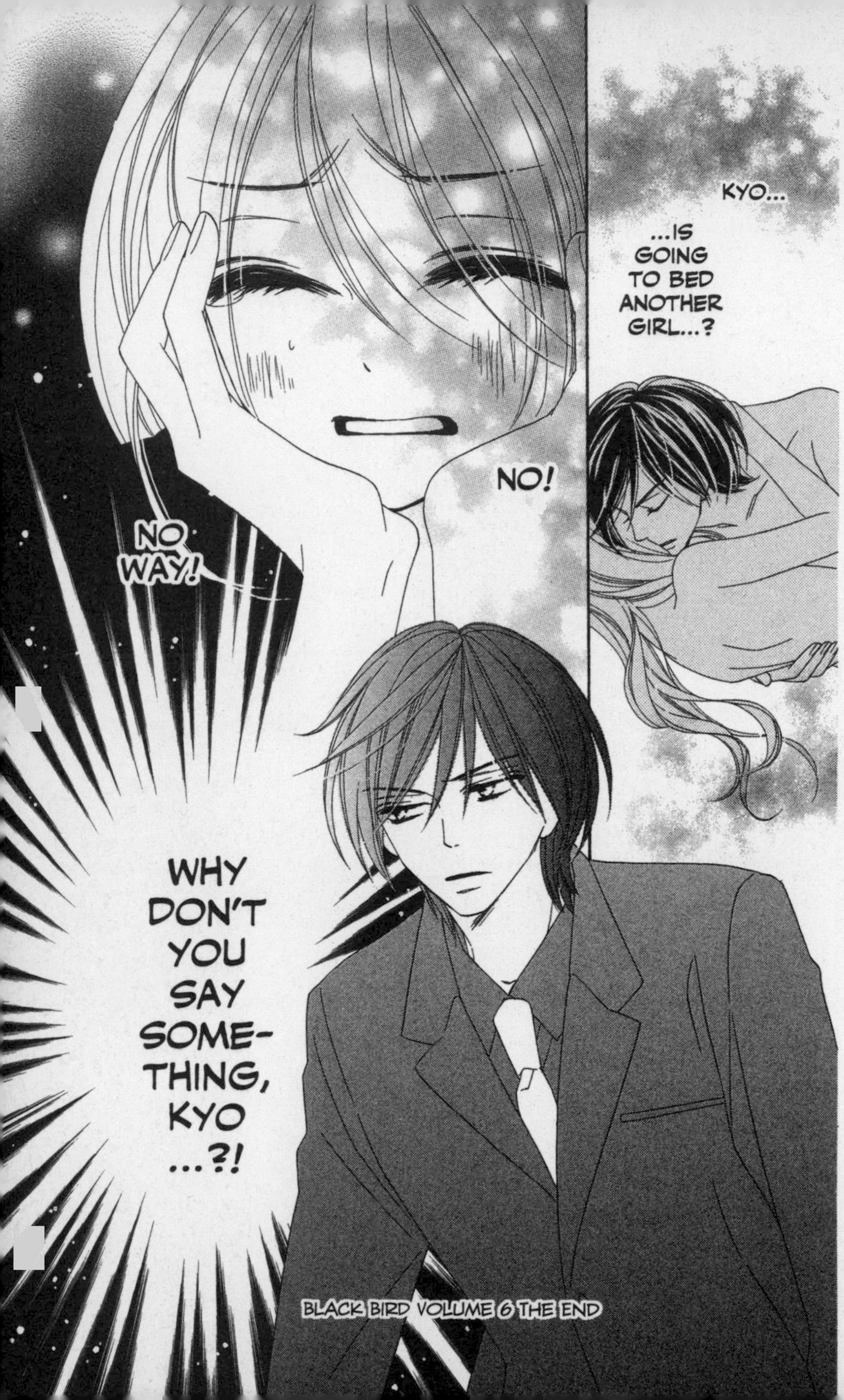
KYO...
...IS GOING TO BED ANOTHER GIRL...?
NO!
NO WAY!
WHY DON'T YOU SAY SOME-THING, KYO ...?!
BLACK BIRD VOLUME 6 THE END

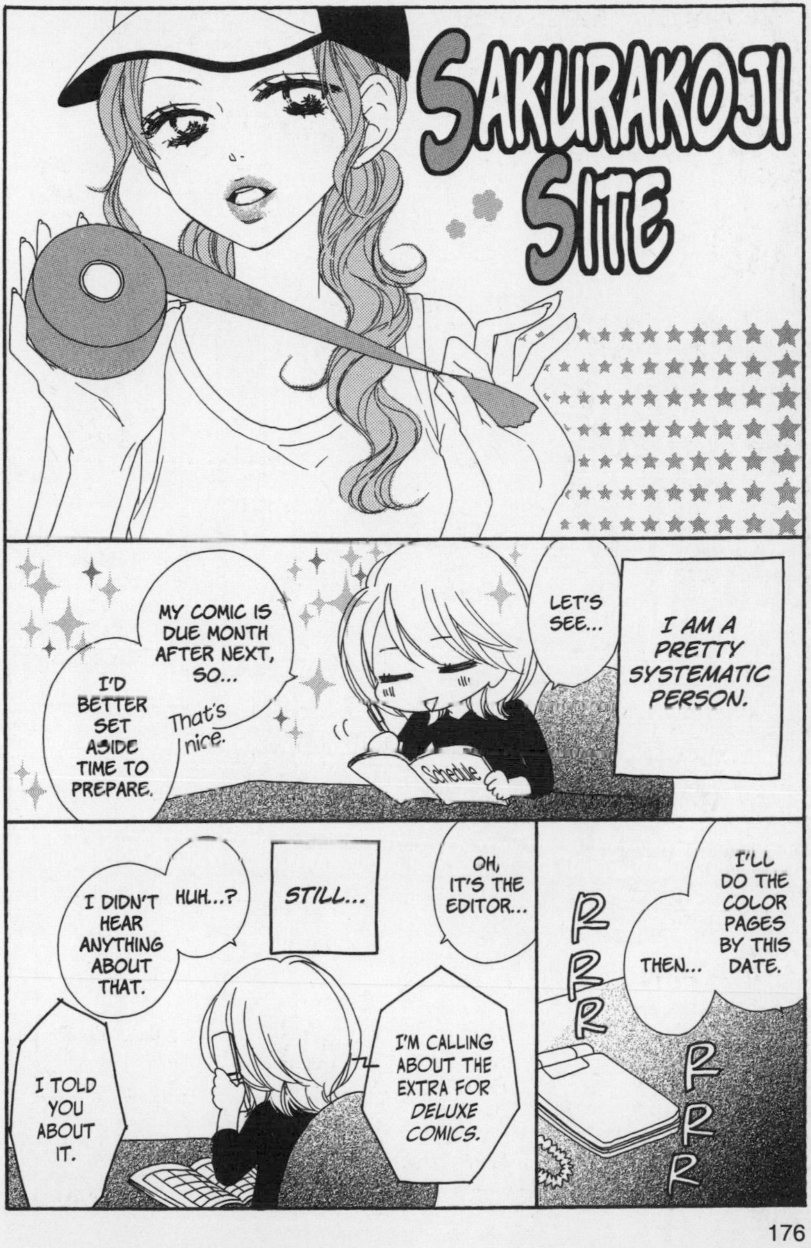
SAKURAKOJI SITE
I AM A PRETTY SYSTEMATIC PERSON.
LET'S SEE...
MY COMIC IS DUE MONTH AFTER NEXT, SO...
That's nice.
I'D BETTER SET ASIDE TIME TO PREPARE.
Schedule
I'LL DO THE COLOR PAGES BY THIS DATE.
THEN...
RRR
RRR
OH, IT'S THE EDITOR...
STILL...
HUH...?
I'M CALLING ABOUT THE EXTRA FOR *DELUXE COMICS*.
I DIDN'T HEAR ANYTHING ABOUT THAT.
I TOLD YOU ABOUT IT.

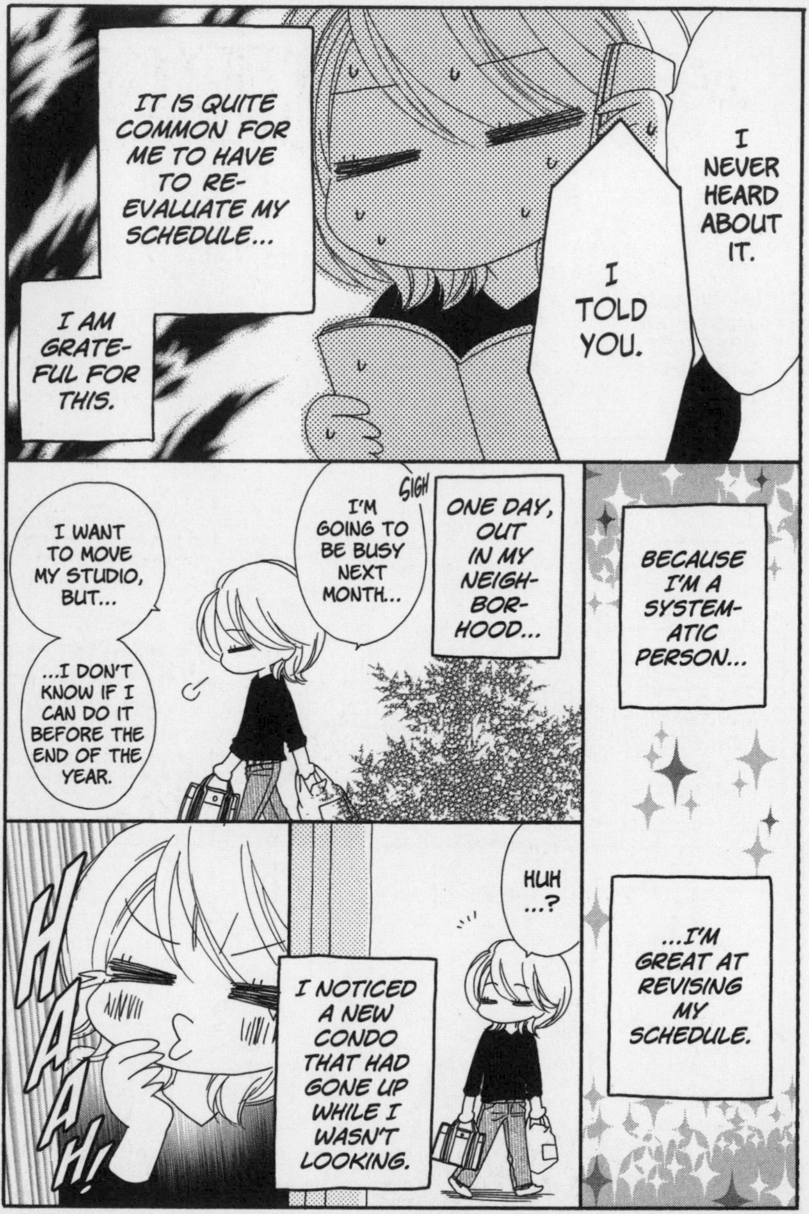
I NEVER HEARD ABOUT IT.
I TOLD YOU.
IT IS QUITE COMMON FOR ME TO HAVE TO RE-EVALUATE MY SCHEDULE...
I AM GRATE-FUL FOR THIS.
BECAUSE I'M A SYSTEM-ATIC PERSON...
...I'M GREAT AT REVISING MY SCHEDULE.
ONE DAY, OUT IN MY NEIGH-BOR-HOOD...
SIGH
I'M GOING TO BE BUSY NEXT MONTH...
I WANT TO MOVE MY STUDIO, BUT...
...I DON'T KNOW IF I CAN DO IT BEFORE THE END OF THE YEAR.
HUH ...?
I NOTICED A NEW CONDO THAT HAD GONE UP WHILE I WASN'T LOOKING.
HAAAH!

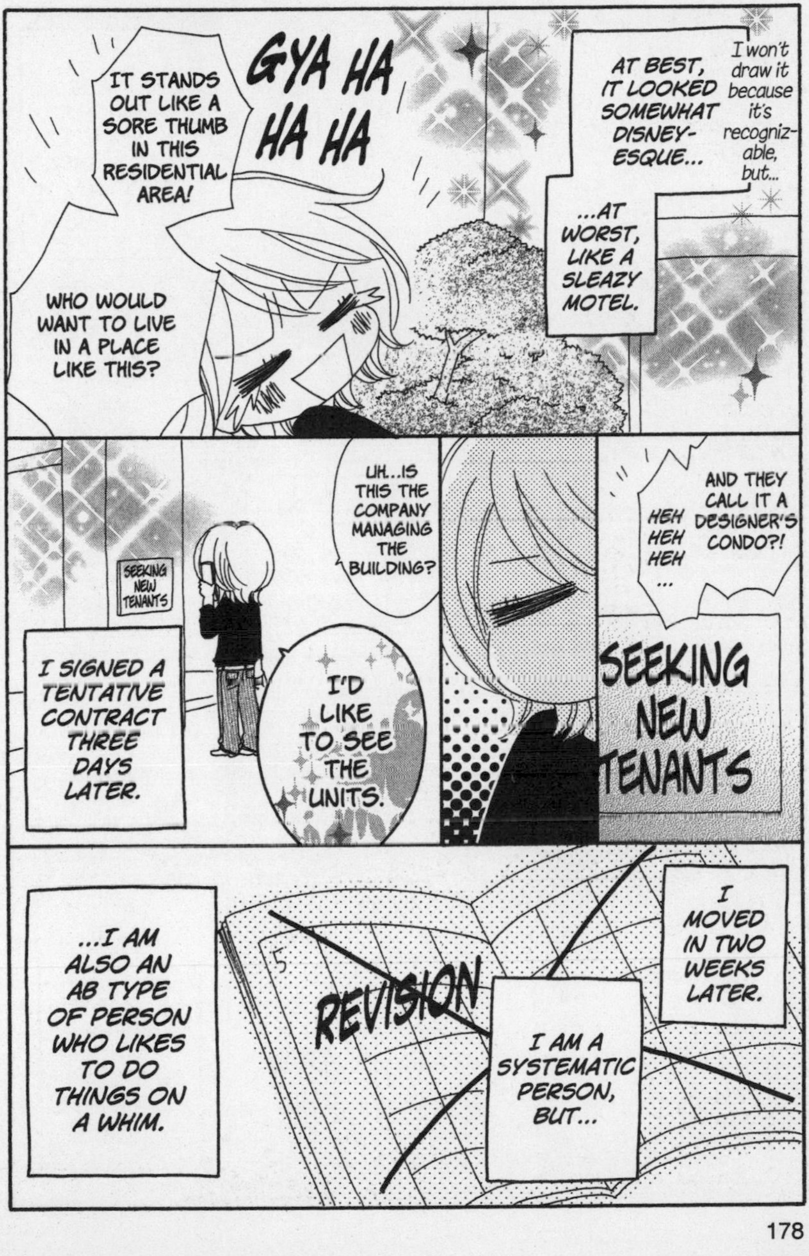
AT BEST, IT LOOKED SOMEWHAT DISNEY-ESQUE...
I won't draw it because it's recognizable, but...
...AT WORST, LIKE A SLEAZY MOTEL.
GYA HA HA HA
IT STANDS OUT LIKE A SORE THUMB IN THIS RESIDENTIAL AREA!
WHO WOULD WANT TO LIVE IN A PLACE LIKE THIS?
AND THEY CALL IT A DESIGNER'S CONDO?!
HEH HEH HEH ...
SEEKING NEW TENANTS
UH...IS THIS THE COMPANY MANAGING THE BUILDING?
SEEKING NEW TENANTS
I'D LIKE TO SEE THE UNITS.
I SIGNED A TENTATIVE CONTRACT THREE DAYS LATER.
I MOVED IN TWO WEEKS LATER.
I AM A SYSTEMATIC PERSON, BUT...
5
REVISION
...I AM ALSO AN AB TYPE OF PERSON WHO LIKES TO DO THINGS ON A WHIM.

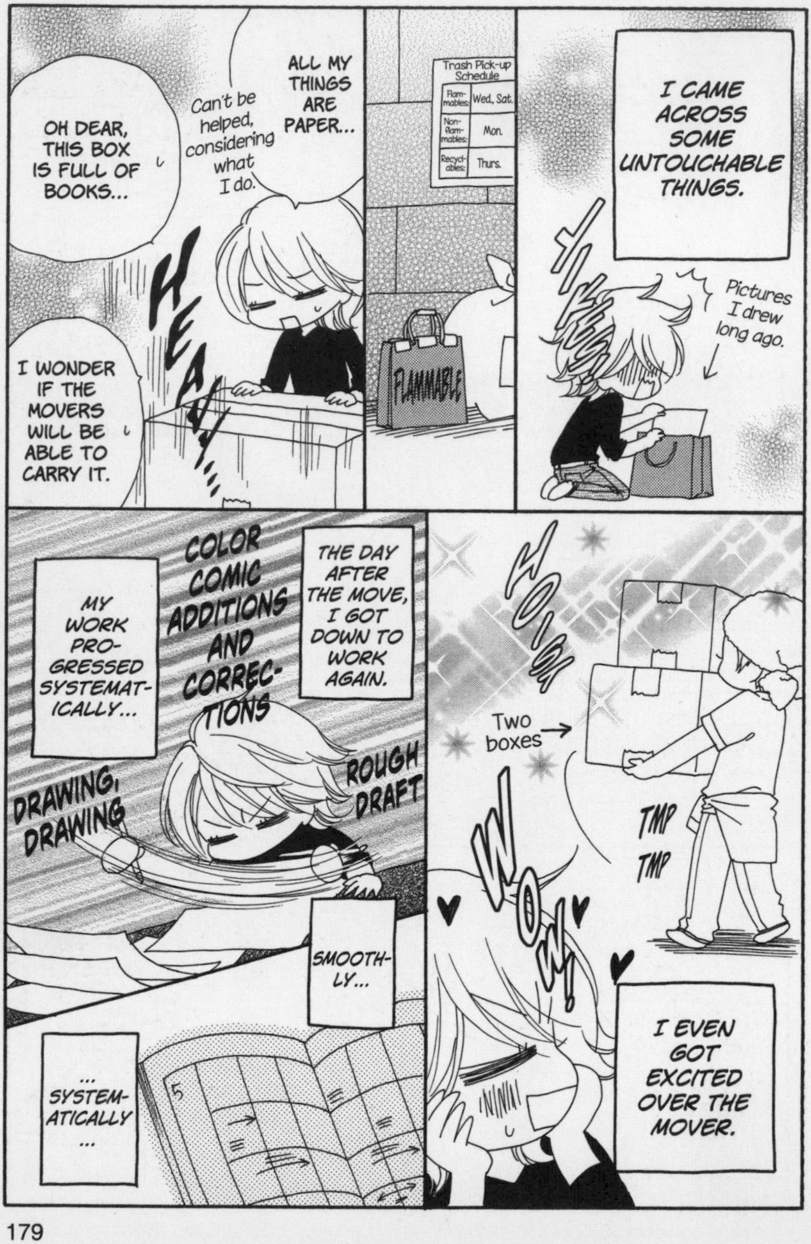
I CAME ACROSS SOME UNTOUCHABLE THINGS.
Pictures I drew long ago.
Trash Pick-up Schedule
Flammables: Wed., Sat.
Non-flammables: Mon.
Recyclables: Thurs.
FLAMMABLE
ALL MY THINGS ARE PAPER...
Can't be helped, considering what I do.
OH DEAR, THIS BOX IS FULL OF BOOKS...
I WONDER IF THE MOVERS WILL BE ABLE TO CARRY IT.
Two boxes
TMP
TMP
I EVEN GOT EXCITED OVER THE MOVER.
THE DAY AFTER THE MOVE, I GOT DOWN TO WORK AGAIN.
COLOR COMIC ADDITIONS AND CORREC-TIONS
MY WORK PRO-GRESSED SYSTEMAT-ICALLY...
ROUGH DRAFT
DRAWING, DRAWING
SMOOTH-LY...
... SYSTEM-ATICALLY ...

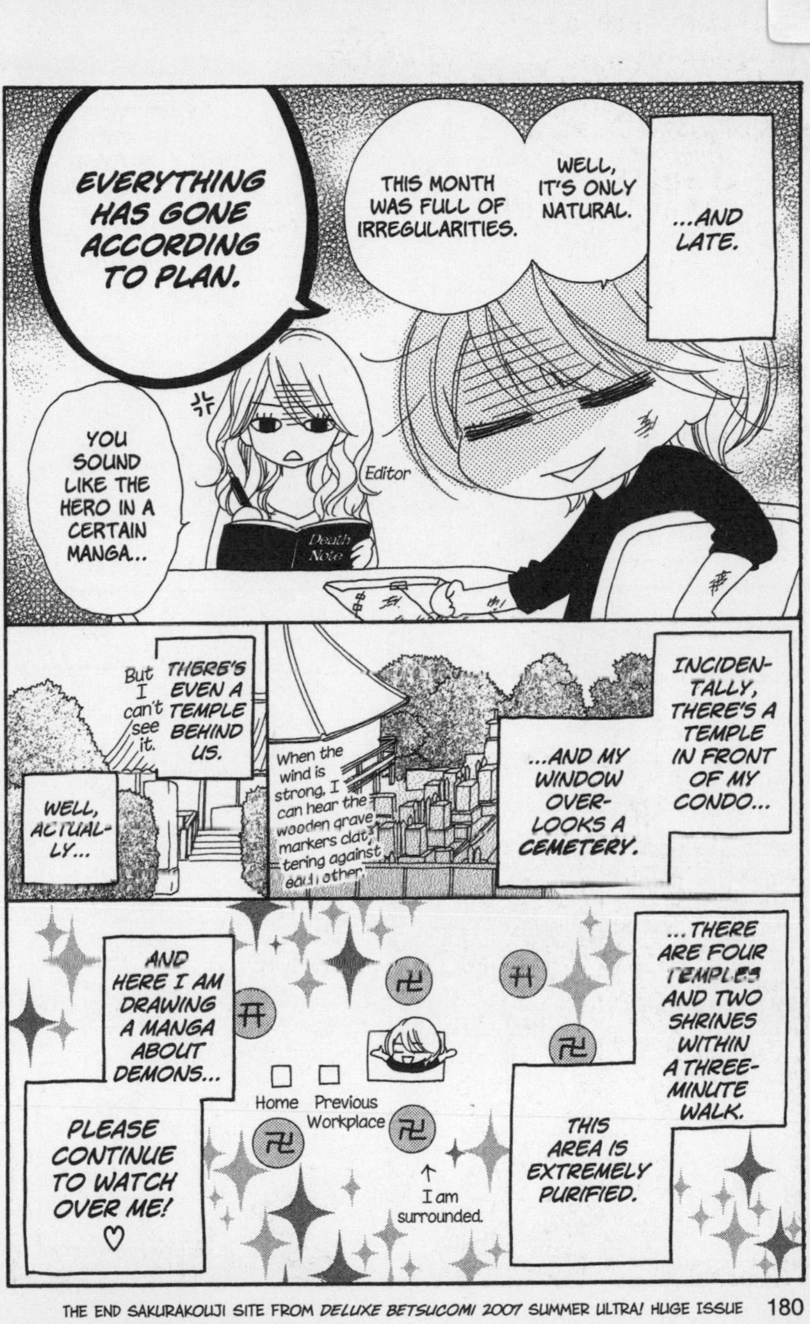
WELL, IT'S ONLY NATURAL.
THIS MONTH WAS FULL OF IRREGULARITIES.
...AND LATE.
EVERYTHING HAS GONE ACCORDING TO PLAN.
Editor
Death Note
YOU SOUND LIKE THE HERO IN A CERTAIN MANGA...
INCIDENTALLY, THERE'S A TEMPLE IN FRONT OF MY CONDO...
...AND MY WINDOW OVERLOOKS A CEMETERY.
When the wind is strong, I can hear the wooden grave markers clattering against each other.
WELL, ACTUALLY...
THERE'S EVEN A TEMPLE BEHIND US.
But I can't see it.
...THERE ARE FOUR TEMPLES AND TWO SHRINES WITHIN A THREE-MINUTE WALK.
THIS AREA IS EXTREMELY PURIFIED.
↑ I am surrounded.
Home
Previous Workplace
AND HERE I AM DRAWING A MANGA ABOUT DEMONS...
PLEASE CONTINUE TO WATCH OVER ME! ♡

THE END SAKURAKOUJI SITE FROM *DELUXE BETSUCOMI* 2007 SUMMER ULTRA! HUGE ISSUE

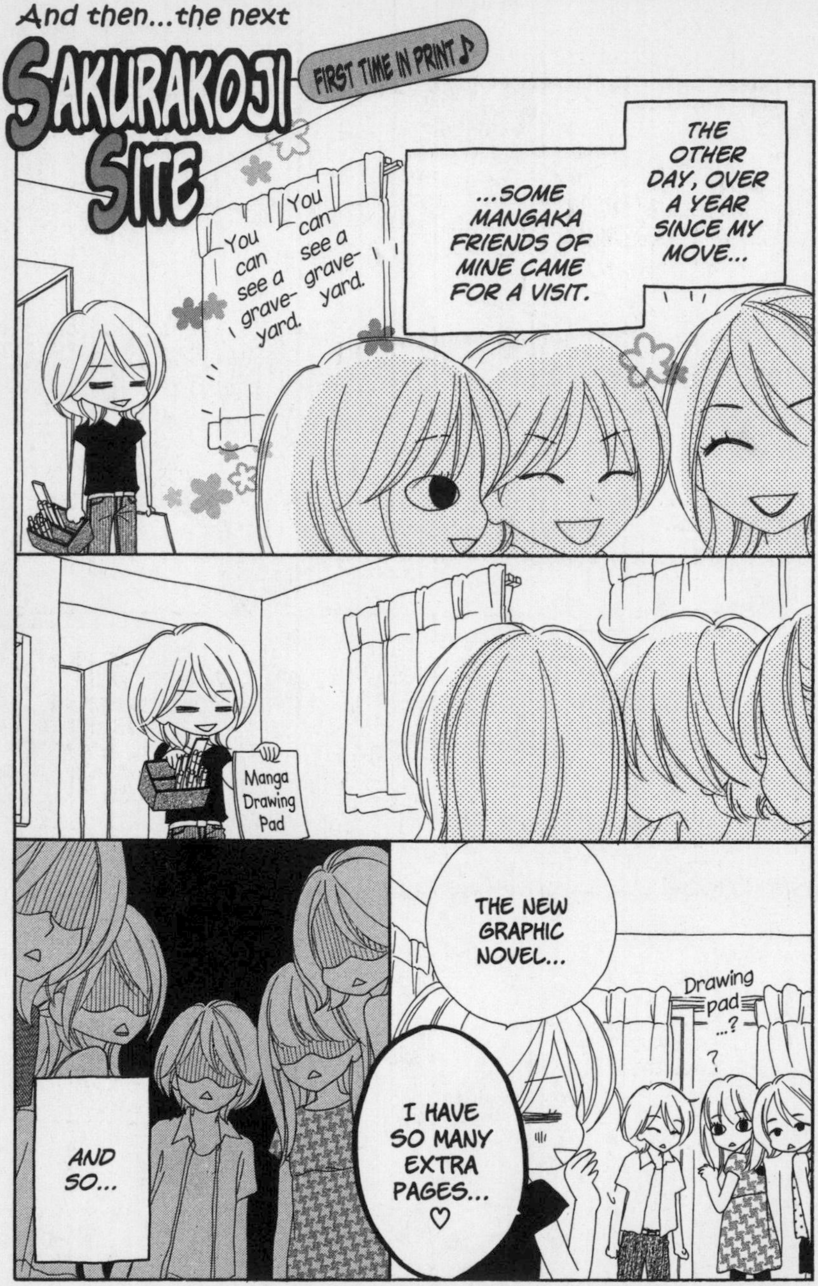
And then...the next
SAKURAKOJI SITE
FIRST TIME IN PRINT♪
THE OTHER DAY, OVER A YEAR SINCE MY MOVE...
...SOME MANGAKA FRIENDS OF MINE CAME FOR A VISIT.
You can see a graveyard.
You can see a graveyard.
Manga Drawing Pad
THE NEW GRAPHIC NOVEL...
I HAVE SO MANY EXTRA PAGES... ♡
Drawing pad...?
?
AND SO...

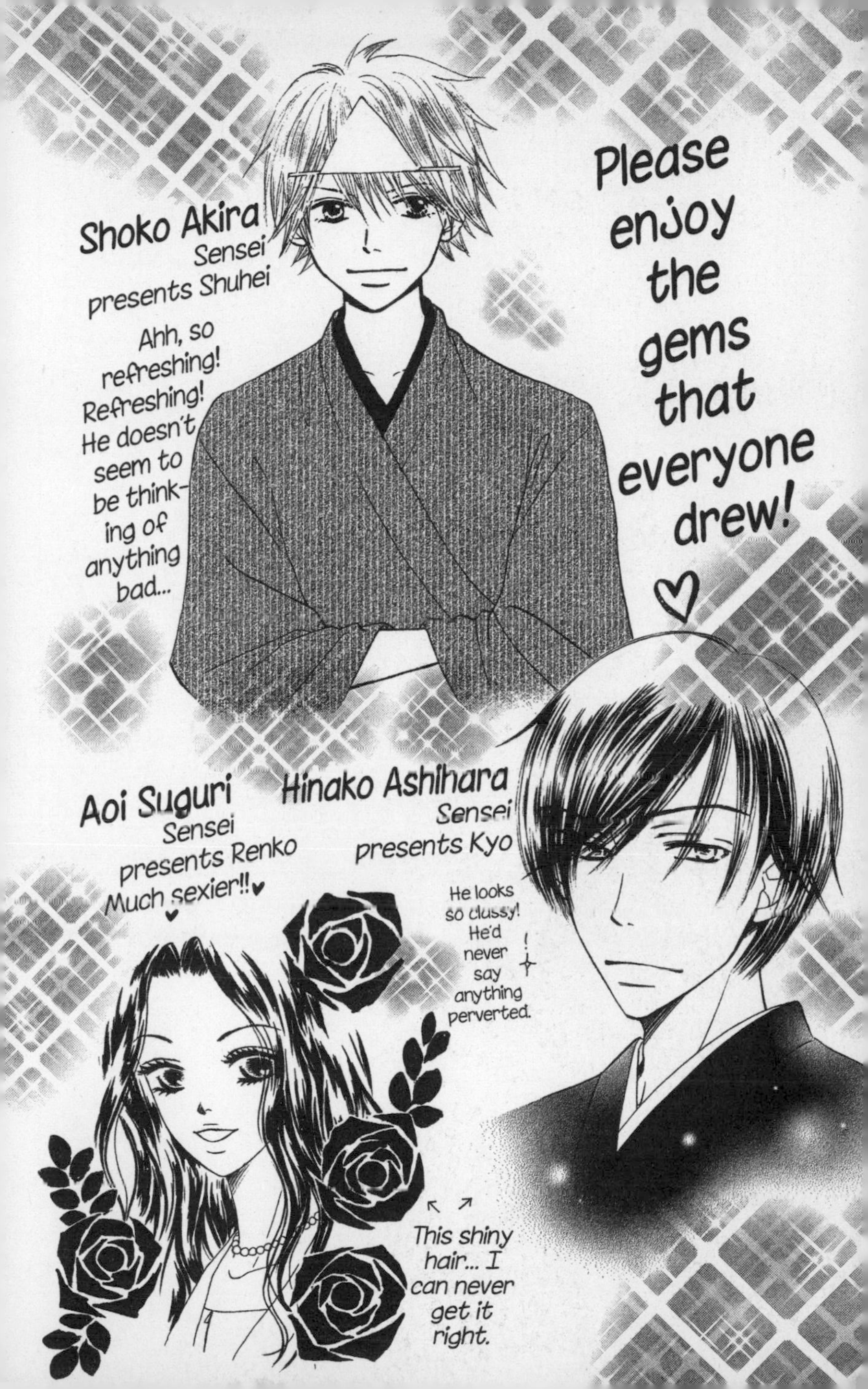
Please enjoy the gems that everyone drew! ♥
Shoko Akira Sensei presents Shuhei
Ahh, so refreshing! Refreshing! He doesn't seem to be think-ing of anything bad...
Hinako Ashihara Sensei presents Kyo
He looks so clussy! He'd never say anything perverted.
This shiny hair... I can never get it right.
Aoi Suguri Sensei presents Renko
Much sexier!! ♥

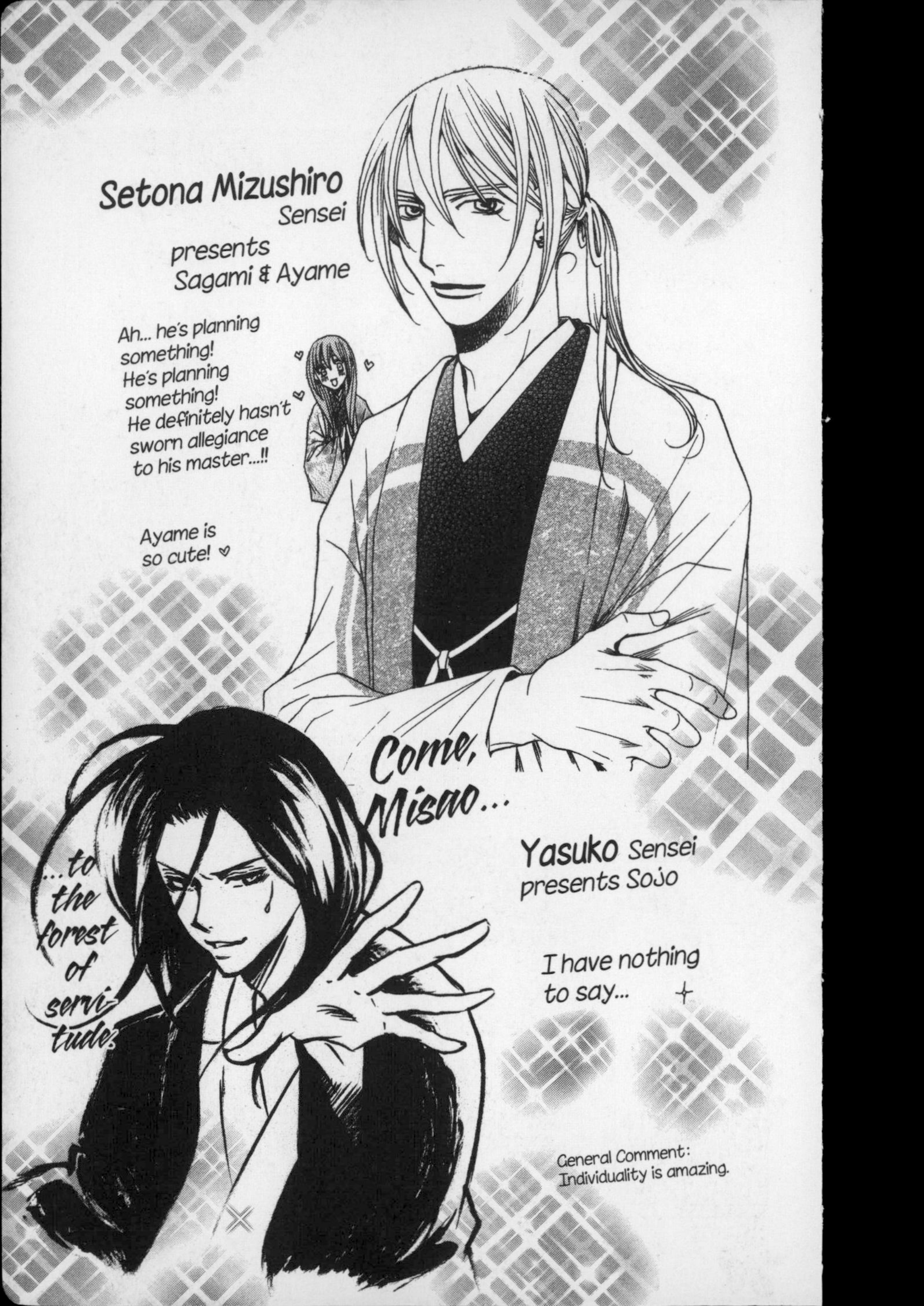
Setona Mizushiro Sensei presents Sagami & Ayame
Ah... he's planning something! He's planning something! He definitely hasn't sworn allegiance to his master...!!
Ayame is so cute! ♡
Come, Misao...
...to the forest of servi-tude.
Yasuko Sensei presents Sojo
I have nothing to say...
General Comment: Individuality is amazing.

When they got here, it was already the middle of the night.

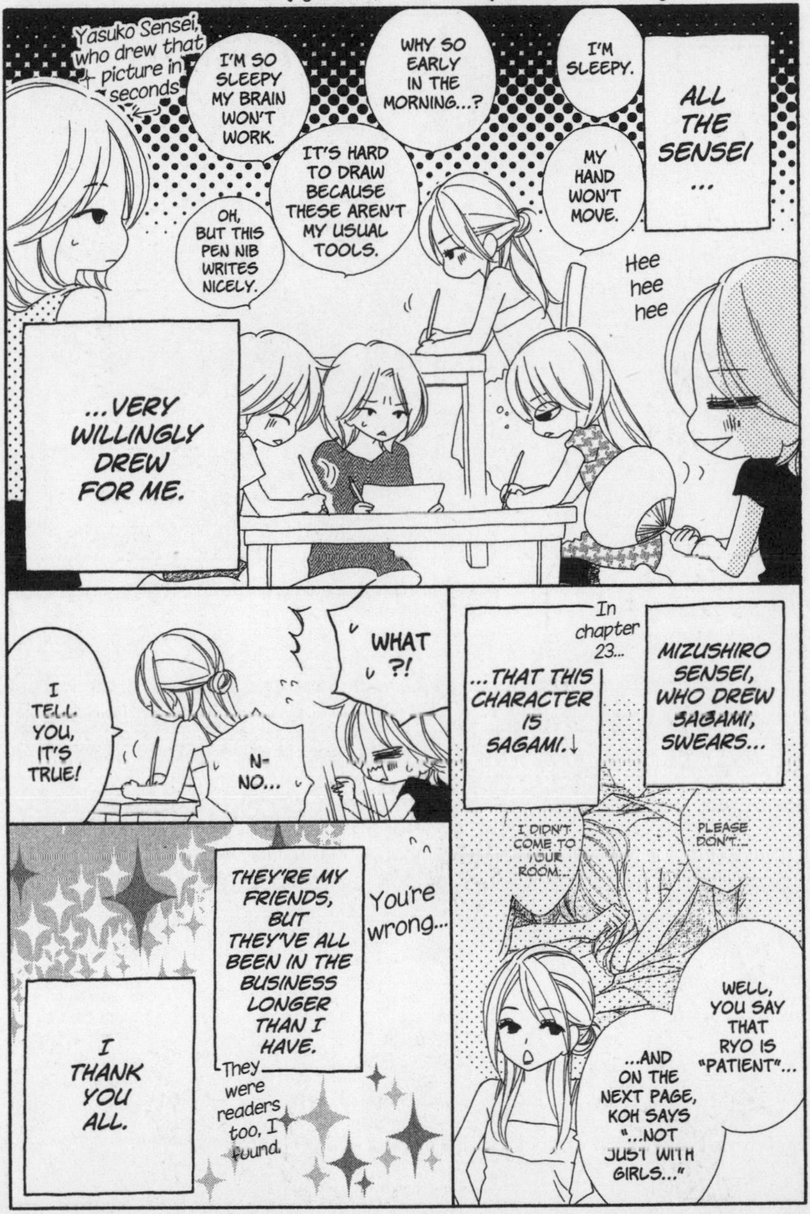
ALL THE SENSEI...
I'M SLEEPY.
MY HAND WON'T MOVE.
WHY SO EARLY IN THE MORNING...?
IT'S HARD TO DRAW BECAUSE THESE AREN'T MY USUAL TOOLS.
I'M SO SLEEPY MY BRAIN WON'T WORK.
OH, BUT THIS PEN NIB WRITES NICELY.
Yasuko Sensei, who drew that picture in seconds
Hee hee hee
...VERY WILLINGLY DREW FOR ME.
MIZUSHIRO SENSEI, WHO DREW SAGAMI, SWEARS...
In chapter 23...
...THAT THIS CHARACTER IS SAGAMI.↓
PLEASE DON'T...
I DIDN'T COME TO YOUR ROOM...
WELL, YOU SAY THAT RYO IS "PATIENT"...
...AND ON THE NEXT PAGE, KOH SAYS "...NOT JUST WITH GIRLS..."
WHAT?!
N-NO...
I TELL YOU, IT'S TRUE!
THEY'RE MY FRIENDS, BUT THEY'VE ALL BEEN IN THE BUSINESS LONGER THAN I HAVE.
You're wrong...
They were readers too, I found.
I THANK YOU ALL.

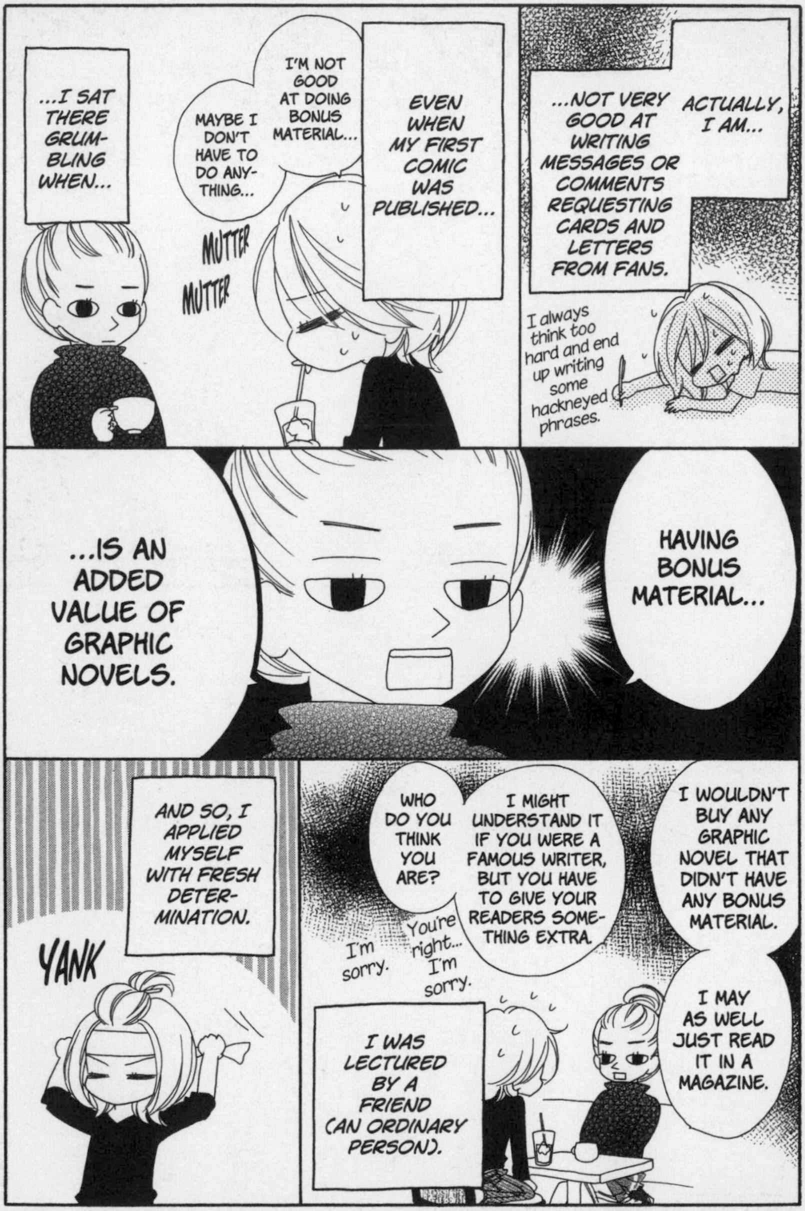
ACTUALLY, I AM...
...NOT VERY GOOD AT WRITING MESSAGES OR COMMENTS REQUESTING CARDS AND LETTERS FROM FANS.
I always think too hard and end up writing some hackneyed phrases.
EVEN WHEN MY FIRST COMIC WAS PUBLISHED...
I'M NOT GOOD AT DOING BONUS MATERIAL...
MAYBE I DON'T HAVE TO DO ANYTHING...
MUTTER
MUTTER
...I SAT THERE GRUMBLING WHEN...
HAVING BONUS MATERIAL...
...IS AN ADDED VALUE OF GRAPHIC NOVELS.
I WOULDN'T BUY ANY GRAPHIC NOVEL THAT DIDN'T HAVE ANY BONUS MATERIAL.
I MAY AS WELL JUST READ IT IN A MAGAZINE.
I MIGHT UNDERSTAND IT IF YOU WERE A FAMOUS WRITER, BUT YOU HAVE TO GIVE YOUR READERS SOMETHING EXTRA.
WHO DO YOU THINK YOU ARE?
You're right... I'm sorry.
I'm sorry.
I WAS LECTURED BY A FRIEND (AN ORDINARY PERSON).
AND SO, I APPLIED MYSELF WITH FRESH DETERMINATION.
YANK

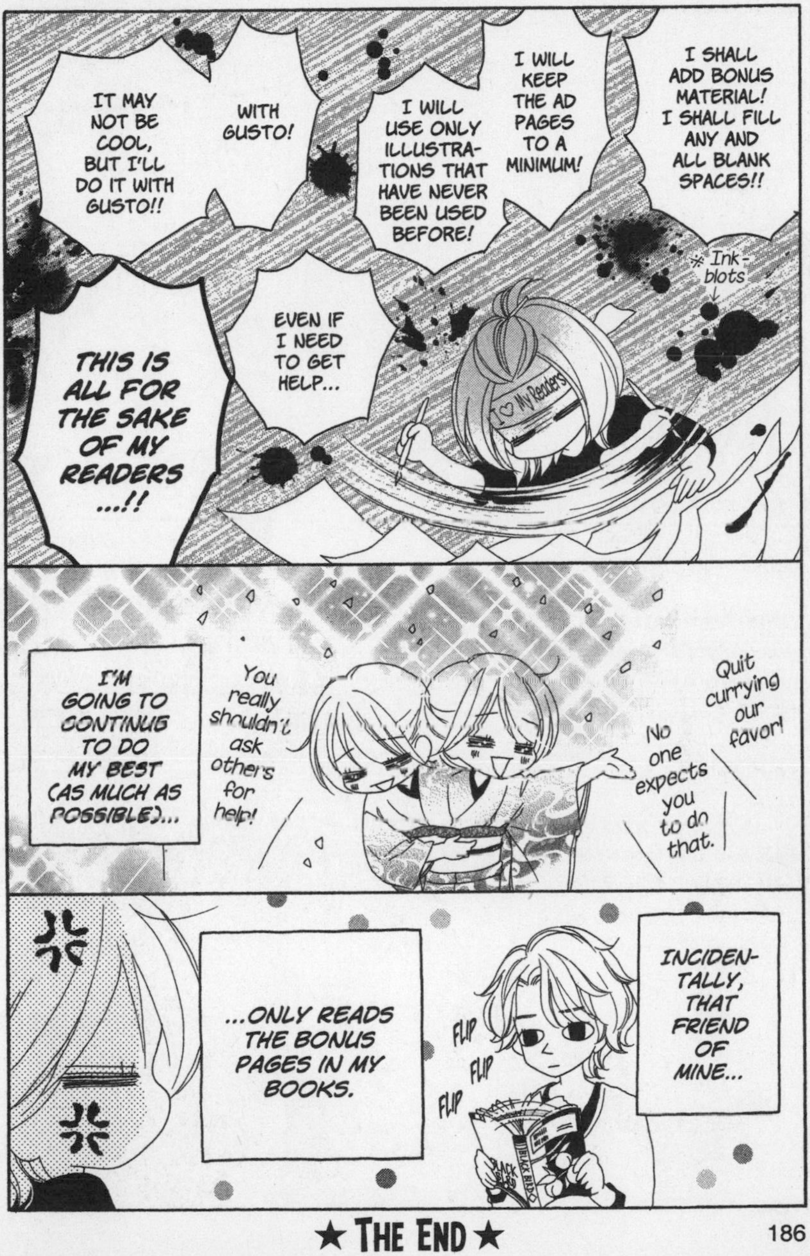
I SHALL ADD BONUS MATERIAL! I SHALL FILL ANY AND ALL BLANK SPACES!!
I WILL KEEP THE AD PAGES TO A MINIMUM!
I WILL USE ONLY ILLUSTRATIONS THAT HAVE NEVER BEEN USED BEFORE!
WITH GUSTO!
IT MAY NOT BE COOL, BUT I'LL DO IT WITH GUSTO!!
※ Ink-blots
I ♡ My Readers
EVEN IF I NEED TO GET HELP...
THIS IS ALL FOR THE SAKE OF MY READERS ...!!
Quit currying our favor!
No one expects you to do that.
You really shouldn't ask others for help!
I'M GOING TO CONTINUE TO DO MY BEST (AS MUCH AS POSSIBLE)...
INCIDENTALLY, THAT FRIEND OF MINE...
FLIP
FLIP
FLIP
...ONLY READS THE BONUS PAGES IN MY BOOKS.

★ THE END ★

I have tried to depict the things around me in the manga essays in this volume.

There are still many others to whom I am indebted.

I hope I will also be able to write about my assistants who help me draw, and designers, and writers someday.

And more than anyone, it is you, the readers, who have made it possible for this series to go on volume after volume!

I shall continue to write stories, squeezing my little wisdom to bring you even a modicum of pleasure. ♡

An Auspicious Day, September 2008
Kanoko Sakurakoji
桜小路 かのこ

GLOSSARY

PAGE 63, PANEL 3: *Marriage meeting*
Called *miai* in Japanese, it is an arranged meeting between a prospective bride and groom to see if there is the possibility of a good match.

PAGE 162, PANEL 3: *Valentine's Day*
In Japan, on Valentine's Day some girls and women give out chocolates to male friends, co-workers and other acquaintances in addition to their lovers.

PAGE 178, PANEL 5: *AB type person*
In Japan it is popular to assign personality traits by blood group. AB is the most volatile and unpredictable of the types.

PAGE 180, PANEL 4: *Symbols on map*
The 卍 symbol represents the location of a Buddhist temple. The 卉 represents a Shinto shrine.

PAGE 180, PANEL 4: *Watch over me*
Yoroshiku (よろしく) is a common Japanese phrase, but here different characters are used to spell the word: *Yo* (夜, night) *ro* (露, dew) *shi* (死, death) *ku* (苦, pain; suffering).

PAGE 182: *Sensei*
An honorific used as a term of respect for manga creators. Doctors and teachers, among others, are also called *sensei*.

PAGE 182: *Shoko Akira, Hinako Ashihara, Aoi Suguri*
Shoko Akira is the creator of *Monkey High!*; Hinako Ashihara is the creator of *Sand Chronicles*; Aoi Suguri is the creator of *Amayakana Fujitsu*

PAGE 183: *Setona Mizushiro, Yasuko*
Setona Mizushiro is the creator of *After School Nightmare;* Yasuko is the creator of *Cherry na Bokura.*

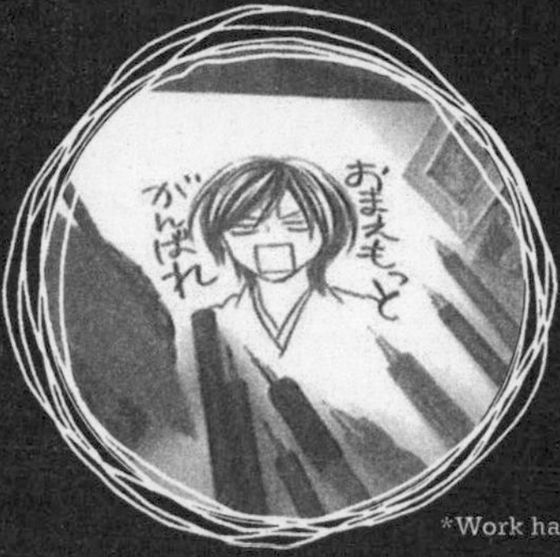
おまえもっと
がんばれ

*Work harder!

Kanoko Sakurakoji was born in downtown Tokyo, and her hobbies include reading, watching plays, traveling and shopping. Her debut title, *Raibu ga Hanetara*, ran in *Bessatsu Shojo Comic* (currently called *Bestucomi)* in 2000, and her 2004 *Bestucomi* title *Backstage Prince* was serialized in VIZ Media's *Shojo Beat* magazine. She won the 54th Shogakukan Manga Award for *Black Bird*.

BLACK BIRD
VOL. 6
Shojo Beat Edition

Story and Art by KANOKO SAKURAKOUJI

© 2007 Kanoko SAKURAKOUJI/Shogakukan
All rights reserved.
Original Japanese edition "BLACK BIRD" published by SHOGAKUKAN Inc.

TRANSLATION JN Productions
TOUCH-UP ART & LETTERING Gia Cam Luc
DESIGN Courtney Utt
EDITOR Pancha Diaz

The rights of the author(s) of the work(s) in this publication
to be so identified have been asserted in accordance with
the Copyright, Designs and Patents Act 1988. A CIP catalogue
record for this book is available from the British Library.

Printed in the U.S.A.

Published by VIZ Media, LLC
P.O. Box 77010
San Francisco, CA 94107

10 9 8 7 6 5 4 3 2 1
First printing, October 2010

www.shojobeat.com   www.viz.com

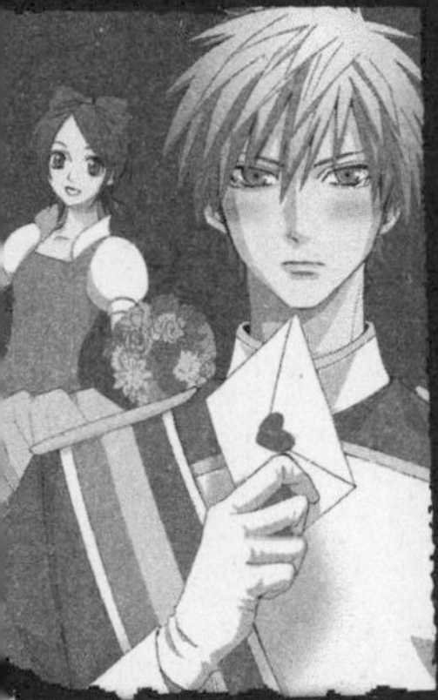

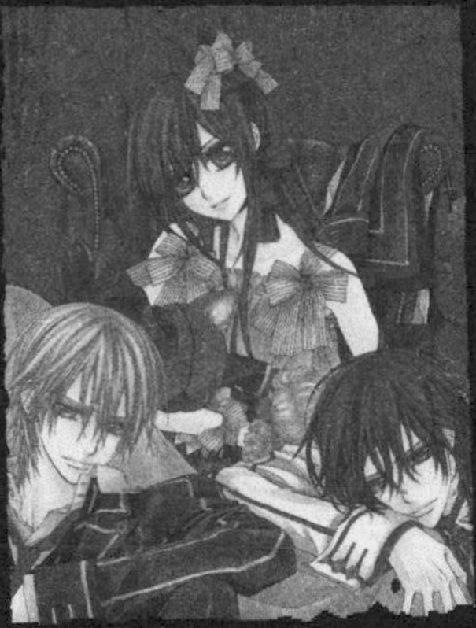

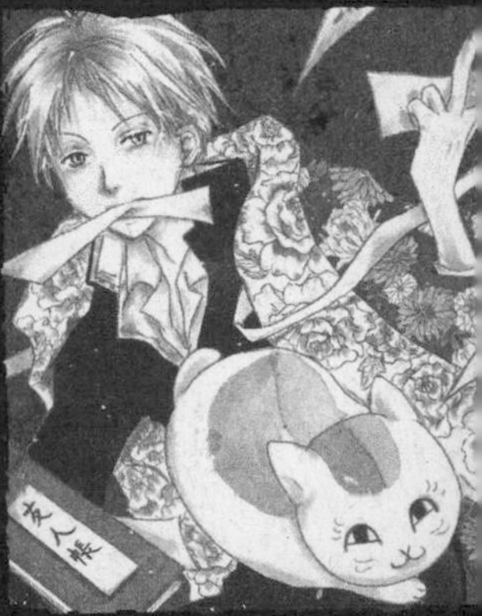
友人帳